HUNTER OR HUNTED?

Technology, Innovation, and Competitive Strategy

Dave Rochlin

THOMSON

Australia • Brazil • Canada • Mexico • Singapore • Spain • United Kingdom • United States

THOMSON

TM

Hunter or Hunted? Technology, Innovation, and Competitive Strategy, 1st edition

Dave Rochlin

Library of Congress Cataloging-in-Publication Number is available. See page 306 for details.

For more information about our products, contact us at:

Thomson Learning
Academic Resource Center
1-800-423-0563

Thomson Higher Education
5191 Natorp Boulevard
Mason, Ohio 45040
USA

To Tara, Alex, and Bradley

There are two kinds of people: those who finish what they start and so on.
—**Robert Byrne**

contents

PART 2   LIFE CYCLES, TIMING, AND EVOLUTION   99

PART 3 COMPETITIVE ADVANTAGE 201

preface

For years, Chicago's Museum of Science and Industry has featured an exhibit, winding its way down the staircase, that presents a series of wall-mounted ½-inch cross sections of a human body. It isn't as macabre as you might imagine. Presenting anatomy in this way reveals remarkable detail about the various parts that make us "tick," but, ironically, looking at the individual slices obscures the fact that an entire body is actually on display. This is no small shortcoming, because what's most amazing about the body is not the function of the individual parts, as intricate as they may be. A true understanding of the body requires grasping the complexity of how all these parts work together.

I have found that teaching, organizing, and applying technology strategy presents a similar obstacle. The body of knowledge that has been developed in the field is overwhelmingly extensive. But it exists primarily in cross section. Far less abundant are cohesive and organized sources that do justice to these "slices" while distilling and organizing the many issues that drive the competitive dynamics surrounding technology and innovation. The result is that most business school or engineering department technology strategy courses (mine included) have traditionally relied on pieces assembled from disparate and, in many cases, unrelated sources in order to develop the best fit to the overall course coverage. In a classroom setting, this can be a bit frustrating for the instructor and student alike, as many of the most insightful materials, while oft-cited, are tightly focused on specific issues and not intended for or suitable for general consumption. Even the more populist and broad-scoped material is typically self-contained, creating a sort of silo-based approach to understanding the competitive dynamics of technology and innovation. Outside the classroom, managers and executives who attempt to draw on this approach on their own can end up being overly attentive to some material without adequate organization, perspective, or context or—worse—without comprehensive understanding of the whole. This imbalance can lead to some ill-advised decision-making. As Alexander Pope wrote, "A little Learning is a dang'rous Thing;/Drink deep, or taste not the Pierian Spring."

After some fairly rigorous due diligence and academic inquiry, the editors at Thomson corroborated my assertion that there is indeed both a need for and a relative dearth of titles in this area. The result is this book, *Hunter or Hunted? Technology, Innovation, and Competitive Strategy*, which is intended to service both students and industry practitioners. As a technology executive, I can't help but wistfully imagine how I might have managed certain initiatives differently had more of the body of knowledge been better organized and easily available to me. As an educator, I find it frustrating to have to rely primarily on disparate and often unrelated materials (no matter how well organized) to help students build an overall understanding of the issues that determine why some firms and technologies thrive while others do not. My students—largely mid-career executive MBAs—have been clear in expressing their interest in leaving my class with an organized toolset that they can refer back to as practitioners in order to make better decisions about technology. I don't believe that they are atypical in this regard.

An important part of presenting a holistic view of innovation, technology, and competitive strategy is blending together contemporary and classical research theory, the historical perspective, and current best practices from industry. I have drawn very heavily from all three perspectives in writing and assembling this text.

On the research side, recent work in areas such as network-based competitive advantage, dominant design, platform management, diffusion, and disruption is combined with the more classical works of economics and management theory. In my attempt to develop a well-researched and comprehensive academic platform, I have relied heavily on the work of a variety of leaders in their respective fields. Included is coverage of the published research, writings, and commentary of Derek Abell, Philip Anderson, Jay Barney, Henry Chesbrough, Clayton Christensen, Michael Cusumano, Michael Gort, Boyan Jovanovic, Steven Klepper, Michael Porter, Everett Rogers, Joseph Schumpeter, Carl Shapiro, David Teece, Michael Tushman, James Utterback, Hal Varian, Eric Von Hippel, and many others who have dedicated themselves to advancing our understanding of the interplay among technology, innovation, and strategy. I am much obliged to them and encourage readers to consider further exploring their works in areas that are of particular interest.

Despite the rapid march of progress, many of the themes and dynamics observed in the recent generations of technology are not new; they are simply manifestations of well-documented historical patterns with some slight modern variation. Investment bubbles have been documented in great detail as far back as the trade-related bubbles of the early 1700s. Diffusion archetypes have been studied and observed relative to the expansion of Cistercian monasteries and Gutenberg's printing press. Patterns associated with disruptive technology have been acknowledged as a decisive factor in military conflicts as far back as one might care to look; an example is the impact of the Welsh longbow on the outcome of the battle of Agincourt in the Hundred Years' War. Likewise, the issues around standards are apparent in virtually every wave of technology from canals to electricity to the roads built by the Romans, while enabling technology has been a key determinant of economic distribution and technology diffusion in many historical cases. These patterns are not coincidental, but rather indicate strong behavioral, sociological, and political underpinnings that need to be considered as part of the overall explanation of technology and firm selection.

Finally, necessity is the mother of invention. Practitioners in industry were tackling issues such as technology stacks, platform management, and total cost of ownership long before they were subjected to academic exploration, explanation, and refinement. Fortunately, many practitioners also thoughtfully sought to explain why the decisions they made and processes they used were good and bad. The ideas and models developed within these pages are based both on my own experiences and exploration and on the contributions of executives and consultants including Bill Gates, Andy Grove,

Michael McGrath, Geoffrey Moore, Jerry Porras, and Jack Welch, as well as firms such as Gartner Group, Forrester, and McKinsey.

Helping to blend these three perspectives (and to make the book an interesting read) are several Voices boxes, which present first-person viewpoints from experts in the areas mentioned above. You will also find some rather unusual juxtapositions and analogies used to illustrate key points. For example, you will discover how the experience of the nuclear power industry applies to IBM's OS/2 programming language, why NASA's approach to the Apollo mission helps illustrate the trade-off between modularity and time to market for Apple, and what tomatoes can teach us about software cycles.

The Three Sections of the Book

The potential impact of technology and innovation should be viewed in relation to their interaction with both internal and external structures (context), industry and market evolution (life cycles), and competitive capabilities (competitive advantage). The three sections of this book cover these three areas, giving the reader a complete picture of how firms can approach technology and innovation strategically.

The first section covers technology from a systemic and contextual perspective. Technology without context is insignificant. Technology should be evaluated based on how it changes and creates value configurations, interacts with other components of value delivery, and changes market spaces and delivery systems. Understanding the potential of a technology and the relative leverage and opportunity for individual firms requires the use of a variety of different models, to put innovation into context and evaluate it as a value delivery amplifier or disruptor.

The second section covers the life cycle and evolution-based perspective. Market, consumer, complement, and competitive behaviors evolve over time, creating and defining the opportunities available to both innovators and incumbents. Life cycle behavior and industry evolution have a significant impact on innovation and strategic technology choice. Developing behavioral/predictive models and methods for determining where various technologies are in their life cycle is an important step in developing appropriate strategy and tactics.

The third and final section covers competitive advantage and the role of technology. Competitive advantage is at the core of any strategy. A fundamental message of economics is that perfectly competitive markets are marginally profitable. Finding, developing, and, in some cases, destroying barriers to competition is a key to superior performance. For established firms, technology can play a large role in the process. For startups or technology-based firms, establishing and managing unique and unusual barriers can make the difference between success and failure.

My intention is to make this book useful to a wide variety of readers in both educational and professional settings. In the spirit of the innovation that will be discussed within, I have attempted to create a hybrid—a book that is appropriate for multiple audiences and that can be used in the business and engineering classroom as well as the conference and board room.

The title, *Hunter or Hunted? Technology, Innovation, and Competitive Strategy*, conveys the complexity and uncertainty that characterize the competitive landscape and strategic choices surrounding technology. It is often unclear whether a new and potentially disruptive technology is an opportunity, a threat, or simply a non-starter. The answer can be any or all of the three and is highly situation-specific. Having worked in and consulted for several firms in emerging technology sectors, I have been in a number of meetings where the business development groups from two companies spent most of the meeting time just trying to determine which of the two sides should be selling to the other. I can assure you that my experience with this is in no way unique and sums up the challenges that executives within the industry face.

I am eager to hear from any of you who wish to comment, suggest changes, or simply establish a dialog on any of the topics contained in the text. Feel free to visit the website http://www.hunterorhunted.com or contact me at hunter@emacula.com.

Acknowledgments

I've discovered that I am hopelessly fascinated by the "new." While I am by no means a technophile (or an engineer, for that matter), I have tended to gravitate professionally toward new products, processes, and technology. I've been fortunate to have had the opportunity to help design, productize, and commercialize a variety of innovative products, from global data management systems to bio-engineered tomatoes. I have also worked in both old-line consumer products and "big six" consulting environments and have gained a respect and appreciation for the power of organizational capability, well-honed processes, customer reach, and executional skill. It takes considerably more than a good idea to create a successful company. It also takes considerably more than a good idea to create a book. So many people have been involved in one way or another in this project that I hesitate to name any for risk of overlooking anyone. If I have, please accept my apologies!

I would like to acknowledge the following reviewers, who contributed their time and expertise, suggested additional materials, offered frank criticism, and in the end helped make this a much better book:

Dolphy Abraham, *Loyola Marymount University*
Louis K. Bragaw, Jr., *Rensselaer Polytechnic Institute*
Mary J. Cronin, *Boston College*
Lynn A. DeNoia, *Rensselaer Polytechnic Institute*
Alan D. Flury, *Georgia Institute of Technology*
Jason L. Frand, *University of California at Los Angeles*
Bernard M. Gillespie, *Marshall University*
Robert D. Gulbro, *Athens State University*
Glenn Hoetker, *University of Illinois at Urbana-Champaign*
Clyde Hull, *Rochester Institute of Technology*
Sanjay Jain, *University of Wisconsin at Madison*
Katryna Johnson, *Concordia University*
Richard Klein, *Clemson University*
Thomas D. Lairson, *Rollins College*
Chung-Shing Lee, *Pacific Lutheran University*

Susan K. McEvily, *University of Pittsburgh*
Nigel Melville, *Boston College*
Steven C. Michael, *University of Illinois at Urbana-Champaign*
Michael Mino, *Clemson University*
Hal A. Rumsey, *Washington State University at Spokane*
James J. Smith, *Rocky Mountain College*

John Szilagyi at Thomson/South-Western was an enthusiastic champion of this project and stuck with it (and me) despite some delays and mid-stream restructuring. Thanks also to the many other team members at Thomson for their assistance, including Judy O'Neill, who helped focus and solicit outside feedback on the manuscript early on. Monica Ohlinger and Joanne Vickers helped to edit, shape, and tighten the text; cracked the whip when necessary; and kept the project on a true course whenever it started to drift. Sally Lifland and her bookmakers team also provided much-needed help in revising and organizing the text and endured the dreaded green pencil with equanimity. Danielle Jatlow helped me select a publisher, and her former colleagues at Waterside Productions provided excellent insight and coaching advice via their technology writers conferences.

I am extremely grateful to Jim Barton, Cathy Benko, Lise Buyer, Adam Fein, Annabelle Gawer, Randy Komisar, Peter Micciche, Cynthia Robbins-Roth, Jim Sayer, and Michael Schrage for their participation, their interest, and, most of all, their valuable time. Minda Lehto provided an early editor's viewpoint and encouraged me to pursue the project. Ranch Kimball was highly supportive and offered some excellent suggestions early on. Catherine Banbury provided some valuable early insight as well. Dave Kellogg's guest lecture in my class and general observations helped persuade me of the need for this book. Special thanks go out to KT, Suzio, and Kelly, three of my most steadfast confidants with regard to this project.

St. Mary's College was vital in providing access to the academic resources and platform necessary to complete and publish this book. My executive students at the college also played an important role, both in serving as a sounding board for various portions of the book and in coming up with some of the more interesting examples used herein. Thanks also to those whose work is cited and referenced herein and to all of the individuals and organizations that provided permission to use data or reprint photos, charts, and graphs.

E. L. Doctorow said that "writing is a socially acceptable form of schizophrenia," while George Orwell wrote that "writing a book is a horrible, exhausting struggle, like a long bout of some painful illness." To these quotes, I'll add my own, which is that "writing sure can make you one cranky bastard." The final and most heartfelt of thanks go out to my family and friends, for supporting and putting up with me throughout the process.

Dave Rochlin
Moraga, California
April, 2005

about the author

Dave Rochlin is a technology executive, consultant, and educator with a broad background in product innovation, information services, networking, consumer technology, and enterprise software. Dave's past experience includes big five and boutique consulting, running e-commerce and hosted software application companies, advising several technology startups, and conducting e-business seminars in Europe and the Middle East. He developed and teaches the e-business and technology strategy course for the executive MBA program in the St. Mary's College of California Graduate School of Business, where he has been a part-time faculty member since 2001. He has degrees from the Haas School at UC Berkeley and The Kellogg School at Northwestern University, where he graduated Beta Gamma Sigma. Dave can be contacted at hunter@emacula.com.

Introduction: The Hunt

*The land may be extremely cold or dry, yet there will be com-
petition between some few species, or between the individuals
of the same species, for the warmest or dampest spots.*
—**Charles Darwin**, *Origin of Species*

The Power of Competition

No force of nature is stronger than competition. The book you hold in your hands, for example, has been shaped by competition in innumerable ways: The paper was selected and purchased based on a quality/price equation set by competitive forces in the pulp market. The trees that became the pulp were from genetic stock that, over time, proved to be stronger, more productive, or perhaps simply more suitable for Weyerhaeuser's tree plantations. The retailer who stocked the book did so with the activities of other retailers in mind and set the price to reflect the choices available to prospective buyers both within the store and from competing retailers. Even the author (sadly) is paid based on the level of competition presented by other would-be writers and the myriad of choices available to both the publisher and end-consumers.

Innovation versus Resource Base

To survive competition, it is essential not only to recognize that competition will inevitably arise, but also to characterize the nature of the competition appropriately. If an Olympic-caliber distance runner declared that he was planning to enter and win the Masters (golf) Tournament because he could run faster than the other golfers, he would elicit either a chuckle or a blank stare from anyone who understands the skills required to win on the golf course. Tiger Woods certainly would not feel a need to put in more time at the driving range. Likewise, an upstart cola manufacturer with a better-tasting product would have difficulty making a credible argument that it could compete against Pepsi and Coke, which control most of the shelf space and distribution of carbonated beverages. Yet, in the technology sector, entrepreneurs often speak of speed to market, uniqueness, and/or product superiority as reasons why they will grab market share and win, when issues such as compatibility with existing infrastructure, interoperability, and total cost of ownership are often more important to the buyer.

Large **incumbents** (well-established organizations) can also be myopic when assessing competition. They may frame customer need in terms of their product offerings rather than offer the full range of possible solutions to customers' problems, giving rise to unanticipated competition. They may also fail to recognize the emergence of entirely new markets. Polaroid's, Encyclopedia Britannica's, and Novell's mischaracterizations of their markets and competitive landscape present excellent case studies in this regard. In each case, competitors met customer needs in new and unanticipated ways, the robustness of the incumbent's feature set was largely irrelevant, and the incumbent firm's fortunes went into long-term decline.

WordPerfect versus Microsoft Word: Good Product, Slippery Slope

Over the course of the 90s, Microsoft's Word replaced WordPerfect as the dominant word-processing program for PCs, climbing from a 20 percent share of the market[1] in 1990 to a 90 percent share[2] by the end of the decade. Early on, WordPerfect had taken hold among legal professionals, a market resistant to changes in technology because of its large interest in backwards compatibility and its small interest in retraining. WordPerfect was offered in a vertically tailored legal edition and, as late as 1997, held over a 50 percent market share in corporate law offices,[3] despite Microsoft Word's overall 80 percent market share.[4] By 2000, however, Microsoft's share of the corporate law market had climbed to 87 percent,[5] despite WordPerfect's continually favorable reviews, its significantly lower price point, and its commitment to specifically tailor the product to the legal customer.

As surprising as it may seem, quality, low price, and customer features were not the most influential factors in the word-processing software decision-making process for law firms and corporate law departments (so much for Marketing 101)! Since most clients were sending attorneys documents written in Microsoft Word, *compatibility* with clients became a key issue. In other words, market share in *adjacent segments* helped Microsoft to dominate the professional segment, regardless of whether its software was the "best" choice for the legal professional. Additionally, the market had shifted from single applications to office suites, allowing the seamless integration of data among various desktop applications. Finally, the rise of Microsoft's Windows operating system as a standard favored Word over WordPerfect, which focused development efforts on the competing OS/2 standard. While WordPerfect's owners—Novell and later Corel—assembled various programs and introduced a suite to compete against MS Office, Microsoft's overall solution represented a better choice for users, was more tightly integrated into the dominant new 32-bit operating system (Windows 95), and represented an easier training and support solution for IT departments. This readily trumped the specific advantages of WordPerfect for the legal community.

Charles Darwin's observation while aboard the HMS *Beagle*—and subsequent theory of natural selection—introduced the concept of survival of the fittest and natural selection as the driving mechanisms that determine which species and attributes win out. Darwin observed that a variety of strategies were utilized by virtually all plants and animals to improve their chances of continuing as species. More importantly, he observed that nature's long-term winners were those that benefited from mutation and variation (innovation) over time, rather than adaptation or control of the environment. Whether in beak size, eyesight, fur, or coloring, favorable mutations gave those species a greater chance of success. This view of the world, when applied to business entities rather than species, is certainly encouraging for the typical technology startup, which has traditionally relied on innovation to compete and win.

In contrast, in the Pulitzer Prize–winning book *Guns, Germs, and Steel*, Jared Diamond looked specifically at the history of human populations and concluded that **innovation** happens everywhere and that other factors—namely, natural resources and production capabilities—determined which groups developed the capabilities necessary to dominate the modern world.[6] As Diamond points out, 16th-century Spain didn't produce physically superior or smarter children, but its ability to produce food and domesticate livestock eventually led to the rise of a society that could send conquistadors to enslave the New World. In this sense, Spain's cattle were perhaps the world's first true "cash cows." Using Diamond's observation about resources as an allegory for business strategy would probably make most of the Fortune 500 CEOs sleep a bit easier, since, in most cases, they have vastly superior resource bases and capabilities.

These contrasting viewpoints—dominance based on innovation versus dominance based on resource base—raise an interesting question: When it comes to developing a successful long-term business strategy, does technological innovation lead to success, or is technology a tool to be used by those firms that already possess advantageous resource bases? The answer is not black or white. For every eBay, which provides proof of the former, there's a Ford Motor Company, which provides evidence for the latter. While many of the Fortune 500 seem to be virtually unassailable (for a variety of reasons to be explored in later chapters), others—such as Xerox, Polaroid, and Kmart—have fallen from grace. Still others, such as Oracle, Microsoft, Cisco, and even Wal-Mart, were not so long ago young startups that managed to leverage technology to become what they are today. Beyond the Fortune 500 are a variety of successful and profitable technology companies, such as Siebel Systems, SAP, and Intuit, that have managed to dominate their respective markets, even as thousands of others have failed in similar attempts.

The poet Edgar Guest wrote the often-misappropriated line "There are ways uncounted to lose the game, but there's only one way to win."[7] Strangely enough, this provides some guidance in determining how technology is best incorporated into a business strategy, a question that is the central focus of the chapters that follow.

An E-Tale

1998 was a great year to be an e-tailer. While Jeff Bezos was still a year away from being crowned *Time* magazine's man of the year[8] (and three years away from starring in Taco Bell commercials), Amazon.com already appeared to be a spectacular success as an online retailer, selling $600 million worth of books, music, and movies, a 400 percent increase over 1997. Amazon carried a $4 billion market capitalization and was regularly referred to in the press as "the next Wal-Mart," a retailer with over $100 billion in sales that same year.

The Pioneers

Pioneering e-tailers in other vertical markets were feeling equally optimistic. Reel.com received national attention for selling over 300,000 copies of the video *Titanic* and was purchased for $100 million by Hollywood Video. CDNow hit the $50 million sales mark, and Egghead Computer completed its transformation from a besieged physical-world retailer with an obsolete format to what Piper Jaffray termed "a bold company that saw a brick-less future and forthwith reinvented itself as a leading Internet retailer of computer-related and other products."[9] The entire industry hit the $8 billion sales mark, with sales expected to more than double in 1999 and then double again the following year.

The basic business premises of these e-firms—selling books, CDs, toys, software, etc.—weren't particularly revolutionary. Building the necessary technology to sell these products over the Internet is what made these companies innovators. Amazon.com, for example, built much of its website and back-end systems from the ground up.[10] The expectation was that Amazon would use technology to compete by offering a unique customer experience, as well as developing an operational infrastructure with low-cost attributes. It invested almost $50 million in product development in 1998 alone, much of which went to support its massive technology organization. While Amazon claimed in its original S-1 filings that it would be licensing, rather than developing, technology as a core strategy, by 1998 it had changed its position, focusing more heavily on proprietary internal development.[11] Amazon also made several acquisitions, the most notable being Junglee, a developer of virtual database technology, which further extended its proprietary technology platform.

Most other first-generation e-tailers were embarking on similar technology strategies, designed to give them similar dominance in their respective categories. At the time, building these systems was no small challenge. The Gartner Group estimated that over 75 percent of e-commerce initiatives would fail because of poor execution. This assertion was backed up by several well-publicized disasters involving some of the world's largest and most technologically adept retailers. Wal-Mart, for example, struggled mightily to move online throughout 1998 and 1999 and didn't get a suitable e-store launched until late 2000. The initial e-commerce site of Toys "R" Us was a major fiasco, with frequent site crashes and January deliveries of Christmas orders. A 1999 Andersen Consulting study found that 25 percent of all purchase attempts on e-commerce sites in general failed, and that traditional retailers attempting to sell online were able to deliver goods on time only 20 percent of the time.[12] These are especially astounding numbers when you consider that the perception of high-level customer service is integral to the brand identities of offline retailers.

For early e-tailers, margins were in line with those of physical-world retailers and were acceptable, given the growth expectations for these early entrants. EToys and CDNow, for example, had 19 percent gross margins, compared to 25–30 percent margins for their brick-and-mortar counterparts. E-tailers expected margins to rise as they filled their virtual shelves with higher-margin goods and started exerting some buying leverage over their suppliers. On the inventory side, a physical-world retailer might spend as much as $3 million building and stocking a new store, making the economics of e-tail seem attractive by comparison. Egghead, for example, was able to reduce its inventory costs by 85 percent when it shifted from physical locations to a virtual retail strategy.[13]

Amazon.com was rumored to have positive float on its inventory, meaning that it sold its inventory before it had to pay for it. This was in stark contrast to Barnes & Noble, which carried an inventory of almost $1 billion—roughly 30% of its annual sales. Overall, these first-generation e-tailers looked like attractive bets.

If there was an overarching concern, it was how the pie would be divided and which of the new e-tailers would generate the best customer responses and business propositions. While Amazon.com claimed that there was "plenty of room for everyone," it enthusiastically broadcast its successes in music and video to the press and was laying the groundwork to begin selling in several more categories. Many vertical retailers banded together in a joint marketing effort designed specifically to meet the Amazon challenge.[14] Despite this in-fighting, the combination of technology and first-mover advantage was supposed to be enough to propel many of these companies to leadership positions in the new economy. These firms had the technology, margins, branding, and market share to become winners in their respective categories.

In a world without competition, it might have turned out that way.

Those Who Followed

By 1999, however, new e-tailers were coming out of the woodwork. The success of the first group attracted both attention and capital. Pioneers invariably break a trail, which makes it easier for others to follow. This was certainly the case in **e-commerce**. There were now hundreds of well-funded Internet retailers, and, in most categories, the top e-tailers saw their market share decline, while acquisition cost per customer increased by 50 percent or more.[15] Differentiation became more difficult, and many of the newer e-tailers, as well as some of the older ones, adopted aggressive price/promotion strategies or cost-focused pricing models as a way to attract consumer attention and market share. Many of these models were unsustainable, but the abundance of capital and its close link with market share led to some artificially low pricing models and aggressive marketing programs.

One of the most prominent and damaging examples of this new breed was Buy.com, which advertised "the lowest prices on earth." It guaranteed that it would have prices significantly lower than the already discounted prices of the early e-tailers and even went so far as to buy website addresses such as "www.10percentoffamazon.com" to reinforce this message.[16] To counter the obvious flaw in its pure retail model (lack of margins), Buy.com claimed that it would make a profit via advertising, although there was scant evidence to support the viability of this strategy. By selling goods essentially at cost, Buy.com was able to grow to over $500 million in sales by 1999. This gave the company substantial market share (at the expense of Outpost.com, CDNow, and other early innovators) and allowed it to attract significant venture capital. Buy.com eventually went public in early 2000.

Tools for the Trade

Most of these aggressive price-based competitors were destined to fail, and even many well-capitalized efforts soon began to falter. In the process, however, they managed to do substantial damage to the other early e-tailers. At the same time, something even more competitively challenging began to happen—it began getting easier to build and operate online stores. The rapidly increasing demand for the technology to build online stores led to an explosion in the number of consultants, developers, and service providers with experience and a focus on e-commerce. Technology developers surveying the e-tail landscape by mid-1999 easily concluded that they would be better off providing the technology to others, rather than competing as e-tailers themselves.

Not only did this focus on providing technology fuel even greater competition; it also removed some of the technology risk and enabled the category leaders—old-line companies such as Sears, Best Buy, Target, and Office Depot, as well as traditional catalogers such as Sharper Image and Land's End—to build online operations without worrying about whether they could acquire sufficient technological competency. With relatively competitive web infrastructure available, these companies could rely on their many other skill sets and advantages, including known and trusted brands, vendor relationships and clout, large customer bases, merchandising experience, logistics infrastructure, and broad-reaching advertising/co-op vehicles, to capture customers online.

By 2001, with a few notable exceptions, most of the early innovators and their imitators had disappeared, either having been taken over by old-line companies, having been taken under by second-generation competitors, or simply having shut down in the industry's shakeout. As the industry has stabilized, it has become largely dominated by existing retailers, and many of the innovators are but a footnote in the growth of the industry.

Learn from History or Repeat It?

While hindsight is 20-20, it's clear that this whole scenario follows a predictable pattern in technology. Many other technology-driven and technology-dependent industries, from motion pictures at the beginning of the 20th century to Internet service in the 1990s, have gone through similar cycles of competition, with similar results. The names and players may change from industry to industry, but the market forces that conspired to take down some early innovators have remained to form a predictable pattern of competitive responses and life cycle.

John Steinbeck once wrote, "Ideas are like rabbits. You get a couple and learn how to handle them, and pretty soon you have a dozen." This certainly applies to the ideas behind startups. When a promising technology idea is attached to talent, it can often attract capital. Even if a new idea represents an unproven opportunity and entails more risk than an established firm is willing to take on, the abundance of **venture capital** presents a funding mechanism for innovation.

As Part 2 of this book will illustrate, venture capitalists are, by nature, risk-tolerant investors, since they are essentially involved in identifying and managing high-risk/high-return opportunities in a diversified portfolio. The potential of the first venture will often draw additional capital to the new technology segment. *Red Herring* magazine reported that in the fiber-optic switching category (necessary infrastructure for the building of broadband networks), for example, 198 companies raised about $6.8 billion in capital in 2000.[17] Average valuations for optics-related companies rose from $5.2 million in 1998 to $30.4 million in 1999 and $126.1 million in 2000.[18] As one venture capitalist put it, "There's been a lot of overfunding going on in the business, on both the systems and components side, because there has been so much in the sector from a valuation standpoint."[19]

In many cases, this capital acceleration occurs far ahead of realization of the potential of an innovation, proving its profitability. **Liquidity events**, in particular—such as an early player being acquired for a significant premium over the venture investment—draw venture capital to technology segments like bees to honey. In the optical switching market, the acquisition of a small firm called Cerent by Cisco Systems for over $6 billion was one of the catalysts that fueled what has since been called the "optical bubble." These events may occur far in advance of profits or even demonstrated commercial viability. Once this cycle begins, however, the additional capital provides fuel for a firestorm of future competition in the still-unproven segment.

Waiting to consume this capital are groups of entrepreneurs and engineers—some more talented, some less—who want to share in the riches. Invariably, the new groups believe that they can do it better. After all, what entrepreneur doesn't believe this? Self-confidence bordering on arrogance is considered one of the most common traits of the entrepreneur.[20] Even if the entrepreneur originally has the most prudent of business plans, with a detailed feature-laden product roadmap and a plan to make money from day one, the onslaught of competition puts incredible pressure on both ship dates and pricing. Under this pressure to compete, external forces—such as market share, time-to-market, and installed base—can easily replace the original prudent plan as the central focus.

As competitors multiply, sooner or later pragmatic entrepreneurs looking at the competition will decide that the market has become too crowded and unattractive to take a realistic run at the category. To use a gold rush analogy, eventually there are so many prospectors panning for gold that all the good claims have been staked, and the possibility of striking it rich no longer seems like a sure thing. The 300 tons of gold extracted during the California gold rush comprised an attractive market for the first 1500 miners, but, with over 100,000 miners digging and most of the best claims staked, returns diminished rapidly.

There were two answers to this dilemma in the gold rush era: Look for the next big strike, or supply prospectors with the tools they needed. While some headed to Australia, and later Nova Scotia or South Africa, in search of the next "mother lode," others stayed and simply moved upstream in the supply chain. California's famed "Big Four"—Mark Hopkins, Leland Stanford, Collis Huntington, and Charles Crocker—all came West with the gold rush but made fortunes as merchants, not miners, on their way to eventually financing the transcontinental railroad. Operating out of Sacramento, Huntington and Hopkins sold picks and shovels, Stanford sold groceries, and Crocker sold everything else.[21]

In the modern era, companies such as UUNET in Internet service and Affymetrix in biotechnology supply the tools, focusing their technology and infrastructure primarily on creating technology solutions for others to use in crafting products for the end user. UUNET, for example (ownership by WorldCom aside), provides at least part of the underlying network infrastructure for many of the leading Internet service providers (including AOL, MSN, and Earthlink) rather than competing directly in the consumer ISP space. Affymetrix provides the pharmaceutical industry with DNA chip arrays, used to more efficiently match molecules to gene-specific characteristics in screening for potential new drugs.

As in the preceding e-tale, the emergence of tools enabled additional competition and removed certain pieces of technology as differentiators. Without technology, other industry-specific factors become more important. In the case of ISPs, the emphasis shifts to customer service and marketing. In the case of pharmaceuticals, refinement and preclinical and clinical trialing become more important. This transition often favors larger, entrenched firms, which might have lagged in technology investment but usually have much more powerful and refined business value chains, including customer and channel access, brand names, low-cost procurement capabilities, and support systems.

Studies of railroads, electricity, and early telephony indicate that the innovation **boom-bust cycle** has been a common feature of the economic landscape during the post-industrial period of the last century and a half.[22] The common conditions leading to this pattern are technology diffusion, followed by overexpansion, leading to marginal profitability, resulting in eventual consolidation and standardization, driven by the most capitalized firms with the best cost structure and most complete business systems. The history of the railroad industry provides a clear illustration of this phenomenon.

Working on the Railroad

The lure of the West and the success of the Big Four, as well as the success of the Union Pacific and several other early railroads, created a vibrant speculative market for new railroads in the late 19th century. Much of the capital was financed by large construction companies, which took stock in payment and resold the securities to raise the cash for construction. The construction companies—focusing on their own profitability and short-term returns on investment—did not concern themselves with the long-term needs (or, unfortunately, the long-term construction quality) of the railroads they were both building and essentially raising funds for:

> If the road returned large immediate profits on construction, it made little difference whether or not the railroad would be able to pay dividends in the future. The controlling interests received all that they had any expectation of making, and were then satisfied with whatever fate might hold in store. Obviously, the majority of Western railroads were over capitalized. But that fact in itself did not cause anyone immediate worry. Railroad building was being promoted on the assumption that railroads were an economic panacea, and would create wealth through their mere existence.[23]

In the 1880s, 71,000 miles of new line were built, representing roughly 30 percent of the total line in use at the *peak* of the railroad industry in 1916.[24] At this same time, $7.5 billion in capital was committed, against a gross revenue stream of less than $1 billion.[25] The pursuit of marginal lines and short-term overcapacity on major routes were fueled by standardization (of equipment and track) and availability of capital. When capital became scarce, a great number of the new railroads ended up in receivership and, eventually, in the hands of larger companies, such as Union Pacific.

Confronting Competitive Evolution

The innovation boom-bust cycle is driven by several factors, foremost among which is competition. A basic premise of economics is that market forces work against **excess return**. When a firm has a competitive position that allows overly advantageous pricing, it tends to under-deliver on product and over-deliver on price. Whether high profits are made in financial markets or through the sale of computer memory chips, they result in an expansion of supply (and suppliers) that drives down prices and makes the excess profits disappear. Once excess profits are removed, only the more efficient suppliers (in terms of either costs or matching consumer preference) can compete. Basic economic theory holds that competition is in most cases a virtual certainty and that all industries move toward a point of **rational rate of return**, where weaker players exit and the industry is relatively stable or unattractive.

This doesn't mean that the fate of individual firms is a preordained certainty. The role of executive leadership is to fight this overwhelming force, and it is a fight that can be won. To the extent that underlying competitive forces are the same for new technology as for existing industries, the solution to this problem is also the same: Create barriers or temporary advantages that prevent competitors from duplicating or substituting for the value the business creates for customers. This concept—known as competitive advantage—is a fundamental underpinning of most corporate strategy. Companies from Microsoft to The Coca Cola Company enjoy competitive advantage in some form or another, leading them to capture both profits and market share.

As anyone who has managed a business knows, establishing a competitive advantage is easier said than done. Even in well-understood market spaces, developing competitive advantage involves a thorough understanding and continuous refinement of the **value chain** (to drive cost out and put value in). It also requires a complete understanding of a firm's customers and how to uniquely position the firm to meet their needs. All this must be done while anticipating the competition. Where technology innovation departs from the normal pursuit of competitive advantage is in its lack of clarity over the ultimate value chain and customer.

In his book *Only the Paranoid Survive*, Andy Grove focused extensively on what he termed **strategic inflection points**, those points at which technologies totally change the competitive playing field in an industry.[26] Two significant characteristics of inflection points follow:

1. The old rules—the set of success factors governing winners and losers in an industry—change, and they change in ways that are poorly understood.

2. Nobody can quite tell when the change takes place, even in retrospect; the switch from the old to the new is amorphous.

This does not bode well for developing competitive advantage. Traditional methods for establishing competitive advantage can't apply in industries where the emerging value delivery mechanism is yet undefined.

The Need for Completeness

While anticipating and maneuvering against competitive evolution, it is equally critical to focus on the factors that influence the overall diffusion of and demand for new technology. Market growth and mass adoption depend on the development of new value delivery systems, standards, and interconnectivities. While Henry Ford might have believed that "Cars must come before roads,"[27] both "rules for the road" and the roads themselves are just as important to the adoption of the automobile. A similar observation can be made about the development of railroads, electricity, telephones, "talking" motion pictures, personal computers, and the web. If the systems, infrastructure, and rules governing how a technology is used haven't yet been established, the market is almost certain to be small and slow to develop, consisting primarily of early innovators, technophiles, and enthusiasts, rather than mainstream buyers. Both new and old firms will have difficulty in identifying where to focus effort and in identifying critical gatekeepers, and the result will be unappealing customer value propositions.

When Sega developed the Saturn game console, for example, its strong distribution channels and network of game developers in Japan meant that consumers could comfortably buy the hardware, knowing that it was an accepted standard around which a supporting market of complementors and complementary products (game software) would develop. As a result, the Saturn was a highly successful product in Japan. In the United States, however, Sega failed to build support from software houses or retailers and faced competing value configurations, which led to the ultimate failure of the platform.

Open standards, in particular, can vastly accelerate adoption by removing risk and facilitating choice for customers. Purchasing a DVD player, since one standard exists, is an easier decision than purchasing a game console, where multiple platforms that don't share software create additional decision-making issues. The paradox for a smaller **challenger firm**, whether first in or following the leader, is that while standards accelerate the penetration of the technology, they are seldom good for the challenger, as they favor firms with established business systems. Yet, with competing standards (an oxymoron if ever there was one), the cycle of competition has time to play itself out long before the market gains enough speed to appoint winners.

Technology and Institutional Change

Finally, new organizational structures, processes, and behaviors arise as a byproduct of innovation. The ubiquity of cell phones and instant messaging, for example, has changed how a variety of communication activities take place. Similarly, automobiles have created massive change in how communities develop, and television is considered to be a factor in the decline of a variety of social institutions.[28] Even computer networking has been accompanied by changes in the form of greater decentralization and a less hierarchical work force.[29] These influences cannot be ignored in attempting to introduce new technology.

Changes in underlying institutional patterns can act as a barrier if they are perceived as overly negative—as is often the case when jobs are at stake, business or personal interests are impacted, or major economic dislocation may result. At a minimum, they can slow the transition process for even the most attractive of innovations, since users may have a propensity to just substitute the new technology for the current/traditional technology until new social/economic structures emerge that intensify use of the new technology.[30]

Conversely, institutional changes can create a one-way path toward new structures and technology adoption by removing the path of retreat. In Los Angeles, the post–World War II embrace of the automobile resulted in the decline of the street-car system, creating a dependency on the automobile. Similarly, the decline in the use of money in favor of debit/credit cards may someday make us a "cashless" economy. This will require everyone to embrace "plastic" money and the underlying networks that make it possible, and will make it quite difficult to revert to traditional currency once the trucks, safes, banks, and other currency-related infrastructure have disappeared.

Lastly, technology-induced social change can create unanticipated issues, leading to a backlash against the innovation. The unanticipated behavioral issue in the trend toward plastic money is the increase in consumers' spending beyond their means.[31] In the case of genetically engineered foods, concerns over biodiversity and lack of control have dampened enthusiasm and acceptance, despite the agronomic benefits.

Like the issues surrounding competitive behavior and completeness, the issues arising from changes to longstanding social, economic, business, and other institutions need to be considered in order to understand the characteristics of technology diffusion, consumer adoption, and market evolution.

About This Book

The purpose of this book is to offer a strategic guide for determining and understanding the factors that influence the long-term success and viability of both new technologies and the firms that produce, purchase, or otherwise appropriate them. It is intended to assist managers in both incumbents and startups in planning accordingly. The potential opportunities and pitfalls differ substantially based on a variety of factors, including a firm's timing, resource base, external connecting points, technology portfolio, and capital. In the ensuing chapters, we will

❑ Develop a set of tools for identifying the potential impact of technology and the circumstances under which a new technology (or a firm pursuing it) can be potentially destabilizing,

❑ Measure new technologies against a life cycle of competitive innovation and diffusion,

❑ Identify the competitive implications for firms either developing or being affected by the technology, and

❑ Suggest appropriate strategies for navigating through periods of potential technological change.

For those involved or considering becoming involved in technology startups, this book should help clarify the strategic decision-making process. Capital and time are precious commodities. Individuals who anticipate the development of the competitive landscape can make better decisions about how aggressively to pursue markets, whether and when to pursue a consumer-facing or business-enabling opportunity, which core technology to focus on, and whom to align or partner with. Not every company should aspire to be the next Microsoft; for most, this is unrealistic. Positioning a company to sell out at a good return or to successfully dominate a niche is an equally admirable strategic goal and, for many, the best option.

For those in established firms, this book will provide help in determining how and when to leverage technology, which startups and new technologies pose potentially crippling or fatal threats, and how and when to respond. As we'll examine later on, it has become increasingly accepted that while large companies have the advantage when it comes to incremental innovation—including closeness to customers, category expertise, and supplier relations—smaller companies are more likely to come up with the **disruptive technologies** that cause the largest shifts in the status quo. The corollary to this is that large companies are in a constant state of peril, and vigilance is essential. As former Intel Chairman Andy Grove says, "Only the paranoid survive."

While the models and strategies that will be presented here are partially the result of a rigorous review and application of both emerging and classical economic and management theories, this book is designed to be used for practical application by investors, entrepreneurs, and managers involved in the technology sector. The book was developed with substantial input from a variety of sources, including leading venture capitalists, technology executives, successful entrepreneurs, and unsuccessful entrepreneurs. The result is a blend of practical application, academic research, and historical perspective, intended to assist the practitioner in planning and executing strategy.

The Three Perspectives

All the topics covered in this introduction will be examined in much greater detail later in the book. The objective of this initial introductory material is to highlight the three different perspectives necessary to identify the appropriate strategies for surviving and thriving in the face of changing technology. This book is divided into three parts, each of which is devoted to one of these three perspectives.

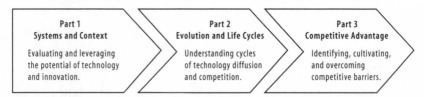

Part 1 Systems and Context	Part 2 Evolution and Life Cycles	Part 3 Competitive Advantage
Evaluating and leveraging the potential of technology and innovation.	Understanding cycles of technology diffusion and competition.	Identifying, cultivating, and overcoming competitive barriers.

Part 1: Systems and Context

Industry leverage points, market competitive structures, value configurations, component architecture, and market definitions all need to be considered in defining the risk and opportunity for both innovators and incumbents. They represent the systemic context in which a technology provider attempts to affect change and the ecosystem that the technology either exists in or disrupts. Part 1 focuses on methods of assessing the impact of firm size and resources, technology delivery systems, competencies, competitive dynamics, market definition, and other factors on a firm's strategic decision making.

Part 2: Evolution and Life Cycles

New technology must also be looked at in the context of its evolutionary life cycle. Whether a firm is first in, improving on someone else's idea, or an incumbent, the best way to attack and respond depends on how far along the technology is in a predictable life cycle of diffusion and competition. Decisions on whether to launch a new business directly, sell out, partner, focus on product improvements, or rapidly build market share are highly dependent on the anticipated development of both competition and demand.

Part 3: Competitive Advantage

Existing and potential barriers are an important element in survivability and the generating of superior long-term performance. Competitive imbalances allow firms to thrive in what would otherwise be hotly contested and therefore unattractive markets. Part 3 of the book looks at the strategies and tactics for both creating and disrupting competitive barriers.

Together, Parts 1 through 3 focus on making sense of the many factors that influence the opportunities and threats presented to various firms by new technologies.

A prominent and peculiar landmark in the middle of Silicon Valley is the Winchester Mystery House. Built by the heiress to the Winchester rifle fortune in the early 1900s, the house defies common sense, with windows in the floors, hallways that dead end, and stairways that run into the ceiling. While many people consider the unexpected twists of Silicon Valley to be just as mysterious as those of the famous house that sits at the center of it, the technology sector itself is not so mysterious that the basic laws of economics and competition don't apply. If anything, the availability of capital, potential windfalls for the winners, and the mobility of the work force increase the speed and intensity at which these basic laws take hold. As John Seely Brown has pointed out, "Competition is intense because in Silicon Valley, people know so much about their competitors. The amount of knowledge available about the players in the valley is incredible."[32] This relatively free flow of information in many technology sectors accelerates and nourishes competitive intensity.

Hunter or Hunted?

By now, the reasoning behind the title of this book should be self-evident. While technology-driven competition is predictable in its intensity, even the most agile of firms can find themselves at the wrong end of the rifle scope. A successful and dominant incumbent firm, intent on maintaining or growing its market share, may quickly have to face a disruptive new technology that threatens the viability of its entire market. An aggressive and ambitious startup may suddenly discover that a vanquished technology competitor has partnered with or sold out to a vulnerable incumbent, creating a configuration that puts the startup on the defensive. In both cases, the hunter becomes the hunted.

Many of literary great Jack London's stories from "the great white North" focus on characters who are conquered by the very wilderness that they've come to tame.

"Whatever we're hunting, I suggest we stop!"

Cartoon by Jerry King

Suddenly (usually too late), they comprehend that they haven't really understood their adversary at all. In these stories, it is generally hubris and a lack of understanding of the harsh and unforgiving climate that lead characters to their untimely end. This is often the case in the business arena as well.

As it was for the characters in Jack London's stories, the realization that one is no longer the hunter, but the hunted, can be chilling for a firm. By anticipating and understanding the life cycle of competition and employing the appropriate strategies, firms can maximize their opportunities against the force of technology-oriented competition. Doing so requires the right tools. In order to help develop these tools, this book will explore competitive dynamics, technology delivery systems, competitive life cycles, and appropriate strategies and tactics.

part 1

SYSTEMS AND CONTEXT

B iologists use the term *ecosystem* to describe the complex interactions of the plant and animal communities in an area along with the nonliving physical environment that supports them. The interrelationships are both symbiotic and competitive, and the fates of individual organisms and entire species may be determined largely by the ecosystem in which they subsist.

Businesses can also be thought of as inhabitants of an ecosystem. They exist as part of a complex network of interactions among suppliers, competitors, customers, partners, government agencies, external resources, and environmental factors. It follows that successfully introducing technology and innovation into a business ecosystem necessitates a deep understanding of the ecosystem's requirements.

Since profiling the ecosystem is a precursor to developing a strategy, Part 1 of the book will develop a variety of methods of placing technology and innovation in both a contextual and systemic framework. A new technology can be positioned in relation to an overall system of value creation, a firm's resource base, alternatives in the marketplace, necessary partnerships and complementary assets, and the overall product delivered. All of these determine strategic options for firms with a potential stake in the innovation.

Chapter 1 examines the impact of the size of the firm on factors such as behaviors, mortality, and agility. Large, well-established, "incumbent" firms and newer start-ups are radically different in composition and capabilities—and, consequently, strategic posture.

Chapter 2 focuses on technology delivery systems. Customers need complete solutions for value to be created. A firm's contribution to delivering a solution and competition between overall solutions are significant factors in the fate of individual firms.

Finally, Chapter 3 looks at the overall market in which a firm is attempting to compete. Market structure and industry definition are dynamic processes, and technological innovation plays a key role. Developing a framework for understanding and anticipating key technology-driven changes can help firms of all sizes compete more effectively.

Risk and Behavioral Patterns Among Startups and Incumbents

You show me the people who control the money, the land, and the weapons, and I'll show you the people in charge.
—**George Carlin**, *Braindroppings*

Why Size Matters

A common assignment in math, computer science, and biology classrooms involves modeling the behavior of predators and prey and their interrelated mortality rates over time. Referred to as Lotka-Volterra models, these models are more familiarly known as *sharks and minnows* or *deer and mountain lions simulations*. What makes creating these models so challenging for students is that while predator and prey populations are very different, their mortality rates are interrelated for a variety of reasons, including the facts that they might compete for resources, assist each other (symbiosis), or kill each other. The following Lotka-Volterra equation illustrates this relationship:

$$\frac{dN_1}{dt} = N_1 R_1 \left(1 - \frac{(N_1 + \alpha_{1,2} N_2)}{K_1} \right)$$

where

N_1 = Number of individuals of species 1

N_2 = Number of individuals of species 2

R_1 = Intrinsic growth rate of species 1

R_2 = Intrinsic growth rate of species 2

K_1 = Carrying capacity of species 1 when species 2 is absent

K_2 = Carrying capacity of species 2 when species 1 is absent

$\alpha_{1,2}$ = Competition coefficient (the effect of an individual of species 2 on an individual of species 1)

At the risk of grossly oversimplifying the intricacies of population modeling, we can summarize this equation by saying that the general assumption is that most populations reach equilibrium when, because of resource constraints, there are fewer predators than prey (as many as 750 deer for every mountain lion, for example). Typically, at equilibrium, predator birth and mortality rates are also low relative to those of prey. The behavior of each species is impacted by that of the other.

How does this relate to technology-driven competition? While the actual equilibrium numbers and factors in the economic arena will vary based on behavior and resources, the general underlying finding is the same: Markets are both stable and dynamic, with lots of startups (prey) that come and go rather quickly and a few incumbents (predators) that comprise a more constant population. Additionally, the startup and incumbent populations can be expected to behave quite differently from each other. In nature, the evolution and behavior of predators and prey differ radically. These differences are governed by the realities of their respective mortality rates. In business, where firms are usually run by individuals at least as self-aware and intelligent as sharks and minnows, it's no surprise that startups, with their high mortality rates, need to behave radically differently than incumbent firms. Unlike those in the wild, however, entrepreneurial minnows in the business world can aspire to become sharks themselves, so the analogy is far from a perfect one. Nevertheless, in anticipating the direction, behavior, and strategies of technology-induced competition, it's critical to take into account the size of the firm. There have been several serious attempts to apply Lotka-Volterra models to technology diffusion.[1] The significance of the distinct benefits and liabilities attributable to incumbents and startups makes size an important starting point in examining the impact of context on strategy. Indeed, firm size does matter.

Behavioral Patterns

The debate over whether incumbent firms have the upper hand in innovating or are burdened by their size and inertia has been an active one. Introducing technology innovation and the accompanying strategic, product, and process changes into a large enterprise is often compared to "making elephants dance," implying that large companies are unlikely to be nimble enough to substantively innovate.

Unquestionably smaller companies are more nimble, but this isn't necessarily advantageous and is not the only measure of the potential for driving innovation. The preceding section established that large and smaller firms have different characteristics and exhibit different behavior. As a result, the strategic challenges and options available to each are also different. As a result of their size and short-term operating history, smaller firms face daunting challenges in taking on incumbents, while incumbent firms face challenges in initiating or reacting to technology-induced changes as a result of the characteristics typically associated with larger established firms.

Resource and Usage Specificity versus Flexibility

Large incumbent firms have significant assets to bring to bear on a new product category, but they also suffer from a need to protect their existing franchises. If a firm is publicly traded, it is particularly encumbered and can't divert cash with the speed or flexibility called for when a real threat or opportunity emerges. One way of thinking about this problem is to determine which of a firm's investments, assets, and resources are firm specific, as opposed to nonspecific, and which are assigned to specific uses, as opposed to more general (flexible) uses (see Exhibit 1-1).[2] **Firm-specific resources** are the physical and intellectual assets applied by the incumbent firm. **Usage-specific resources** are the products and services against which resources are applied. Cash, for example, is a firm- and usage-flexible resource that may be invested indiscriminately (and thus would appear in quadrant A of Exhibit 1-1), while manufacturing capability is, in many cases, a firm-specific resource tied to a specific use (quadrant D). An example of a firm- and usage-specific resource investment is Gillette's $200 million technology investment in the Sensor razor. The technology developed was designed to address a specific market opportunity and extend a product set already pursued by Gillette (disposable razors), and much of the technology and research and development (R&D) involved in developing the Sensor were specific to Gillette's manufacturing capabilities. Large firms tend to be heavily biased toward investment in firm- and usage-specific rather than firm- and usage-flexible resources, since they are considered to have more influence on the firm's competitive position in its current markets, leverage the firm's existing asset base, and provide a more predictable return on investment. Gillette's six-point share boost and higher margins in the $5 billion shaving market attest to the motivation behind this bias.

EXHIBIT 1-1 ■ Resource Specificity Matrix

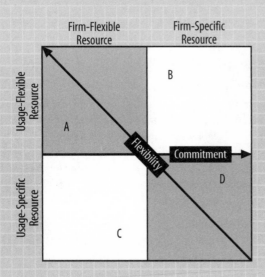

SOURCE: P. Ghemawat and P. del Sol, "Commitment versus Flexibility?" Copyright © 1998, by the Regents of the University of California; reprinted from *California Management Review*, Vol. 40, No. 4. By permission of the Regents.

Innovation in large firms is also based largely on in-house technology, with large elements of the firm's tacit and specific knowledge.[3] The firm's technology prowess can be thought of as a set of building blocks, with the current configuration leading to the next logical innovation. IBM, for example, found that its chance of success was high in taking technical risks in core computer markets where it had a strong and applied technology base; however, it had only limited success in incubating new businesses in unfamiliar markets such as those for medical and scientific instruments.[4] This is why incumbents are considered to be more adept at incremental change—a notion that will be reviewed in greater detail in Part 2 of this book.

Creative Activity versus Adaptive Response

Just as the behavior of minnows may not be optimal for sharks, technology-driven "young" industries have some characteristics that explain why incumbents may not consider such technology and innovation to be a part of their internal R&D investment scope. These characteristics include

❏ Unpredictable demand because first-version products are crude and long-term cost is unknown;

❏ Alternative and unproven technical approaches, which change rapidly; and

❏ An emphasis on new resources and skills over well-honed ones.

These qualities create a marked difference between the attributes of potential new markets and those of more stable existing markets.[5]

Startups, on the other hand, are more nimble and flexible, but have finite funding and often lack the infrastructure necessary to become viable ongoing concerns. Economist Joseph Schumpeter identified archetypes of startups and incumbent firms over the course of his research in the first half of the 20th century. Schumpeter labeled the focus of the archetypal startup as *creative activity* and that of the successful incumbent as *adaptive response.*

■ *Creative Activity.* Schumpeter's view of the creative process is summed up as follows:

> *Entrepreneurship—bringing the radically new into the economic system—has been the province of bold individuals because, in a world of limited knowledge, it is necessarily an unpredictable and extra-rational activity. Because of limited knowledge, "planning" is incompatible with innovation; progress depends on the ability of individuals to command resources and direct them in unconventional and surprising directions.[6]*

In other words, the path of innovation is often spontaneously determined and inconsistent with the highly controlled strategy-driven planning processes of large corporate entities.

Schumpeter also stated:

> We have seen that, normally, the modern businessman, whether entrepreneur or mere managing administrator, is of the executive type. From the logic of his position he acquires something of the psychology of the salaried employee working in a bureaucratic organization.[7]

This incumbent behavior has often been noted and has provided fertile ground for innovation consultants, yet it is often mischaracterized as a fatal weakness of large businesses. As demonstrated earlier, systematically leveraging the infrastructure (in terms of what assets a large firm has and how they are employed) can be both strategic and productive for an incumbent firm. It does present blind spots, however, in the incumbent's view of the potential evolution of the market and its ability to respond to it. These gaps, when not recognized and addressed, can be fatal. IBM's decision not to partner with Xerox in its launch of the first Xerox machine is an example of the inability to envision new market structures.

The Birth of the Xerox Machine

The path of Xerography from patent in 1937 to commercialization of the Xerox machine in the 1960s reveals how easy it is for large companies to become bogged down in existing business models and market definitions. After startup Xerox developed an initial commercial version of its process, it sought an incumbent channel partner to help launch the product in the office market.

Kodak and IBM were both offered—and rejected, much to their eventual dismay—the opportunity to bring the first Xerox machine (the Xerox 914) to market. IBM commissioned the management consulting firm Arthur D. Little to study the market potential of the 914. The consultants reported back to IBM:

> It has been extremely difficult to identify particular applications for which it [the 914] is unusually well suited in comparison with other available equipment. . . . Although it may be admirably well suited for a few specialized copying applications, the 914 has no future in the office-copying-equipment market.

Since the existing economics of the non-Xerographic process involved the purchase of a $300 machine on which less than 100 copies a day were made, the $2,000 price tag for the 914 seemed untenably high. Because of the superiority of the Xerox process, however, and lesser "variable costs" associated with the required paper and other supplies, customers who purchased Xerox machines actually used them to make an average of 2,000 copies per day, 20 times the pre-Xerographic usage rate. The technology, which made little sense in the industry's traditional business model, instead redefined it, and Xerox became a **category killer**.

SOURCE: Adapted from H. Chesbrough and R. Rosenbloom, "The Dual Edged Role of the Business Model in Leveraging Corporate Technology Investments" in L. Branscomb and P. Auerswald, *Taking Technical Risks: How Innovators, Executives, and Investors Mange High Tech Risks* (Cambridge, MA: MIT Press, 2001).

■ *Adaptive Response.* Fortunately for incumbents, Schumpeter's adaptive process (further developed by economist Israel Kirzner) predicts that a "great rush" follows the entrepreneurial process, where potential users and beneficiaries of a new economic opportunity seek to participate and control it. In other words, while true innovation and creativity may be stifled in large companies (as many corporate refugees will attest to), the end beneficiary of innovative technology is often still these same large enterprises, *if* they are sufficiently nimble to co-opt it.

Acquisition versus Internal Innovation

One way nimbleness manifests itself in large companies is through **growth by acquisition**, a strategy currently employed by many firms (including technology stalwarts such as Cisco, Microsoft, Hewlett-Packard, and Johnson & Johnson). Technology consultant Jim Pinto asserts, "It is difficult, if not impossible, to generate real innovation amidst the bureaucracy of a large company. The only way to get it seems to be by buying smaller companies."[8]

This isn't necessarily a fault in large enterprises. From a corporate CFO's perspective, the low probability of success and high uncertainty surrounding early innovative ventures make them best left off the corporate income statement. Once the future is more certain and technological and market uncertainties have been resolved, however, competitive forces dictate that incumbents will acquire needed technology capabilities accordingly. The acquirer's risk at this point becomes less technical than managerial.[9]

The consequences of combining entities are significant for both small and large competitors. Trying to go it alone can be difficult for a startup, even without the specter of competing firms aligning with large incumbent ones. Executives in small firms who focus on the innovation ineptness of much larger potential competitors miss the more important point of whether the larger incumbent is acquisition savvy. Once entry occurs via the purchase of new technology capability, the balance of power can shift immediately and quite dramatically. This is true even for the larger incumbent firms, as the capabilities of competitors can change overnight via acquisition.

One such example is Royal Philips Electronics' decision to acquire Systemonic A.G., a company that markets 802.11 wireless local area network (WLAN) chipsets. The growth of 802.11-based wireless networking has developed into a potentially significant change in the way devices interact, and it cannot be ignored by incumbents. As a Royal Philips spokesperson stated:

> *This market is beginning to mature and is going to demand larger players to service it. We're not among the first, but we certainly won't be the last to make this kind of announcement. I think in the next year you'll see some other smaller players either partner, get acquired, or go away. We see [our acquisition of Systemonic] as a home run because we have a huge capability to pull together IP and connectivity technologies enabling broadband access, network processing, and WLAN.*[10]

While Systemonic may have been previously viewed as one of many venture-backed startups, with narrowly focused technology and additional cash needs, the acquisition immediately changed the dynamics of the industry. As Systemonic's CEO affirmed:

> *Philips provides the consumer and communications expertise, global sales and marketing reach and manufacturing strength that will give our team the solid foundation to make our vision of wireless connectivity in the home, office and on-the-go come alive faster than ever.*[11]

Systemonic's $30 million in venture capital represented only one of many "bets" in the wireless industry, and Royal Philips was able to buy in on a bet that was ready to pay out, rather than having to make more speculative bets internally.

Stopping short of outright acquisition, licensing and joint ventures also allow incumbents to participate and control innovation in an adaptive fashion. While some technology entrepreneurs act to undermine established firms, others cooperate with incumbents and reinforce existing market power.[12] The desirability of these alternatives depends on the extent to which they give the incumbent a proprietary position (in the case of licensing) and the incumbent's proficiency in navigating the conflicts and management challenges (in the case of joint ventures).

The Winner's Curse

Schumpeter asserted as far back as the 1930s that it is very difficult for large companies to generate true innovation. A few notable exceptions are still routinely celebrated (3M and Intel come to mind), since they have been able to overcome the widely recognized **innovation inertia** that plagues most large organizations.

Barriers to Internal Innovation

A number of factors contribute to inertia undermining a large firm's innovation potential. The most successful large companies will seek to minimize these factors, which include long and often inflexible planning and budgeting cycles, an emphasis on predictability of earnings, a need to focus full attention on the core business, a tendency toward herding behavior, complacency, and overreliance on the status quo.

■ *Long and Often Inflexible Planning and Budgeting Cycles.* Midcourse corrections that deviate from the approved plans or budgets of large and publicly traded companies are difficult to make "on the fly." Recasting and rolling up budgets is a cumbersome and time-consuming process. Accounting firm KPMG, for example, found that its clients described their typical planning processes as highly iterative, inefficient, and ineffective.[13] 3M has addressed this problem by allowing some research time to be spent on nonspecific innovation and by encouraging departments to make this research available for use by any business unit, instead of compartmentalizing projects.[14]

■ An Emphasis on Predictability of Earnings. Wall Street closely watches earnings numbers, and many funds invest based on the ability of executives to meet earnings targets. Any unanticipated variance is typically met with swift retribution in the form of analyst downgrades and declines in the firm's stock price. As John Challenger, CEO of the nation's largest outplacement firm, said, "It's like standing in front of a train when bad earnings come out. The market is very harsh and punitive when a company does not meet its earnings expectations."[15] Other research indicates that investors actually react more harshly to companies that miss their expected numbers than to those that report lower earnings or even losses.[16]

■ A Need to Focus Full Attention on the Core Business. As pointed out by the consulting firm McKinsey:

> Top managers, already struggling to maintain contact with existing customers, markets, and employees, are faced with a growing information overload. In some cases, new ideas are suppressed too quickly; in others, top managers champion projects whose true potential hasn't been assessed accurately.[17]

The full plate of specific efforts on most large organizations' resource specificity matrices leaves little room for opportunistic or unpredictable innovation. Thus, size favors more predictable innovation in the form of line extensions and well-understood product roadmaps.

■ A Tendency to Herd Together. Because they read the same trade magazines, use the same research and consulting firms, attend the same educational programs, go to the same trade shows, and recruit personnel from within the industry, executives tend to define their businesses in a standard fashion.[18] This inhibits their ability to "think outside of the box" on either a process or a product level and results in standard solutions to many of the problems and products in any given industry. Guy Kawasaki, chairman of Garage Technology Ventures, laments that typically the best way to get to the top in large companies is by "keeping your head down,"[19] which implies following this approach. Business guru Tom Peters states that successful companies recognize that the most important innovations come from "the wrong person in the wrong group at the wrong time for the wrong reasons,"[20] highlighting the importance of an organizational culture that challenges conventional thinking.

■ Complacency. As marketing experts Al Reis and Jack Trout have pointed out, "Success leads to arrogance, and arrogance to failure."[21] When managers become successful, they tend to become less objective, substituting their own judgment for what the market wants. They may also develop a heightened aversion to risk. This complacency, combined with the psychological tendency to seek out information that confirms rather than challenges beliefs, leads to a lack of impetus to innovate.

■ *Overreliance on the Status Quo.* Throughout the 20th century, established firms have resisted radical innovation because of their investment (in terms of both capital and organizational design) in existing technologies and their delivery. When it comes to technology innovation, James McGroddy describes large companies as chess players at the poker table, more interested in modeling and planning their next ten moves than in placing bets.[22] Clayton Christensen further points out that customers tend to exacerbate this desire to maintain the status quo by insisting on a known paradigm, while new entrants to an industry have a clean slate to work with.[23]

The paradox is that while most of the above-mentioned factors tend to inhibit true **disruptive innovation**, they are also what make the large incumbents successful in the first place—that is, they represent the **winner's curse** or "competency trap." A continuous stream of new products and line extensions, designed to expand a well-defined franchise, is the lifeblood of growth in large companies. The same method of operating that allows large companies to expand the footprint of their franchise, as they seek to control more and more of the chessboard, prevents them from making radical innovations (often referred to as disruptive change) in the market. One of the best documented examples of this paradox occurred in the personal computer industry of the late 1990s. While Compaq continued to focus on making incremental progress in expanding products and channels to meet its stated goal of gaining twice the market share of its nearest competitor, Dell was busy pioneering a direct channel that took advantage of a build-to-order method of selling computers. Dell has built an infrastructure that allows it to wait to assemble computer systems until it has received an actual order, leading to customizable configurations, rapid product line changes, and inventory levels one tenth those of many competitors.[24] With few channel issues and existing product lines to protect, Dell was able to develop this new model for selling PCs. This ultimately proved to be a more critical and significant innovation. By 2000, Dell was the market share leader,[25] and CEO Michael Dell was talking about dominating the market.[26]

Skunkworks and Internal Development

For the dominant industry players, a big concern of management should be how to overcome the factors driving the winner's curse. One way this can be accomplished is by allowing a core group of employees to operate outside of the normal operating structure of the organization. These types of arrangements are called **skunkworks**, a term with origins in the classic comic strip "L'il Abner." Proponents of skunkworks believe that they break down many of the barriers that create predictability and control in large corporations, thus allowing true innovation. These barriers include complete technical specs, customer input, defined functional roles, defined processes, and large teams. Ironically, in large organizations these factors are typically considered to be prerequisites for successful project completion![27]

Why "Skunkworks"?

The term *skunkworks* originated from cartoonist Al Capp's classic comic strip "L'il Abner." One of the features of Capp's imaginary backwoods Dogpatch was an outdoor still called "the skonk works," in which Kickapoo Joy Juice was produced from old shoes and dead skunks. Kickapoo Joy Juice "was a liquor of such stupefying potency that the hardiest citizens of Dogpatch, after the first burning sip, rose into the air, stiff as frozen codfish."[28]

As a joke, engineers at Lockheed-Martin applied a variation of the name to their Advanced Aeronautics Development Program. While the name may have been a joke, the work that came out of their skunkworks was not. The purpose of the lab was to isolate engineers and machinists so that they could focus on making incremental leaps in technology, primarily for use in the Cold War. Lockheed's skunkworks has produced some of the most innovative airplanes in history, including the SR-71 Blackbird and U-2 spy plane. The term *skunkworks* stuck and has become the standard industry description for internal groups taken out of the mainstream corporate organization and given the freedom to innovate without regard for the sponsoring organization's rules of operation.

One of the best recent examples of a modern organization employing a skunkworks has been the brokerage firm Charles Schwab. In order to keep abreast of potential consumer technologies, Schwab has historically encouraged efforts to explore trading solutions using new technologies, without imposing the constraints of pricing strategy, integration, and planning methodologies that characterize the base business. Some of its forays into out-of-the-box thinking, such as PC-based trading in the 1980s, were not particularly successful. Others—in particular, Internet-based trading—turned out to be highly appealing, based on consumer technology developments.

Schwab's early success in Internet-based trading created several issues for the company. The skunkworks, operating independently of the rest of the organization, had a separate account for each customer (even if the customer also traded by phone) and a separate pricing structure, which was substantially lower than Schwab's base pricing. The online pricing was based on that of competitors in the online trading market, which were not necessarily seen as significant threats to the core offline business. The result was an online business that was much more successful than it might have been if Schwab had merely taken its offline model to the Internet—the more likely outcome without a skunkworks. Other examples of effective skunkworks-created products that became major components of a company's innovation and evolution include Apple Computer's Macintosh and Sun Microsystems' Java programming language.

EXHIBIT 1-2 ■ Advantages and Disadvantages of a Skunkworks

Advantages
- Ability to explore alternative pricing, partnering, and new approaches
- Potential access to capital and joint ventures
- Flexibility in results and profit timing

Disadvantages
- Consistency in product lines, branding, and channels
- Integration issues
- Possible loss of internal innovation capabilities

While it is tempting to include cannibalization among the disadvantages, the entire point of a skunkworks is to innovate before competitors do.

The dark side of the skunkworks strategy is also illustrated by Schwab's Internet efforts. As it became clear that the Internet would play a significant part in Schwab's future, the separate account tracking and the channel-based pricing discrepancy became major problems for the company. Eventually, Schwab lowered all prices to the Internet rate and re-integrated the accounts. The decision was a difficult one, given the expense and potential revenue losses associated with the re-integrating effort. Some of the advantages and disadvantages of a skunkworks are listed in Exhibit 1-2.

As technology consultant Michael Schrage points out, overreliance on skunkworks can also be a sign of managerial weakness:

> *A skunkworks is not a sign of great management championing inno-vation; skunkworks are instead a signal of management that has given up on innovation. When an enterprise goes skunk, what's the real message? Top management effectively acknowledges that their corporation is incapable of internal organic innovation and must set up a different organization with different people, different val-ues, and different incentives. In other words, management launches a skunkworks because it has failed to create an organization that can innovate without skunks.*[29]

A variation on the skunkworks concept is **corporate venturing**, which involves a more formal separation of an incumbent sponsoring company and an innovator. This strategy creates an entity capable of behaving like a small startup while accruing bene-fits for the incumbent. Corporate venturing and venture capital investment (intro-duced in the next section) will be considered in greater detail in Chapter 4.

The Risk-Tolerant Nature of Startups

Unlike the incumbents described above, startups exist in a system designed for high risk and high return. This creates an opportunity to innovate in areas left mainly unex-plored by incumbents and makes competing against Microsoft less daunting than it sounds. Rather than the controlled growth and tightly managed expectations preferred by executives in publicly traded companies, CEOs in startups seem resigned to uncertainty and risk as facts of startup life. Leading venture capitalist Vinod Khosla believes, "It takes a certain amount of fearlessness and naiveté to be a successful entrepreneur ... you have to have the big idea, but you also have to be foolish enough to believe that you can pull it off."[30]

Encouraging and Diversifying Risk

The fearlessness of startups is due in no small part to the composition of the typical startup's board, which includes the venture capitalists that have invested in the business. While VC funds are not necessarily highly risk tolerant, they rely on a diversified portfolio to diminish risk, rather than managing risk at an individual company level.

Although few VCs release details on portfolio performance, the efficacy of the portfolio approach can be seen by examining the investment results of a venture firm called Technology Funding. The firm publicly released details of previous performance as part of a prospectus for a new fund called Technology Funding Venture Capital Fund VI. Over the course of the 1990s, several of its funds made investments in 29 IT and communications companies, for a total of $48 million. The total return was at an annualized 3.40% rate (poor for a venture fund, but more than compensated for by TFI's success in biotech and medical technology sectors). The firm's results showed that, as of March 1998,

- ❑ 8 companies were still actively held in the portfolio,

- ❑ 7 had been liquidated at a complete or near complete write-off,

- ❑ 6 had gone public, and

- ❑ 8 had been disposed of (via merger or sale).

If the active (nonharvested) investments are put aside, the top two winners in the portfolio accounted for only 14 percent of the initial investment in the group of 21 companies, but contributed 60 percent of the portfolio value post-event. These two winners, Geoworks and UTStarCom, made up for a host of other nonperformers.[31]

These results are consistent with other research that indicates a **skew-distributed outcome**: A small number of innovations and innovators are responsible for most of the total value realized by venture funds. In studies covering over 1,000 startups, the top 10 percent of the firms typically realized roughly 60 percent of the total value. The top 10 percent of patents were even more impressive, realizing roughly 90 percent of all of the eventual value captured.[32] This explains why venture funds actively seek returns of 500 percent or above—they need to make up for the many nonperforming investments in their portfolio. Founders are wise to understand this expectation prior to accepting significant venture capital. The box on page 29 highlights how disproportionate rewards and market confusion play into the venture capitalist's decision to invest.

For incumbent firms, the implications of venture funding are also profound. Venture capitalists place bets on ideas and in areas where incumbents are unwilling to invest. If the target sector happens to threaten one of an incumbent's revenue streams, the business may fall victim to a seemingly irrational wave of competitive activity and a

> ## Placing Bets

Bill Frezza of Adams Capital describes a broad rule of thumb for attracting venture capital including, among other things, a potential exit valuation of $100 million at the time of IPO, as measured by those of comparable businesses in the same sector, and a plausible chance of giving first-round investors a tenfold return on their money. He observes that, considering the high failure rate of early-stage companies, disproportionate rewards are the key to attracting the high-risk money.

Jim Breyer of Accel Partners points out that confusion is what creates opportunity for venture capitalists and venture-backed firms:

> *Perhaps the defining characteristic of what we look for, taking all things into account, is confusion. Confusion is an enormous positive for the businesses that we participate and invest in. Massive confusion indicates to us that established leaders such as Microsoft, Cisco, and Intel are unlikely to put together a detailed, implementable plan on their own. They can buy into the market, but they won't innovate.*

SOURCES: MRS bulletin, August 2002; and U. Gupta, *Done Deals: Venture Capitalists Tell Their Stories* (Boston, MA: Harvard Business School Press, 2000).

proliferation of potential competitive threats, especially if the sector becomes "hot." Ultimately, however, venture funding may also promote the development of new technology-driven opportunities—in the form of infrastructure improvement or new markets—that can later be acquired by the incumbent.

The Liability of Newness

While incumbents may face a winner's curse, startups have their own set of challenges that threaten their survival.[33] These challenges are primarily related to the technology itself, market uncertainties, and a host of infrastructure issues in the area of organization (roles, responsibilities, workflow), external relationships (with suppliers, partners, complementors, and other stakeholders), and processes related to developing products that customers want and need. Employees of startups often lament that they work harder, but not necessarily more efficiently, than they would in a larger firm. While lack of processes might appear to enable a startup to accomplish more, it creates issues regarding prioritization, organizational support, and tools and structures needed to share critical information. These issues manifest themselves in a variety of different types of risks, including early technology risk, market risk, systemic risk, and management risk.

■ *Early Technology Risk.* While a firm may have a promising idea or invention, it may not be able to move from this phase to actually **productizing** the innovation (turning it into an actual product or service). This can be due to a variety of factors, including difficulties in establishing a cost-effective manufacturing process, insufficient quality and reliability to cost-effectively service the market, problems with adapting the product for existing or planned distribution systems, and inability of the team to complete the product.

The inglorious landing of NASA's $250 million Genesis project exhibits the technology risk inherent in newness.

SOURCE: NASA.

■ **Market Risk.** Gauging demand without formal channels and customer experience against which to refine hypotheses can lead to building and launching products that simply don't interest the market. Customer trial may not indicate intent to repurchase, success with early adopters may not lead to mainstream product acceptance, and unanticipated competitive offerings may alter expected customer behavior. While market risk exists for all firms, startups have less-developed processes for minimizing this risk and also suffer from a lack of reputation and permanence, which creates a higher hurdle for acceptance of new products.

■ **Systemic Risk.** Even a successfully productized technology that has potential market appeal can be "frozen out" of the market if the young firm lacks the ability to access sales channels, create appropriate bundles, or gain the necessary support of third parties. The latter portion of this chapter and Chapter 2 will further discuss the ability to fit the startup and its products into product and value delivery systems for end customers as an important element of market penetration.

■ **Management Risk.** If developing a workable and realistic business plan is in itself a challenge, executing the plan is an even greater challenge and source of risk. Mistakes are magnified, and a startup's survival can depend on such seemingly routine activities as making a key sales hire, adhering to product management best practices, and managing supplier relationships. Effective decision making, implementation, communication, and general team-related processes are critical. Unlike incumbent firms, which have cultures, practices, and processes in place, startups need to create them—a very difficult task, which many executives may not be capable of.

While these issues differ markedly from the inertia factors for incumbents, startups must work equally diligently to minimize the impact of these risks of newness on their chances of success. A product milestone focus, frequent target market/customer inter-actions, a strong network, a tight team, and good hiring and deal execution practices can reduce these risks. Not coincidentally, these are the very areas on which venture capitalists tend to focus in evaluating and later supporting their portfolio companies.

RANDY KOMISAR ON

THE CONTRAST BETWEEN STARTUPS AND INCUMBENTS

Randy Komisar is a Consulting Professor of Entrepreneurship at Stanford University and a partner at well-known venture capital firm Kleiner Perkins Caufield & Byers. He is the author of a best-selling book on entrepreneurship, *The Monk and the Riddle*, pub-lished by Harvard Business School Press, and is also the subject of a Harvard Business School Case Study on innovation in building new businesses. Randy was previously CEO of LucasArts Entertainment and Crystal Dynamics. He currently serves as a direc-tor or advisor to a number of public, private, and nonprofit organizations.

Randy believes that large and small companies excel at different types of innova-tion. Large-company success relies on leveraging established policies and proce-dures designed for managing complex and large-scale operations:

> *Large companies are particularly good at incremental and customer-driven innovation. They value and are structured to solicit extensive market feedback, and have well-developed processes and ecosystems to support existing businesses and markets. They also have resources and expertise that makes them highly capable of taking products from concept to market.*

> *They don't do as well in breakthrough "game-changing" innovation. While large companies excel at process, this type of innovation is not process driven. To the extent that large companies have the flexibility to adjust their market definition, M&A, joint ventures, and partnerships are legitimate R&D substitutes for this in large companies. On a risk-adjusted basis, this may make more sense for them.*

In looking at venture-funded startup companies, on the other hand, Randy sees organizations that are free of traditional large-company constraints and are encour-aged by investors to pursue uncertain paths:

> *Start-ups are valuable because of their speed, innovation, vision, and willingness to flirt with disaster. Following a plan is not the key to start-up success. You have to set a course and constantly question its appro-priateness, zig-zagging to avoid the minefields that pop up around every turn while staying as true to your compass as possible.*[34]

Randy says:

> *Teams who come together in a startup to develop a new product and new business have a heightened level of confidence that they know what the market needs. Because the startup's initial concept is built*

around the confidence in a better solution rather than market consensus, relying too heavily on market feedback can lead to paralysis.

Randy emphasizes that these differences are driven primarily by the risk profiles of the two types of firms and their respective shareholders:

Large companies have quite a few "false negatives." While new products tend to succeed, risk aversion leads to many potentially successful innovations being shelved. Fundamentally, large companies err on the side of not making mistakes. The more uncertain the technology, the less likely established companies are . . . to pursue it. Their culture is typically not built around tolerating failure or rewarding risk taking.

On the other side, the higher risk acceptance in the VC-fueled innovation industry leads to a lot of false positives. The portfolio-oriented business model means that less screening is necessary, since the market results will determine the winners. It is a laboratory model, where failure is much more tolerated and built into the overall industry's financial model.

Finally, Randy points out that organizational models differ dramatically between the two types of businesses. While large companies focus on continuity and leadership development, startups often require leadership changes and the acquisition of skills and talent from outside the company as they progress:

Small companies exist on a continuum. The move from pure technology development to productization requires a change in competencies, new capital, and managing a different kind of risks. The next progression—to market and ecosystem development—again requires different skills and a change in focus. Large companies are beyond this in maturity, and focus on institutional maintenance and fine-tuning existing processes.

The Power of Complementary Assets in Technology Adoption and Organizational Viability

It is often said that innovation is the lifeblood of firms. If incumbent firms are risk averse and not prone to develop truly innovative technology, why are they still incumbents? The primary reason is that the delivery of any product or service to a customer requires a series of value-creating activities, of which technology innovation is only a part. These activities are often represented in the form of a value chain, which identifies the various activities needed to successfully deliver a product to market.

For example, a novel compound from the Brazilian rainforest with cancer-curing properties is in itself relatively worthless. To exploit the technology, a firm would need to employ R&D to refine the compound, test it in a laboratory setting on animals, use clinical trials to determine its efficacy and effects on human populations, and follow FDA approval procedures (see Exhibit 1-3), as well as develop manufacturing processes and sales procedures.

EXHIBIT 1-3 ■ Value Chain for Getting a Drug to Market

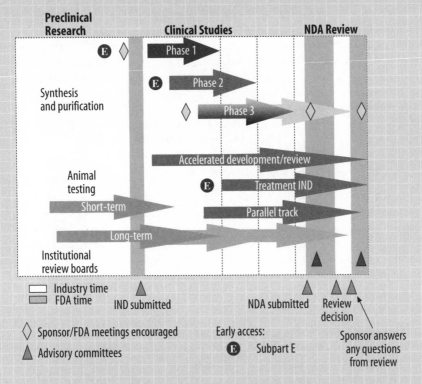

Note: NDA = new drug application; IND = investigational new drug application.

SOURCE: USFDA-CDER, http://www.fda.gov/cder/handbook/develop.htm, accessed on July 21, 2004.

Likewise, an inventor of a new soft drink would need to execute purchasing, manufacturing, distribution, and sales strategies in order to get the product into the hands of consumers. When a firm is attempting to exploit a technology-related innovation (or other intellectual property), these other value-chain activities are the ones that require complementary assets. **Complementary assets** include sales force; distribution channels; brand; customer relationships; manufacturing expertise; a current installed base of users; interdependency between new products and existing products; public perception; and everything else that isn't categorized as technology or intellectual property. Examination of the list makes it clear that these complementary assets are almost always held by incumbent firms. As a result, the relative importance of these assets is one of the most critical variable determinants of strategy and competitive threat for both startups and incumbent firms.

Like many other new technologies, the technology associated with talking motion pictures took time to become entrenched in the market. Those holding the necessary complementary assets controlled the diffusion.

> ## Talkies and the Motion Picture Business

The release of the movie *The Jazz Singer* in 1927 is identified as one of the defining milestones in motion picture history, as it was the first "talking picture." Warner Brothers and Thomas Edison's motion picture subsidiary both usually get partial credit for introducing talking motion pictures. While it is true that Edison was a film and sound pioneer, as early as 1905 the French inventor Leon Gaumont was showing off his "chronophone," while Augustine Lauste was experimenting with a "photocine-mataphone." While these systems were far from perfect, the rate of improvement and adoption of the technology was quite slow. Talking pictures can be classified as a disruptive technology, with significant additional value for consumers and cost savings for theaters, which no longer had to hire live musicians. So why didn't any new studios emerge to capitalize on this potential market opportunity?

Since the technology for talking motion pictures required both "head" and "end" equipment (a situation not uncommon among many of today's network infrastructure providers), coordinated agreement by both film producers and theaters was required to actually deliver the motion pictures to market. The existing studios also had the content—as most of the movie stars of the day were under long-term contract. Without the stars and theater distribution—two important complementary assets—a new studio would have found it quite challenging to get talking pictures produced and screened.

As the established studios began expanding into the movie house market in the early 1920s, they began to have both the necessary control over the distribution system and the interest to push through the deployment of sound delivery technology. Though Harry Warner, one of the Warner brothers, once said, "Who the hell wants to hear actors talk?" perhaps he really meant, "Why the hell do *I* want to *let* the public hear actors talk?" Once it was clearly in their own best interest, the Warners introduced the technology change on their terms.

SOURCE: S. Eyman, *The Speed of Sound: Hollywood and the Talkie Revolution* (Baltimore, MD: The Johns Hopkins University Press, 1999).

Since many technology-based firms are focused on intellectual property (chip design, code, processes, etc.), they may incorrectly assume that complementary assets are less important or easily acquired. Professor David Teece's examination of EMI—an audio recording company that, as a byproduct of its research into pattern recognition, invented the CAT scan (technology used for imaging and mapping the human body)—identified an important distinction between enterprise value creation and innovation. EMI, despite a significant technology lead in this new market, was forced to exit in less than a decade.

> *We can now see very clearly why EMI failed, despite having created an order-of-magnitude technological breakthrough. The scanner that EMI developed was of a technological sophistication much higher than would normally be found in a hospital, requiring a high level of training, support, and servicing. EMI had none of the requisite complementary assets and capabilities, could not easily*

contract with them, and appears to have been slow to realize their importance.[35]

The technology pioneered and possessed by EMI was only one of many factors necessary to win in the healthcare equipment arena.

VentureOne tracks the performance of startups over time, and a review of its database shows a correlation between the extent to which complementary assets drive a sector and the end results for startups in that sector. As Exhibit 1-4 shows, in the information technology and healthcare sectors, where complementary assets are most important, VC-backed firms are much less likely to remain independent over time. Generally, these firms either go public (and thus can afford to build the complementary assets), are acquired (most likely by companies with the assets), or go out of business. Thirty percent or less of the IT-related and healthcare companies were independent after 10 years, while almost 50 percent of the other companies were independent over the same time frame.

The importance of complementary assets to a technology-based startup can be characterized in one of three ways: Are complementary assets

❑ Important and inaccessible?

❑ Important and accessible, but expensive?

❑ Unimportant or able to be bypassed?

EXHIBIT 1-4 ■ The Fate of Startups by Sector

		Date Founded				
		1990–1992	1993–1994	1995–1996	1997–1998	1999–2000
Healthcare	IPO	33%	21%	14%	5%	—
	Merger/Acquisition	27	22	12	8	3%
	Out of Business	14	16	10	6	3
	Independent	26	41	64	80	94
IT-Related	IPO	24	20	15	5	—
	Merger/Acquisition	31	29	28	18	4
	Out of Business	15	14	8	7	8
	Independent	30	37	48	70	87
Other Products/Services						
	IPO	22	21	15	5	—
	Merger/Acquisition	14	14	12	11	7
	Out of Business	15	17	12	12	15
	Independent	49	49	61	72	77

SOURCE: Based on data from VentureOne.

Important/Inaccessible Complementary Assets

Lack of access to critical complementary assets can have a profound impact on the viability of technology-based startups, and it can be a powerful competitive tool for entrenched incumbents in shaping markets.

As an example, consider one of the early and now-defunct leaders in the cable Internet market: a firm called @home. It built and provided the central network infrastructure, substation equipment, and service organization for cable-based delivery of broadband Internet access, but lacked the most important element in providing the service—a physical cable into the homes of potential consumers. This is often referred to as the last-mile problem. This particular "last mile" was controlled by major cable operators such as AT&T, Comcast, and Cox, which had invested substantial capital in building infrastructure in exchange for a near-monopoly in their trading areas. In order to gain access to the lines, @home funded much of the equipment capital cost (in the form of substation and Internet infrastructure) and then gave the cable operators in excess of 50 percent of the revenue generated from the service. For the cable operators, the arrangement proved to have short-term financial benefits, while allowing them to learn about and evaluate the technology. Since they controlled the lines, there was little risk of @home cutting them out of the market. @home, on the other hand, had a very tenuous position: Its gear was installed in cable company facilities, and its knowledge base could not be protected. On @home's withdrawal from the market, AT&T was able to deploy a network in a matter of weeks. AT&T's complementary assets (existing cable lines, service crews, and billing relationships) provided it with a lower cost structure, while the technology transfer occurred without financial gain for @home.

Anticipating the consumer migration toward broadband and the power of the major cable companies, AOL in the 1990s became an aggressive lobbyist for creating government-mandated open access to cable lines. Eventually, AOL acquired Time Warner, gaining access that it could not otherwise have hoped to get through Time Warner's cable properties. Not all firms can make $100 billion acquisitions, however, underscoring the risk for startups in targeting markets where an entrenched incumbent has a set of complementary assets that cannot be duplicated. AOL's situation also demonstrates the insulation that unique complementary assets can provide to incumbents against new entrants, even ones with a "better mousetrap."

Important/Expensive Complementary Assets

One area of seemingly continuous innovation and investment is that of enterprise software. As shown in the simplified enterprise software value chain in Exhibit 1-5, a firm with an enterprise software application needs to excel at solution sales, application integration, and vertical market customization—not just core software development—to create valuable customer applications.

Software is most valuable when it can be installed in customers' environments, solve their problems, and work with their other systems. For a firm to succeed in the enterprise software arena, it must look well beyond its code and gain access to the necessary

EXHIBIT 1-5 ■ Simplified Enterprise Software Value Chain

complementary skills. This can be very challenging, since the sales/solution provider and application integration markets are dominated by very large professional services organizations, including BearingPoint, Accenture, and Deloitte. Only the largest of software organizations, such as Oracle, IBM, and Microsoft, can afford to deploy organizations to compete against these firms. Costs aside, the reputations of these firms and their existing relationships with Fortune 1000 companies would make it difficult for a new entrant. Reputation plays a key role in decisions regarding enterprise software. So what is the rest of the industry to do? The Chasm Group stated:

> *Successful companies create well-defined value chains where all players in the chain understand their role and make good money in the process. . . . This typically means aggressively partnering with the other participants not just at a corporate level, but through active market planning, product management and field selling.*[36]

With capital in limited supply, partnering becomes critical to acquiring complementary assets for many startups. While many eventually (post-IPO) build the most critical of these assets, the pre-IPO firm must focus heavily on strategic relationships to deliver its products and/or services and evaluate a range of go-to-market strategies, as NCompass Labs did with its content management software. This approach (to be discussed further in Chapter 2) is a practical one, since the startup's core strength may lie in the technology area anyway.

NCompass Labs Knows Its Limitations

The small technology firm NCompass Labs started out as a university web browser project in Canada in 1995. The company, seeing that the browser market was beyond its reach (think Netscape and Microsoft), began exploring other technologies and eventually focused its efforts on content management—a category of software designed to simplify and automate many website publishing and organizational tasks. The area was evolving quickly as user needs and technology changed, and this discouraged the incumbents from developing solutions—moving targets present extra risk. Eventually, NCompass found itself marketing a solid and well-regarded product called Resolution, which was built to integrate with customers' Microsoft NT–based web server platforms.

Microsoft, with its increased emphasis on ".net"—an initiative to provide fully integrated web building products—realized that content management was an important component of its strategy. Without assuming a technical or cash risk in advance, Microsoft was able to add this capability simply by buying NCompass Labs in 2001 (after evaluating other choices as well). NCompass could not hope to compete against Microsoft's reach, channel, support, and brand, and the revenue potential for Resolution was much higher as part of Microsoft, which could tap into these complementary assets to expand NCompass's market. This made NCompass much more valuable to Microsoft than it was as an independent company. Microsoft was able to quickly enter what was developing into an important new market segment.

Unimportant/Bypassable Complementary Assets

When complementary assets are unimportant or widely available, a technology provider has a significantly greater amount of leverage and, therefore, can retain a larger portion of the "value." Building the complementary assets (if necessary) is easier, and finding partners and setting terms on a favorable basis is more realistic, given the lack of leverage of the partners.

For example, a company that had patented a unique multifold box for packaging and merchandising small items (such as toys, videos, and software) would be able to directly contact a wide base of customers and would have a number of paperboard manufacturers to choose from. As a result, it would be able to maintain attractive margins in the traditionally low-margin packaging supplier business. Typically, in these cases intellectual property represents a large proportion of the price of the item relative to actual variable manufacturing costs.

When Technology Is Easily Imitated or Substitutable

The analysis above of complementary assets assumes that the technology provider has a defendable technology, based on patents, trade secrets, or other types of insulation from competition. If the underlying technology is not protectable (as in the case of @home and EMI), then rapid imitation should be expected. (This market behavior will be examined in greater detail later in Part 2 of the book.) With merely a temporary lead, the technology owner can rely only on speed (when complementary assets are unimportant) or on securing contractual partnerships with the asset owner and otherwise locking up market share (when complementary assets are tightly held). Incumbents can be expected to quickly imitate or duplicate noninsulated technology, once it shows market potential. Partnering with the complementary asset holder before they recognize the opportunity can create a barrier to imitation by these incumbents. Conversely, incumbents with valuable complementary asset bases should be cautious about long-term commitments that lock them out of markets they could develop themselves, unless the terms (as was the case with @home) are highly favorable.

Strategy Based on Core Strengths

Some world-class incumbent firms have both strong complementary assets and a technology platform. Possessing a brand, a means to deliver the brand to market, and proprietary technologies that are built into products or services represents a strong competitive position. Most firms, however, are weighted more heavily toward one or the other and should focus their efforts on the dimension that provides the most opportunity for the firm. For startups and even many more mature technology-focused firms, this often means avoiding overinvesting in some complementary assets.

When Technology Is the Platform

For technology providers, underlying technology assets can be thought of as a **platform**. Capturing value depends on effectively productizing and distributing the technology in key market sectors, thereby maximizing the value of the intellectual property. As discussed previously, many of the variables associated with successfully capturing value are complementary assets, and not the core focus of startups. The distribution of revenue and profits can be highly dependent on access to these assets, and the choice of an appropriate strategy for gaining access is a function of their uniqueness and cost.

While many startups are tempted to enter distinct vertical markets in order to accelerate their market entry and capture greater portions of the product revenue, they may do so at the expense of the firm's technology platform, as shown in Exhibit 1-6. Take as an example the artificial sweetener Aspartame (originally marketed by Monsanto's Searle unit as Nutrasweet). One of the single largest markets for sweeteners is the soft drink market. The sugar in soda accounts for roughly 10 percent of the calories consumed by the average teenager.[37] Consumers in the United States drink, on average, over 50 gallons of soda annually![38] For those marketing a sugar replacement, clearly the soda market is an attractive target. On the other hand, the market has very costly shelf space and other distribution barriers, and brands are highly important and time consuming to build. Even "overnight successes" (such as Red Bull) can take a decade to catch on and still garner relatively small market share. Faced with this market, nine years remaining on its patent window, and an expertise in pharmaceuticals, Searle decided to market Nutrasweet as an ingredient rather than entering the soda business, since entering the business directly would require investing significant resources in

EXHIBIT 1-6 ■ When Technology Is the Platform

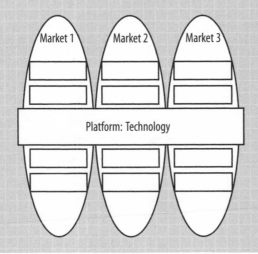

skills specific to the soda market. In hindsight, choosing an ingredient market worth perhaps $2 billion instead of the $50 billion soda market—despite a patented technical advantage—seems like a rational decision for Searle to have made. But many firms, particularly in technology industries, are unable to come to this same conclusion about their own products. Even Searle couldn't resist trying to go directly to market with Simplesse, a fat substitute, by launching its own Simple Pleasures brand of ice cream.

By avoiding oververticalization and the need to build or acquire the complementary assets to compete in the soft drink market as a soda marketer, Searle was able to capture a much larger share of the market much more quickly, grow Nutrasweet sales much faster, and focus efforts on other segments and initiatives. Anticipating the loss of patent protection, Searle expended resources turning the patented intellectual property into brand equity (by investing in developing the Nutrasweet brand name) so that at least some of the technology value would remain associated with Searle, despite the lower barriers to competition. The firm might not have been able to pursue this strategy if it had been focused on establishing its own soda brand.

In contrast, Searle did go more directly to market with Equal sweetener and was successful with that strategy. Unlike the soda (and ice cream) market, the sweetener market had relatively few competing brands, Searle had easier access to channels, and the product itself was a much larger component of the value delivered to the consumer. In this case, the complementary assets were less of a factor (relative to the intellectual property), and so their acquisition was a more reasonable use of resources.

When Complementary Assets Are the Platform

Conversely, how should a holder of complementary assets approach technology? Much like technology, a set of complementary assets can be used as a platform when the goal of the firm is to maximize revenue by driving products through the asset platform, as shown in Exhibit 1-7. Partnering is equally important in this case.

EXHIBIT 1-7 ■ When Complementary Assets Are the Platform

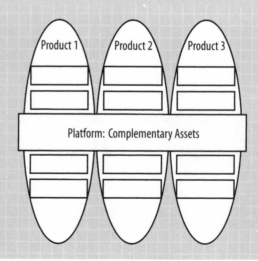

The Walt Disney Company, for example, has movie production, distribution, and marketing assets, which it has used to develop a variety of branded characters.[39] While Disney is vertical in some "products" (videos, theme parks, clothing), in order to maximize its assets it also needs to be horizontal, partnering with others to leverage them. Some of this partnering is simple character licensing to firms with additional complementary assets, such as those in the frozen foods industry. In other cases, partnering is with firms that have technology competencies that Disney lacks, but that do not have access to Disney's assets. Pixar, for example, the maker of *Toy Story* and *Monsters, Inc.*, is well ahead of Disney in digital animation technology, but has brought its movies to market using Disney's important distribution and marketing assets.

When Technology Is a Complementary Asset

In some cases, technology itself can become part of the incumbent's complementary asset base. In the late 1980s, Frito-Lay, for example, invested heavily in direct store delivery system technologies that helped move products to market more efficiently. This distribution system became one of its core competencies. Many manufacturing processes/systems, such as Intel's manufacturing expertise, also serve this role for their owners.

An important strategic assessment management should undertake is determining when a technology drives the company's product platform (and thus is subject to outward-focused productization), when it is used to develop a complementary asset base (and thus allows the asset owner to bring in and productize new technology), and when it is neither. As an example of the latter, in the 1990s Del Monte Foods divested itself of and then outsourced both its can manufacturing operations and IT services, since neither was providing a leverageable platform and both were tying up capital assets in providing services that could be easily acquired on the "outside."

EXHIBIT 1-8 ■ Summary of Complementary Assets

If complementary assets are	Technology providers/developers should
Important/Inaccessible	Aggressively seek partners.
	Reconsider chosen markets.
Important/Expensive	Partner.
	Build complementary assets only if there is sufficient time and capital.
Unimportant/Bypassable	Execute multiple partnerships.
	Consider building complementary assets.
If complementary assets are	**Complementary asset holders should**
Important/Inaccessible to Others	Seek technology to expand franchise.
	Negotiate from power with technology owners.
Important/Expensive for Others	Partner.
Unimportant/Bypassable	Lock up attractive technologies.

Exhibit 1-8 outlines the approach firms should take, depending on the accessibility of complementary assets and whether they are the asset owners. Exhibit 1-9 factors in the leverage obtained by firms that own either a unique complementary asset or a unique technology. Earlier in the chapter, it was pointed out that nimble firms can co-opt technology, even if they don't develop it internally. Exhibit 1-9 points out that firms that leverage their size and experience so as to make market access difficult for smaller technology firms can control markets and co-opt technology on favorable terms.

One of the challenges of truly disruptive technologies, however, is that they can lack specificity and relevance to the incumbent's complementary assets, either bypassing them or rendering them unimportant. The ability to determine when this is the case is critical. Mapmaker Rand McNally, for example, had valid concerns that electronic tools such as Internet-enabled interactive mapping, and eventually GPS and location-based services, would replace its printed map products and distribution system. All of these technologies seem potentially disruptive to printed map products and could also be construed as eliminating Rand McNally's complementary asset base. Consumers' gradual movement toward interactive mapping has not completely undermined the company's base business and complementary assets, however, nor has it eliminated the value of the Rand McNally brand. Attempting to leverage these assets might have been more prudent than embarking on a startup trajectory into interactive areas, which

EXHIBIT 1-9 ■ Who Profits Most from Innovation?

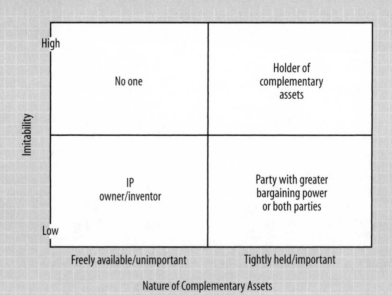

SOURCE: Based on D. Teece, "Profiting from Technological Innovation," *Research Policy*, Vol. 15, 1986.

eventually led Rand McNally into Chapter 11 bankruptcy. Chapter 3 will focus on developing tools for recognizing when these table-turning shifts occur and how to address them. Along with Chapter 7, it will also discuss how incumbents can deal with the uncertainty surrounding potential disruptions.

CHAPTER SUMMARY

This chapter began with a look at population modeling, used as an analogy to highlight the fact that incumbent and challenger firms are distinctly different in nature. The stability of large firms comes from their existing business infrastructure, capabilities, revenue base, and product sets, which both enable and (in most cases) require that innovation be more specific and incremental to their current markets. While this can lead to an inability to make more dramatic (disruptive) leaps in technology, proper adaptive response will allow incumbents to co-opt many of these innovations once they show potential. This approach is often dictated by internal organizational issues, the clear return on investment in incremental opportunities, and an inability to take on the kind of risk inherent in startups. One way to avoid both these internal issues and the need to co-opt innovation is through the use of skunkworks, which are not constrained by these limitations. Corporate venturing can also be used to develop innovation without the typical internal constraints of successful firms. Alternatively, a strong and valuable complementary asset base will often give incumbent firms an additional opportunity and motive to gain access to external innovations and, ultimately, to benefit from them. The exception to this is when a radical innovation de-emphasizes the importance of or eliminates a firm's complementary assets.

Startups should take more innovative approaches to technology development, given their risk profile, lack of revenue base, and funding mechanisms. This, however, does not eliminate the need to eventually acquire internal organizational skills and complementary assets in order to take the technology to market. Depending on the complexity, importance, and accessibility of these assets (as well as access to capital), the startup can either build them, partner for them, or sell out in order to leverage the technology. Even if it has developed a complementary asset base that is marginally competitive with those of incumbents, a startup can unwittingly overinvest in these assets, creating a situation in which it can no longer fund the expansion and support of the technology platform necessary to gain widespread adoption of the innovation.

Technology Value and Delivery Systems

*Always remember that the purpose of all software is to provide
you with a sufficient level of computing power so that your
hard drive gets filled up and you need to buy a new computer.*
—**Dave Barry**, *Dave Barry in Cyberspace*

Beyond a Better Mousetrap

Chapter 1 demonstrated that there is more to successful technology introduction than simply "building a better mousetrap." The size and resources of a firm determine its capabilities, and issues such as access to key resources and the freedom to operate within a market matter just as much as intellectual property does. Clearly, innovative technology is of little value to a firm that cannot get it to market, either on its own or through partnerships.

This view of technology from a market and institutional context also reveals that the importance of an innovation is related to the overall market delivery system it influences or changes, creating value for end users. This chapter will explore how the value of a technology relates to its role as an embedded piece of an overall technology delivery system.

While the classic economic measure of a technology's incremental value is the increase in product/service demand driven by increased utility or cost reductions, the impact of technology change is often widespread and complex and can be qualitative rather than quantitative.[1] As a result, a whole spectrum of measures can be used to evaluate the potential value of a technology, including cost reductions, new feature sets, new applications, greater efficiency, and customer utility. Whatever the measure, however, it is rare for technology to deliver value without context.

A better mousetrap

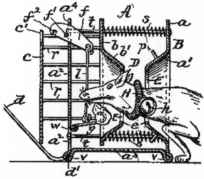

SOURCE: Patent No. 883,611, issued March 31, 1908, from
http://www.bpmlegal.com/wmouse.html.

For example, a patented new way of dimpling golf balls is valuable only if the balls can be put into mass production, used in conjunction with standard tees and golf clubs, and approved for play by the sanctioning golf organizations. If it does not satisfy the contextual conditions, the technology is merely an interesting physics experiment. Likewise, a new method of wireless data transmission depends on the availability of spectrum, and a new computer operating system depends on both hardware/chipsets to run it and applications software to make it useful. Even a company's development of an internal IT application is valuable only in the context of its alignment with other systems and processes of the firm. The constraints in these examples relate to a number of factors, including *market factors* (e.g., the influence of sanctioning bodies for golf), *environmental factors* (e.g., the impact of the type of grass surfaces used by golf courses), and *institutional factors* (e.g., the availability of the assets necessary to put the golf ball into mass production). There are also several constraining factors related to the technology system itself (e.g., the ball's performance in relation to existing clubs and tees), which is the primary focus of this chapter.

Whether a firm is evaluating technology as an incumbent, leveraging technology as a challenger, or determining how to get technology to market as a startup, the overall systemic context is critical. As Harvard professor Marco Iansiti has pointed out, "When inevitable inconsistencies arise between technology and existing system characteristics, the results will be delays, the need for additional resources, longer lead times, and poor R&D performance—even industry exit."[2] This is not to say that technology should always be designed around existing systems. Pioneering new delivery systems is at the heart of innovation and leads to true disruptive change. For example, cable television would not exist if all television manufacturers and broadcasters had continued to focus on only broadcasting and receiving signals over the airwaves; airlines' issuance of directly booked e-tickets is not consistent with historical methods of booking travel through travel agents; and circuit-based telecommunications will eventually be replaced by IP-based systems. What is important to recognize is that technology needs context, whether it can be found in an existing delivery system or requires the building of another.

Developing tools for understanding new technology as part of an overall technology system will greatly simplify the often difficult process of understanding what it is that a specific technology does to add value. It will also illuminate how the organization and roles of various technologies and their providers in the delivery system impact the capture of that value, the distribution of profits, and influence within the industry. These tools will form a framework for answering a variety of critical questions relating to the introduction of new technology into the marketplace, including the following:

❑ Where is the technology positioned within its overall delivery system?

❑ Does the technology really matter?

❑ Where does the power lie within the system?

❑ How does this power influence the adaptation, profitability, and sustainability of the technology?

❑ Does the new technology create new market opportunities?

❑ Does it enable new competitors?

❑ Does it threaten existing competitors?

❑ Does it change the structure of the industry (in terms of delivery channels, profitability, and scale, for example)?

These questions should be addressed by anyone engaged in strategic decision-making processes related to the adoption of a new technology and should also be carefully considered by technology vendors seeking to determine the market opportunity for their new technologies.

Product Completeness and Modularity

The examples of different platforms in Chapter 1 focused primarily on market verticalization—taking an existing product platform, packaging it, and using appropriate channels to provide a complete solution and meet the needs of a particular market segment. Such verticalization often requires some partnering. A meeting of the minds is necessary between an incumbent with the means to reach and sell products to a segment and a technology provider with a solution that the segment wants. Relative leverage between the potential partners determines the distribution of revenue and thus the likely outcome for both parties. For example, cellular phone manufacturers partner with telecommunications carriers, rather than building their own cellular networks and marketing channels.

In order to meet the needs of the market and the partners, however, the product platform itself needs to provide a complete technology solution. While cellular phone manufacturers must ensure the connectivity of the phones they manufacture, the phones themselves are an integration of various components, chipsets, and software, without which partnerships with telecommunications carriers would not be possible. This product integration is at the heart of the R&D process for many major technology companies.[3]

The need for a complete solution at the product level comes with its own set of associated competitive issues and strategy. If the patented golf ball dimples discussed previously require that a special club face be used rather than the existing standard, for example, the ball is not likely to be accepted by golfers unless the golf ball maker also has a viable strategy for migrating golfers to new clubs or modifying their existing ones. Addressing the interplay with the other technology components of golf is an integral part of delivering the technology to market.

The need for complete products, coupled with the inability of most firms to invest in and excel at supplying all of the pieces or subsystems, has led to a **modular approach** to product design in many industries. Car manufacturers, for example, dictate the design characteristics for car tires, but design their manufacturing process so that the tires can be built by outside vendors. The tires are simply added on at the factory. This modularity means that outside parties, unaffiliated with the car manufacturer, can provide tires that are used as part of the automobile. The complexity of the various components that deliver a complete solution for high-tech products has led to the widespread use of the modular approach in high-tech markets.[4] Commonly referred to as *modularity*, *open architecture*, or *open systems*, this open approach allows for faster development and greater choice of component technologies, leading to superior complete solutions in most cases.

A key distinction between the modular approach discussed here and the approach used by Disney and Aspartame (see Chapter 1) is that a formal relationship between the technology owners need not be in place. The relationship that does exist is often contentious, with aggressive jockeying for industry influence and profits. IBM discovered this in the 1960s when it first migrated from a proprietary integrated technology approach to a modular approach to computing. Previously, computers had been built as stand-alone systems, lacking backward compatibility, migration capabilities, interoperable software, interoperable operating systems, and compatible processors. The computer manufacturer acted as a master contractor for the closed system and maintained tight control. IBM's rationale for switching to modularity was to allow a variety of different companies to share the burden of innovation, to create an easier upgrade path for customers wanting to purchase new hardware, and to enable the development of a whole line of mainframes with different combinations of hardware, software, and peripherals. The company anticipated that all of these developments would grow the market and increase IBM's lead. Indeed, a major benefit of modularity is the rapid innovation it fosters.[5]

An unanticipated consequence of modularity for IBM, however, was the rise of an industry of "IBM-compatible" products, which often took profits away from IBM. These products were not necessarily built with IBM's best interests in mind. By substituting a product architecture built on standard component interfaces, modularity intentionally creates a high degree of independence and a loose coupling of suppliers.[6] This creates competitor, supplier, and customer dynamics that can influence the fate of the firm.

The Technology Stack

One of the most useful tools for assessing technology delivery and determining the competitive structure of an industry in a modular world is the **technology stack model**, which puts technology into the context of a complete delivery system. Delivering a complete product generally requires that new technology be used in conjunction with other technologies. Thus, the set of relationships among technologies, the alternatives, and the interdependencies reveals a great deal about the opportunities created by the technologies and the prospects of the companies that introduce them.

As an illustration, a technology stack model can be applied to the field of plant biotechnology, where patents are granted on individual genes, the ability to alter the behavior of a gene, vectors for introducing changes into a gene, and markers used for measuring whether a gene has actually been successfully introduced into a plant (gene expression). To genetically engineer a tomato that doesn't spoil quickly, a biotechnology firm must have access to all four technologies—one of the tomato's spoilage-causing genes, a method for somehow influencing the gene in a positive way, a method for inserting the altered gene into a young tomato vine, and a way of measuring that the process was successful. Exhibit 2-1 shows how one company put together its technology stack in order to develop genetically altered tomatoes. In this case, the gene identified was widely available via the USDA, the change mechanism was proprietary but not unique, and the vector and testing mechanism were unique and (unfortunately, for DNA Plant Technology) owned by Monsanto.

Since one firm (Monsanto) owned the patent on the only known reliable method of introducing altered genes into a tomato, it clearly had an inside track for development and significant leverage over competitors in the field. For the other necessary technology components, there are either choices or only limited barriers to access. Although DNAP owned a patented change mechanism, the leverage and value represented by its technology component was limited by the existence of an alternative method. A firm building a proprietary but not unique solution may have some advantage (if the solution is relatively better), but not as dominant an advantage as it would have with a truly unique technology layer. The price it can charge for licensing the technology to others is limited by its value relative to other solutions; the price for a unique technology (assuming that the firm owning it believed in modularity and wished to share) would be relatively higher.

Clearly, the conditions of availability and the interplay of stack layers are critical to determining profits and competitive position in an industry, as well as the value and likelihood of adoption of technology. A complete technology stack is crucial to directly tailoring the genetic makeup of crops.[7] Based on the stack shown in Exhibit 2-1, it should be no surprise that Monsanto, which endeavors to own the technology in key layers of agricultural biotechnology, has captured roughly a 90 percent market share of the global transgenic seed market.[8]

EXHIBIT 2-1 ■ The Technology Stack of DNA Plant Technology's Tomato

	Stack	What It Does	Who Owns It
Gene	ACC Synthase Gene	Controls ripening (ethylene production)	USDA; license available to multiple companies
Change Mechanism	TranSwitch Patent	Shuts off gene	Proprietary; other methods exist
Vector for Plant Introduction	Cauliflower Mosaic Virus	Inserts gene into a plant's DNA	Monsanto
Agent for Testing Success Rate	Kanamycin Resistance Marker or ALS	Successful plants survive antibiotic exposure; others die	Monsanto; other methods under development

Ownership of layers gives firms significant control. In the case of agricultural biotechnology, the strength of IP control of key layers means that few firms can gain freedom to operate across all layers, a key requirement for a complete product.[9] Agricultural biotechnology is an extreme case, with clearly defined rights and few alternatives for firms aspiring to design and build innovative complete products. This lack of freedom to operate has meant that, unlike the semiconductor and pharmaceutical biotechnology industries, the agricultural biotechnology industry so far has been structured around a relatively small number of tightly woven alliances, each organized around a major life sciences firm and each vertically integrated from basic R&D to marketing.[10] As later discussion will show, this industry structure, with tightly controlled layers, may be one of the limiting factors in category diffusion.

Standard-Bearers and Layer Ownership

While technology standards as a source of competitive advantage will be discussed in greater detail in Chapter 10, it's worth noting that the existence of alternatives does not in itself ensure that no one firm will be able to leverage market power, nor does strong patent protection of the "best" solution ensure success. If the industry participants rally around or by default choose a particular solution that gives the solution's owner a significant market share, then this in itself is enough to influence the technology stack. Quite often, the standard most widely favored by technology users is an open one, so that choosing the standard doesn't benefit a particular for-profit enterprise or transfer profits to the supplier of the dominant layer technology. This isn't always the case, however. IBM is widely credited with launching Microsoft's current dominance by choosing Microsoft's MS-DOS as its operating system for PCs; in a similar fashion, the motion picture studios embraced Dolby as a sound standard, though Dolby is an independent firm.

The advantages for industry participants of rallying around a specific platform provider are primarily oriented toward the leadership role the standard-bearer assumes in

❑ Creating an architecture with adequate modularity,

❑ Coordinating the activities of various firms on other stack layers, and

❑ Setting a future platform direction that allows firms to confidently produce their next generation of platform-compatible products.[11]

Where standards are open and no formal standard-bearer exists, lack of coordination can severely restrict market growth. This was the case with the UNIX operating system in the 1980s and 1990s. UNIX was described as having "as many authors and personalities as the graffiti spray painted on a Los Angeles freeway . . . and the underlying baggage of having to form coalitions to meet agreement."[12] This both slowed market development of further key standards and opened the door for other operating systems. Lack of leadership also creates a market opportunity for a firm to develop modular but not standards-based products, as will be discussed in a later section on multi-layered solutions. There is a clear tradeoff between selecting a standard-bearer at the risk of ceding economic leverage and using an open standards approach that may create confusion and slow diffusion.

Large incumbents are typically seen as potential standard-bearers because of their influence over the stack participants and their access to channels and customers.[13] This role can be used by an incumbent to create an even more dominant position. Controlling the overall architecture is in itself a potential source of proprietary technology, even if the stack layers are primarily open. The opportunity for the standard-bearer in this case is to keep a proprietary layer firmly entrenched in an otherwise open solution that is widely supported. Microsoft and Intel have done this through the basic **Wintel architecture**, which is at the dominant center of the personal computer market and is well positioned in the server market. As will be discussed further in the next section, these two firms benefit from this architecture because they have kept control of proprietary layers. IBM, on the other hand, had architectural control of the market early on, but failed to hold onto either the microprocessor or the operating system as a distinct proprietary layer. Consequently, a world of IBM-compatible computers has done little for IBM.[14]

Influence of Stack Position and Control on Profitability

Expanding the stack view to include the entire array of solutions in each layer helps clarify the dynamics of competition as well as the distribution of profits and power in an industry. Witness the personal computer market and web server market referenced earlier. As shown in Exhibit 2-2, in the PC market, Intel and Microsoft (Windows) are both highly dominant in their particular layers, as most PC solutions include both Intel and Windows. This dominance ensures that most of the profits accrue to Intel and Microsoft. Microsoft—with virtually no competition—had a

EXHIBIT 2-2 ■ Dominance in Web Server and PC Market Layers

	Web Server Market				PC Market				
Applications	Depends on segment				Microsoft		Others		
Middleware	IBM Websphere	BEA J2EE	MS .Net		Active X		Java		
Database	IBM/DB2	Oracle	SQL	my SQL	N/A				
Operating System	Microsoft Windows		Unix	Linux	Microsoft Windows				Mac
Hardware	HP	Dell	IBM	Sun	HP	Dell	IBM	Other	Mac
Processor	Intel		Sun	Mac	Intel			AMD	Mac

EXHIBIT 2-3 ■ Microsoft Key Business Segment Margins (in millions of dollars)

	Revenue	Operating Income	Margin
Client (Operating Systems)	10,394	8,017	77%
Server Platforms	7,140	1,121	16%
Information Worker (Desktop Software)	9,229	6,486	70%
Business Solutions (Enterprise Software)	567	(309)	(55%)

SOURCE: Microsoft SEC 10K filing, year ending June 30, 2003.

77 percent gross margin for its operating system segment in 2003,[15] while Intel—with a bit more competition and higher manufacturing costs—had a 57 percent margin.[16] Both of these contrast quite favorably to the margins of downstream PC makers. Dell, for example, has a gross margin of less than 20 percent. Apple Computer, in contrast, avoids the Wintel solution by providing its own operating system for the Macintosh and using a processor supplier with less leverage (Motorola). This reduced stack pressure allows Apple to achieve a much higher gross margin of over 25 percent, but at the cost of using a nonstandard solution, which has relegated the firm to a very small market share. In the web server market, where greater competition exists on most layers, Microsoft does not have such dominance either in profit margin or in market share (Exhibit 2-3).

The ability to broadly diffuse an architectural layer can lead to large profits for the firm that controls the layer.[17] In contrast, when a solution becomes more standardized, competing alternatives lead to limited supplier leverage and additional "commoditization" puts pressure on suppliers to deliver better price and performance at the expense of margins.

Influence of Stack Position and Control on Technology Adoption

Far from simply influencing profit distribution, the layer dominance possessed by Microsoft has also allowed the company to influence the layers above and below it in the PC technology stack. Other firms relying on the standard Wintel stack as part of their architecture must await Microsoft's product changes before making their own and must respond with products that match the changes in Windows. Virtually all PC software produced is in some way influenced by Windows, and once written for Windows, this software further solidifies Microsoft's dominance. While this is the source of much ongoing litigation, options outside of the courts for breaking free of this influence are extremely limited.

Platform leadership is defined as "the ability of a company to drive innovation around a particular platform technology at a broad industry level."[18] Platform ownership ensures that a standard-bearer has the opportunity to continue to shape the development of an industry around its solutions. To ignore the requirements of the next release of Windows would be a mistake for software developers downstream (above Windows in the stack), since it is clear that Windows is the dominant operating system on which their applications will be run. Since the software will be developed to run on the next release of Windows, Microsoft can dictate how many of the software's functions interact with the operating system, creating a virtuous circle (or notorious circle, depending on your viewpoint), which continuously reinforces the Microsoft architecture. Upstream, if the interaction between the processor and the OS requires certain coding or chip design, then both Microsoft and Intel must design for compliance with each other. Since their interests are aligned, this does not present a threat, although both support each other's rivals as well.

Dependence on Partnerships and Integration

With the complex interplay among various technology providers and the need for their solutions to come together in a coordinated fashion, maintaining relationships is an important facet of success in a stack-based architectural model. As Harvard Business School's Carliss Baldwin and Kim Clark point out, "[Modularity] transforms relations among companies. Module designers move in and out of joint ventures, technology alliances, subcontracts, employment agreements, and financial arrangements as they compete in a relentless race to innovate."[19]

Geoffrey Moore describes learning how to partner as one of the biggest challenges for high-tech executives, surpassed only by the challenge of learning to *compete* in markets dependent on partnerships.[20] It's no surprise that elements of the organizational structure of technology firms in Silicon Valley are markedly different from those of their "old economy" counterparts. Large business development organizations, partnership groups, industry education functions, and even **evangelists** are all in place to promote technology adoption and control the interfaces between layers of technology stacks. In many cases, the structure of these firms actually mirrors the architectural approach—with flatter organizations designed to create and dissolve alliances and interact with fewer and simpler rules.[21]

For a firm to effectively leverage its new technology for long-term viability, possessing the organizational capabilities and skills to develop partnerships—both formal and informal—is key. Without these capabilities and skills, the firm cannot effectively integrate its technology into complete solution stacks that meet customer needs. Even for a large incumbent, innovating and commercializing new technology is faster, costs less, and entails less dependency on core competencies when the firm emphasizes partnering and integration with other firms. Corning Glass, for example, was able to tap into the fiber optics and telecommunications business by partnering with Siemens. Corning's technology layer in telecommunications is glass fiber manufacturing, and by partnering it was able to direct this core skill toward a high-growth market and become a significant part of the technology solution for the telecommunications industry.[22] Polaroid, on the other hand, was less inclined to partner and develop the third-party relationships it needed to succeed with digital photography technology.

> *Polaroid and the Shift to Modularity*

Up until the late 1990s, Polaroid was a highly successful provider of "instant photography." Polaroid was described as having a "veritable fortress of patents," which covered most of the core platform technology associated with instant photography.[23] From this platform, it developed a variety of products according to its own specifications (much like IBM in the early 60s). Polaroid formed few third-party relationships, as it had a strong and uncontested key technology layer that allowed it to capture the value in each layer of the instant photography stack.

The development of digital photography technologies, however, created a significant shift in the instant photography market and the skills necessary for success. Without the patent-protected, inimitable technology platform that the firm had enjoyed in instant photography, Polaroid's proprietary digital stack had to compete with many modular open system solutions. These other solutions could be built with components from best-of-breed providers, such as lenses from Nikon, chips/software from Intel, and printing/processing from Hewlett-Packard. Recognizing this, the CEO of Polaroid stated,

> *We're not going to do this by ourselves. We are going to need alliances, partnerships, ventures with other companies, especially in the digital arena where relatively few folks have the breadth and scope to do it alone. . . . Even beyond that you have the systems integration kinds of opportunities that present themselves, especially in the commercial arena.*[24]

However, in the more open and modular world of digital photography, Polaroid lacked the skills to develop these technology alliances and influence the market to accept it as a standard-bearer. Polaroid's past practices and early digital approach made it an unlikely candidate to be embraced in this fashion by the market. The company clung instead to a model of large-scale internal invention and a **razors and blades approach**, which was inconsistent with the open modular approach being developed elsewhere in the industry. Consequently, Polaroid has not been able to convert its success in the instant photography market to success in the digital photography market.

Adopting a Layer-Based Platform Strategy

As discussed in Chapter 1, a firm choosing to develop a technology platform needs to focus on **productization** of the technology—finding a "collection of common elements, particularly the underlying technology elements, implemented across a broad range of products."[25] The Monsanto tomato discussion illustrates that technology platforms can encompass more than one layer of technology (Monsanto has both the vector and the market layers). What the Monsanto case does not illustrate, however, is that the key to platform strategy is often to leverage the technology platform broadly (horizontally), whether internally or externally.

In adopting a modular approach, therefore, a firm must learn to focus on segment penetration and technology dissemination, rather than market share of the end products produced internally. For Palm Pilot and Research In Motion (RIM), for example, the movement toward a platform focus has meant allowing others—such as Handspring in the case of Palm and Nokia in the case of RIM—to compete for end users in the sale of handheld products and placing greater emphasis on share of operating system and penetration of core technologies. Similarly, Motorola's move from a proprietary bundled architecture to a modular platform-based strategy in its cellular phone business has created a need to focus on overall installed base, even if many of the phones embedded with Motorola technologies are sold by competing firms.[26] The goal is diffusion and horizontal market share—an important part of developing and maintaining modular leadership.

Unbundling the BlackBerry's Bundled Architecture

The problem addressed by the Canadian company Research In Motion with its BlackBerry product is a simple one, crucially important to e-mail users: how to access and synchronize corporate e-mail while on the road. By offering an e-mail server, handheld device, OS platform, and even wireless access, the BlackBerry device/service gives the corporate road warrior an easy way to access e-mail residing on the corporate e-mail server. The service is always "on" and presents users with the kind of real-time e-mail connectedness they are used to in their office.

Facing intense competition at each layer of its stack (as shown in the following table), RIM elected to partner, rather than build connectivity.

	RIM	Potential Competition
Servers	E-mail synchronization server	MS Exchange, IBM/Lotus Domino
Devices	BlackBerry	Palm, Handspring, Compaq, phone manufacturers
OS	Proprietary	Palm, Windows CE
Access	Motient, others	Carrier networks

Given that the competition was formidable and well-developed and well-tested technology already existed, why has RIM, a small device manufacturer, emerged as the early winner in this market?

The real challenge in this case is the architecture—putting the technology together for easy interoperability between layers. Palm, which leads the PDA market, was the logical company to do this, but focused on web connectivity rather than messaging. This allowed BlackBerry to file key (although contested) patents covering this interoperability. Without a clear and simple open systems alternative, BlackBerry has been able to win a significant amount of business by giving users a complete solution.

As a standard stack develops, the proprietary bundled architecture strategy presents potential risks for BlackBerry, unless RIM is confident of its patent coverage or can transition its closed system into an open one. While defending its patent coverage aggressively and selling its own devices, the firm is also moving toward the latter layer-based strategy by negotiating with Nokia (the world's largest mobile phone manufacturer) to offer the BlackBerry operating system on Nokia phones, by partnering with major carriers, and by opening and promoting its OS to third-party applications developers. As RIM's chairman put it, "If you want BlackBerry with our device, fine. If you want it with another device, fine."[27]

Both the strength of RIM's patents and its ability to gain horizontal market share are important variables in its long-term market position.

Multi-Layered Solutions

There are two significant issues that adopters of the modular approach confront:

1. It takes time for market standards to develop and complementors to emerge.

2. Incumbents are favored as the overall system architects.

These issues are particularly significant for startups, which have an incentive to disrupt the status quo and can't always afford the luxury of waiting for the market order to develop.

Using a complete **multi-layered approach** (also referred to as a *bundled architecture*[28]) is a way around these issues. By removing the chicken and egg issues surrounding technology stacks, this solution opens new markets more rapidly and gives a non-incumbent a chance to take a leading role. In established markets, debates over whether vertical integration or modularity is advisable often center on the issues of value capture, flexibility, complements, and capital in relation to choices available on each layer. In some cases, modular markets can actually move backward, toward a more bundled approach, as dominant layer owners emerge and consolidate their position, locking new entrants out. In the case of new technologies, however, where clear standards don't exist and consumer need does, a simple single-vendor solution is often requisite to remove ambiguity while ensuring that the primary consumer need (the **killer application**) is met. Wang's word-processing workstations, RIM's BlackBerry pager, Palm's Palm Pilot, and Apple's Macintosh are examples of technology innovators that captured distinct markets by providing complete bundled architecture solutions.

Although the solution provider need not offer a proprietary solution of its own at each layer, it should take on the role of assembling various technologies to offer the customer a complete solution, whether or not the individual technologies are market-leading (or industry-endorsed) open systems standards. Consulting firm McKinsey refers to this as a **network orchestrator** role:

> *A network strategy thus enjoys important advantages. . . . First, the orchestrator chooses both its partners and the standard, instead of waiting for the market to embrace the standard it has chosen, and then hoping that the applications providers come around. Since market-based standards are harder to erect, broader in sweep, and thus fewer in number than proprietary networks, companies have a better chance of launching networks.*[29]

The early success of Atari, a pioneer in the console-based video game market, was based on setting standards for a modular stack, from microprocessor to cartridge design, rather than waiting for standards to emerge. The console-based gaming industry has continued to succeed in growing and launching new platforms by using multi-layered proprietary technology networks. Each manufacturer determines what chips, operating systems, and hardware are most appropriate for its bundled offering.

The Long-Term Issues of Bundled Architecture

Over time, early bundled architectures become ripe for attack from open systems.[30] Once standards are established and a dominant design emerges, a vertically integrated or self-determined multi-layered solution can be a risky strategy. Several problems can arise—including higher costs, fewer complements, slower innovation cycles, and perceived technology risk—which make bundled architecture difficult to maintain for the long term.

■ **Higher Costs.** A dominant standard design leads to "dramatic decreases in product cost."[31] These cost reductions result from the standardization and interchangeability of technologies at each layer, an increase in the number of firms supplying the technologies at each layer, scale economies enabled by standardization, and greater market penetration. Pursuing a go-it-alone platform, with increased vertical integration and less concern for standards, leaves a firm with less sales volume on which to justify and amortize R&D. The possibility of achieving cost reduction through economies of scale in manufacturing or competitive supplier bidding is also reduced.

A striking example of the cost of a closed platform was shown in a Stanford study of comparative technology choice in the Department of Defense.[32] The study tracked the results of two similar satellite control projects. One, code-named "Stream," adhered to "COTS" (Commercial Off The Shelf) technology, while the other, code-named "Sword," was built on a more conventional (for the military) custom software platform.

> *The resulting differences were staggering. For example, Stream's system cost $1.25 million (mostly Dell computers and COTS software); Sword's cost $40 million. Stream required annual maintenance of $200,000 per year; Sword required $2 million. Stream took six months from the time the acquisition was approved until it became operational in late 1999; Sword took 32 months from approval until it became operational in mid-2000.[33]*

■ **Fewer Complements.** Developers of third-party applications and complementary products suffer from the same scale-related issues mentioned above, making accessories higher priced and less abundant for customers. A comparison of add-on hardware and software products for Mac- versus PC-based computers makes it clear that less choice at higher cost is one of the issues associated with proprietary solutions. One of the constant dilemmas for the console gaming industry has been the question of availability of software titles from third parties. Since game development requires some incremental investment for each particular console supported, developers hesitate to support newer or less-established platforms. Microsoft's Xbox's disappointing initial sales numbers were widely reported to have been caused by a lack of third-party software, a pattern often repeated throughout the history of the console gaming industry.

■ *Slower Innovation Cycles.* When multiple firms compete for business in an open market, innovation happens at a more rapid pace, new products are less costly to implement, and entrepreneurial firms have fewer barriers to entry. Since the proprietary standards–based system is less attractive to complementors, less effort is put into innovation for these product stacks. The market will simply "flow around" these products, as it did around Wang's word processor and Digital Equipment's Vax computer line, two closed architecture but dominant tools that did not evolve at a quick enough pace.

■ *Perceived Technology Risk.* As the market develops around standards, the multi-layered or bundled architecture provider can appear to be out of step if the layers used in its solution don't match up with the standards being deployed by the remainder of the industry. An early provider of rewritable DVD players, for example, would have needed to make a variety of specification- and technology-related architectural decisions (recording speed, software, hardware, etc.) to assemble a product that would enable a customer to record to a DVD. The alternative was to wait for market standards to emerge, at which point the opportunity to ship an innovative product would be limited. As an industry grows, however, if the early innovator's solution is different from and not interoperable with that of other device manufacturers, the innovator's market share will suffer.

Another potential effect is that the entire market will develop more slowly because of customer uncertainty, which limits the diffusion of the technology. In the midst of the rewritable DVD battle, Wolfgang Schlichting of IDC commented,

> *Confusion over format compatibility is sending shockwaves to potential buyers—consumers, PC buyers, and OEMs—and that is resulting in lower rates of acceptance in the PC world. Standards confusion will continue to make market conditions challenging for all players. Consumers need assurances about DVD compatibility.*[34]

As Exhibit 2-4 shows, a number of possible DVD-recording technologies were in use in 2002. Apple, which put a DVD burner in its desktops relatively early, adapted a DVD–R standard, while Microsoft, Hewlett-Packard, and Dell later lined up behind the DVD+R standard. By 2004, many manufacturers had given up and started producing dual-standard drives in order to try to attract consumers, despite the additional licensing costs.

Another example of the impact of technology risk is in the satellite radio industry. While the FCC is working toward interoperability, customers must make a bet—in the form of a radio purchase—on whether their provider will be in business for the long term. Both of the leading companies in the industry in 2004—XM and SIRIUS—carry significant debt, have large operating losses, and are far from a sure thing. A consumer purchasing a radio—or a channel partner such as GM, Ford, or BMW agreeing to use the technology—risks having a piece of decorative but nonfunctional hardware if the satellite provider goes out of business. If an interoperable standard for satellite radio emerged, however, the customer would need simply to believe in the category, without being concerned about whether a particular provider would survive.

EXHIBIT 2-4 ■ DVD Recording Format Compatibility Chart
(C=Compatible, N=Not Compatible)

	Normal DVD Player	DVD-ROM Drive	DVD-R(G)		DVD-R(A)		DVD-RAM		DVD-RW		DVD+RW	
	Read	Read	Read	Write	Read	Write	Read	Write	Read	Write	Read	Write
DVD-R(G)	C	C	C	C	C	N	C	N	C	N	C	C
DVD-R(A)	C	C	C	N	C	C	C	N	C	N	C	N
DVD-RAM	N	N	N	N	N	N	C	C	N	N	N	N
DVD-RW	C	C	C	N	C	N	C	N	C	C	C	N
DVD+RW	C	C	C	N	C	N	C	N	C	N	C	C

- **DVD-RAM** supports dual-sided media, which come in protective caddies that make them incompatible with other types of players.
- **DVD-R** stands for DVD-Recordable. DVD-R is a write-once format. There are two types of DVD-R: DVD-R(A) for authoring and DVD-R(G) for general-purpose use.
- **DVD-RW** is the first rewritable released in general-purpose format. It uses phase-change technology similar to that of CD-RW to record content.
- **DVD+RW** is a higher performance DVD-RW alternative.

Solutions to the Long-Term Issues of Bundled Architecture

Despite the negatives mentioned in the previous section, firms like RIM, which wish to open new technology markets, will sometimes decide to follow the integrated stack path. Doing so can allow them to circumvent incumbent barriers, get into a market early, and potentially shape its future direction. In order to avoid becoming a mere footnote in the evolutionary history of the industry, a firm can employ a number of tactics to counteract the problems of bundled architecture. These tactics include leveraging potential cost savings, differentiating the product, designing a better product via interoperability, and expanding or opening the platform to embrace an open systems approach.

■ *Leveraging Potential Cost Savings.* While costs in general are higher for many proprietary stack components, areas may exist where a vertically integrated provider has the advantage. In 2002, for example, the cost of the Motorola G4 microprocessor used by Apple in its Macintosh line was roughly half the cost of the Intel Pentium 4 processor used in most advanced PCs.[35] (One could argue that, however, in order to compete on the very high performance end, consumers would have to exercise the option of buying a dual processor, doubling the cost.) The lower Motorola price reflected Motorola's comparative lack of leverage over Apple (relative to Intel) and the reduced product variation and more compact integration requirements that come with having only one customer. The simplicity of designing for and supporting a single customer can be an advantage if it translates into a simpler, low-cost product design.

■ **Differentiating the Product.** The greater control over design and production for a multi-layered solutions provider creates the opportunity to differentiate the product and compete on factors other than price. Apple has leveraged this strategy on a design basis by offering colors, a single form factor machine, and unique shapes for the Mac and iMac. With regard to features, Apple came to market early with DVD writers and firewire (data transfer) technology and has maintained a focus on functionality that has historically made its product more suitable than the PC architecture for graphics and layout-oriented work. All of these factors have insulated Apple from some of the price-based pressure associated with the PC market, while positioning Apple to better service certain market segments.

■ **Designing a Better Product via Interoperability.** Controlling the direction of development and integrating multiple layers have the potential to yield a superior customer solution. Part of the Palm Pilot's distinction early on was that it combined an operating system designed specifically around the simple personal information management functions that a PDA is designed to serve (primarily calendar and address book), a pen-based "handwriting recognition" system, and the architecture for synching the information contained in the handheld device with PCs. Palm was able to develop a set of design rules for the system as a whole, which resulted in a product that functioned exceptionally well for its focused application.[36] It functioned so well that, in its first 18 months, the Palm Pilot was the fastest-selling computer product ever.[37]

■ **Expanding or Opening the Platform to Embrace an Open Systems Approach.** Despite the tactics just suggested, the higher costs, fewer complements, slower innovation cycles, and perceived technology risk of bundled architecture work against the long-term proprietary stack approach for the early innovator. As alternative standards arise, the long-term viability of the firm exerting a high degree of layer control is at risk. One solution is to eventually migrate away from this strategy toward an open architecture approach. The RIM BlackBerry example illustrates how a vertically oriented offering can be opened to expand the market and work toward a standard platform. While this can mean a painful loss of control (as the IBM example from the 1960s illustrated), it may ultimately leave the firm better positioned for the long term. For a firm attempting to make the architectural transition from bundled to open, the focus of future development needs to change from a vertical orientation (e.g., "What product(s) should we release next?") to a horizontal one ("How can this technology be expanded to be incorporated into other category stacks, as well as the next generation of new products?").

The challenges involved in making the switch are considerable, as Polaroid discovered with digital photography. Organizationally, the technology company making this switch will need to retool to move toward a focus on a new set of customers, much different and technically focused support requirements, and a different view of what "domain" (market segment) expertise is necessary to plan for and penetrate new markets. Selling chips to electronics manufacturers requires different skills than does selling novelty electronics to consumers, and selling software directly to enterprises requires different skills than does providing tools to other software vendors to use in developing software. The tight interoperability that made an early multi-layered vertical approach attractive can become a liability from a stack perspective, as it can present a barrier to the leveraging and porting of distinct portions of the stack to other companies. Modular architecture is considered most useful when the platform leader specifies publicly how to connect components to its platform and focuses on interfaces. These interfaces may be lacking for a firm with bundled architecture. At the same time, the firm may also lack the skills and infrastructure to protect its core proprietary intellectual property. This can lead to loss of control over the technology, even as its adoption is accelerated across different applications. Intel and Microsoft have been particularly adept at designing architectural interfaces while protecting their core technology,[38] but these are not necessarily skills honed by firms with more closed, traditional systems. Incumbent firms and buyers that are considering using the platform layer of a formerly vertically oriented technology company should take all of these challenges into account. A healthy level of skepticism is appropriate when a vertical and proprietary stack-oriented firm announces that it is now in the "platform business."

Modular Evolution and Stack Reintegration

While technology firms may find a multi-layered or nonstandard technology solution useful in opening and accelerating new markets, eventually they will face a choice between surviving in a narrow specialty position—with the risk of being out of sync with the industry standard—and attempting to open up the core elements of the technology in order to capture a larger share of the overall industry. As discussed earlier, each choice has its own set of challenges. Apple Computer is widely criticized for its decision not to go with the open platform approach for its operating system, instead focusing on a more vertical proprietary approach. This approach led to early success but, in the long run, made Apple a niche player. To Apple's credit, it has successfully employed the tactics mentioned previously to thrive as a niche player, but it is mired at a market share of less than 5 percent.

In contrast, for firms that become successful platform suppliers first, eventually the opportunity to partially re-bundle or offer additional layers may emerge, if the modular layer gives the layer owner sufficient market influence. The dominant enterprise resource planning (ERP) vendor SAP appears to be moving in this direction, with its integrated NetWeaver stack. The interoperable stack is intended to leverage SAP's platform, allowing expansion into other layers of enterprise software, such as business intelligence and human resource applications. The stack evolution in Exhibit 2-5 was illustrated by one of SAP's executives in an interview with *SAP Insider* magazine. As will be discussed, Microsoft has used its dominance not just to become entrenched as provider of the operating system standard, but also to capture new application layers and promote an entire multi-layered framework. If Apple had been a horizontal OS supplier first, it might have been able to eventually return to a bundled architecture, but as a much larger market participant.

EXHIBIT 2-5 ■ Evolving SAP Stack View

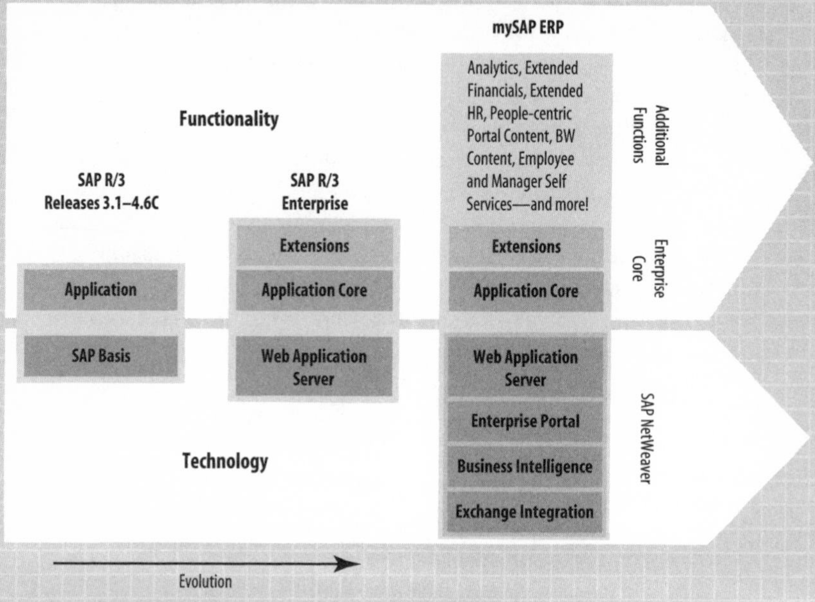

mySAP ERP

Functionality

Analytics, Extended Financials, Extended HR, People-centric Portal Content, BW Content, Employee and Manager Self Services—and more!

Additional Functions

SAP R/3 Releases 3.1–4.6C

SAP R/3 Enterprise

Extensions

Extensions

Enterprise Core

Application

Application Core

Application Core

SAP Basis

Web Application Server

Web Application Server

Enterprise Portal

Business Intelligence

Exchange Integration

SAP NetWeaver

Technology

Evolution

SOURCE: "Does My SAP ERP Render SAP R/3 Enterprise Obsolete? And If Not, How Does an SAP R/3 Customer Pick the Right Upgrade Path?" *SAP Insider*, April-June 2004, http://www.sapinsideronline.com/searchspi/search.htm?page=article&key=37900.

While some platform giants move toward offering bundled solutions, other large verti-cally integrated manufacturers may never fully embrace standardization and modular-ization in the first place. This was the case with GM and Ford in the early automotive industry[39] and also describes Monsanto's approach to transgenic crops. The affinity that the largest incumbents tend to have for vertical integration, scale barriers, and pro-prietary solutions hints at why platform leaders have potential interest in reorienting toward this model as the opportunity presents itself over time. This issue is discussed more fully in the next section.

Layer Encroachment

In *The Prince*, Machiavelli wrote, "The forces of a powerful ally can be useful and good to those who have recourse to them . . . but are perilous to those who become depend-ent on them." This sentiment, echoed by Sun Tzu in *The Art of War*, essentially points out that while firms benefit from developing powerful allies, they must always be wary of them.

The Dominant Provider Threat

One of the larger threats for a complementor above or below a dominant layer provider is that the more dominant industry participant will leverage its dominance to extend its market scope to adjacent stack layers. The tight integration of Microsoft Office products with the Windows operating system, for example, allowed Microsoft to encroach on, and eventually come to own, the basic software applications layer of the PC market. As mentioned, this is not an isolated case; Microsoft has been accused of doing this in virtually every market in which it participates, by leveraging its dominance in operating systems.

When a platform owner decides to compete with previously complementary and noncompetitive offerings, it clearly has some distinct advantages. However, it is important to reiterate that the dangers of competing on many layers include the loss of innovation and complement support, so in some cases this is not a prudent strategy. An additional risk for a platform leader is that developing a reputation for stepping out of product boundaries into complementors' territory creates a competitive dynamic that prevents the overall stack from growing at a fast pace. The perception of a level playing field is important in fostering complements and innovation.[40] Nintendo and Sony would have had much less long-term success in the console gaming market without the support of a variety of third-party game developers. It is important that these firms maintain an equitable playing field when they do in some cases compete against game developers. Another example is Oracle's decision to stay out of the business information (BI) layer, which uses advanced analytics and reporting to leverage databases. By allowing BI firms such as Cognos and Business Objects to thrive, Oracle has created additional value for the core database-driven products. In other cases, the lure of additional profits may make the negatives inherent in competing on many layers acceptable to a dominant technology provider.

Taking a Proactive Stance Against Layer Encroachment

Rather than relying solely on the attitudes and ambitions of partners, a complementor can proactively avoid layer encroachment. There are three primary methods used by complementors to achieve this goal:

1. *Focus on offerings that enhance the platform or other layers.* Growing or adding value to primary markets of the dominant technology layer provider makes a firm a more valuable complementor. This has been the case for the BI tool providers mentioned earlier. In the gaming market, Konami's "Dance Dance Revolution" (DDR Max) helped secure Sony's leadership by offering music software and a dance pad peripheral that increased both the value of and the demand for the basic PS2 platform. This made Konami a valuable ally, worth much more than this particular application might be worth to Sony.

2. *Find areas outside the core competency of the firms on other layers.* When a layer owner can easily acquire the skills or assets needed to develop a product offering on an adjacent layer, the offering becomes a logical candidate for bundling; product offerings requiring access to assets or skills that are harder to come by are less attractive. Despite AOL's large market share, for a long time

the company was not a threat to broadband providers, since AOL did not have the requisite core assets to compete in the broadband market. Its merger with Time Warner, which owns cable assets, was motivated partly by AOL's desire to control or at least compete on this layer. In the gaming market, we can contrast the DDR Max product with a peripheral called "Eyetoy," which is a motion-detecting camera for controlling video games. Because the requisite hardware competency is well within Sony's core, the Eyetoy is much more likely to be absorbed into Sony's PlayStation stack.

3. *Form relationships to keep other layer providers in check.* By retaining some influence over the standard, complementors can keep layer owners in check. For example, if Intel entered the PC business, many existing manufacturers would no doubt retaliate by switching to AMD for a much larger portion of their chips. Many of Intel's complementary partners have an active interest in seeing that AMD remains a vibrant competitor, in order to keep Intel honest. Without AMD, Intel would be more tempted to leverage the power of its position to capture value on other layers.

As illustrated by the AOL/Time Warner merger, another method of layer encroachment is to use acquisition to capture value on additional layers. For the firm wishing to expand its presence to other layers of a stack, acquisition of noncore competencies or a set of complementary assets can be the key to more rapid and successful expansion. Microsoft has used this strategy on several occasions, to acquire installed base and brand name (Hotmail), core industry knowledge (NCompass Labs), and tools and distribution channels (Vicinity). For the threatened firm, when a dominant layer owner indicates an interest in moving upstream or downstream, selling out rather than competing head on is always an option worth considering.

Layer Substitution and Platform Shifts

From the point of view of the owner of a dominant technology layer, the path to greater profitability and control over a market is to jealously guard the technology while encouraging others to adopt a stack that employs it. Other stack participants, however, see their lack of influence or control over a highly dominant layer provider as threatening profits and viability. A natural reaction is to try to bypass or create substitutes for dominated layers, thus removing the imbalance in power. This sentiment has the potential to garner broad support, as there are many more complementors than dominant layer owners. The actual "overthrow" of a layer, often referred to as a **platform shift**, can represent a complete redistribution of power within a technology solution space.

The ubiquity of Windows in the PC operating system environment has made Microsoft dominant in the industry, and only by removing this source of power do many competing firms believe that they can set direction and capture greater profitability. A technology that bypassed or replaced Microsoft's OS layer would offer a significant way to redistribute profits and influence. In the late 90s, Sun Microsystems set out to do just that. Its Java programming language—described by Sun as "write once, run anywhere"—was designed to be operating system neutral. By inserting a new layer, called a Java virtual machine, that interacts with the underlying operating system (Mac, Linux, UNIX, or Windows), it effectively decoupled the OS from the applications layer, making Microsoft's dominance of the layer potentially less relevant. As CNET reported, "Java could allow computer users to run numerous applications without Windows, a scenario that Bill Gates once said 'scares the hell out of me.'"[41]

As an analogy, imagine the invention of a universal airline mileage converter, which would allow a traveler to use any earned mileage credits with any airline. Such an invention would destroy the loyalty-related benefits of mileage programs for specific airlines and instead create loyalty to the mileage converter program. This product, however, could never be launched without the agreement of the airlines, which would naturally be reluctant. Since Sun was attempting to insert Java *above* Microsoft in the technology stack, rather than replacing the layer, it needed some cooperation from Microsoft to make sure that the two layers were compatible. Microsoft wisely worked for incompatibility by creating and distributing its own version of Java. This effectively fragmented the Java layer and removed the threat.

In cases where the layer is completely replaced (i.e., a disruptive shift), it can be more difficult for the previously dominant technology layer provider to defend its competitive position. For example, a study of the disk drive industry revealed a significant shift in the leading device manufacturers as the standard drive size decreased from 14 inches to 8 inches, 5¼ inches, and eventually 3½ inches and smaller.[42] Two-thirds of the makers of 14-inch drives never introduced an 8-inch drive, and those that did were several years behind. When the market shifted again, to 5¼-inch drives, one-half of the 8-inch drive manufacturers failed to make the shift. In each case, the replacement standard market was dominated by new entrant firms. Another example of layer disruption's enabling new competitors was General Motors' ability to successfully enter the locomotive market post World War II by manufacturing diesel-electric engines rather than steam-powered engines, disrupting the locomotive power plant. As in the disk drive industry, the dominant steam engine firms were several years behind in introducing the new technology or didn't make the shift at all.[43] In both cases, the previous incumbent was harnessed with commitments (and a dominant market to serve) on its old technology layer and failed to focus on assuming the leadership position in the emerging one. When the new layer eventually replaced the old layer altogether, it no longer held the dominant position.

A shift in platform provides an opportunity not just for a new platform provider to emerge, but also for a variety of industry participants to change the competitive status quo. Customer relationships can become unlocked, and other "lock-ins," such as switching costs (discussed in more detail in Chapter 10), can become less important. A platform shift represents a significant opportunity for redistribution of influence in a technology stack, and for new entrants to gain traction. Once again, a look at the influence of broadband connectivity on AOL provides an example. As the preferred dial-up connector and browsing solution for half of the Internet users in the United States, AOL has had significant leverage over advertisers. More importantly, it determines the selection of dial-up Internet connectivity solutions (called point of presences, or POPs) for its users. A POP is a set of modems in a nearby physical location that allows an Internet user to phone a local number and connect to the Internet without incurring long distance charges. This layer is competitively contested, solutions are standard, and AOL has negotiated attractive long-term arrangements. Customers choosing AOL effectively allow AOL to choose their POP provider for them. As broadband connections replace dial-up services as a layer in the Internet stack, the power is shifting away from AOL to the telecommunications and cable companies that control broadband connectivity. While the cable companies clearly benefit, others that will also benefit include Motorola, which offers cable modems and can capture market share in the modem area through its relationships with Comcast and AT&T; Linksys, which offers routers for distributing broadband access to multiple machines; and a variety of competitors on AOL's content and application layers. These competitors had been locked out of 50 percent of the market, since dialing in meant that customers were accessing AOL's services first and, in many cases, using the AOL-designated stack.

Voices

PETER MICCICHE ON

MODULARITY AND TECHNOLOGY STACKS

Peter Micciche has been a CEO at several top-tier, venture-funded, early-stage software companies. A long-time technology executive, he was previously president of leading business information tool provider Cognos Corporation and has served in a variety of senior executive, sales, marketing, and business development roles in the software industry.

Peter sees technology stacks as a method of understanding both markets and participant influence. He believes that anyone who manages a firm that produces products or services that are part of a stack can't look at the firm's layer in isolation.

> You have to look at all of the components to understand a technology stack's significance. For example, in many software stacks, the core piece is the transactional data layer, which really is about the flow of money in and out of various technology users' bank accounts. Since banks ultimately manage the flow and warehouse all of the transaction data, they are in a powerful position vis à vis technology providers.

> As a technology provider, you need to ask "How do I create a more powerful competitive position within a stack?" Particularly, how are you in a position where you can influence the creation of standards that vendors above you in that stack must adhere to and thus essentially . . . control the end product.

While this is true for virtually all technology providers, approaching a technology stack as an entrepreneurial startup is situation specific and a function of the firm and its investors' objectives. Peter points out:

> It all depends on your ambition. You can be an opportunistic participant and essentially put a band-aid on an obvious hole in the stack, or you can make a large bet with a chance to control the game board. These bets are often in the hundreds of millions of dollars, with larger payouts.

You have to decide from the outset what you are playing for and how aggressively to engage.

Peter also points out that the issue of power and influence is as critical to technology buyers as it is to industry participants:

There are also strategic implications for technology buyers in supporting various technology solutions. In selecting vendors, you are also choosing to support specific platforms and their inherent standards. CIOs typically recognize this and understand how their support shapes the future of markets. . . . The most successful CIOs are able to educate the CEO on the strategic implication of decisions. At the same time, CEOs have become much more aware of this since the rise of the Internet, which has created a greater dependence on e-business infrastructure.

In discussing the practicalities of managing modularity, Peter emphasizes the need for organizational acumen:

Effective partnering is critical, since you need to work with other companies in the ecosystem. You need to understand not just technology integration, but what the customers require. This means that product marketing, as well as corporate development, plays a critical role.

Finally, Peter is an enthusiast of open rather than bundled architecture as a method of engaging the market:

Openness invites participation from others who can add to the value chain and fosters the opportunity to build an industry around oneself. Tightly integrated stacks discourage others from investing in playing.

Overall, he believes that one of the key roles of software executives is to focus on the complete solution for customers. This involves a holistic view of where a given technology might fit into existing systems, who needs to support it, and whether the technology is geared toward horizontal or vertical application. All of these are key considerations in defining a firm's technology stack.

Stack Implications for Technology Buyers

While much of the preceding discussion appears to apply most readily to technology providers, incumbent firms that are buyers of technology (are there any that are not?) can also benefit from an understanding of stacks and the relative positions occupied by various vendors. For the purchaser, there are a variety of risks—a general technology risk, a proprietary development risk, a monopoly and oligopoly risk, and a platform shift risk—associated with the chosen vendor's position within a technology stack.

General Technology Risk

A solution that was costly to purchase, integrate, and roll out can turn out to be a dead end if the technology proves to be incompatible with the dominant open system or unsupported by complementors. As discussed earlier, this concern has delayed adoption of rewriteable DVD hardware. Another example occurred in the early 1980s, when Xerox developed a remarkable line of proprietary office workstations. Unfortunately for Xerox, the industry's complementary product suppliers lined up behind the IBM-compatible PC architecture. Over time, any external customer that had invested in the Xerox line found itself increasingly isolated from the majority of the industry, as well as the many products in the IBM PC stack.[44] A similar situation has arisen for purchasers of Macintosh computers; many software packages no longer support the Mac platform, since Macintosh users constitute a smaller market and the platform is not in sync with the dominant modular Wintel architecture. Even in the automotive world, technology risk must be endured in choosing nonstandard product bundles. Michelin's attempt to introduce metric-sized TRX tires in the early 1980s, for example, left some car owners unable to find replacement tires, as the standard was never widely adopted. In all of these cases, a departure from the standard architecture left the buyer in the lurch.

Proprietary Development Risk

For firms developing proprietary firm-based technology to meet specialized needs or market opportunities, the choice of components should take into account the position of the vendors in the overall industry. Two contrasting initiatives at snack food company Frito-Lay illustrate why this matters. Frito-Lay pioneered handheld computing in the 1980s in order to offer its salespeople better field tools for keeping their accounts' shelves stocked with the right mix of snack foods. At the time, no standard for handheld wireless computing existed, so Frito-Lay was something of a ground-breaker in this area. Because of the expected benefits in pricing flexibility, reduced out-of-stocks, more accurate accounting, and increased productivity, the company felt confident that the payoff would be worth the investment, despite the absence of vendor or solution standards. In this case, the project was a success for Frito-Lay, and the chosen hardware vendor (Fujitsu) has been a stable ongoing participant in the handheld market. In developing a decision support system, however, Frito-Lay (as well as several other packaged good companies) selected a hardware, software, and database solution from Metaphor Computer Systems, a spin-off from Xerox's Palo Alto Research Center (PARC). In this case, the hardware diverged from the Intel/IBM PC standard, the desktop tools diverged from the dominant applications for word processing and spreadsheets, and the mainframe approach was overtaken by client/server architecture. Eventually, IBM bought Metaphor, leaving the earlier product configurations unsupported. Although the Metaphor decision support tools appeared to be moving toward an industry standard, the choice by Frito-Lay and others of proprietary multi-layered bundled architecture led to many of the negative consequences discussed earlier in the chapter and proved to be a poor decision.

Monopoly and Oligopoly Risk

Firms that gain excessive power through layer control in dominant architectures can exert leverage on solution providers (some of whom are customers) and end users alike. Technology buyers must be aware of this potential risk and avoid it when possible. In an antitrust case against Intel, for example, the FTC found that Intel refused to do business with three companies—Digital Equipment, Compaq Computer, and

Intergraph—unless they agreed to license certain technology patents to Intel on favorable terms. Intel's blackballing would have had severe consequences for each company. In a very different type of situation, Chrysler, after a detailed supply chain analysis of the components of its Jeep Grand Cherokee, found that one engine component, made only by one local foundry, relied on a casting process that required a particularly unusual grade of clay. This clay was, in turn, provided by only one supplier, which was not reciprocally dependent on this segment of the business. Since Chrysler standardized on a stack of technology solutions with a thin but proprietary layer (the clay), the small clay supplier was in a position to threaten the short-term production of Chrysler's most profitable product line simply by switching more capacity to kitty litter production.[45]

While avoiding dominant suppliers isn't always feasible, selecting a technology solution with a monopolistic or oligopolistic component has a potential downside. Customers should be braced for the possibility that the vendor in the monopoly/oligopoly position may try to maximize its market position through suppression of competition, substantial price increases, deliberate incompatibility with other technologies, price discrimination, or forced product bundling. If a component technology is particularly important to the buyer or a group of buyers, then a dominant layer owner will usually find ways to make the buyer pay.

Platform Shift Risk

As mentioned earlier, when a platform shift occurs, the set of industry complementors and viable products may also change rapidly. The primary risk to buyers is that they can end up with poorly supported legacy systems (as occurred in many cases with the platform shift from client/server to IP-based computing). This lack of support is manifest in an evaporation of complementors and further platform innovation, higher costs to acquire necessary resources, and an uncompetitive solution. Much like buying an automobile at the end of its model life, buying technology when a platform shift is imminent is a risky proposition; a buyer should consider waiting for the new architecture.

CHAPTER SUMMARY

Dave Barry's quote at the outset of the chapter lampoons the dynamics between hardware and software layers in personal computing. The primary reason these two are interrelated is that they are part of an overall technology system that provides value to end users. This contextual view of technology is an important one—whether the delivery system considered is external, internal, or related to technological interoperability. With its focus on technology in the context of its value delivery, a stack model can be used to understand the overall architecture and connection points between the various technology components used to assemble and deliver a complete solution. The model is also useful in determining where the potential power and influence lie in the set of relationships. Power arises as a result of architectural leadership, control of standards, or customer and channel influence, all of which typically accrue to incumbents. The results can be skewed profitability, customer and supplier leverage, and influence over future product direction.

To succeed in the world of modularity, technology providers must have the skills and capabilities to partner, work cooperatively with third parties, and integrate technology with other components of the stack. Relationships must be managed, and rules governing architecture must be clearly understood or, in the case of a standard-bearer, created. Providers also need to focus on broadly disseminating their technology solutions, rather than holding them tightly and pursuing only internally orchestrated products.

Firms desiring to accelerate introduction of their product/service to capture emerging market opportunities—or those simply unwilling to cede the standard-bearer role to an incumbent—can achieve early success by offering a bundled architecture: a complete solution with self-selected vendors or standards on each stack layer. While this approach has time-to-market, category-shaping, and interoperability advantages, in the long run higher costs, less third-party support and innovation, and slower market development will lead to a potentially uncompetitive position. A bundled architecture strategy needs to be followed by either defined niche positioning or, preferably, migration toward an open systems approach. Unfortunately, the elements that make a firm's product offering successful with a bundled approach make it difficult to later switch to an open architecture posture.

Over time, dominant layer owners may be tempted not only to preserve their current position, but also to expand their franchise into adjacent markets. They are often in a strong position to do so, particularly if an adjacent layer is easily absorbed or offers little value-adding innovation. At the same time, maturing markets also present threats for the incumbent. Layer displacement via bypass or a platform shift can lead to a reconfiguration of technology stacks. Firms that stand to benefit should work toward such layer displacement, while incumbent firms with favorable positions should focus on preserving the status quo—in both current and successive generations of technology.

Finally, analyses of technology stacks are useful to technology buyers, since an understanding of vendor position relative to the overall set of solution choices can help buyers pinpoint sources of risk associated with particular technology strategies and initiatives.

Market Definition and Disruption

Can't sell a hand plow anymore. Fifty cents for the weight of the metal. . . . Disks and tractors, that's the stuff now.
—**John Steinbeck**, *The Grapes of Wrath*

Gauging the Impact of Emerging Technology

Over 100 years ago, Charles H. Duell, commissioner of the U.S. Patent and Trademark Office, allegedly proclaimed, "Everything that can be invented has been invented." It's safe to say that history has proven Duell wrong. In fact, the opposite seems to be true. The more that is discovered, the more that is left to be discovered. As a result, the pace of innovation has reached staggering proportions. Prior to 1987, a total of 683,000 patents were issued in the United States. In contrast, over 187,000 new patents were issued in 2003 alone.[1] Some of the fastest-growing areas have been electronics, drug discovery, nanotechnology, and, of course, computer technology. It's no wonder that, on the information technology front, many CIOs feel like hunted animals, being stalked by vendors.[2]

With all this innovation, how does a company know when a new technology is something to be embraced (or at least closely watched) or when it represents just another file in the patent office? Chapter 1 showed that a firm's size, capabilities, and resources influence how it should attempt to diffuse or exploit innovative technology. Chapter 2 examined how technology, as part of an overall product delivery system, determines competitive position and industry structure. Yet neither chapter provided a complete picture of the full impact of an innovation. The impact of technology is also determined by its interplay with firm-specific factors, such as its value relative to the overall business structure of the firm, as well as external factors, such as whether it gives rise to new competition, changes relationships between buyers and sellers, or redefines the potential market. Emerging technology, when it changes significant variables for a firm or redefines an entire market, can create major changes in competition, market size, and industry attractiveness. Incumbent firms need to anticipate or at least make informed decisions about how to react to these shifts, while challenging firms can drive these shifts or use them as an opportunistic point of entry. Consider the following scenarios:

❑ A company has invested heavily in centralizing its customer call centers in the midwestern United States. It discovers that advancements in Internet infrastructure, remote customer relationship management (CRM) automation software, and data warehousing have triggered the growth of outsourced services in India and the Philippines. As a result, firms in India can remotely service U.S.

customers, tapping into a large base of well-educated, English-speaking workers with computer skills, whose wage rate is one-fifth that of comparable workers in Indiana. Also, these offshore firms are said to have an annual employee turnover rate of only 6 percent versus 34 percent in the United States, thus creating a more stable workforce.[3] The result is falling prices, higher quality/service expectations, and a doubling of total industry capacity.[4]

❑ An airplane manufacturer finds that it is losing market share to a new competitor. The competitor uses virtual design technology to produce airplanes faster, cheaper, and with fewer design flaws and quality issues. The virtual design method reduces cycle time for engineering change requests by more than 50 percent and defects by more than 80 percent, while simplifying the manufacturing process and reducing inventory-carrying costs by streamlining relationships with suppliers.

❑ A leading lab-based medical diagnostics firm sees a variety of lower cost, more effective diagnostic tools being developed and is unsure how to act on these emerging technologies. In the near term, the development of specially designed CD-ROM disks and software may allow personal computers to act as centrifuges, giving doctors the ability to provide results to patients in real time.[5] In the long term, the firm expects nanotechnologies to lead to the development of inexpensive test chips, which could permit instant testing for a variety of genetic diseases via immediate DNA matching.

❑ A global media company recognizes the explosive growth potential of the Internet. Concerned about threats to market share, it invests $150 million to build a series of content websites. Equally concerned about interactive television, it also spends $100 million on interactive television trials. Other media groups facing the same dilemma receive pressure from their boards to merge with new media companies. Virtually none of the efforts has resulted in a long-term business opportunity. The more aggressive firms end up with weaker balance sheets and little else to show for their efforts.

The last two scenarios, in particular, reveal the ambiguity inherent in determining a new technology's potential for redefining markets and competitive sets. Clearly, gauging which new technologies are most disruptive to current business models, change profit potential, or enable potentially dangerous competitors is a difficult yet important survival skill. This chapter will review a series of different concepts and models that can be employed to help determine what technology will influence an enterprise, how it will affect the business, and in what areas innovating companies will have the largest impact. Later chapters will discuss two more critical variables—the timing of the introduction of emerging technology and the interplay between technology and competitive advantage.

Identifying Points of Leverage

The Joad family from Steinbeck's *The Grapes of Wrath*, cited at the beginning of the chapter, would have been well advised to pay attention to the disruptive technologies changing the nature of the farming business in the 1930s. While the drought-driven Dust Bowl contributed to the demise of the small Plains farmer, technology also played a part. The tractor was a significant labor-saving device that created a major substitution of capital for labor in farming, essentially rendering sharecropping and the small family farm obsolete. As another character says to Tom Joad, "One cat' [Caterpillar Tractor] takes and shoves ten families out. Cats all over hell now. Tear in and shove the croppers out."[6] Interestingly, the parallel development of another technology—new "double cross" corn hybrids, promoted as offering high potential economic benefits to farmers— did not save the family farm.

This, in a nutshell, is the dilemma facing executives today, particularly those in companies that depend on technology to differentiate or create additional efficiencies in their operations: When is new technology a tractor, and when is it simply a corn hybrid? The logical starting point in determining which technologies to pay attention to is to focus on those that influence areas core to the success of the enterprise.

In the pharmaceutical industry, for example, the duration of patent protection is a major factor dictating the profitability of firms. When a drug comes off patent, generic competition can immediately and dramatically reduce sales and margins. Eli Lilly's Prozac, for example, dominated the market while its patent was valid, but the antidepressant's sales steadily and significantly decreased once a generic version became available in August 2001. Lilly was forced to reduce profit estimates three times in 2002 as a result of these sales losses.[7] For the top-selling pharmaceuticals, a six-month patent extension could be worth as much as $1 billion (see Exhibit 3-1). In Eli Lilly's case, the almost $900 million incremental revenue of a six-month extension of Prozac, at a 90 percent margin, would be worth roughly $800 million in profits. In contrast, a significant savings in manufacturing or accounting costs would have much less impact on a firm's financial results. A 25 percent reduction in the manufacturing costs of Prozac would have saved only $60 million per year.

The cartoon below illustrates one way that pharmaceutical companies extend patents; another way is through technology investments that get products to market earlier, extending the patent life on the front end. After patents are issued, drug companies often must complete complex clinical trials and FDA-approval processes before they get the go-ahead to market products to the general public. Technology that accelerates and adds efficiency to this process has significant potential value to these firms. Eli Lilly, for example, has implemented computer-based algorithms, advanced database technology, and gene-sequencing software to speed drug development. It has also been active in leveraging online trial techniques, which might accelerate approval of new drugs.

The concept of a **point of leverage** (also referred to as a *critical success factor* or *point of pain*) goes beyond

SOURCE: TOLES © 2000 The Buffalo News. Reprinted with permission of UNIVERSAL PRESS SYNDICATE. All rights reserved.

the level of an industry to that of individual firms. This resource-based view of firms acknowledges that not only are different industries impacted in different ways by new technology, but all firms *within* an industry do not derive equal value from an

EXHIBIT 3-1 ■ Added Revenues and Costs to U.S. Consumers of a Six-Month Extension in Patent Protection of Billion-Dollar Drugs in 2000

Drug Names	Manufacturer	2000 U.S. Sales	Added Revenues	Added Costs to U.S. Consumers
Prilosec	AstraZeneca	$ 4,102,195,000	$ 1,435,768,250	$ 676,862,175
Lipitor	Pfizer	$ 3,692,657,000	$ 1,292,429,950	$ 609,288,405
Prevacid	TAP	$ 2,832,602,000	$ 991,410,700	$ 467,379,330
Prozac	Eli Lilly	$ 2,567,107,000	$ 898,487,450	$ 423,572,655
Zocor	Merck	$ 2,207,042,000	$ 772,464,700	$ 364,161,930
Celebrex	Pharmacia	$ 2,015,508,000	$ 705,427,800	$ 332,558,820
Zoloft	Pfizer	$ 1,890,416,000	$ 661,645,600	$ 311,918,640
Paxil	GlaxoSmithKline	$ 1,807,955,000	$ 632,784,250	$ 298,312,575
Claritin	Schering-Plough	$ 1,667,347,000	$ 583,571,450	$ 275,112,255
Glucophage	Bristol-Myers	$ 1,629,157,000	$ 570,204,950	$ 268,810,905
Norvasc	Pfizer	$ 1,597,091,000	$ 558,981,850	$ 263,520,015
Pravachol	Bristol-Myers	$ 1,203,474,000	$ 421,215,900	$ 198,573,210
Neurontin	Pfizer	$ 1,131,678,000	$ 396,087,300	$ 186,726,870
Oxycontin	Purdue Pharma	$ 1,052,771,000	$ 368,469,850	$ 173,707,215
Cipro	Bayer	$ 1,023,657,000	$ 358,279,950	$ 168,903,405
Total		**$30,420,657,000**	**$10,647,229,950**	**$5,019,408,405**

SOURCE: Public Citizen, "Patently Offensive: Congress Set to Extend Monopoly Patents for Cipro and Other Drugs," *Congress Watch*, November 2001.

innovation. For example, as the *Wall Street Journal* pointed out, "Information technology is essential for retailers, but not in the same way for every retailer. Wal-Mart needs technology to cut inventory and warehousing costs. . . . Neiman Marcus and Saks need to keep tabs on upscale customers to get them to spend more."[8]

A vendor developing a new class of integrated point-of-sale and customer relationship management (CRM) tools would find that a certain subset of retailers—those for which customer relationship leverage was most critical—would present the most vibrant market opportunity. For an incumbent firm, a decision to invest in CRM tools and technology should be less dependent on the activities of other retailers and more focused on whether a customer relationship–driven strategy is likely to have a significant impact on the particular firm's results, based on its positioning and market strategy. As technology executive Lise Buyer says, "The solution has to solve a major point of pain."

LISE BUYER ON

THE POINT OF PAIN

Lise Buyer has been a top-ranked technology analyst in the Credit Suisse First Boston Technology Group, a venture capitalist with Technology Partners, and, more recently, a member of Google's IPO Committee. As a result, she has had the chance to see more than her share of business plans.

Like many venture capitalists, she concentrates on four key areas in evaluating startups:

- Is the market opportunity large?
- Is the business/technology defendable?
- Does the business model work?
- Is the team in place to execute?

As Lise points out,

> *Virtually every business plan attempts to address these questions (with varying degrees of success), but many plans contain a fatal flaw in logic: By simply identifying a large market and estimating an attractive set of sales and market share figures, the business plan's architects ignore the intensity of potential customers' motivation to try something new (and take a chance on a new company). While everyone in an industry may have the same problem—which could be solved by the new venture's product or service idea—the problem may just not be big enough or important enough to be a priority for firms in the target market.*

According to Lise, "The argument that this is a big industry and we'll sell them 'stuff' is the wrong approach—the solution has to solve a major point of pain." Lise suggests that the would-be entrepreneur consider the following question: "If a purchasing manager has 50 purchase orders on his or her desk, what is it that will make [the manager] sign yours? Often, the entrepreneur's technology approach is sound, but the opportunity to solve a major problem simply lies in a different market or application."

Identifying points of pain is a key sales and marketing activity in the information technology sector for firms of all size. Many software firms include "pain sheets" as part of their standard sales tool kits, in order to help technology salespeople zero in on these opportunities and emphasize them to potential buyers.

Identifying Levers of Innovation: The Classic Five Forces Model (Plus One)

How can the impact of technology on a firm's competitive position be assessed? As a starting point, the firm should be viewed within the context of its external dynamics. Harvard Business School professor Michael Porter revolutionized industry analysis with the introduction of the **five forces model**, a systematic method of examining not just competitive intensity between firms, but also other external factors that can influence the attractiveness of an industry. As Porter put it, "Competition in an industry is rooted in its underlying economics, and competitive forces exist that go well beyond the combatants in a particular industry. Customers, suppliers, potential entrants, and substitute products are all competitors that may be more or less prominent."[9]

To facilitate examination of the impact of external forces on industry attractiveness, the model can be presented on horizontal and vertical axes, as shown in Exhibit 3-2. The horizontal axis of the model can be thought of as "supply chain" oriented. Interplay between a firm and its suppliers and customers determines the distribution of profits and profitability. Since profit at the most simplistic level is revenue minus costs, it is clear that the ability of a supplier to drive up costs—or of customers to drive down prices (and hence revenue)—plays a large part in determining a firm's profit potential. Andy Grove, former chairman of Intel, has expanded on the five forces model, describing complementors as a sixth force that also influences the attractiveness of an industry for particular firms. As discussed in Chapter 2, technology success often relies on aligning multiple layers, not all of which are controlled by the innovating firm. Thus, the availability of complementary products and technology and the power of complement providers are important determinants of overall profit distribution. The vertical axis relates to competition. Even if an industry has high profit potential because of weak supplier and customer leverage, the intensity of market share competition among rivals, the quality and quantity of competition, and the alternatives available in the industry also determine the industry's overall attractiveness.

EXHIBIT 3-2 ■ Six Forces Model

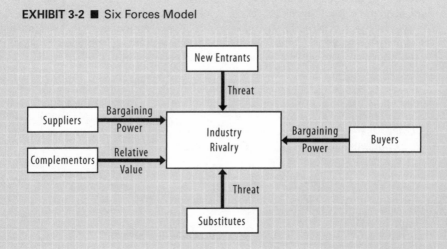

The forces model has been criticized as being a somewhat static snapshot, while the business environment is dynamic, especially when it comes to technology. Once the key leverage points and overall attractiveness of a market are understood, however, the impact of a new technology on the status quo can be gauged, leading to an assessment of the disruptive potential of the technology.

Horizontal Forces and Profit Distribution

As Exhibit 3-3 graphically illustrates, supplier leverage, customer leverage, and complementor dynamics create the forces on the horizontal axis of the model. These forces all affect profit distribution in an industry.

■ *Supplier Leverage.* The more leverage suppliers have over an industry, the more opportunity they have to shift industry profits into their pockets. Their leverage typically derives from a combination of limited choice, proprietary technology, the importance of the component input, customer demand for specific supplier inputs, and switching costs. For example, OPEC's dominant position in the oil market creates significant profit leverage over the air travel industry, since fuel is an important and irreplaceable supply component. The cost of fuel represents 15 to 25 percent of the operating cost of an airline,[10] basically making major airlines beholden to OPEC for their profits.

Chapter 2 touched on the most extreme case—monopoly or oligopoly—where little choice exists for buyers. One of the key opportunities from a technology perspective is to reduce supplier power in a market where it presents an obstacle to a firm's profitability. Conversely, one of the key threats is technology that increases supplier power. Alternatives to crude oil–dependent airplane engines would certainly benefit the airline industry. Similarly, new software that facilitated porting Oracle customers' applications and databases to other platforms would reduce Oracle's leverage over its installed base. This would significantly reduce supplier power and thus would be a

EXHIBIT 3-3 ■ The Horizontal Axis of the Six Forces Model

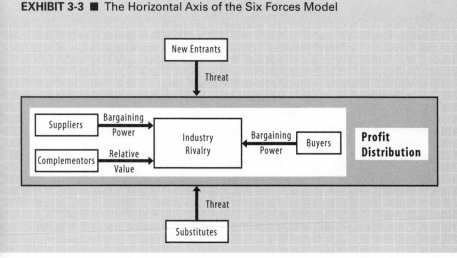

significant development for firms heavily dependent on database technology. Conversely, downloadable music technology has the potential to strengthen supplier power and weaken record labels' profits, by reducing the dependence of musicians (the suppliers) on record companies during the early phase of their careers. This would negate some of the record companies' negotiating leverage.

One way for an organization to overcome supplier power is to **backwards integrate**, or gain control of its inputs by taking control of activities formerly supplied by suppliers, and to self-supply. Technology that helps firms backwards integrate in the face of strong suppliers is likely to have a large impact and be extremely attractive to an industry. The Enron-induced California energy crisis in 2001, for example, created severe problems for many energy-intensive manufacturers, which were 100 percent reliant on Pacific Gas and Electric (PG&E), the local utility, for their power. As PG&E was forced to pay higher prices, it simply passed them on to its customers, who had no short-term alternatives for supply. Some of the largest PG&E customers were manufacturing facilities; power was a key input for these firms, yet they faced competition from manufacturers outside of the PG&E power grid. The Shasta Paper Mill, a typical PG&E customer, saw its energy bill more than double and had no choice but to shut down.[11] Improved technology for micro-turbines, fuel cells, and co-generation plants,[12] however, allowed many campuses and other facilities to self-supply power, avoiding this potential squeeze. If Shasta had been able to leverage alternative technology and supply its own energy, perhaps it would still be in business.

■ *Customer Leverage.* The leverage of buyers also has an impact on the attractiveness of an industry. Buyer power is a factor when only a few buyers with significant volume exist, the product they are buying is not a critical input, and the buyer accounts for a significant portion of the seller's volume. This is how Wal-Mart continues to drive prices down, and why automobile manufacturers get good deals on tires. Information technology has recently become a threat to industry attractiveness in some cases, as buyers are using technology to create global electronic marketplaces and develop purchasing groups and consortiums in the hope of increasing their relative power.

Porter points out that the ability to influence the end consumer's purchase decision is also a significant source of buyer power, if the typical buyer in an industry is an intermediary.[13] Aldi, one of Europe's most successful retail chains, sells only Aldi-branded goods, with the promise that anything carrying an Aldi label is both good quality and a good value. Doing so enables Aldi to aggressively negotiate prices with manufacturers. Industry participants are motivated by the opportunity to realize significant volume gains by selling through the Aldi chain, which is their only path to Aldi's customers. Aldi does not feel pressured to do business with particular vendors in the industry, since all products carry the Aldi name. This gives the firm significant buyer leverage. In other cases, branded manufacturers that use a heavy marketing–oriented pull-through strategy (such as Coca-Cola and Levi's) are able to negotiate with much greater leverage over buyers. Customers expect buyers to have these products on their shelves; therefore, buyers have far less leverage. Particularly when a firm sells through channels, technology that reduces buyer power by co-opting the ultimate end user and circumnavigating the channel's relationship can be tempting to adopt.

Such **disintermediation** (removal of an intermediary) is likely to be resisted by a firm's current intermediary buyers. In relatively obvious cases, this threat is simply labeled **channel conflict.** Existing channel buyers pressure producers to make a choice between selling directly to consumers and selling through distribution channels. Because of this pressure, Levi's, for example, has chosen to redirect Internet customers to both online and offline retail partners, rather than sell blue jeans directly to consumers, as the company did not want to risk losing or damaging these channels. Dell, on the other hand, relies heavily on the Internet in pursuing a direct model for selling PCs and has made channel-related sales only a small portion of its business. By doing so, it has avoided the need to cater to large retailers' requirements for inventory and special deals and has removed buyer power as an issue.

More subtly, the rise of technologies that create greater consumer influence can severely weaken channel-based buyer power and make a market much more attractive. One industry where this is (slowly) occurring is the motion picture industry. For independent filmmakers, getting a film into distribution means dealing with a highly concentrated studio system, which essentially controls the theater and aftermarket channels. Only through pre-production demand can a filmmaker hope to obtain negotiating leverage. This is why filmmakers often earn more on sequels than on the original (even if the product is poorer) and why established novels command the highest price for screenplay rights. Unknown Haxan Films—producer of *The Blair Witch Project*, a low-budget horror film—was able to create intense interest via the Internet prior to negotiating a distribution deal. When Artisan Entertainment picked the film up, it was with an unusually significant commitment to support the film. Not only has the use of the Internet reduced channel/buyer power; the cost of a film itself has been reduced 90 percent by the move to digital photography, allowing filmmakers to remain relatively debt-free and therefore less reliant on unattractive deal terms.

■ *Complementor Dynamics.* Often, complementors supply the other products in a stack needed for a technology to gain market acceptance, but they can also simply provide the supporting infrastructure that accompanies a product. Automobiles need gasoline, computers need processors, and actors need playwrights. Andy Grove thinks of complementors as "fellow travelers" with aligned interests,[14] but has pointed out that new technologies can cause the paths of the travelers to diverge—in some cases, quite rapidly. This outwardly congenial approach probably helped lull major PC manufacturers into supporting the "Intel Inside" campaign. While the campaign helped grow the PC-based market as a standard, it also shifted most of the hardware-related profits into Intel's pockets. In addition to influencing the layer power discussed in Chapter 2, the relative importance of complementary inputs greatly impacts the attractiveness of a given industry.

In the Internet service provider (ISP) market, the relationship between connectivity providers and developers of browser and e-mail tools was originally highly complementary, and both were necessary to the growth and diffusion of the Internet. Since users need an interface, connectivity providers were reliant on the development of browser and e-mail software to offer service to consumers. Conversely, the browser and e-mail software developers would not have had much success if users had not been able to get connected to the Internet through an ISP. Originally, the large ISPs (through their market share) were powerful relative to the complementary tool developers. When Netscape and Microsoft began to offer simple developer's kits for creating a browser-driven connection, however, they enabled ISPs of all sizes to offer similar products and thus reduced ISP power. As with PCs, the effective commoditizing of the market by the complementor resulted in a highly competitive and unattractive market.

The lesson from these examples is that a more appropriate stance toward complementors would be that of **co-opetition**, a phrase coined by Professors Adam Brandenburger of Harvard and Barry Nalebuff of Yale. While acknowledging the need for complementors to cooperate in order to open markets, Brandenburger and Nalebuff recognize the nature of the competition between complementors in dividing profits. Technology that creates a more powerful and concentrated complementor (like Intel) or dilutes the power of the firm (as Netscape did to the ISPs) can have as large an impact on a firm's future results as the power of either a supplier or a customer. As Brandenburger and Nalebluff say:

> When a complementor enters the game, the pie grows—that's win-win. But then there is a tug-of-war with your complementor over who is going to be the main beneficiary. If your complementor gets less of the pie, it leaves more for you, and vice-versa. . . .
> Complementors may be your friends, but you don't mind if they suffer a little. Their pain is your gain."[15]

Vertical Forces and Competitive Intensity

As mentioned earlier, the vertical axis of the six forces model (depicted in Exhibit 3-4) is concerned primarily with rivalry, competitive choice, and the impact on industry and firm profit potential. Strategic issues to be concerned with on the vertical axis tend to focus on market entry and questions such as the following:

❑ What barriers will keep other new entrants out of the market?

❑ What substitute products will put pressure on my market share?

❑ How intense is the head-to-head competition?

New entrants can threaten an industry's attractiveness by increasing competitive pressure and industry capacity. Erecting barriers to keep competitors out makes intuitive sense as a way for existing firms to improve profits. An increase in alternatives, or substitution, provides customers with additional means of "solving the problem." Customers' propensity to switch is typically related to price performance, as it is in the relative relationships between leather and vinyl, real crab meat and imitation crab meat, and, perhaps, Oracle and MySQL databases. If the "superior" product's price differential increases by a large degree, then the substitute will begin to deliver better price performance and capture market share. For example, the CTO of Sabre Holdings, in building a new online shopping application, faced a choice between a $160,000 per CPU Oracle license and a $495 MySQL license. As *Forbes* magazine reported, "Customers will balk at ever-escalating prices for mainstream products and will opt whenever they can for bargain-basement software based on freely available

EXHIBIT 3-4 ■ The Vertical Axis of the Six Forces Model

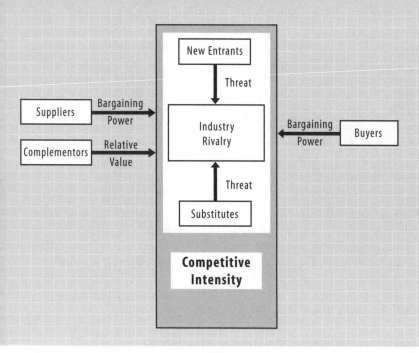

code such as MySQL or the Linux operating system."[16] A market without substitutes offers much more opportunity for price maximization.

The size of the threat of increased rivalry often depends on the strength of complementary assets rather than technology-based issues. A strong brand name, for example, can dissuade consumers from trying a new, unknown product; provide defense against price competition; and help secure distribution channels. An incumbent's strong sales force, distribution channel, and buyer relationships can keep a new product out of distribution or limit its trial among target customers. Experience, know-how, and economies of scale also play a large role, creating advantages for existing firms over new firms wishing to enter the market. Even customer perceptions can prevent substitutes and rivals from encroaching. In theory, cubic zirconium, with the same appearance and many of the same properties as diamonds, should have captured the engagement ring market long ago. But consumer perceptions about both the quality and the emotional meaning of diamonds have prevented this near-perfect substitute from damaging the diamond industry. This is no accident—the diamond cartel De Beers spends upwards of $400 million a year on marketing to foster this perception of diamonds as a gift without substitute.[17] Similarly, Larry Ellison and Oracle have promoted a perception (whether true or not) that MySQL is neither scalable, secure, nor reliable enough for large firms running mission-critical applications.[18] Non-technology-related assets provide at least partial insulation from many substitutes and new entrants. However, they can also create a false sense of security that keeps a firm with a leading position from taking innovation seriously as a threat.

In some cases, technology can totally change an industry's attractiveness and competitive intensity by eliminating barriers and redefining the competitive space, through either substitution or new entry. As an example, consider the pay phone market. Traditionally, dependence on real estate assets and territorial rights (complementary assets) provided insulation for firms, once phone locations had been established. But pay phones have become less valuable as cellular phones have become more widely used, redefining the nature of remote location phone access. More than 600,000 pay phones have disappeared in the United States (a 30 percent decline), and telephone companies are either giving up the pay phone business, seeking out government subsidies, or trying to leverage the assets in other ways.[19] Similarly, the development of laser eye surgery for treating myopia has created an alternative to disposable contact lenses. This development is a potential threat to firms that mass-produce lenses, regardless of how strong their lens franchise is, as it redefines the market for vision correction (see "Lasik and the Optometry Business," later in the chapter.)

Technology issues relating to market entry and substitution are often associated specifically with the resource bases of an individual firm, rather than an entire industry. Cost-reducing production technology might have a large impact on a "private label" producer, for example, and significantly less impact on a branded manufacturer. Similarly, the owner of a pay phone franchise located in a rural area, where current technology does not allow for cost-effective mobile phone service, may be much less affected by cellular phones than is a franchise located in a major city.

Beyond the Static—Defining Market Spaces Dynamically Using the Three-Dimensional Model of Market and Business Definition

Determining the severity of technology threats on the vertical axis of the six forces model can be complicated. Not only do the firm's resource base, complementary assets, and specific market definition need to be factored in; developments outside of the firm also need to be considered. While some technology-induced market changes are obvious—such as the way the diffusion of cell phones has reduced the need for pay phones—other such changes—such as the impact of laser eye surgery on contact lens sales—are more difficult to gauge.

An excellent model for understanding the impact of innovation on a firm's market was developed by Professor Derek Abell. His model defines businesses using a three-dimensional framework:[20]

1. Customer groups served (customers and markets serviced; i.e., "who")

2. Customer functions served (products and services offered; i.e., "what")

3. Technologies utilized (the way 1 and 2 are executed; i.e., "how")

Exhibit 3-5 shows the model visually as a three-dimensional market space that is dynamic over time.

EXHIBIT 3-5 ■ Three-Dimensional Market Space

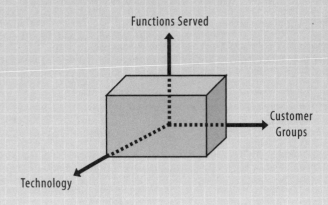

This model is significant in its departure from the tendency to define a firm's business as simply products and/or services offered and markets served. As Abell says:

> *The danger is that business definition may be perceived as a choice of products on the one hand, and markets on the other. In reality, the product should be considered simply as a physical manifestation of the application of a particular technology to the satisfaction of a particular function for a particular customer group. The choice is one of technologies, functions, and customers to serve, not products to offer.*[21]

This perspective puts an emphasis on understanding how new underlying technology can reshape the choices available to current and potential customer segments (market spaces) in solving problems, even if it does not appear to compete in existing markets against existing products.

Threats to a well-defined market space are most likely to be recognized by entrenched competitors. If a new firm wishes to enter an existing market space with relatively undifferentiated products and no unique technology edge, then it will probably face retaliation from incumbent firms. In this situation, various incumbent barriers and advantages may act to reduce the likelihood of success for the newcomer, including[22]

❑ Economies of scale

❑ Availability of complementary assets

❑ Capital requirements

❑ Experience-related advantages

❑ Developed channels

This list provides an explanation of why directly taking on a firm such as Microsoft or Cisco will more likely lead to retaliation than success. As one of the directors of Juniper Systems said, "Anyone who tries to compete with Cisco head on will get their heads handed to them."[23]

The logical way around this problem is **flanking** the competition—moving into a competitive area or new market space that competitors do not occupy and possibly are not even aware of. Small firms usually grow by differentiating themselves from current industry leaders rather than taking them on. An obvious benefit of innovative technology is that it changes the characterization of the market and thus avoids head-on competitive challenges. The change can affect just one variable (the technology used to deliver previously well-defined products to a well-defined market) or several (the technology variable and also the product offering or market). In either case, the change in application of technology can make the new product seem quite different from the old. Performance, value delivery, physical attributes, sourcing, or any number of other factors could create what appears to be an entirely new category, forming an opportunistic point of entry for the innovator.

For example, when the Macintosh was launched by Apple Computer, it represented a new operating system/hardware configuration radically different from that of the IBM PC. This configuration made the desktop computer more accessible to the home and educational markets. Those associated with the launch considered the Macintosh a product designed to "change the world."[24] As illustrated in Exhibit 3-6, Apple's impact on the market space was far different from that of a vendor that simply offered a lower cost configuration by including a different chipset or OS designed to emulate that of Intel or Microsoft (e.g., Cyrix- or Linux-based machines). Currently, the optometry industry is in the process of assessing the "world-changing" potential of laser eye surgery, but the phenomenon may be better described by Exhibit 3-6b than Exhibit 3-6a.

EXHIBIT 3-6 ■ Radical versus Incremental Shift in Industry Definition

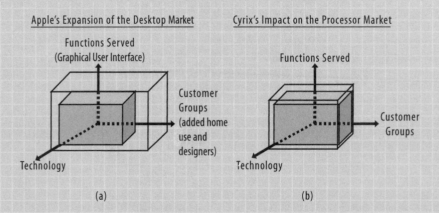

Apple's Expansion of the Desktop Market

Functions Served (Graphical User Interface)

Customer Groups (added home use and designers)

Technology

(a)

Cyrix's Impact on the Processor Market

Functions Served

Customer Groups

Technology

(b)

> ## Lasik Surgery and the Optometry Industry

Laser eye surgery is an interesting new medical technology that has gained favor in the last several years. It addresses a major market—60 percent of all Americans need some sort of vision correction[25]—and has generated almost $2 billion in annual vision market revenue in the United States.[26] Each vision correction patient spends an average of $150 a year, an attractive ongoing revenue source for lens manufacturers and optometrists. Patients who get laser surgery, however, do so in the hope of no longer contributing to the annual revenues of the traditional contact lens and eyewear segments.

In the three-dimensional model, laser surgery would be seen as bringing about a two-dimensional expansion of the market, as new technology introduced a new functionality to address a well-defined customer base. Application of the model immediately leads to a series of strategic questions for contact lens and eyeglass manufacturers, such as the following:

❑ Can we get access to the technology?

❑ Does the new "product" (large capital equipment) fit into the business model and capabilities of our company?

❑ Most importantly, how much of our customer base is likely to erode, and can we innovate to avoid this erosion?

By focusing on these areas, an incumbent can attempt to quantify the threat, as well as gauge the appropriate response. If the core technology is accessible and can be used by the firm and if the economics of the new segment are highly attractive, the firm may choose to enter the new market rather than work to discredit the new technology. Indeed, this is the tact taken by Bausch & Lomb, which sells Lasik equipment and is one of the leaders in the industry. Seven percent of Bausch & Lomb's revenue came from this segment in 2002.[27] If, on the other hand, the technology is unavailable or will not give the firm a representative market share based on its current competitive advantages, then it constitutes less of an opportunity and more of a threat. In this case, the size of the threat is a determinant of how aggressive the response should be to improve the selling proposition of contact lenses versus surgery.

The laser surgery industry has stabilized at roughly 750,000 patients, with 1.5 million procedures performed each year in the United States (see table).[28] This represents less than 1 percent of the total consumer population and 3 percent of total vision-related spending. Since U.S. population growth and immigration add roughly 1.5 million new candidates for vision correction per year, the net effect of the threat is simply to remove some of the growth in the category. Because it repesents a relatively limited market segment, many suppliers in the industry believe that laser surgery will not apply cost pressure to the lens market, and lens suppliers should have only limited concern. Of more concern to lens suppliers in the short term is the switch in business models caused by new disposable lens manufacturing technology. The pertinent question for the long term is whether successive generations of laser technology will create a more accessible and economical substitute.

Annual U.S. Vision Market Consumer Population

	Population	Share
Laser Surgery	750,000	1%
Contacts	35,000,000	22%
Glasses Only	130,000,000	77%

Retail Revenue Trend—Laser Surgery and Contacts (in millions of dollars)

	2001	2002	2003
U.S. Laser Revenue	$ 1,400	$ 1,400	$ 1,500
U.S. Contact Lens Revenue	$15,900	$16,200	$16,600

Contact Lens Segment Share Trends

	2001	2002	2003
One-Day Disposables	3%	3%	3%
Weekly Disposables	60%	61%	64%
Monthly/Quarterly Disposables	20%	23%	24%
Traditional	17%	13%	9%

Source: Figures are estimates, based on data from K. Croies, "Will Custom LASIK Boost Growth? Analysts Say Yes, but Also View Emerging Technologies and Favorable Demographics as Growth Generators," *OptiStock Refractive Surgery Edition*, September 2003, http://www.optistock.com/mw/2003_09all.htm; and Vision Council of America website, http://www.visionsite.org.

Evaluating the Potential Impact of Changes on the Technology Axis

In cases where products/markets served seem to be relatively unchanged by a new technology, evaluating the impact of the technology on the status quo requires testing against a number of conditions. Ohio State's Jay Barney bases this evaluation on a set of four resource-oriented questions:[29]

- ❏ Is the technology valuable?
- ❏ Is it rare?
- ❏ Is it difficult to imitate?
- ❏ Is it without substitutes?

Barney's purpose in asking these questions is to identify potential sources of competitive advantage. This model will be revisited in Part 3, which deals specifically with the issue of competitive advantage, since a great deal of the strategic planning process involves finding ways to answer "yes" to the imitation and substitution questions. As the Porter model illustrated, eliminating imitations and substitutes through the use of technology can make a firm's competitive situation more attractive. For now, however, the focal point of these questions is the impact of a technology change on overall industry attractiveness, as well as a firm's position in the market. As a result, the discussion will center on the issues of value and rarity; the impact of asymmetry, when a lack of imitations and substitutes gives one or more firms a unique capability, will be covered in later chapters.

A Question of Value: Innovations That Have Minimal Impact

A technology change may have little or no impact on a market. All new products are not necessarily good ideas, and many innovations are simply technologies in search of a market, with little potential attractiveness. For technology to alter the competitive structure of an industry and position of a firm, it needs to pass the value test. Thus, before considering whether a new technology is scarce, is heterogeneous (unavailable to all firms), or creates more intense competition through increased imitation or substitution by competitors, a firm needs to determine whether it has some value.

Value can be looked at from the perspective of its impact on several different constituents. In terms of *customer impact*, a technology with either a direct favorable consumer utility or a secondary favorable response through its impact on cost structure or service delivery will force a firm to adapt and adopt in order to maintain the competitive status quo. From an *incumbent's internal viewpoint*, a valuable technology will exploit an opportunity or neutralize threats in the firm's competitive environment.[30] From a *challenger's viewpoint*, the converse is true: A technology has value if it threatens the status quo or opens up new opportunities.

As unnecessary as this exercise may seem, the sad fact is that not all new technology has value. An example of a technology that lacks value from the incumbent perspective would be a traditional (or even new) billing system that provides only limited functionality. For a challenger, a non-valuable innovation might be an aftermarket improvement to an outdated system or one that embeds a standard rejected by the market. Finally, for an end-customer, a low-value technology would be an innovation that had little customer utility or appeal. Some extreme examples in the latter category are featured annually in the Ig Noble Prize award list, developed by the Annals of Improbable Research and the Harvard Computer Society. Past winners include Under-Ease—airtight underwear with a replaceable charcoal filter that removes bad-smelling gases before they escape—and Pawsense—software that detects a cat walking across a computer keyboard. Hanes is probably not too concerned about charcoal-filtered underwear stealing market share, nor is Microsoft likely to be overly worried about the introduction of Pawsense.

As mentioned previously, the value of an innovation must be considered in relation to the specific resource base of the firm on whose behalf it is potentially to be applied. While a firm may not find value for itself, a competitor's ability to derive value from a different resource configuration, complementary assets, or capabilities could make the technology highly "impactful." For example, improvements in satellite technology would be of little use to a cable operator, but could create opportunities for satellite broadcasters, ultimately causing major shifts in product/market definition and overall share.

The Issue of Rarity

■ *Asymmetry.* Naturally, rare technology that has value presents unique opportunities for firms to create competitive disparity. Both the life cycle observations in Part 2 of this book and the competitive advantage review in Part 3 will cover asymmetrical availability and technology barriers in more detail. Valuable and rare technology does not create a sustainable competitive advantage as frequently as some expect, as firms can generally find ways to gain access to or imitate technologies. On the other hand, it takes only one such event to destroy an incumbent company's hard-won competitive position, so firms should be in tune with the new patents, theories, and proofs of concepts that may eventually displace their product configuration.

■ *Structural Change Caused by Consumer Preferences.* Even without asymmetry, innovation can have a destructive effect on a firm's competitive position. A widely available technology that does not create a competitive advantage for any specific firm can still take away an incumbent's advantage and expand or contract the revenue and profits of an industry. When a valuable technology is widely available, it may lack strategic leverage, but still it must be evaluated for its potential impact on customer choice. Ignoring customer preferences has never been a particularly attractive strategy, and successful firms have at their foundation a keen understanding of and insight into customer need.[31] This means that firms must often respond to customer preferences, whether or not the response can leverage a unique capability.

Take, as an example, responses to the ubiquitous Internet pop-up ad. A major annoyance to many users of the Internet, this type of advertisement appears in a new browser window as a result of code written into a variety of websites. The new advertising window often seems to appear out of thin air or is tucked under other open browser windows, so that it is never quite clear which site spawned the ad. Growing irritation with these ads has given rise to a host of "pop-up killing" software, designed to prevent these ads from downloading to users' PCs. This technology is certainly attractive to many users, and it is widely available. In fact, it quickly became one of the applications most often downloaded by Internet users. EarthLink, one of the largest Internet service providers, added pop-up killing software as a feature for its users, after identifying a need to grow into the revised market definition created by consumer interest in non-invasive Internet browsing. EarthLink tried to leverage this advantage over AOL, its top competitor, but AOL was able to quickly respond with similar software in its next release. The homogeneity of this technology, due to its easy replication, meant that it did not create an opportunity to alter rivalry. Nor did the technology fundamentally alter the basis of competition in the industry—new ISP firms could not use it to create an opportunistic entry point based on a promise to eliminate pop-up ads (although they might have, if EarthLink, AOL, and others had chosen to ignore it). The technology did, however, redefine the overall product offered to customers and potentially increase its attractiveness (by eliminating a consumer nuisance). A firm not adopting the change might lose market share as a result.

■ Structural Change Caused by Substitution or Lower Entry Barriers. In addition to changing customer preferences, a widely available (non-rare) technology can also have a high impact by increasing rivalry. The Porter model points out that increased availability of substitutes—whether imitation crabmeat or alternatives to Intel processors—puts pressure on the price performance equation of an existing product. Likewise, more direct competition leads to competitive pressure. A prominent illustration of this phenomenon is the way eBay has lowered entry barriers significantly for those wishing to sell many categories of products. There are no significant technology barriers to selling on eBay—the e-commerce capability can be imitated by anyone willing to pay $.35 to list items—so the technology tool is not a source of competitive advantage for any one firm or person. It can, however, potentially create structural changes in the industry, by moderating prices in categories with traditionally tightly controlled distribution and lowering costs by eliminating the need for entire sets of service attributes (such as a storefront or sales force). *Forbes* reported that in the network router market, for example, eBay sellers were undercutting Cisco's traditional channels by as much as 50 percent or more on price.[32] This could have an impact on the ability of these channels to maintain historical margins, as well as on Cisco's business, since these channels can serve important sales, service, inventory-carrying, and integration functions.

Assessing Problem Size: Matching Reaction to Threat/Opportunity

After determining how an innovation can provide new sources of value and to what extent the innovation is available to the industry, a firm must still consider the magnitude of the potential change. Since industry participants define their businesses differently, not all changes—even disruptive ones—are of large consequence to all incumbents. Some innovations may grow or change the category along vectors of little interest to established firms.

Category Disruption

Technology may be disruptive enough to completely change the competitive basis of an industry.[33] If a technology creates new sources of competitive advantage, such as new highly desired features, a lower cost basis, or a different method of delivering a service, then it has the ability to significantly disrupt the industry and a firm's position in it. In the pharmaceutical industry, a firm with a new and much more efficacious drug—or simply a new delivery mechanism—could capture most of an illness segment if it had the patent protection (and complementary assets) to do so. Even drug discovery technology itself—such as advanced genomics capability—could create a change in the fundamental competitive basis of the industry if it allowed some firms to "out-innovate" others in drug development. As mentioned earlier, this sort of change is rare, and firms can often find ways to gain access to or at least closely imitate technologies. More often, it is an unwillingness to change rather than an inability to gain access to innovation that leads to a loss of position or failure to move with the category definition.

A well-documented example is the case of Encyclopedia Britannica, a 200-year-old company that had a dominant share of the $1 billion encyclopedia market throughout most of the 20th century. In the early 1990s, Microsoft's multimedia capabilities allowed it to produce a CD-ROM–based encyclopedia called Encarta, using content licensed from Funk & Wagnall's. The traditional product—a bound encyclopedia in multiple volumes—was expensive to produce, was difficult to update, and, of course, lacked sound and media. While adding new features, Encarta also eliminated $800 of the overhead associated with traditional encyclopedias, in the form of printing, shipping, and sales commissions. Application of CD-ROM technology resulted in an encyclopedia that could be profitably sold for $50 instead of $1500. For consumers, the money saved on the encyclopedia could be used to buy a PC, which could then be used for many other educational applications as well as Encarta.

Microsoft's technology advantage was somewhat short-lived and imitable, which meant that Britannica, by switching to selling its product on CD-ROM, probably could have maintained its market share dominance. Multimedia development redefined the encyclopedia market on the technology axis (see Exhibit 3-7), and the move to a primarily digital distribution model enabled a superior price/value substitute that appealed to many consumers. Additionally, the emphasis in the reshaped market was on a large mass market and customer-installed base, rather than on a high-revenue-per-customer model. Britannica had a difficult time adjusting to these new market realities.[34] While the scope of the market was much larger, the total number of potential dollars was smaller, since the overall value chain had been reduced by eliminating paper production–related issues and costs.

EXHIBIT 3-7 ■ Redefinition of the Encyclopedia Market to Include CD-ROM–Based Encyclopedias

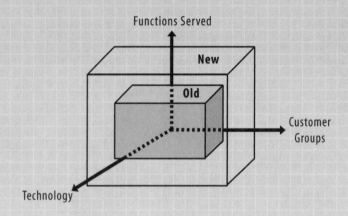

This example demonstrates the importance of responding to changes in market definition, regardless of the homogeneity of the technology. If Microsoft had had an inimitable technology for producing CD-ROM–based encyclopedias, Britannica would have faced a serious threat to market share. Even without inimitability, a threat to the existing business model and revenue base still emerged. More importantly, the change in the customer group and how it was served removed a key complementary asset for Britannica—its sales force. With CD-based distribution, the PC distribution channels available to Microsoft created a new source of complementary assets and redefined the market with significantly different characteristics unfavorable to Britannica.

Segment-Specific Disruption

Evaluating the potential impact of new technology and appropriate strategic posture becomes much more ambiguous when the technology in question threatens a segment but not a majority of the market. The reason segmentation exists is to more closely tailor products (and messages) to the needs of certain user groups. Since these groups have different needs and characteristics, an innovation may come along that appeals to some but not all of the larger market. Many product categories are relatively complex from a demand perspective and can be mapped as distinct consumer "spaces," with an emphasis on different product variables. **Conjoint analysis** is sometimes used to define the mixtures of variables comprising product bundles that meet the needs of a segment.

Exhibit 3-8 shows three hypothetical PC bundles that might be seen as offering equivalent "utility" to one segment, based on testing consumers' preferences by offering them a variety of tradeoffs and asking which option they prefer. While some consumers in the segment value (and would pay extra for) more memory and a rewritable drive, as offered by Toshiba in bundle 2, others prefer a DVD drive, and most have some price sensitivity. The research indicates that consumers would be willing to accept slower processor speed to keep the price point down, and many would forgo a CD-RW or DVD drive if the price gap grew too large.

EXHIBIT 3-8 ■ PC Bundles with Equivalent Utility

	Bundle 1	Bundle 2	Bundle 3
Brand	Compaq	Toshiba	Gateway
Processor Speed	1.7 GHz	1.5 GHz	2.0 GHz
Memory (RAM)	512 MB RAM	256 MB RAM	128 MB RAM
Hard Drive	60 MB	80 MB	40 MB
Price	$799	$899	$599
Optical Drive	DVD drive	CD-RW	CD-ROM

SOURCE: Based on Sawtooth Software, "Academic Aids—Introduction to Conjoint Analysis,"
http://www.sawtoothsoftware.com/curr1.htm.

Certain segments might be disrupted as a combination CD-RW/DVD drive became available. Bundles 1 and 2 could both become unattractive, and if Compaq and Toshiba neglected to make the move, they could rapidly become uncompetitive. A supplier of CD drives without DVD technology would also be adversely affected. Bundle 3 would still offer the same tradeoff between low price and disk features, however. As a result, Gateway might not be impacted, assuming it was serving customers who showed a much higher preference for low price and high processor speed. (*Note:* When applied to the rapidly evolving PC market, conjoint analysis illuminates the wisdom of Dell's build-to-order PC business model. Technology changes cause PC bundles to become uncompetitive rapidly, leaving companies with a large inventory of poorly configured bundles if they are pre-assembled.)

New Segment Emergence

Another possibility is for new segments to emerge that engage part of a company's market but don't eliminate it. Any study of consumer preferences related to automobiles would reveal a series of tradeoffs that consumers will make among price, performance, comfort, cargo space, and mileage. Consumers can be grouped into clusters according to their tradeoff preferences. For example, the utility of a powerful, spacious, large-capacity SUV makes up for a lack of handling and mileage for some consumers, while others see handling and comfort as most important and are willing to trade off price and cargo room to get them. Car manufacturers compete aggressively to identify and offer a vehicle targeting each of the meaningful segments. If a manufacturer developed an SUV with higher mileage and carlike handling, a whole group of buyers would migrate to the new vehicle. Some would be SUV purchasers unhappy with their SUVs' mileage, and some would be mileage-oriented buyers unhappy with the size of their fuel-efficient vehicles. This new segment would create a new market opportunity (as the Macintosh did), but also redistribute the market away from other segments. In the latter case, the incumbent manufacturer would be faced with lost sales and some difficult choices regarding how to respond to the innovator, but not the total collapse of the business. Consider Chrysler's success with the Jeep Grand Cherokee in the early 1990s. Redesigned with a carlike "unibody" construction and performance characteristics and sporting a variety of luxury trims, the Jeep redefined SUVs and quickly took market share from traditional trucklike SUVs, as well as sedans. Since competitors essentially needed to add a new class of vehicle to compete in this new space, they were slow to react, giving Jeep (and Chrysler) new life. Similarly, the Hummer H2, a large military-inspired SUV with low mileage and weighing over 6,000 pounds, appeals to a more extreme, trucklike SUV customer segment, at the expense of more practical vehicles.

At first blush, it would seem to be important to react quickly to technology-induced innovation that alters the value proposition and distribution of customer demand in a market—even if the redistribution is only a partial one created by the discovery of a new segment. Still, as the Lasik illustration demonstrated, it's possible to overreact to segment-specific innovation. In the case of laser eye surgery, the market has changed in only a minor fashion, and several contact lens–making firms were better served by developing next-generation disposables than by investing in laser surgery machines. The proper response depends on the size of the threat/opportunity, the cost versus payout implications of allocating resources to the new segment, and the fit of the new market definition with the firm's set of core competencies. At the same time, if the new segment represents an opportunistic entry into the incumbent's market, the incumbent needs to be wary of ceding profits and market share to a competitor without a contest, since this can provide a beachhead for expanding into the larger market. Even if cable television operators cannot offer competing satellite-based technology, simply ignoring the new segment would have been unwise. The cable industry's short-term reaction has been to try to minimize the impact of satellite (by limiting local channel access). In the long term, it's developing alternative digital delivery technologies that will address some of the same customer wants (e.g., hundreds of channels).

Multidimensional Shifts and Myopia

Determining the impact of a new technology becomes much more complex when redefinition on the technology axis is accompanied by a shift in the product and/or customer dimension. These more radical market space shifts usually fit into the category of disruptive changes, which are difficult to recognize, gauge, and react to.

Firms often don't recognize the potential of a new space, since it doesn't seem likely to have an impact on the firm's business. Ken Olson, the founder of Digital Equipment Corporation, is widely reported to have said, "There is no reason anyone would want a computer in their home," not recognizing that technology change and new functionality would create a new market for computers among consumers. Xerox is almost mythological for its myopic view and inability to capitalize on inventions, including graphical user interfaces and the Ethernet. Harvard professor Ted Levitt, in his classic piece about "market myopia," wrote:

> It is impossible to mention a single major industry that did not at one time qualify for the magic appellation of "growth industry." In each case, its assumed strength lay in the apparently unchallenged superiority of its products. There appeared to be no effective substitute for it. It was itself a runaway substitute for the product it

so triumphantly replaced. Yet one after another of these celebrated industries has come under a shadow.[35]

Even when an existing firm recognizes the potential of a new space, the change may not seem relevant to the firm and its customer base—particularly if the offering of a "different package of attributes"[36] does not fit with the incumbent's internal organization or current value delivery system. For example, Merrill Lynch was widely criticized for reacting too slowly to the development of Internet-based trading in the late 1990s, while competitor Charles Schwab was considered to be an innovator. Schwab customers, however, were the prime segment to take advantage of "self-service" trading tools, since Schwab conducted a relatively impersonal transaction–based business built around the middle-class mass market. Merrill customers, on the other hand, were wealthier, had larger accounts, and were used to the personal brokerage relationships and proprietary research offered by Merrill. In the short term, Internet trading seemed less relevant to Merrill customers, and Merrill would naturally be slower to react. Compounding the problem was Merrill's higher commission structure and broker-based culture, which was inconsistent with the Internet-trading segment. Schwab did not have these internal issues, with brokers paid on salary and a technology-driven culture.

Finally, since short-term economic interests can be aligned against a shift in business definition, the shift can be difficult to react to—even when recognized. A "competitive" product with different channels, lower quality, different price points, a different delivery mechanism, and different skill sets makes for a difficult business case. When a new innovation seems to be focused on a distinct market or segment and has a radically different pricing structure and feature set, it is easier for a firm to simply dismiss the challenge than to dismantle its current business model or even supplement it with another. Such was the case with Brittanica, mentioned earlier in the chapter. Cisco's and Juniper's differing views on carrier class routers demonstrate the difficulty of establishing a clear view of markets when both new customers and new technologies are in play.

Juniper versus Cisco

Despite predictions to the contrary, Juniper Systems has yet to be mowed over by Cisco Systems, the $20 billion gorilla of the networking industry. The nature of the competition between Juniper and Cisco, as well as its likely evolution, depends on whether Juniper's product family represents a one-dimensional or two-dimensional shift in the industry space.

Cisco and Juniper both agree that Juniper flanked Cisco in the high-end router market—specifically, the expensive "carrier class" routers that move traffic along the Internet's backbone. Juniper sells routers with enough capacity, speed, and reliability to satisfy the needs of telecommunications firms and ISPs. Juniper's products go for as much as $1 million each and are now used by over 90 percent of the major service providers.[37] Cisco, traditionally focused on corporate "enterprise class" networks, has much lower average price points and a different set of performance characteristics.

Where the two differ in opinion is in whether Juniper's strategy has been simply to go after a market on which Cisco hasn't focused attention (different customers served) or whether Juniper's technology is also superior to that of Cisco for these customers (different technology).

While Juniper is adamant that key differences in architecture (dedicated processors for control and forwarding of data packets) and software make its product a superior telco solution, Cisco does not see the technology as a threat. One of Cisco's executives was quoted as saying that Juniper's technology contains substantial flaws, and Cisco seems to feel confident in its ability to replicate anything that Juniper does. Juniper, in turn, sees Cisco as using non–state-of-the-art technology and being far behind Juniper in innovation for the segment. In any case, as the carrier market continues to evolve, both companies are now focused on it, and Juniper cannot rely simply on avoiding head-to-head competition.

Multidimensional shifts are much more difficult than one-dimensional shifts to compete against, since they require not only a technology competency but also the resources and skills to align with the change in the product and/or service offered or the customer group served. Christensen describes a multidimensional shift as a radical change in value proposition that results in a totally different product definition, which has more value for new consumer sets than for existing ones.[38]

The Role of Uncertainty in Innovation—Signal versus Noise

As mentioned earlier, one of the most difficult tasks for managers and executives in incumbent firms is to distinguish genuine threats from the ubiquitous innovation that generates the majority of the 100,000-plus patents issued each year. Intel's former chairman Andy Grove refers to the genuine threats posed by the emergence of disruptive technologies as creating strategic inflection points for firms and industries. True threats don't always take the form of frontal, "Desert Storm"–type assaults; they can be covert actions that topple market leadership because they weren't identified soon enough.

On the other hand, excessive hype ensures that many "paper tigers" and untenable technologies are trumped up as the next threat to the status quo. Grove identifies this as a **signal versus noise** issue:

> *Most strategic inflection points, instead of coming in with a bang, approach on little cat feet. They are often not clear until you look at the events in retrospect. Later, when you ask yourself when you first had an inkling that you were facing a strategic inflection point, your recollections are about a trivial sign hinting that the competitive dynamics had changed.*[39]

This is not a particularly comforting observation, since developing strategy in retrospect is not the role of the executive office.

Successful market entry for new disruptive competition often takes the form of a flanking move, to avoid head-on competition with the incumbent. As a result, many of the

First-generation
Motorola
cell phone—
disruptive
technology?

technologies that represent the most serious concerns for a business don't even appear to be in the competitive domain. Motorola's development of portable cellular phone technology, for example, was not met with great concern by competitors such as AT&T. The former CEO of Motorola said, "Nobody believed us, especially the competition. They didn't believe that the world was waiting for a portable."[40] As Part Two will discuss, compounding the problem is the fact that first-generation products often perform so poorly that it is difficult to take them seriously as a threat. Certainly, the first cell phones, such as the one depicted here, did not portend the low cost, compactness, and performance that have made the mobile portion of the phone industry so powerful.

Levels of Uncertainty

While entirely eliminating uncertainty is never possible, adopting an appropriate posture toward possibly disruptive technology is important in order to set an effective strategy. Based on level, the uncertainty surrounding a new technology may be classified in one of four discrete categories: a clear path, alternative paths, a range of paths, and true ambiguity.[41] Looking at just the home Internet broadband market, we can find examples in all four categories:

❑ The use of standard packet-based Internet protocols (TCP/IP) is a *clear path* of future technology.

❑ DSL and cable represent *alternative paths* of connectivity in the consumer market.

❑ Issues and solutions relating to home media networks (digital rights management, security, and privacy) may take a *range of paths*, since there are competing technologies and standards in multiple areas of the stack.

❑ The future of video on demand is truly *ambiguous*, with fundamental questions about business models and architecture still undetermined.

For a router and modem manufacturer, these differing levels of uncertainty make it relatively easy to plan for some of the technologies (those with clear paths, such as using IP protocols) and establish contingencies for others (such as DSL versus cable). It is virtually impossible to plan with certainty for others (such as products relating to the delivery of video on demand), however.

Appropriate Strategic Postures

The appropriate strategic posture for a firm depends on the level of uncertainty. The three postures can be classified as shaping, adapting, and reserving the right to play.[42]

A **shaping strategy** refers to making large commitments and putting in place large initiatives in order to "shape" the market's acceptance of a technology. By doing so, a firm can remove some of the uncertainty surrounding the technology, while steering the industry toward its preferred solution. This is a "big bet" strategy, requiring the dedication of significant resources, and is typically most appropriate for large companies. Warner Brothers, for example, in order to create momentum for DVD technology, began releasing products on DVD and soliciting cooperation from consumer electronics manufacturers early on. The motivation was to establish a royalty-free DVD standard (which would favor the studios, since they own the content), while allowing Warner Brothers to penetrate new distribution channels and reduce its dependence on large rental chains and cable operators.

As Warner's Warren Lieberfarb (often referred to as the "father of the DVD") pointed out:

> *I decided that if we were going to compete, we had to change the rental model. My conclusion was you had to be able to sell movies at places where the customer does conventional shopping, like Wal-Mart, and make up in volume what you lose in margin. . . . In 1994, Philips advised me that they and Sony were going their own way. They had a compact disc and if you wanted to use it, you'd have to get a license from them, and any improvements you made belonged to them. They invited Matsushita to join them. They were out to make it impossible for us to compete. . . . [In response] the executives of every studio except 20th Century Fox got together to enunciate disc specifications that would satisfy them as major producers of movies. These were not requirements—just a perfectly legal "wish list."*[43]

The end result was an unprecedented rapid conversion to DVD, using a variety of standards—including regional encoding to allow global distribution at different times—that clearly favored the studios. For a modem manufacturer, a similar strategy for video on demand might involve steering the industry toward server-side technology, which favors remote distribution and high-bandwidth transfer, rather than client-side technology, which places less emphasis on the transfer of bits and bytes and more emphasis on local storage. Shaping strategies are more appropriate when two alternative paths or a narrow range of alternatives are available, since the shaper has a reasonable chance of success.

In contrast to a shaping strategy, an **adaptive strategy** involves waiting for the market to evolve and then reacting appropriately. This often makes sense for smaller firms and in cases where the technology path is uncertain. While this strategy doesn't require the kind of large and speculative bet that shapers make, it also has risks. The primary risk is that the market will reshape itself in a way that is less attractive to the adapting firm or locks the adapter out. Firms face some risk by waiting, particularly when a high level of uncertainty exists. Consider the major record companies, which were very slow to embrace any sort of digital music initiatives, despite the development by several pioneering firms (such as Liquid Audio) of players and encoding systems designed to protect the labels' and artists' digital rights and assets. Since other environmental requirements had developed that favored the digital distribution of music—namely, broadband connectivity, digital encoding on CDs, and the ability to play music CDs on computers—the lack of label leadership resulted in the rise and adoption of the MP3 format as the preferred digital technology standard. This technology has many disadvantages for the record labels, including lack of quality, absence of digital rights management, and an open standard that allows the companies no control. Worldwide sales in the recorded music industry dropped 15 percent in

2001 and 2002 and another 7 percent in 2003, a drop attributed by many to the rise of the MP3 format. The record industry provides a major contrast to the DVD industry, where aggressive management of technology resulted in double-digit growth.

Executives generally wish to avoid the sort of negative reshaping that has plagued the music industry. Firms lacking the wherewithal to shape an industry can employ a third strategy called **reserving the right to play**. This strategy entails making limited incremental investments and establishing partnerships in new areas with the potential to become disruptive. For the incumbent, the objective is to gain organizational skills and knowledge, information, cost advantages, or key relationships that improve visibility into potential new technologies. The incumbent can also gain an inside track, which may allow it to acquire potentially disruptive businesses while they are still small and to do some limited shaping, both externally and internally. At a minimum, right-to-play participation allows the incumbent to favorably influence standards. Had the record labels participated sooner in digital music initiatives with RealNetworks, Liquid Audio, and others, they could have helped push these technologies forward and might have been much more alert to the threat presented by MP3-type formats and Napster-type file-sharing services, rather than reacting after the damage had already been done.

For innovators, a correct assessment of the incumbent's posture toward uncertainty is an important piece of the strategic roadmap. An incumbent that is aggressively shaping an industry clearly intends to make the industry as attractive as possible for itself. This situation is potentially limiting for the innovative technology provider. It also creates tremendous competitive pressure, which greatly reduces the chances for success. For example, retail chain Circuit City invested well over $100 million in an attempt to develop an alternative to standard DVDs called DivX. While this technology offered some additional digital rights features that were economically attractive and consumer controversial, the standard was competing against Lieberfarb's industry-driven initiative and so was unlikely to succeed. If, on the other hand, an innovator's technology is embraced by an incumbent, it is likely to be saddled with a set of conditions that limit the upside and flexibility of the innovator. While this reduces some of the risk particularly for startups, it comes with some loss of control and reorients the innovator's exit strategy. When incumbents assume an aggressive shaping posture, the choice presented to the startup may be to either align with or compete against the large, industry-dominant incumbent. A startup should be realistic about its options in such a case.

When the incumbent is less sure of its intentions and acquires technology simply to reserve the right to play, the innovator may suffer less loss of control and limitation of upside, but still should not expect much assistance from the incumbent in facilitating adoption of the new technology. While the innovator may consider itself in partnership, the decision to reserve the right to play indicates that the incumbent almost certainly has placed multiple technology bets, is likely sharing best practices and knowledge with various initiatives, and may actually be working against the interests of the innovating firm.

CHAPTER SUMMARY

Predicting the future is a tough business. As Shakespeare wrote in *Hamlet*, "We know what we are, but know not what we may be." Yet, given the rapid pace of innovation and development of new technologies, engaging in informed prognostication is important to maximizing the success of an enterprise and is arguably the foundation of strategy. For the would-be entrepreneur, not only is it important to have a view of the future; it is equally important to have an understanding of how other firms view the future. The capability of large firms, in particular, to shape the future through their actions and inactions must be considered in trying to bring innovation into the marketplace.

This chapter introduced a variety of tools for analyzing where technology and innovation are likely to take an industry and how they are likely to affect individual firms. Identifying a firm's critical success factors is important, since innovation can be evaluated based on its potential impact on the activities that contribute most to the success of the firm.

The nature of the influence of these factors can be clarified by applying Porter's five forces model, which systematically organizes the variables impacting firm and industry attractiveness. These include both competitive pressure—in the form of substitutes, industry rivalry, and new entrants—and the distribution of economic gains among members of a value network or supply chain.

Abell's three-dimensional model of industry and market definition was introduced as a tool for identifying how an addressable market's overall definition can be changed by technology, thus impacting Porter's competitive intensity–related vertical axis variables— substitutes, new entrants, and industry rivalry—while also perhaps creating new growth opportunities. Different functionality, new customers and channels, and new technology create different value propositions and can change the shape, size, and distribution of share in a firm's markets. While a technology's uniqueness and insulation are key variables in creating major competitive shifts between individual firms, they are not required to structurally change markets. Even widely available technology can cause structural changes that make markets more competitively contested or alter market definition.

Quantifying the size of a shift is necessary to develop an appropriate response. Complete redefinition of what is valued requires dramatic action, while segment-specific changes may not be worth pursuing at all. In the most ambiguous case, where significant but not complete market erosion is envisioned, a firm must determine how the tradeoffs involved in pursuing or not pursuing a piece of the new segment will affect the business. If the resources and core competencies necessary to compete in the new segment are beyond the firm's capabilities, then either partnering or simply ceding the segment might be necessary. The danger of this strategy is that a competitor with an uncontested segment can often use that segment as a beachhead for expanding into other business. Ideally, a firm will be able to leverage existing resources (whether complementary assets or technology-based resources) to participate in the new segment.

Uncertainty makes the strategic decision-making process more complex. In the case of new technologies, it is almost a given that decisions will need to be made in an environment of uncertainty. Rather than simply taking an inactive adapting position, dominant firms can attempt to reduce uncertainty in one of two ways. By shaping the direction of technology, firms with large resource bases can attempt to define a future environment that favors their position. Alternatively, through participation in partnership and pilot programs, firms can reserve the right to play in order to reduce uncertainty and react quickly as technology changes markets. For innovators, adopting a strategic posture that takes into account the behavior of the incumbents is equally important.

part 2

LIFE CYCLES, TIMING, AND EVOLUTION

P art 1 of the book looked at innovation in the context of value delivery systems. A new technology can be positioned in relation to an overall system of value creation, a firm's resource base, alternatives in the marketplace, necessary partnerships, complementary assets, and the overall product delivered. All of these determine strategic options for firms with a potential stake in the innovation. Yet this systemic view is dynamic over time—an innovation's value changes as the industry and markets it serves evolve.

Part 2 will cover technology evolution and industry life cycle concepts, as well as the impact of timing on innovation and strategic technology choice. Chapter 4 will give an overview of how life cycles develop and the factors that contribute to their progression. Chapters 5, 6, and 7 will look at the evolution of new technology over the key phases in the progression—innovation and imitation, diffusion and standardization, and industry adoption—and focus on the competitive dynamics, economics, and market behavior likely to characterize each period.

An Introduction to Technology Life Cycles and Their Drivers

"There ain't no rules around here! We're trying to accomplish something!"

—Thomas Edison

The Influence of Timing

Timing is an important variable in assessing whether an innovation is poised to change an industry's status quo and competitive landscape. The timing within an emerging technology's life cycle also dictates which firms are best positioned to take advantage of a change and when and how firms should commit to a new technology.

A startup may seize a market opportunity where no one else has yet ventured, but once a monolithic competitor such as GE or IBM enters, the window of opportunity may rapidly close. GE may look at a new technology-driven opportunity as unattractively small and fraught with risk, yet a venture capitalist may see upside in the same opportunity. A new feature or quality benchmark may be enough to excite adventurous buyers, yet stop short of creating a market large enough to build a successful business around. In these ways, a firm's capabilities and resources are either well- or ill-timed relative to the opportunity a new technology offers.

As a starting point, looking at behaviors that drive both consumer demand and supplier decision-making will illustrate the important role that life cycle timing has in overall market dynamics.

Demand-Side Behavior

Consumers, whether they are aware of it or not, make life cycle–based decisions continually. In buying an automobile, for example, the model year is a key consideration. In the first year of a new model design or a model redesign, a car may have a novelty factor, as well as some features unavailable in competing models. This factor will drive many shoppers into the showroom. At the same time, such models are often of lower quality than those made in either succeeding or preceding years, prompting the Center for Auto Safety in Washington to advise consumers, "Don't buy any new vehicle in the first year of production."[1] The more radical the change in a model's design (and thus the more appealing the novelty factor), the more likely the quality issue is to arise.

A 2002 study by J.D. Power found that model redesign typically leads to an initial decline in quality, after which second-year quality *increases* significantly—a cycle well known to consumers. Many consumers will choose to wait, understanding this product life cycle phenomenon and the price they might pay to drive a car with leading-edge design. Conversely, for those who buy the last model year of an automobile line, obsolescence and resale value become issues, even though quality and reliability may be at their peak. This equally well-known portion of the life cycle causes many consumers to delay their purchase or demand additional discounts.

When a new class of consumer electronics becomes available, many consumers will wait, expecting prices to come down and choices to expand and hoping to gain greater clarity on whether the new product will become a well-supported standard (such as DVD) or an idea destined for the junk heap (such as DivX, Betamax, or 8-track tape). Still others will immediately run out and buy anything new and different (such as TiVo or plasma televisions) without regard for the long term. Similarly, even with motion pictures, there are those who absolutely must see a new movie on opening weekend, while others wait to see what the reviewers and their peers have to say before deciding whether to go to a theater or to "wait for the DVD." These consumer decisions and behaviors are based on "rules" developed through both observation and research into the implications of various choices. For example, the rule that new consumer electronics will drop in price over time leads many to wait, whether or not the particular item conforms to the rule. (Exhibit 4-1 shows the predicted path of the prices of plasma and LCD TVs.) Marketers need to be aware of and establish programs that take into account—and, when appropriate, overcome—these behaviors. Moreover, identifying customer segments likely to contain early purchasers who will influence other buyers will lead to greater success. As with consumer electronics, new information technology and other innovations follow predictable life cycles, with implications for buyers.

Supply-Side Behavior

The demand side time-based behavior discussed above is based partially on expected supplier behavior. Much like consumer behaviors, there are supplier behaviors relating to timing of market entry, overall capacity, and product performance.

A simple illustration of supplier time-based behavior emerges in examining the choice of crops planted by farmers. Often, a high-price year for a particular crop will cause many farmers to switch to that crop. In the case of processed tomatoes, the industry follows a self-induced five- to seven-year cycle of expansion and contraction.[2] High prices (driven by undersupply) attract new growers/processors, and the subsequent oversupply drops prices and drives many out of business or into other crops, leading the cycle to repeat itself (see Exhibit 4-2). The DRAM (Dynamic Random Access Memory) market has followed a similar supply-driven boom and bust cycle. An attractive market leads to overcapacity, followed by price declines. Eventually prices rise, encouraging additional fabrication capacity construction, leading the cycle to repeat.[3]

EXHIBIT 4-1 ■ Price Drops Are the Expected Rule in Consumer Electronics

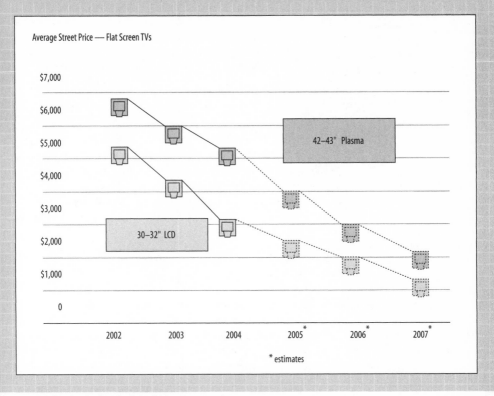

Average Street Price — Flat Screen TVs

SOURCE: Based on data from Pacific Media Associates.

EXHIBIT 4-2 ■ California Canning Tomatoes Price and Supply Decisions

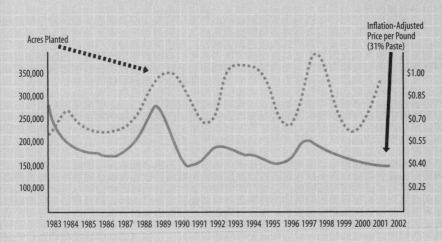

SOURCES: California Tomato Growers Association and Morningstar Farms.

There are, of course, differences between new technology markets and established commodity markets. The high potential growth rate of emerging market categories attracts capital to fund startups, while the uncertainty around the future of the category often delays entry by incumbent competitors. Also, necessary complements and infrastructure may not yet exist and be slow to develop because of this uncertainty. While commodity markets are predictable and attract only "low-risk money," the nature of VC-funded startups is to take a higher risk approach, given the great uncertainty about what technology and technology providers will emerge as commercially triumphant. The introductory chapter alluded to the fiber-optics networking bubble and the oversupply of technology firms chasing the "brass ring" in this emerging category. This environment of competitive disorder, market uncertainty, investment exuberance, and instability has a major impact on both competitors in the market and individuals/firms planning to buy from the market. The fundamental value proposition and underlying market structure for a new technology may not be known. The process of determining them is actually part of the new technology life cycle. In an emerging technology market, unlike an established commodity market, the quality and nature of the "product" offered may go through several transitions.

Clearly, with an understanding of the market and competitive characteristics of new technology life cycles, the managers in firms affected by them can make better decisions. For consumers, awareness of the life cycle presents a chance to understand and evaluate the tradeoffs between "being first" and waiting for lower-risk/higher-return products. For incumbent firms ever vigilant about new competitive or market-changing forces, an understanding of the dynamics of new technology life cycles provides guidance about when and how to react to potential threats and opportunities emerging from both existing competitors and startups. Finally, for startup firms, greater insight into what is likely to occur along the journey—and even the appropriate definition of the destination—will help them along the road to success.

Distinguishing Discontinuous from Incremental Change

Technological innovation can be classified as either discontinuous or incremental. **Discontinuous innovation** (also referred to as *disruptive innovation*) upends the nature of what is valued and how value is delivered in an industry or in some cases creates completely new market areas. **Incremental innovation** usually derives from development of production processes, distribution changes, or simple line extension and has no significant impact on market structure.[4] The cycle of change for discontinuous innovation follows a far different, less certain, and longer path than that for incremental innovation. According to the resource-based view developed in Part 1, incremental innovation strongly favors incumbents. Discontinuous innovation has a much more variable impact on both startups and incumbents.

Both incremental and discontinuous innovation follow generally identifiable, but contrary, cycles. A steady flow of line extensions and attempts to wrest away market share represents a far different scenario than the potentially fundamental and far-reaching changes brought about by discontinuous change. The future impact of wireless networks on telecommunications, for example—and on the existing industry order—is far more uncertain and potentially impactful than that of improvements in existing wired infrastructure.

Discontinuous innovation eventually gives way to incremental innovation as industries mature in a process that will be outlined over the course of the next few chapters. This, in turn, eventually creates the opportunity for a next generation of discontinuous change. These interrelated life cycles are important from a strategic planning perspective.

Behavior, Technology Diffusion, and Adoption

As discussed in the first section of this chapter, buyers, for a variety of reasons, can be grouped into different segments based on their propensity to adopt new technology. The terms *technophile* and *luddite* describe the extremes, but they do not represent the only buyer groups. This behavioral stratification has a profound impact on the fortunes of innovative firms. Innovation is a race against time; the longer the delay in gaining a mainstream and widespread market, the higher the potential for competition and the less opportunity for a firm to press the advantage of uniqueness. Historically, the gap between invention and market acceptance has led to a sharp rise in competition prior to a sharp rise in sales, as Exhibit 4-3 illustrates. More recent technology, such as flat screen and digital television, has shown similar behavior, although more time-compressed.

In some cases, such as for cell phones and CD players, the infrastructure, standardization, and complement needs of an invention delay adoption. As discussed in Part 1, this is not surprising, given the disparity between the component nature of technology and the market's need for a complete solution. This is only part of the story, however. In the case of discontinuous innovation, new technology makes the old obsolete. The move from one paradigm to the next requires that both suppliers and buyers embrace the change. The placement of word-processing PCs in offices, for example, forced many users of Wang word processors to give up on a technology that they knew well. Teleconferencing tools require employees to change the way they hold meetings and reduce face-to-face contact. Railroads made the Erie Canal—and river towns in general— less important. Although it seems obvious in retrospect that innovations such as railroads and the automobile have positive benefits and should be readily embraced, paradigm shifts (Schumpeter's "creative destruction") are often resisted. Take, for example, the letter shown in Exhibit 4-4, allegedly written by Martin Van Buren to President Andrew Jackson in 1829 on the topic of railroads.

EXHIBIT 4-3 ■ Examples of the Gap Between Invention and Market Acceptance

	Year of Invention	Year of Commercialization	Year of Competitive Intensity	Year Sales "Take Off"
Automobile	1771	1890	1899	1909
Vacuum Cleaner	1907	1911	1928	1934
Ballpoint Pen	1888	1948	1957	1958
Home VCR	1951	1974	1975	1980
Cell Phone	1970	1983	1985	1986

SOURCE: R. Agarwal and B. Bayus, "The Market Evolution and Take Off of Product Innovations," *Management Science*, 2002.

EXHIBIT 4-4 ■ Martin Van Buren on the Radical New Invention Called "Railroads"

To: President Jackson,

The canal system of this country is being threatened by the spread of a new form of transportation known as "railroads." The federal government must preserve the canals for the following reasons:

One. If canal boats are supplanted by "railroads," serious unemployment will result. Captains, cooks, drivers, hostlers, repairmen and lock tenders will be left without means of livelihood, not to mention the numerous farmers now employed in growing hay for horses.

Two. Boat builders would suffer and towline, whip and harness makers would be left destitute.

Three. Canal boats are absolutely essential to the defense of the United States. In the event of expected trouble with England, the Erie Canal would be the only means by which we could ever move the supplies so vital to waging modern war. As you may well know, Mr. President, "railroad" carriages are pulled at the enormous speed of 15 miles per hour by "engines" which, in addition to endangering life and limb of passengers, roar and snort their way through the countryside, setting fire to crops, scaring the livestock and frightening women and children. The Almighty certainly never intended that people should travel at such breakneck speed.

Martin Van Buren, Governor of New York

Van Buren's comparison of canals to railroads also highlights the fact that old paradigms are often both well understood and finely honed, while new ones are neither and can look almost absurd by comparison. When the Defense Advanced Research Projects Agency (DARPA) recently offered a $1 million prize to any team that could build a robot vehicle capable of maneuvering a 150-mile course through the Mojave Desert, its objective was simply to push unmanned vehicle technology forward, even if no vehicles could actually finish. DARPA sponsored the event in response to a 10-year lack of progress by defense contractors in advancing driverless technology, which the Department of Defense has said will one day revolutionize warfare and reduce battlefield casualties. The most successful vehicle traveled less than 5 percent of the course, with many entries running into walls or ditches within sight of the starting line. Based on these early results, it would be easy to dismiss this avenue of innovation altogether, particularly since existing contractors and defense customers are committed to the multibillion-dollar Humvee and assault tank programs they have in place.

The combination of a less-than-perfect "first version" of new technology and an institutionalized dependence on and fondness for the "mainstream" has always opened the door for attacks on new technology. The book *Seabiscuit* describes the state of the automobile industry circa 1903:

> *The horseless carriage was just arriving in San Francisco, and its debut was turning into one of those unmitigated disasters that brings misery to everyone but historians. Consumers were staying away from the "devilish contraptions" in droves. The men who had invested in them were the subject of cautionary tales, derision, and a fair measure of public loathing. In San Francisco in 1903, the horse and buggy was not going the way of the horse and buggy. For good reason. The automobile, so sleekly efficient on paper, was, in practice, a civic menace, belching out exhaust, kicking up dust,*

The DARPA challenge highlights the rough spots
on the road to progress.

DARPA

becoming hopelessly mired in the most innocuous-looking puddles,
tying up horse traffic, and raising an earsplitting cacophony that
sent buggy horses fleeing. Incensed local lawmakers responded with
monuments to legislative creativity. . . . In some towns, police were
authorized to disable passing cars with ropes, chains, wires, and
even bullets. . . . Doctors warned women away from automobiles,
fearing slow suffocation in noxious fumes. [5]

The S Curve of Innovation Adoption

The overall set of buyer dynamics and typical buyer adoption behavior cycle can be described by an S curve. This simple model illustrates that technology diffuses over time in a nonlinear fashion. The rate of adoption of an innovation typically starts off slowly, increases as the innovation takes hold, and then slows again as the innovation reaches saturation (see Exhibit 4-5).

The inflection point occurs when growth is at its maximum, after which growth decreases and the "growth in growth" turns negative. A study of historical adoption rates of 27 products (including the innovations mentioned in Exhibit 4-3) found that an average of six years passed before competitive concentration occurred and another eight years before the inflection point was reached.[6] While this time delay appears to be shrinking, even a modern, earth-shaking technology such as the World Wide Web exhibited S curve characteristics, with three to four years (from 1995 to 1998) passing before the industry took off and seven years before the inflection point was reached (in 2002).[7] The first reference to the behavioral S curve is generally attributed to Gabrielle Tarde—a sociologist, not an economist[8]— based on his observations of human and group behavior 100 years ago. The concept has been applied and tested across a wide variety of new innovations, including software, canals, and even Cistercian monasteries.[9]

EXHIBIT 4-5 ■ The S Curve of Consumer Adoption and Diffusion

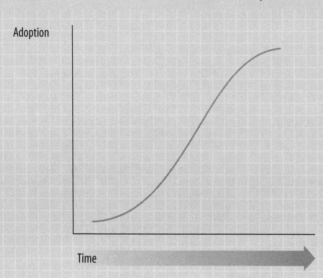

Consumer Segmentation and Adoption

The behavior and characteristics of the buyers of an innovation are markedly different at different points in time. The overall S curve can be segmented into five distinct populations—an idea developed by Everett Rogers[10] and made popular by Geoffrey Moore.[11] Innovators and early adopters represent the bottom part of the S. The early majority is responsible for the initial takeoff of the innovation. The late majority and laggards are at the top tail of the S; they join in after the point of inflection. The S curve can be reconstructed as a normal distribution curve in Exhibit 4-6. Although the time values of the mean and standard deviation will differ for various innovations, the curve is generally thought to be symmetrical and characterized by a normal distribution, with roughly 15 percent innovators and early adopters, 70 percent "mainstream market" majority, and the other 15 percent laggards.

Technology suppliers must appeal to the innovator and early adopter customer segments in order to gain a foothold for a new product. Unfortunately, the skills and features that win over these segments don't necessarily translate well to the more mainstream market. **Innovators** are typically emotional, risk-taking technophiles, who often embrace change for change's sake.[12] **Early adopters** are more closely integrated into the market and often have influential opinions. Like innovators, they embrace change and seek to establish a new order.[13] The **early majority**, however, has a significantly different profile from the first two groups. These mainstream users are heavily integrated into the current market system. They typically are more deliberate and make more practical and less emotional decisions regarding purchases.[14] This behavior has earned them the label "pragmatists,"[15] in contrast to the earlier, more intuitive and adventurous buyers, willing to take a chance on something new.

EXHIBIT 4-6 ■ The Normal Distribution of Consumer Types

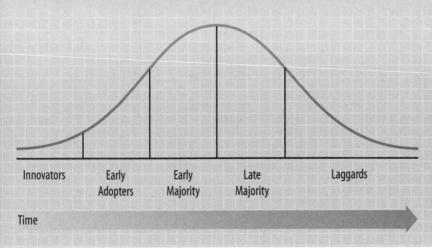

Moore describes a "chasm" between the early and mainstream markets, created by the need to address these markets in different ways in order to speed a product or innovation toward broader market acceptance. This change in emphasis poses a problem for innovating firms, since incumbents are often much better equipped to meet the desire for complete products and low-risk purchases. The innovating firm's lead in an early adopter market can vanish as the innovation goes mainstream. While speed and newness can capture the early market, this market segment is also the most fickle and will often abandon yesterday's innovation for the "next new thing." An innovator must be prepared to make the leap and compete in the mainstream in order to have long-term viability. Even if this necessity is recognized, success in the early market often is achieved at the cost of competitive positioning in the maturing high-growth market populated by the early majority. This issue and its implications will be examined further in the ensuing chapters.

Industry Evolution

The preceding section hints at—and later chapters will examine—the interplay between demand and supply when a new innovation is introduced into an industry. Implicit in examining buyer risk profiles and behavior in purchasing a new product or service is the assumption that supply side risk and entry strategies change over time. As with diffusion behavior, this **industry life cycle** takes the form of an S-shaped curve.

The look at new automobile models earlier revealed that early production experience can create higher costs and lower quality, while over time capacity increases, prices drop, and quality improves. As competing business models and technology approaches give way to an orderly and mature market, both buyer behavior and the supplier focus evolve. This progression leads to evolving competition and competitive issues as well.

Early in the cycle, innovation—particularly discontinuous innovation—requires capital, since money is spent in advance of revenue. The availability of and conditions placed upon capital for innovation are key drivers of early phases of the industry life cycle and evolving competitive landscape. The remainder of the chapter focuses on these issues.

The Role of Venture Capital in Industry Evolution

Chapter 1 discussed Schumpeter's assertion that innovation is largely an entrepreneurial activity. Whether or not innovation is solely the domain of startups, startups and entrepreneurs clearly play a key role in the innovation process. Liquidity constraints discourage entrepreneurial activities, so the availability of external funding is a catalyst for stimulating entrepreneurial activities.[16] Thus, it is clear that venture capital—one of the primary sources of funding for technology entrepreneurs—is a necessary part of the innovation/commercialization process. A variety of research[17] has found that VC-backed firms bring products to market faster, have more frequent and effective IPOs, and have higher valuations than do non-VC-backed firms. While this capital may be an important component, it also creates some idiosyncrasies in the competitive evolution of innovative technology, since venture capital operates according to rules that are distinct from—and sometimes seem to confound—the rules of rational business behavior.

Startup firms seeking financing for innovation face a number of problems that can often be solved by venture capital.[18] Most startups have a very high degree of uncertainty, which creates a higher variability in outcome than is desired by traditional financial institutions. Furthermore, the technology focus of the innovation often creates a large information gap between entrepreneurs and traditional financiers, whereas the staff of VC firms have a general understanding of new technology and appropriate due diligence processes. Startups often have ideas as their primary assets, and a profile based on **soft assets** is difficult to raise traditional funds for. Finally, the future of many startups is partially determined by overall and segment-specific market conditions. This requires the financier to play a proactive role in harvesting the investment at the appropriate time.

Although many VC-backed endeavors would never have been funded through other sources, venture capital is neither available nor desirable to all entrepreneurs. Most startups do not employ venture capital, nor would they be attractive candidates for venture funding. The vast majority of entrepreneurial startups are sole proprietorships in the service industry with limited opportunity for growth.[19] Venture capitalists do not fund laundries, family-run restaurants, or hair salons; they exist to fund and commercialize disruptive technologies. Even VC-backed firms often go through some self-financing and **angel investor** (private) mechanisms prior to seeking out VC funds.

A Venture Capital Primer

A venture capital firm typically has an amalgamation of discrete closed-end investment funds, managed by a combination of individuals with financial and relevant technical knowledge. The venture capital firm sets up the investment funds as limited partnerships and often operates multiple funds, each of which is managed separately. Typically, the funds are at least partially homogenous—concentrating investment in a few particular areas that the partners believe hold promise for significant growth and in which they can acquire a critical mass of knowledge, visibility, and diversification.

Usually, the inside partners contribute some capital as well as lending expertise in the technology area that the fund focuses on. The firm acts as general partner and sells units of interest in the funds to limited partners (generally wealthy individuals, pension funds, and corporate investors). As the general partner, a VC firm manages the funds and makes investment decisions. In soliciting limited partners, the VC firm will specify both a subscription target and an investment policy for the fund. Investments are made in firms showing promise in the targeted area. This promise may take the form of a technology breakthrough, a general idea of where a breakthrough may occur, access to key resources, a particularly attractive team, or a particularly innovative and protectable way of solving an important problem.

The valuation of the innovating firm for investment purposes is arbitrary, particularly in early-stage investment rounds. A VC firm will submit a term sheet outlining how much it is willing to invest, what percentage ownership in the venture it expects in return, and various other conditions. These conditions may include board seats, liquidation preferences, changes in the management team, and even the direction of technology development. Most often, a startup will need additional rounds of funding at various milestones on the path to achieving its end objectives. The VC firm also has a hand in defining these milestones and the terms under which additional capital will be invested, since they affect the valuation of the firm's stake in the startup.

The limited partners pay the VC firm an annual management fee of roughly 2 percent of their investment. The VC also typically receives 20 percent of all upside beyond the original investment made by all partners. As liquidity events occur, the fund realizes a gain (or recognizes a loss), and this is used to pay investors as well as give the VC its 20 percent upside. Most liquidity for limited partners is not realized until a fund's termination. A VC firm opens and terminates funds—some appealing to retail investors and others to institutional investors—on a regular basis.

The Venture Objective

In order to understand the flow of venture funds and the role that venture capital plays in fostering innovation, disrupting the status quo of industries, and generally creating mayhem in organized markets, it is important to understand the end goal of VC firms. Quite simply, they exist to invest money and generate returns through liquidity events. A liquidity event occurs when a fund is able to recognize a gain and return capital to investors. Whether through an IPO, acquisition, or other exit strategy, VCs look for liquidity events from the most successful companies in their portfolio to make up for the many other investments that don't bear fruit. Driven by this quest, venture firms establish timetables and goals that are aggressive and reflect the higher degree of risk associated with a higher potential return. As mentioned previously, VCs do not invest in stable, low-growth opportunities.

The higher risk associated with individual investments requires funds to adhere to a portfolio management approach in order to generate a predictable return. In some ways, this is no different from the way fund managers invest in a number of stocks to reduce the beta (risk) associated with individual investments. There are two primary differences:

1. Each startup has a much higher chance of failing; therefore, the successful investments must yield correspondingly higher returns.

2. The VC firm takes a much more active role in the management of investments to ensure that returns are generated within the VC's time frame.

Unlike traditional stocks, VC investments have a "hit or miss" nature. If a fund invests in 20 companies, in order to get a decent overall return it needs a return as high as 1000 percent on the more successful elements of its portfolio (not at all unrealistic). If only 3 of the 20 companies in the portfolio return this kind of gain, the fund will be a success, despite the 17 nonperformers. Realistically, of course, some of the 17 "losers" will provide some return on investment. Some will be sold or merged, and others will have a liquidation value. A highly simplified, typical VC fund might have 20 investments of $10 million each, with a 7-year time frame for generating returns. In that fund, the returns might be as follows:

	Number of Firms	Dollars Invested	Dollars Returned
Successful	3	$30,000,000	$300,000,000
Moderately successful	3	$30,000,000	$30,000,000
Failed	14	$140,000,000	$10,000,000
Total	20	$200,000,000	$340,000,000

In this case, the three successes make up for the lack of results in the other businesses. By returning capital on the three moderately successful firms and taking only a small liquidation position on the remaining 14 firms, the fund is able to generate an annual internal rate of return of over 9 percent.

Venture Capital Behavior

Game theory is the study of how groups of people interact. Part psychology and part economics, game theory is applied (although far less frequently than it should be) in business in the design of bidding strategies and negotiation tactics, when one side can gain leverage by specifying the rules of the game. In auctioning broadband PCS spectrum in the mid-1990s, for example, the FCC successfully applied game theory, employing a "simultaneous ascending auction"—multiple rounds of sealed bids with complex minimum bidding requirements—to ensure that it maximized revenues.[20] The FCC's purpose in this case was to overcome possible signaling and cooperative bidding that would minimize the cost of spectrum to those bidding on it.

One of the most famous examples of game theory and the impact of market rules on individual choice is known as the **prisoners' dilemma**. Imagine that two people are arrested for robbing a bank. The police have caught them with handguns, but don't have sufficient evidence for a bank robbery conviction. So they sequester the two prisoners in separate rooms, in the hope of extracting a confession and minimizing cooperation. If one prisoner confesses and the other doesn't, the confessor will go free while the other will get 10 years in jail. If both confess, each will get a reduced sentence.

If neither confesses, they both will get 180 days for illegal firearm possession. The joint table of outcomes is as follows:

	Prisoner 1	Prisoner 2	Total Time in "the Slammer"
Only Prisoner 1 confesses	Goes free	Gets 10 years	10 years
Only Prisoner 2 confesses	Gets 10 years	Goes free	10 years
Both confess	Gets 3 years	Gets 3 years	6 years
Neither confesses	Gets 180 days	Gets 180 days	1 year

The table shows that by far the optimal outcome for the two prisoners would be for neither prisoner to confess. Each would get 180 days and be released. In reality, however, most prisoners will confess, since no matter what Prisoner Two does, the outcome for Prisoner One will be better if he confesses. The following table looks at the outcomes from the perspective of just Prisoner One.

	Prisoner 1 Confesses	Prisoner 1 Doesn't Confess	Advantage of Confessing for Prisoner 1
Prisoner 2 confesses	Gets 3 years	Gets 10 years	+7 years
Prisoner 2 doesn't confess	Goes free	Gets 180 days	+180 days

Prisoner One, looking only at his outcomes, will conclude that confessing is the superior option. Whether or not Prisoner Two confesses, Prisoner One's individual outcome will always be better. The lesson from this is that as long as each prisoner pursues an individual goal and is unable to cooperate, the prisoners' mutual goal will suffer. Mathematician John Paulos has pointed out that this analysis can be readily applied to a variety of real-world situations:

> Action in one's self interest doesn't always best serve one's self interest. . . . [This] dilemma often arises in situations where we fear we are going to be left behind if we don't watch out for ourselves. . . . A similar situation can arise in a legitimate business transaction, or, indeed, in almost any sort of exchange.[21]

Significantly, this example destroys one of the basic assumptions underlying the orderly world of economics—that individuals behaving rationally create an aggregately rational market. The prisoners' dilemma has been shown to apply in a variety of real-world situations, from competitive pricing and advertising to public works funding. The principle is critical in understanding and anticipating the flow of venture capital. Even when venture capitalists behave rationally for their own benefit, their behavior isn't necessarily in the best interests of the industry or its competitors. VC firms operate with a focus on their own self-interest and policies that don't maximize returns for the industry as a whole or for the particular ventures receiving venture funds. As John Zider wrote in the *Harvard Business Review*,

> One myth is that venture capitalists invest in good people and good ideas. The reality is that they invest in good industries—that is, industries that are more competitively forgiving than the market as a whole. In 1980, for example, nearly 20% of venture capital investments went to the energy industry. More recently, the flow of venture

> *capital has shifted rapidly from genetic engineering, specialty retailing, and computer hardware to CD ROMs, multimedia, telecommunications and software companies. . . . The apparent randomness of these shifts among technologies and industry segments is misleading; the targeted segment in each case was growing fast, and its capacity promised to be constrained in the next five years. Each fund invests in perceived high growth segments to reduce the technology risk, since high growth markets are much more forgiving than those with little growth.*[22]

Absent from this simple risk-reducing approach is a consideration of the impact of individual investment decisions on overall overfunding and valuations in the segment. This **capital market myopia**[23] has been observed among venture capitalists as far back as 1985 and certainly occurred much earlier with other funding mechanisms, as illustrated by the experiences of the South Sea Company in the 18th century.

▶ Bubble History: The South Sea Company

With a weakness most culpable, he lent his aid in inundating the country with paper money, which based upon no solid foundation, was sure to fall sooner or later.

—**Charles Mackay**, 1841[24]

Those alarmed by current budget deficits and national debt might be interested to know that government deficit spending is nothing new. Back in 1711, the British government's debt had risen to 10 million pounds, a staggering sum at the time. In a deal to get the debt off the books and restore public confidence in the government, the South Sea Company was incorporated. The South Sea Company arranged to assume the British federal debt, in exchange for a temporary 6 percent annual interest payment from the government (to be paid by import taxes) and a monopoly on trade to the South Seas. It was assumed that the trade would capitalize on "the immense riches of the eastern coast of South America"[25] and would be highly lucrative, allowing the company to pay off the debt rapidly. After the first voyage in 1717, stock was also sold to the public amid great enthusiasm, with the promise of high dividends. The stock rose rapidly, despite little in the way of actual company revenue. As speculative fever rose, secondary offerings were made to ever-higher prices, and soon the public was paying 300 pounds for a capital position representing 100 pounds. In secondary markets, the shares traded even higher, commanding anywhere from 7 to 10 times their underlying value.

As public interest in the venture mounted and tales of early investor liquidity events multiplied, new companies were formed based on a wide range of other similar but highly speculative trade ventures, from Swedish iron to salt to horse insurance. From September 1719 through August 1720, 190 of these English ventures had their initial public offerings.[26] All of these, including the South Sea Company, eventually collapsed, and many fortunes were made and lost during the years that the South Sea Company existed. As Charles Mackay, who documented the South Sea bubble, pointed out, "In times of great commercial prosperity there has been a tendency to over-speculation . . . the success of one project generally produces others of a similar kind. Popular imitativeness will always, in trading nations, seize hold of such successes . . . ."[27] Many other bubbles— from tulips in the 1600s to dot-coms in the late 1990s—provide ample evidence of this.

The Drivers of Venture Capital Investment

The preceding section explained how a market may seem irrationally competitive to an incumbent firm, yet quite rational to a funder. The three primary forces driving continued venture investment in new sectors are liquidity events, category definition and herding behavior, and portfolio management, all of which tend to overconcentrate investment in the sectors considered attractive, or "hot."

Liquidity Events

In periods of high venture capital supply (more or less a continuous phenomenon since the late 1980s), any promising emerging sector will naturally attract high amounts of capital. Once venture capital has been raised, there is pressure on the fund managers to deploy it. Undeployed funds will not earn a return for investors, while the management fee will slowly eat away at the principal. This leads to a supply of sector-specific capital that drives new venture creation. Investment in the Winchester disk drive sector in the early 1980s provides an example. The rapid growth of disk drive revenue, the projected growth of the PC market, and the superiority of the small high-capacity drive created an attractive investment story. A total of $400 million in capital was invested in 43 companies, with 12 of them going public, in an industry that already boasted several strong incumbents (IBM and Seagate among them).[28] Such an abundance of firms—many with inflated market caps based on growth expectations—is bound to create overcapacity and price pressure. In the case of the disk drive business, many of the market leaders went bankrupt, as margins plummeted.

In terms of the prisoners' dilemma, it is understandable how each venture firm, acting independently and faced with a decision about investing in this arena, will decide to enter it, despite the overall diminishing returns to the industry. For the individual fund, a small return is better than no return. It has been hypothesized that, in times of significant expansion in venture capital, VCs will invest even when they know that the industry is in a bubble, with a correction coming in the future.[29] One strategy used by VC firms to avoid this correction is simply to sell enough at the "top" to make an adequate return, passing the correction risk on to other less savvy investors.

Liquidity events tend to trigger investment barrages, such as the one behind the fiber-optics networking bubble mentioned in the Introduction. Cisco's $7 billion stock purchase of Cerent in 1999 signaled the start of the industry's obsession with the telecom and networking sector. The VC community soon set its sights on the fiber-optics networking industry, and almost 200 companies, with an average valuation of over $125 million, raised roughly $7 billion in 2000. These companies, in turn, helped finance and were financed by telecom providers in a complex symbiotic relationship attracting hundreds of billions of dollars in capital for telecom infrastructure build-outs. This led to apparent hyper-growth in revenues, triggering yet more investment.

The end result was that the sector became a self-powered cash magnet, until the liquidity supply ran down. As *The Economist* magazine reported in 2003,

> *Despite all these apparently healthy signs, over the past couple of years the industry has become notorious for fraud, bankruptcy, debt and destruction of shareholder value. Exactly how much money has gone down the telecom drain is hard to quantify, but many estimates hover around the $1 trillion mark. Dozens of firms have gone bankrupt, including Global Crossing, 360networks, Williams Communications, Viatel and WorldCom, whose bankruptcy last year was the biggest ever. Hundreds of thousands of workers in the industry, and particularly at telecom-equipment makers, have lost their jobs. What explains this paradox of an industry in chaos amid strong demand, growing traffic and record revenues? The short answer is that although the industry has continued to grow, it has not done so in the manner, and above all not to the extent, that those in the industry expected. . . . As it turned out, the bets made during the technology bubble of the late 1990s were spectacularly wide of the mark.*[30]

Category Definition and Herding Behavior

Even without early liquidity events, venture capital firms tend to "herd" together in selecting which opportunities are worthy of investment. As one well-known engineer has said,

> *The electronics industry is driven by fads, just as the fashion and toy industries are. The industry is periodically swept by programming language fads: Forth, C++, Java, and so on. It's swept by design fads such as RISC, VLIW, and network processors. It's even swept by technical business fads such as the dot-coms. No area is immune. If one big-name VC firm funds reconfigurable electronic blanket weavers, the others follow. VC's either all fund something or none of them will. If you ride the crest of a fad, you've a good chance of getting funded. If you have an idea that's too new and too different, you will struggle for funding.*[31]

This phenomenon has also been observed in mutual fund investing.[32] In both cases, it is driven by two factors:

1. With relative reporting transparency, a tightly knit industry, a free flow of information, and the need for entrepreneurs to shop their ideas, astute independent investors observe similar if not the same data and thereby reach the same conclusion on where to invest.

2. Less astute investors simply mimic the ones perceived to be astute in order to both look smart when things go well and share the blame when they do not.[33]

Investment information cascades into a self-perpetuating **hype cycle**. (See "Gartner's Hype Cycle" on pages 140–141 for further insight into the effect of early, excessively optimistic expectations.) Each investment actually reinforces the next investor's decision to join in, rather than dissuading the investors as the economics of diminishing returns would predict.

Portfolio Management

The model VC portfolio shown on page 112, in which the possibility of three successes fueled investment in a total of 20 companies, applies not just to one firm. If this portfolio model is extended to, perhaps, a total of five major VC funds making similar investments, as the herding observation would predict, then the portfolio-oriented VC process will finance 100 companies in an attractive technology sector—creating an extremely concentrated competitive environment. Even accounting for overlap in investment, we can reasonably extend the model to predict that 50 or more companies are destined to fold or to be absorbed, while just 10 firms will be wildly successful.

For the various VC fund managers, the risk is ameliorated by the breadth of their holdings. For an individual entrepreneur or employee of a startup, however, the risk is high, and the odds of "striking it rich" are quite long. Fortunately (for VCs, at least), entrepreneurs are nonplussed by these long odds, and their employees also under-perceive the risks involved.[34] The presence of VC funding actually increases the attractiveness of a venture to quality staff, ensuring a steady supply of qualified and dedicated personnel and feeding the rigorous level of competition. The result of this exuberance and the corresponding concentration of both capital and talent is a significant oversubscription of new ventures in any promising area of emergent technology. This explosion of firms and its implications and aftermath are primary features of the early life cycle to be explored in Chapter 5.

Corporate Venturing

There is a widely held belief that individual companies do not do as good a job as the capital markets in driving disruptive innovation, and markets can change much more rapidly than can corporations.[35] This creates challenges for incumbents, particularly when capital resources are turned toward discontinuous opportunities that impinge on the market space carved out by the incumbent.

Acquisition is one way that incumbents can continue to succeed in selected markets. It represents one type of liquidity event sought by VC firms and is a risk-reducing strategy relative to the venture capital process. However, research indicates that an acquisition strategy has risks as well. Studies by Mercer[36] and KPMG[37] showed that more than half of all acquisitions ended up *eroding* shareholder value; the Mercer study found that only 17 percent were considered to be successful. *The Economist* summarized these results by saying that acquisitions have a "higher failure rate than the marriages of Hollywood stars."[38] Compounding the problems of cultural integration and poor visibility into the acquisition target before purchase is the tendency for acquisitions to be expensive relative to the underlying value of the target. The technology life cycle eventually creates a period of opportunistic acquisition—but for a targeted company early in the cycle, the price may be steep. Cisco Systems, for example, which has relied heavily on acquisition, spent $15 billion on 18 startups in 1999.[39] The fact that these were primarily stock transactions based on Cisco's highly inflated stock price may have made them more palatable; nevertheless, they illustrate the lengths to which companies go to acquire desired technology.

An alternative to acquisition is corporate venturing. By setting up an internal fund designed to foster innovation inside and outside of the company, a firm like ChevronTexaco can attempt to use "incubation rather than acquisition."[40] Corporate venturing can ease some of the constraints, assumptions, and risk aversion that prevent incumbents from succeeding in more disruptive innovations. It can also persuade entrepreneurs within large companies to remain, thus preventing good ideas from "leaking" out of the company.[41]

> ## ChevronTexaco Corporate Venturing

ChevronTexaco manages a corporate venture fund "to create additional value from internal capabilities and to facilitate innovation within ChevronTexaco." The investment philosophy is to "make direct and venture-fund investments in companies with early to mid-stage technologies that could enhance ChevronTexaco's core operations . . . [and] invest in technology companies in the energy and power sector to gain early access to important innovations." The fund also invests in seed-stage development and later-stage commercialization of technologies, competencies, and intellectual properties that have significant market potential beyond ChevronTexaco, but its primary focus is on helping leverage ChevronTexaco's competitive assets and on participating in new sectors that may become meaningful.

Because of the scarcity of fossil fuel and its direct and indirect costs, it is safe to predict that other fuel technologies will eventually arise as alternatives. ChevronTexaco's corporate venture structure allows the firm to meaningfully participate in and learn about a variety of next-generation technologies, including nanotechnology for solar, fuel cell, and hydrogen power, any of which could eventually become a discontinuous innovation.

ChevronTexaco's corporate venture fund follows these guidelines in governance:

❑ The Fund invests in select seed-stage commercialization efforts within ChevronTexaco, providing business development assistance and funding for promising opportunities. Once development milestones are achieved, the commercialization effort may be spun out of ChevronTexaco as an independent company or continued internally with company support.

❑ The Fund's investments are managed as independent businesses with explicit rules of interaction with ChevronTexaco.

❑ The Fund seeks external management and capital as appropriate to reduce risk and to validate the technology commercialization efforts of its portfolio companies.

❑ The Fund's activities are not limited to power and energy related segments.

❑ The Fund initially maintains more than 20 percent of spinout companies' equity.

The combination of focusing on businesses somehow related to the core competencies of the firm and striking a balance between participation and overcontrol means that learning can be retained by ChevronTexaco, even if the eventual venture isn't. The company also obtains a window of understanding into potentially relevant, "hot" sectors, since entrepreneurs call on the firm to "sell" their technology, ideas, and business models.

SOURCE: ChevronTexaco Technology Venture website, http://www.chevrontexaco.com/
technologyventures/invest_tech/internalventures.asp.

Not all corporate venturing is strategic; in some cases, it is driven by other motivations, such as pure return on capital. Corporate venturing can be divided into four distinct types: ecosystem, innovation, harvest, and private equity venturing.[42]

Ecosystem (Complement) Venturing

Most firms need to have a network of partners in order to be successful. As discussed in Chapter 2, delivering complete solutions is difficult without fostering complementary partners. Part of the role of the "standard-bearer" is to make sure that a sufficiently vibrant ecosystem exists and that innovations securing the position of the incumbent are encouraged. Xilinx, for example, launched a $100 million ecosystem venture fund in 2005, specifically dedicated to accelerating, broadening, and strengthening Xilinx product adoption. The fund targets startups that are developing high-speed digital signal processing, embedded processing, and/or high-speed connectivity, which either support Xilinx's core programmable logic device (PLD) technology or create vertical market applications. This, in turn, increases the value of Xilinx's position in the semiconductor industry.

Innovation Venturing

As mentioned numerous times, innovation is more likely to occur outside of large corporate structures. Putting aside funds for exploration into disruptive technologies via a traditional entrepreneurial/startup model can help overcome this barrier. The ChevronTexaco example illustrates how this strategy allows much more radical (and risky) ventures to exist alongside a large, well-controlled, and predictable enterprise. Innovation venturing also creates greater visibility into developing sectors and potential disruptions, an extremely important factor for incumbents.

Harvest Venturing

In some cases, the portfolio of technology within a company far exceeds the company's ability to commercialize the technology and extract value from it. Bell Labs and the Palo Alto Research Center (PARC) are examples of firms whose pure research delivered a stream of interesting and potentially lucrative innovations that could be better exploited outside of the corporate hierarchy. Universities also face this dilemma. Harvest venturing is less beneficial than other types to the core business, but does allow for larger R&D budgets and overall growth.

Private Equity Venturing

Private equity venturing is perhaps the least strategic of the types of corporate venturing, with purely financial goals. The assumption is that the company's core expertise will allow it to uncover and guide opportunities, so the investments are typically related to the company's core business. Ecosystem venturing often leads to private equity venturing as well, since the partners are likely to see numerous attractive business plans and management teams, some of which fall outside the ecosystem definition. The primary advantage of this approach is to create an **opportunity cost of capital**. Internal capital requests—for new equipment, new facilities, infrastructure, global expansion, and even marketing—are rampant, and a high external rate of return on investments creates a greater awareness of required ROI hurdle rates for determining whether internal capital investment makes financial sense.

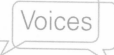

JIM SAYRE ON

CORPORATE VENTURING

Jim Sayre is president of Cargill Ventures, the venture arm of Cargill, one of the world's largest and most innovative agricultural and food-related technology firms. Jim was previously director of mergers and acquisitions for Cargill, so he has a hands-on view of both acquisitions and corporate venturing as tools for expansion and innovation.

Jim points out that while Cargill's venture group is a business unit with a for-profit mindset, it also exists to accelerate core businesses' access to and adoption of key technologies. Cargill operates with a well-defined methodology for identifying investment targets:

> First, we go to R&D and business units with interesting technologies we've uncovered and ask them to assess whether the technology may be relevant to the industry (not just Cargill) and to perform technical due diligence.

> Next, we determine whether we as an investment group think that opportunity has an attractive ROI.

> After this is done, we then look at the relevance with Cargill, in what we can contribute to accelerate the growth of investment target. Naturally, this presumes that an investment will be mutually beneficial for both the target and . . . Cargill.

This disciplined approach leverages incumbent strengths, while also creating a pipeline of new technologies for use by Cargill. Most importantly, these opportunities have been carefully scrutinized for applicability, feasibility, and business potential.

In this way, corporate venturing activities are also complementary to internal corporate R&D efforts.

> My experience with technology and innovation is that some of the best and smartest technologists are inside of the company rather than outside in the marketplace, but they are doing things which are much more consistent [with] the core business rather than second-order technology.

> *You want to have a web of interaction across your marketplace. This includes understanding and participating in areas that are relevant but not necessarily applicable to achieving your short-term mission.*

Jim stresses that returns from venture funding typically come 6–10 years out. Corporate venture funding allows large firms to free themselves of the 3- to 5-year constraints of typical strategic planning and look at more radical "second-order" technology. Since these types of technologies are the most likely candidates to have a disruptive influence on markets, corporate venturing protects large firms from the competency trap.

Finally, Jim points out that every corporate venture fund has a different objective and operating method:

> *Executive objectives, key measures, staffing decisions, and compensation structure all dictate the approach and risk profile of a corporate fund. Outbound, innovation, and ecosystem venture strategies all have applicability depending on objectives, but the key is to align the people and structure with the strategy.*

While access to a corporation's knowledge base, internal team, and complementary assets can be an advantage, a corporate venture fund that doesn't allow both the investment team and the portfolio companies to be free of certain corporate constraints will be less effective.

Since corporate venturing generally has many disadvantages, including less upside for entrepreneurs, less discipline regarding milestone-based funding, and less freedom for truly model-breaking exploration,[43] large firms must counter by pressing their advantages, including the access to know-how and resources, the ability to call on complementary assets, and the willingness to mainstream innovation that shows promise.

CHAPTER SUMMARY

While a variety of tools for industry analysis were introduced in Part 1 of the book, it is important to keep in mind that virtually all industry factors, including competitive intensity, market definition, supplier concentration, and complement power, are fluid over time. Examples discussed in this chapter demonstrated the impact of timing on both supply- and demand-based decisions, in everything from plasma screens to tomatoes. Assessing technology against life cycle patterns is a key factor in developing technology strategies that take into account this fluidity. This overview introduced several fundamental concepts that drive both technology diffusion and the competitive evolution that comes along with it.

Innovation can be classified as either discontinuous (disruptive) or incremental, depending on the extent to which it reinforces current industry paradigms or changes them. From the perspective of anticipated market and industry structural development, distinguishing between these two types of innovation is a precursor to addressing the appropriate strategy to pursue.

For discontinuous change, there are strong demand-side behavioral factors that determine the appropriate speed and product orientation, as well as barriers to successfully introducing, gaining acceptance of, and growing the market for new technology. While predictable, these behaviors are not static, but rather change as the innovation diffuses beyond the earliest adopters toward the mainstream.

These behaviors evolve in part out of observations about supplier development in relation to innovation. One of the primary supply-side influences for new technology comes from the abundance of capital that accumulates around any technology seen as potentially lucrative and industry changing. The capital leads to business formation and business behavior that are in some ways irrational, with major implications for competition and competitive strategy in what may earlier have been orderly markets. Recognizing this, some incumbents have introduced separate capital arms in order to participate in disruptive technology while also managing current stakeholder interests.

Chapters 5 through 7 will approach these issues in greater detail by developing a model of an innovation's life cycle and tools—for firms both large and small, leaders as well as laggards—to use in determining appropriate strategic actions, reactions, and options. The next chapter will kick off this process by outlining the hectic early period of innovation and rapid imitation that characterizes new technologies, particularly disruptive ones.

Innovators and Imitators

Meanwhile, let us not forget that every invention and every discovery consists of the interference in somebody's mind of certain old pieces of information that have generally been handed down by others. What did Darwin's thesis about natural selection amount to? To have proclaimed the fact of competition among living things? No, but in having for the first time combined this idea with the ideas of variability and heredity. The former idea, as it was proclaimed by Aristotle, remained sterile until it was associated with the two latter ideas. From that as a starting point, we may say that the generic term, of which invention is but a species, is the fruitful interference of repetitions.
— **Gabrielle Tarde**, *The Laws of Imitation*

Who's on First?

Johannes Gutenberg invented the printing press with replaceable letters in the early 1400s. With its wooden and later metal movable-type printing, the Gutenberg press brought down the price of printed materials and made books available to the masses, leading to a rise in the number of books in circulation from thousands to millions over the course of the 15th century. It remained the standard until the 20th century and is widely considered to be one of the most significant inventions of all times—even contributing to the spread of Christianity by way of the printing of the Gutenberg Bible. During subsequent centuries, many of the newer printing technologies, such as offset printing, were based in one way or another on Gutenberg's printing machine.

Unfortunately for Gutenberg, he lacked capital and needed to borrow money to develop and commercialize the technology. He eventually formed a partnership with a wealthy local named Johan Fust, for the purpose of completing his press and printing the now-famous Gutenberg Bible. Fust eventually brought suit to recover the money he had advanced to Gutenberg, and, as a result of Gutenberg's insolvency, the rights to the machinery and movable type became Fust's property. Use of the invention spread rapidly. By the end of the 15th century, over 1,000 printing presses were in operation, but Gutenberg was not among the primary beneficiaries of this diffusion.[1]

Someone creates the prototype for every new idea, product, technology, or category. Certain firsts, such as the Wright brothers' flight, Edison's electric lamp, and, more recently, Dean Kamen's Segway scooter (to name just a few), are both celebrated and introduced in ways that ensure a good return for the inventor. It's not always the creator who is remembered or rewarded, however. Moreover, since "history is often written by the victors," this isn't always apparent. The first car powered by an internal, gasoline-driven engine, for example, was built by a Frenchman named Etienne Lenoir in the 1860s. Yet Lenoir died penniless, while Gottlieb Daimler and Karl Benz—who started at least a decade later—and Henry Ford—who started 30 years later—are considered the "founders" of the automobile industry. Eli Whitney is known for the cotton gin, but other types of cotton gins were already in use long before Whitney's.[2] In more modern times, Oracle was not the first relational database company, IBM did not produce the first personal computer, and Amazon was not the first online bookseller.

There is a lot more to succeeding as a technology pioneer than simply being first. Many other factors, including the strength of intellectual property (IP) and franchise protection, the importance of complementary assets, the ability to develop an idea into an applied product, the speed with which imitators can create more attractive variations of an invention, the timing of market introduction vis-à-vis market interest, the availability of complementors, and the accessibility of capital, all play roles in determining the ultimate success of an innovator's attempt to open up a new market. The technology in Whitney's cotton gin combined with the rise of a new type of cotton, a shortage of labor, and growing demand for cotton to create demand for diffusion of his particular inventive variation.[3] Similarly, the web's diffusion was a prerequisite for many new web-reliant technology startups.

First-Mover Advantage

The idea of **first-mover advantage**—that being first in a market space gives a critical competitive edge—was a driving concept of the new economy and venture investment in the late 1990s. Real-world evidence has since disproved the notion that being the first mover is a guarantee of success, an expensive lesson for many investors in firms such as eToys and Webvan. A Penn State study of 45 distinct new product categories found that well over 50 percent of the pioneering companies failed, and only 20 percent were able to capture and hold market leadership.[4] Not surprisingly, based on the earlier look at complementary assets, the majority of companies able to hold leadership possessed a large set of complementary assets as well as the technology. The backlash from such studies, as well as the observed failures of the dot-com era, has created a movement that asks "What first-mover advantage?" and seeks to disprove altogether the notion that it exists. This thinking is exemplified in the following excerpt from a lighthearted article entitled "He Who Moves First Finishes Last," published ironically in a magazine called *Fast Company*:

> As first-mover fever becomes this year's version of the Macarena, *Fast Company's* Consultant Debunking Unit (CDU) has been asking some tough questions about the concept's validity. With contrary evidence piling up, the CDU wanted to make a last-ditch attempt to salvage some credibility for the first-mover theory. That meant contacting the American Moving and Storage Association (AMSA), in Alexandria, Virginia. We asked "When people are moving to a new home, should they hire the first mover that they happen to contact?" "We encourage people to call around and get at least a few bids," says George Bennett, communications director for

AMSA. Interstate moving rates are no longer fixed, and rival ship-pers are free to compete on price. "In fact," Bennett says, "second movers and third movers may be in an advantageous position, since they can learn about a first mover's quote and then decide to undercut that amount by a few dollars to get the business." So even in moving, it turns out, there's no first-mover advantage.[5]

This position has emerged as an equally extreme response to the earlier over-aggressiveness in investment and build-out based on the idea of being first. Clearly, there is more to establishing first-mover advantage than simply being first. Moving first is fraught with perils that will be reviewed over the course of this chapter. It's important to note, however, that being first does offer a potential source of advantage for certain firms, and simply ignoring the possibility of first-mover advantage may not be a winning strategy for incumbents.

For first-mover status to be an advantage, there must be a tangible benefit to being first. Although this sounds like a tautology, it implies that some conditions make first-mover status more favorable than others. The Penn State team found that first movers were more likely to succeed when barriers, such as protection from technology imitation and customer lock-in, prevented others from following.[6] Other research points to the preemption of critical resources such as suppliers, geography, and technology as a key indicator of the effectiveness of first-mover advantage.[7] Many of these are classic sources of competitive advantage. While Part 3 will look in detail at competitive advantage, a brief discussion is appropriate here. Achieving competitive advantage involves accruing a position that is not readily assailable by the competition. First-moving firms are more likely to be successful if they are able to put in place structures that allow them to maintain the lead established by moving first. As in the children's tale of the tortoise and the hare, the sprint into the lead matters only if the fast-starting firm is able to prevent the slower starters from overtaking it.

Patent Protection

The most commonly assumed source of first-mover advantage is patents and the patent process. It is interesting to note that surveys at both Yale and Carnegie Mellon indicated that patent protection was a weak and ineffective method by which to capture returns from innovation.[8] This is because the patent system was designed for diffu-sion as much as protection of new inventions, as described in the overview that follows. Additionally, the explosion of litigation related to patent ownership and protection emphasizes legal rather than R&D acumen. The issuance of record numbers of patents has also created challenges relating to

Tortoise or hare? It's not where you start; it's where you finish.

SOURCE: Warner Bros. Entertainment, Inc.

both the costs and the feasibility of navigating through mazes of overlapping patent rights. In a study of 136 U.S. semiconductor firms, for example, 56 percent were reported to be involved in at least one patent litigation case. Significantly, firms involved in patent law-suits spent more on R&D, were larger, and owned more patents than "peer" semiconductor firms not involved in patent litigation.[9] Litigation is both expensive and time consuming, and the implication is that patent protection is more effective for large incumbents than for the smaller firms in which disruptive invention is most likely to occur. A semiconductor firm that competes on design innovation, for example, can certainly file for patents to protect intellectual property and build a clear-cut patent case, but having the willingness and resources to defend the patents in the courtroom is equally important.

An Overview of Patents and Patent Protection

When the question is raised "How do you protect technology innovation?" patents are often the first thing that comes to mind. Patents can be quite powerful. Thomas Edison, for example, with over 1,000 patents to his name including one for the electric light bulb, was able to capture a significant commercial interest in some of the biggest inventions of the 20th century. Some of his inventions represented innovation on such a large scale that outside capital was brought in to commercialize them, but Edison's patent portfolio ensured him a significant stake in these ventures. Far from being the abode of an eccentric "mad scientist" or rogue inventor, his lab was a methodical and well-organized operation that was the model for modern industrial R&D.[10]

A significant factor in his success was a deep knowledge of the patent process and patent law. Similarly, Edward Land's instant photography invention involved a portfolio of patents and frequent litigation in order to protect the Polaroid camera franchise.

The criteria for a patentable idea are that it must be *novel, non-obvious,* and *useful.* A patent gives the patent-holder the right to stop others from producing, selling, or using the invention for the life of the patent (typically 20 years in the United States). It is up to the patent-holder to enforce the patent: The government does not go after patent or copyright infringers, and patent-holders must take any infringers to court. There is no global patenting body; a patent must be obtained according to the laws of each country or trading region (such as the European Union).

While patents give inventors an opportunity to profit from their creations, the downside is that they also disseminate technological information to other inventors. In order to apply for a patent, the inventor

Edison's light bulb patent

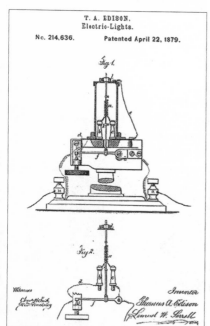

T. A. EDISON.
Electric-Lights.

No. 214,636.   Patented April 22, 1879.

Fig.1

Fig.2

SOURCE: United States Patent and Trademark Office, http://people.howstuffworks.com/patent.htm/printable.

must submit a detailed description of the invention. The detailed description becomes part of the patent office's database, which is public record. Dual concerns—that inventions might become lost if kept secret and that inventors might lose the opportunity to profit from inventions by making them available to the public—led to the creation of patent protection as far back as 15th-century Europe.[11] This tradeoff, in which inventors disseminate information about an invention in exchange for a short-term monopoly on it, is seen as the best way to "advance society" and forms the foundation for the modern patent system.

The nature of innovation in the 21st century and changes in the interpretation of what is patentable make the power of patents debatable. Many types of innovation are now digital rather than tangible mechanical or chemical processes. The entry of patent protection "into the realm of thought and abstraction"[12] certainly has the potential to offer innovators ever-broader patents, such as Amazon's patent on "1-Click" shopping, Priceline's patent on Internet-based "reverse auction" methodology, and Acacia Technologies' patents on video streaming. On the other hand, the broad and nonspecific nature of these patents makes it easy to develop variations on the theme—an acceptable practice if the variation meets the non-obvious standard—and makes defending patents much more difficult.

Other Barriers for First Movers

Patents are by no means the only barriers that can be erected to protect an invention. Customer lock-in, category leadership, and a first mover's organizational capabilities also offer protection to innovators.

> **Customer lock-in** has helped chip designer Xilinx hold a leadership position in programmable-logic chips. First-mover advantage in chip innovation can be significant if customers build entire systems around the chips, making the cost of switching to a new manufacturer prohibitive.[13]

> From a marketing perspective, there is value in establishing in the minds of buyers that the company is a leader.[14] The concept of **category leadership** bestows a variety of positive attributes on the leader, in the minds of both buyers and intermediaries. A study by the public relations firm Manning Selvage & Lee found that a perception of category leadership suggests to people that the firm has both consistency and staying power. Customers ascribe a large variety of attributes to category leaders, including that they stand behind their products (94%), provide high quality (93%), have performance that can be trusted (92%), offer good value (89%), and are an intelligent choice (83%).[15] Whether this is ultimately cause or effect, it indicates that being a category leader creates an umbrella of positive expectation about the product. It also "sets the bar," making it the task of the follower to prove that its product is better. First-moving brands such as TiVo, BlackBerry, and Netflix have immense pools of goodwill which need to be overcome by challengers.

> Pioneering **organizational capabilities** also can create advantages for the first-mover. In addition to applied technical know-how, the knowledge gained from learning about both customers and applied processes can provide significant advantages. Experience can create some of the highest barriers, although

these barriers can erode much more rapidly than some others, particularly in rapidly evolving industries.[16]

When competitive barriers exist—whether because of customer lock-in, a perception of category leadership, organizational capabilities, or a more tangible resource—and are long lasting, being first can be significant. This is the case in the pharmaceutical industry, with its long-lived and clear-cut protective patents. Drug discoveries and patents in the genomics and drug delivery areas are still described in terms of "races," where being first counts. As a Hambrecht & Quist analyst said in describing the biotech landscape, "It's like an Oklahoma land grab out there. . . . Those companies with the best and the most patents will likely be the most successful biotechnology firms in the decades to come."[17] These favorable first-mover conditions tend to be the exception rather than the rule, however, in the knowledge economy in which the First World now operates. David Teece put it this way:

> The gross reality is that most inventions are not patentable, and that intellectual property (IP) in the total scheme of things affords limited protection to innovators. It's like IP consists of islands sticking up in an ocean of new technology. If you can climb onto one of those islands and secure property protection, so much the better, but generally you can't. So you have to learn how to compete where your property rights are at best uncertain, and frequently weak."[18]

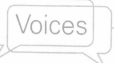

CYNTHIA ROBBINS-ROTH ON

PATENTS, IP, AND INNOVATORS

Cynthia Robbins-Roth, Ph.D., is the founder of BioVenture Publishing Inc. and BioVenture Consultants. Cynthia has been a prominent consultant to the bioscience industry since 1986. She has also written for *Forbes* magazine and is the author of *From Alchemy to IPO: The Business of Biotechnology*.

Cynthia has worked as an advisor or board member for a number of startups and points out that adequate IP protection is a prerequisite for investment in most cases:

> For startups, IP protection reduces the risk for investors that they might be investing in something that others can easily co-opt. The reality is that in most cases, if you have not protected your IP, they will not invest in you.

Having worked extensively with companies developing new drug discovery techniques, drug delivery methods, and compounds, she also sees patent protection as a method of balancing technology risk:

> With new therapeutics, you never know in advance what is going to be successful. So much time—and money—is needed to figure out if you've even got a product that if you don't have strong IP protection, the risk of someone doing an end run is perceived to be very high. You don't want to waste that decade of development time.

Even so, she does point out that successful firms are built on much more than simply a strong idea or patents:

> In the end, you need to have a team that is bright and capable in order to get a product out. You can go ahead and patent everything you want, but if you don't have the right team, it isn't going to generate anything for you.

This is no small challenge. Cynthia points out that specialized and innovative startup companies, because of their heavy focus on pioneering new technology, often have trouble recognizing the difficulties of successfully bringing a product to market and building a business around it:

> My experience with visionaries is that they often under-value the contributions of the nonscientific perspective. They underestimate the challenges to building a business as opposed to running a research project.
>
> They have no clue about the complexity of it, and how much they don't know. They sometimes assume that if they can learn something as complex as, say, immunogenetics, then they can surely learn the business end.
>
> It wasn't until I moved from the lab to the business side that I understood. As a scientist, you have spent a large part of your life in a rarified environment and have no idea about what has to happen to build a business. You tend to think that your initial invention is the hard part, and that it's all downhill from there.

The risk of underestimating the path from invention to market-ready product is exacerbated by pressures from venture capital boards to pursue whatever is the momentum play of the moment:

> One of the challenges for startups is that as the sector looks for the next big thing, there is tremendous pressure on firms from their investors to accelerate commercialization to meet the capital markets' short-term demands, which can be very destructive. There will always be great technology, but how do you generate a sufficient number of competent managers who are very knowledgeable with both the science and business ends and are therefore able to build a company and are willing to stand up to their boards?

The pharmaceutical and biotechnology industries unquestionably possess some unique attributes, such as the decade-long development process, budgetary constraints in the end market, and regulatory issues. Because of the heavy focus on innovation and IP, however, the industries offer some lessons that can be applied broadly to other technology sectors.

Accelerating Diffusion

Invention is the process of demonstrating the feasibility of something new, such as antibiotics, nuclear fission, or videophones. Invention offers conceptual proof, rather than a demonstration of commercial viability. The invention phase is distinctly different from the **innovation phase**[19] of technology (also known as the *commercialization phase*), when the invention is steered toward becoming a commercially viable product.

As discussed in Chapter 4, quite a bit of time can pass between the invention and inno-vation phases. In contrast, the interval between first commercialization and competi-tive entry can be quite short, especially in categories attractive to venture capitalists. The explosion of competitive entry leads to the supporting mechanisms and buyer uptake necessary for the slope of growth to increase and for a category or product to enter its hyper-growth stage (often referred to as a **diffusion period** or a *tornado period*). [20] As Grubler describes in discussing commercialization and diffusion:

> *The [element] which French scholars call* technique *represents the disembodied aspect of technology, its knowledge base. Technique is required not only for the production of given artifacts, but ulti-mately also for their use, both at the level of the individual and at the level of society. An individual must know, for example, how to drive a car; society must know how to conduct an election. Organization and institutional forms including markets, social norms, and attitudes all shape how the particular system of production and use of artifacts emerge and function. They are origi-nating and selection mechanisms of particular artifacts (or combi-nation thereof) and set the rate at which they become incorporated into given socioeconomic settings. This process of filtering, tailoring, and acceptance is technology diffusion.* [21]

The history of the relational database industry illustrates this typical pattern of a slow invention-to-commercialization phase, a rapid commercialization-to-competition phase, and growth accompanying an "established system of use." The concept of a rela-tional database was first described in 1970 in an IBM research publication entitled "A Relational Model of Data for Large Shared Data Banks," by IBM research scientist Dr. Edgar Codd. The article outlined how a system could be developed to let nontech-nical users store and retrieve large amounts of information. Codd envisaged a system where the user would be able to access information with English-like commands and where information would be stored in tables.[22] This came to be accepted as the defini-tive model for relational database management systems (RDBMS). The language developed by IBM to manipulate the data stored within Codd's model was originally called Structured English Query Language, or SEQUEL; the word *English* was later dropped in favor of the term Structured Query Language (SQL).

As expected, quite some time passed between the initial "invention" and the commer-cialization of the technology. IBM had an existing database product called IMS, which was one of its most important revenue-producing (and resource-consuming) prod-ucts. IBM's System R group, tasked with looking at ways to commercialize RDBMS technology, did not produce a usable trial until 1978. Clearly, IBM could have taken advantage of its query language several years sooner than it did. The eventual commer-cialization phase was led not by innovator IBM, but by an early imitator called Oracle. Larry Ellison, who founded Oracle, developed and began selling an SQL-compatible product well before IBM had an SQL product in the market. Ellison had actually learned of SQL through publications by IBM's System R project team.[23] IBM did not release its product until 1980 and really didn't abandon IMS and embrace relational technology as a commercial product until two years later. By this time, other competi-tors such as Ingres and Sybase had also entered the fray.[24]

If an S curve with its early low-sloping tail is the predictable outcome of technology invention, innovation, and diffusion, then an innovator, whether its intellectual property protection is strong or weak, stands to benefit from attempts to accelerate diffusion and to codify its technology as accepted practice or "dominant design." (Both of these will be discussed further in Chapter 6.) If successful, these attempts reduce the ability of competitors to maneuver, as well as the intensity of competition.

From Grubler's viewpoint, attaining a first-mover advantage requires establishing the technique around the technology. Clearly, by waiting for the market to evolve, the first or early innovator invites competition and potential alternatives to emerge. The fact that IBM's reluctance to move on RDBMS allowed Oracle to grab the dominant position is proof of just such a lost opportunity. It took IBM another 20 years to recapture the lead, and it required the billion-dollar acquisition of rival database manufacturer Informix.[25] In this particular case, IBM also suffered from the classic **innovator's dilemma**.[26] By trying to stay focused on an old technology (IMS), it missed the opportunity to pioneer a disruptive new technology (RDBMS). Less encumbered firms can attempt to accelerate the innovation/commercialization process through a variety of methods based on understanding and overcoming the buyer and market psychology that led to the original S curve behavior. Consumer/market resistance points that must be addressed include unknown demand and unclear infrastructure, the lack of standards, the lack of clarity in competitive choice, and budget constraints.

Unknown Demand and Unclear Infrastructure

When the demand for a new product is unclear or the infrastructure to support it is unknown, buyers assume a **technology risk** in selecting the product. For example, a vendor of a new type of radio frequency identification (RFID) chip could make a compelling case for an apparel manufacturer to adopt the technology for inventory-tracking purposes. A savvy manufacturer, however, will look beyond the immediate business case and consider whether the vendor will have enough other customers to stay in business, as well as whether the supporting infrastructure (such as tag readers and software) will be available. If not, the manufacturer could be stuck with "write off" in the form of products with useless RFID chips embedded in them and an obsolete inventory-tracking system integrated into its logistics and operations systems.

A technology vendor, particularly a new one, must overcome these types of obstacles in order to gain a market and accelerate the S curve. One option is to reduce the risk of unknown demand by *offering a contingency plan* to customers, in order to protect them. Young software companies can (and often do) put their source code in escrow to protect customers in the event that the vendor goes out of business. The RFID vendor could offer customers access to the design, so that they would have the option of contract-manufacturing the chips if the RFID company folded. (This is assuming that the production process isn't proprietary and capital-intensive.) Another option is *rewarding customers for taking on the risk*. Beta programs, for example, often give customers discounts or free goods in exchange for taking an early chance on a product. Large customers and channel partners also have the power to secure the fate of a new vendor by *mandating usage*. Wal-Mart, for example, has mandated that vendors adapt RFID to Wal-Mart's specifications, greatly accelerating the category's S curve growth by removing many of the technical risks. Finally, another option is to cross license or license additional sources of a technology. In the semiconductor industry, AMD and Intel have overcome the issues outlined by cross licensing, allowing developers to more confidently plan their products.[27]

The lack of availability of complementary products, supporting firms, and supporting technology is another part of the technology risk delaying adoption. In order to overcome this barrier, a technology innovator needs to focus on developing both a network of complementary assets/complementary products and the appropriate partnerships. The importance of this step can be seen in the need to support a new game platform such as Microsoft's Xbox with game software, the need for widely available replacement filters to successfully launch a new type of Brita water-purifying pitcher, and the need for software developers who can write code supporting a new shopping cart technology so that it will be embraced. In all of these cases, visibility into the future development of supporting infrastructure creates higher buyer confidence.

Tactics such as holding developer conferences and training sessions, releasing software developer kits, establishing partner programs, and making direct investments (via corporate venture capital funds as discussed in Chapter 4) can all raise the comfort level with the infrastructure.

The Lack of Standards

Greater predictability of the standard that will eventually be selected by a market reduces risk and raises buyer willingness to commit. Some assert that consumer confidence in a technology's eventual emergence as a standard is what creates the upward bend in the S curve and the emergence of the mainstream market.[28] Whether it is a contributing factor or the key variable, standards risk must be ameliorated for accelerated growth to occur. The evolution of standardization and the role of dominant design will be reviewed in detail in Chapter 6.

A number of tactics exist for reducing the risk associated with a lack of standards. One is *transferring risk*—making the risk the vendor's rather than the customer's. For example, vendors may offer free upgrades, such as an OS or flash memory upgrade, to meet changes in standards. Cisco, Nokia, and others have built remote upgrade capabilities into products, reducing buyer risk and at the same time making it practical and economical to offer upgrades to customers. *Bundling* the riskiest component of the technology into the product also achieves this goal of risk transfer. Cable ISPs include a modem as part of a bundled broadband package, while cell phone providers often include the phone. As shown in Part 1, offering a complete product stack such as the BlackBerry device also reduces the standards risk. Apple's use of a proprietary "AAC" music format

SOURCE: DILBERT reprinted by permission of United Features Syndicate, Inc.

for the iPod and iTunes doesn't really matter, for example, since Apple is also providing the content, storage, and digital rights management. In this case, aside from appreciating the benefits of tighter vertical integration, consumers will be somewhat indifferent about whether or not the product meets a larger, later standard, as long as it works.

Another tactic for overcoming resistance relating to a lack of clear standards is marketing to **key influencers**. Certain early-adopting groups influence the choices of both other individual buyers and channels. In the hotel industry, for example, concierges are the major gatekeepers to both hotel guests and hotels' internal purchasing decision makers. New restaurants and other tourism and hospitality-oriented companies must go out of their way to gain acceptance from them. In enterprise computing, certain consultants and high-profile journalist/practitioners play a similar role. A favorable review from the *Wall Street Journal*'s personal technology columnist, Walt Mossberg, can influence consumer attitudes toward a new product or service and affect the diffusion process. His influence is so great that it has been the subject of at least one doctoral thesis.[29]

The Lack of Clarity in Competitive Choice

Technology buyers typically like choice—as well they should. A survey by *CIO Insight* found that the top two purchasing tactics used by CIOs to get purchasing leverage are competitive bidding and the request for proposal (RFP) process.[30] The reasons are fairly obvious: These processes give the buyer leverage over vendors and result in the best technology fit at the lowest price. In the absence of competition, it is uncertain whether the buyer is getting a good deal. As a result, buyers may be reluctant to make purchase decisions when they do not have choices. To combat this problem, vendors use as enticements "most-favored-nation" pricing, discounts, or other early benefits such as an invitation to join a "product council."

Budget Constraints

Finally, the last major obstacle to acceleration is that buyers may have only limited funding for purchasing something new. Buyers can't readily budget for something that doesn't yet exist, and building a case for going off budget or resetting spending priorities is a time-consuming process in many organizations. In the IT sector, 70 percent of IT executives believe that their ROI metrics don't adequately capture the business value of their projects, anyway.[31]

Even if a strong business case demonstrates the ROI of a technology investment, making the investment may require a drawn-out process of crossing interdepartmental borders and reallocating budgets. When a hospital purchases a new drug for septic shock, for example, money is saved in the critical care unit, but additional budget is needed in the pharmacy. This makes it a very difficult sell, since the pharmacist simply can't afford it.[32] The typical vendor response to overcome this problem and gain traction for a new market is to aggressively discount. As a later section of the chapter will demonstrate, this discounting is not always necessary or desirable upfront, but can become unavoidable as competition emerges.

While phrases such as "the need for speed" and "Internet time" are, in many cases, relics of the dot-com era, innovators with a potentially real and sustainable advantage can benefit by hastening the market toward the new technology rather than waiting for the S curve dynamics to play out. As the foregoing discussion demonstrated, an important element of the battle is to overcome the high levels of strategic uncertainty and environmental risk associated with early customer adoption. In the relational database market, Oracle was not just the first to move to aggressively commercialize; it was also the first to employ tactics such as cross-platform solutions and portability. Such tactics defused buyer objections and accelerated the market while Oracle was the leader, and before IBM could respond.

Technology S Curves

Consultant Richard Foster developed a second S curve that relates to product performance rather than demand,[33] measuring the value of technology to buyers. This *technology S curve* is driven by competitive entry, improvement on initial innovation, and infrastructure development, all of which add value to the technology.

As you might expect, product performance improves over time. This performance improvement may be mapped to four distinct periods,[34] as shown in Exhibit 5-1. The first period is one of experimentation and innovation, referred to as the era of substitution, or technological discontinuity, when a new technology begins to show signs of replacing an old solution. During this period, improvements are still being made to the old technology, and so the impact of the new product performance paradigm is limited. Early technologies, even if they are disruptive, often show limited promise in their first execution. As an example, Tushman and Anderson point to the continued demand for and progress made on 8-bit microprocessors, even in the face of 16-bit replacements.[35] More recently, 32-bit microprocessors have continued to dominate the PC market, even though 64-bit technology is available.

EXHIBIT 5-1 ■ The Technology S Curve

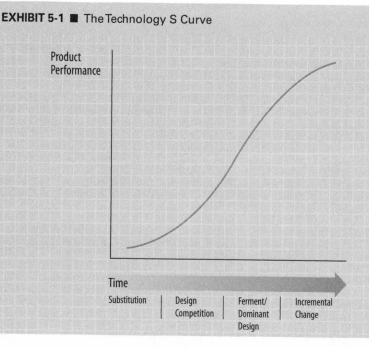

Next, a period of design competition can lead to rapid advancement of the technological breakthrough. While this competition can accelerate product performance, it also creates many of the uncertainties mentioned previously, continuing to limit buyer value. In the quest for digital music, for example, competing codecs (WAV, AAC, MP3, ATRAC, etc.) and hardware have created frustration for consumers. As the *New York Times* reported, "Browse almost any digital-player message board on the Internet, and you'll discover thousands of words detailing frustrations, failures and suggested fixes. Some consumers are learning the hard way that all digital music players and formats are not the same."[36] As discussed earlier, an effective strategy during this period is to take advantage of customer uncertainty by offering to make the decision for the buyer and delivering a complete product to market. Part 1 of the book established that a long and potentially contentious period of design competition can allow a firm to capture a market leadership position by delivering a complete solution, which removes the uncertainty factors.

Eventually, the market "ferments" into a **dominant design**[37] that reflects the solution adopted by the majority of the marketplace. Often, this solution is different from the early leader's complete solution, since the remaining competitors will rally around an alternative in order to avoid being shut out. Occasionally, however, the early solution does become the dominant design. For buyers, suppliers, and complementors, the removal of uncertainty and the market's promise of an orderly organization around a dominant design constitute a "green light" to commit, raising the value of the technology and leading to a much higher buyer performance rating. This, in turn, accelerates market demand.

Finally, product improvement enters a period where only incremental change is possible. The period of disruption is essentially over, and a new paradigm has been established. There is unlikely to be any significant change in market structure after this point. Incremental improvements rather than competing designs become the focus. Technology and product performance may increase, but in a predictable and somewhat linear fashion.

The willingness to pay for technology is a composite of the demand and technology S curves.[38] Buyers are influenced by both behavioral characteristics (modeled in the demand S curve) and the characteristics of the technology itself (modeled in the technology S curve).

Pricing and Demand for First Movers

A general, but erroneous, assumption holds that first movers should always discount their products heavily—losing money in the short term—in order to grab market share in an emerging market. This assumption replaced the earlier "price low" justification of traditional economics literature, which suggested that first movers with an effective "monopoly position" should, in many cases, price low enough to discourage competition, while focusing on cost reduction to gain profitability. In either case, the result is an unprofitable early market, justified by concerns over long-term competitive position. Because competition in emerging markets is not necessarily rational, in neither case is a "price low" strategy always ideal. Pricing decisions for emerging technology should be based on the following:

1. The ability of the innovator to turn a short-term lead into a real first-mover advantage and

2. The elasticity of demand for the product in question.

As discussed earlier, first-mover advantage relies on developing barriers that allow an early entrant to capture and hold on to market share that has long-term value. This concept of lifetime customer value (as well as barriers) will be discussed in detail in Part 3. With an identifiable source of first-mover advantage, "buying market share" through discounting might make sense, since the payout can be harvested later. The much-used analogy of discounting razors in order to sell blades is appropriate in this case. If such an advantage does not exist, then buying market share might still be practical if the resulting "artificial" acceleration of the category helps overcome buyer objections, or if it results in a growth trajectory that allows a firm to raise capital. Implicit in these arguments is that a lower price will stimulate demand for the product.

The degree to which demand is driven by price movement is known as **price elasticity**. In an early monopoly setting or when a product or service is otherwise insulated from competition, appropriate pricing is merely an exercise in understanding consumer demand. Pricing can be either *elastic* or *inelastic*. A product or service is **price elastic** when a small decrease in price greatly increases sales (or a small increase decreases sales). Conversely, a product or service is **price inelastic** when a change in price has little impact on product demand. In an emerging market, either situation may exist. The demand S curves for an elastic and inelastic market are shown in Exhibit 5-2.

An example of an elastic product is music CDs sold by an e-tailer. If the e-tailer raised prices, then shoppers would simply surf to another Internet site. An increase in price by e-tailers in general would simply drive buyers to the substitute—a physical store. Similarly, lowering prices might have a significant impact on the CD seller's fortunes. An example of an inelastic product is the original scientific calculators offered in the early 1970s. Since many scientists were using slide rules, they were willing to pay a very high price for the electronic calculators. A higher price would not have discouraged early purchases, and a drop in price would not have added many more customers early on.

EXHIBIT 5-2 ■ Demand Curves for Inelastic and Elastic Markets

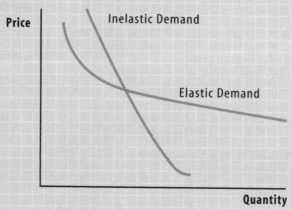

Early Inelastic Demand

In the turn-of-the-century automobile market portrayed in the book *Seabiscuit* (see pages 106–107), many non-price-related factors were in place that served to retard the early sales of automobiles. Many of the necessary accessories (such as bumpers and headlights) needed to be separately purchased and were hard to find. Electric starters had yet to be invented, leaving automobile owners to risk life and limb by hand cranking. Even gas stations were rare. The Buicks sold by Charles Howard (*Seabiscuit's* main character) cost $500 or more, double the average annual salary in 1905. With all these factors in play, a 10 percent or 20 percent discount would likely have had little impact on sales at that time. It's unlikely that a drop to even $250 would have created much additional demand, although it would have been below Buick's cost and removed all profit. Even if a price drop had stimulated some demand, those additional early buyers might not have developed into a repeat buying franchise that would have created eventual profits. With an inelastic price and a limited market, the better strategy would be to try to accelerate the S curve, perhaps by encouraging key influencers to drive Buicks, making the market more likely to assume that the requisite infrastructure will be forthcoming. This is very close to Howard's strategy, which was to seed the market via racing and other high-profile events.[39]

Rogers's and Moore's life cycle segmentation models, discussed in Chapter 4, showed that the post-chasm early majority provides the greatest growth for an innovation, driven by adoption by the mainstream market. A company may be first in the emerging sector, but falter at the point where the market grows fastest and consumer preferences are set in the later growth period. As demonstrated, the cause of inelastic demand in the earlier stages may be that consumer need has not yet developed, that the technology is still crude, or that the necessary infrastructure is not in place to prompt a larger customer base to have interest in the product, even as the price goes down. In this case, addressing mainstream market needs may be more important than attempting to drive early market demand. This is certainly true of electric cars. Amazingly, the basic design of the gasoline-powered internal combustion engine is similar to that of the engine that powered Howard's Buicks 100 years ago, and yet it is still the dominant technology for the automobile. Alternative-fuel vehicles and electric cars have obvious limitations (cruising range, recharging time, remote fueling access) that are more crucial to buyers than the actual price of the vehicle. A UC Berkeley study in 2000, for example, showed that consumers would be willing to switch to electric vehicles only if they were subsidized in the amount of $28,000 to overcome these objections.[40] The study's author remarked:

> *Since the average retail transaction price of an internal-combustion Toyota RAV4 is about $21,000, this would mean that in order to meet California's EV mandate, Toyota would have to give the average consumer a free RAV4-EV plus a check for approximately $7,000. . . . This would be necessary to offset the shortcomings, such as limited range, that are characteristic of EVs.*[41]

It's no wonder that "hybrids" have quickly overtaken pure electrical vehicles, since they are adapted to the existing infrastructure.

Similarly, in the case of a new telephony switch, the cost of integrating the new technology and upgrading the network may make the product worth testing but not deploying—assuming the change is more than just a remote software upgrade (i.e., a "soft switch")—regardless of the actual product cost. This renders the volume from the phone company fixed relative to price and eliminates early access to the mainstream market.

While managers may find it distressing that they cannot drop price in order to stimulate volume, inelastic demand is not always a negative attribute for the early innovator. An inelastic price may simply indicate that a product has disproportionately large or important benefits to certain market segments and thus doesn't need to be priced inexpensively. This creates a significant opportunity for the innovator. When introduced in the late 1980s, Genentech's blood clot–dissolving drug TPA, for example, provided a revolutionary life-saving treatment for stroke victims. As a result, Genentech was able to successfully price it at roughly $2,000 per dose—an unheard-of price for a pharmaceutical at the time.

Early Elastic Demand

Unlike early inelastic demand, early elastic demand is more likely when a low price overcomes many of the risks or shortcomings associated with an emerging technology. This presents an excellent opportunity to accelerate the S curve. In advancing new data features in mobile phones, providers found that bundling text messaging and a browser with the hardware at little or no cost encouraged buyers to give the data features a try, even if the coverage or content availability was spotty. The need to purchase pricey special hardware would discourage this trial, particularly if early versions of the service performed poorly.

Elasticity in an emerging market also comes from the presence of close substitutes. In the case of the drug TPA, a lack of perceived substitutes was crucial in allowing Genentech to price high. For the TPA alternative, Streptokinase, the key to capturing market share via lower pricing was simply to demonstrate that the drug could deliver similar performance and was an adequate substitute for TPA. To this end, the drug was reintroduced with the same intravenous delivery system as TPA. Most of Genentech's subsequent marketing efforts were directed at demonstrating that the two products were not, in fact, perfect substitutes.

Dynamic Elasticity

The focus in the preceding section, as in this chapter as a whole, is solely on the initial emerging portion of the market. As mentioned, early pricing strategy may not have any bearing on what occurs in the growth phase of the market. In the elastic case, the existence of a chasm between emerging and mainstream growth markets will eventually lead to a volume threshold, irrespective of price. In other words, even if the early adopters are price sensitive, price may not have any bearing on later growth markets because of other factors that limit mainstream demand. Presumably, most of the major impediments must be overcome to achieve significant customer adoption, regardless of price. In the inelastic case, the market can become elastic for a variety of reasons. Later buyers may not have the urgency of need that early buyers had. While the early adopters who make good "lead users" are those with needs that foreshadow general demand, they are also the users who stand to obtain the highest benefit from solutions to those needs.[42] Growth-phase customers may be much more price sensitive than the emerging customers. Compounding this problem is the emergence of substitutes as imitators enter the market, which will be discussed in the next section. The degree of competition always needs to be factored into price elasticity; an initial opportunity for **value-based pricing** (pricing based on maximizing a firm's returns) may be followed by competitive pricing pressure and, in many cases, even short-term, below-cost pricing.

In most cases, the optimal initial pricing—whether high or low—eventually becomes subject to competitive pricing pressure. As will be shown, price can drop below the innovator's cost because of increased category competition and differing cost models and assumptions relative to scale and other factors.

Artificial Demand and Hype Cycles

In an early elastic category or segment, an aggressive drop in price can stimulate greater demand. If the lower price is below reasonable expectations of long-term cost, then the aggressive pricing move is designed either to capture long-term customers (so that profits can be made later) or to kick start the market. In either case, the price is effectively subsidized in the short term, as shown in Exhibit 5-3. One of the repercussions of this approach is an unreadable or inaccurate prediction of what long-term demand for the product will be at realistic prices. This artificial curve can give rise to a "hype cycle," as discussed below, and create a flurry of interest from capital markets. A trajectory based on artificial growth projects a larger and faster-growing opportunity than really exists. While the market and its growth rate may be overstated, the artificial demand does represent an opportunity for savvy firms to raise substantial capital at unreasonable valuations, securing for themselves a long-term position in the marketplace.

EXHIBIT 5-3 ■ The Effect of Artificially Low Price on Demand

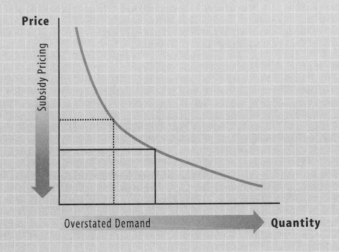

Gartner's Hype Cycle

The research firm Gartner Group uses what it refers to as the hype cycle to identify gaps between early expectations and actual mainstream market adoption of new technology. The hype cycle, as shown below, is a graphic representation of the technology trigger point and eventual maturity, adoption, and practical business application of a specific technology.

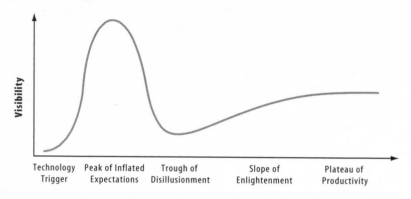

Gartner's research indicates that buyers (and affected incumbents) should keep an eye on potentially high-impact technologies early in the inevitable cycle, but wait to adopt technologies until their value has become clear. The five phases of the cycle are as follows:

1. *Technology Trigger.* A breakthrough, product launch, or other event generates significant press and sudden interest.

2. *Peak of Inflated Expectations.* A frenzy of publicity generates overenthusiasm and unrealistic expectations. In some cases, the technology is successfully applied, but there are typically many failures in both applications and business models.

3. *Trough of Disillusionment.* When the technology fails to meet expectations, it becomes unfashionable. Consequently, the press usually abandons the topic and the technology.

4. *Slope of Enlightenment.* Although the press and analysts may have stopped covering the technology, some businesses continue to experiment through the "slope of enlightenment," trying to understand the benefits and practical applications of the technology.

5. *Plateau of Productivity.* When the benefits of the technology become widely demonstrated and accepted, the technology becomes increasingly stable and evolves in second and third generations. The final height of the plateau varies according to whether the technology is broadly applicable or benefits only a niche market.

SOURCE: Gartner, San Jose, California.

Clearly, the possibility of capturing the early market or a competitive lead must be weighed against the risk of over-hype. For example, the well-hyped IP telephony segment (the transport of telephone calls over the Internet) offered many organizations limited early benefits, with some potential savings but little else in the way of strategic business value. In a few cases, however, such as telephony-intensive overseas call centers, the potential benefit created incentives to proceed with the technology earlier. For call center providers, the almost-free telephony presented an opportunity to exploit wage differentials in various parts of the world. For other customers, waiting for more practical applications and for the performance, technology risk, and business case to become clearer has been prudent.

The preceding discussions of accelerating S curve growth and early-market pricing decisions highlight the need to consider competition as well as the behavior of early markets in the technology diffusion process. The next section discusses the imitation phase of the market, when other firms enter, shaking up the first mover's market.

Imitation and the Industry Life Cycle

The dynamics of an industry's life cycle are such that a new product category can move very quickly from zero entrants to oversubscription (far too many entrants) as the potential of the new category paradigm becomes evident, even if early results are lacking. The aforementioned Buick dealer's early experience did not discourage the growth of the automobile industry. The competitive landscape in the industry went through astonishing growth in the early 1900s,[43] as illustrated in Exhibit 5-4. Similar and far steeper curves have been observed for semiconductors, disk drives, and, more recently, fiber-optics networking and a variety of dot-com sectors. In all cases, the explosion of imitators led to an upsurge in firm failures and a consolidation period, leaving fewer than 10 percent of the firms alive. (This mortality rate will be discussed further in Chapter 6.) There is clearly a perceived incentive (whether misguided or not) for imitators to leap into emerging market segments. Imitation and competition are near certainties for entrepreneurs.

As already discussed, venture capital is a key catalyst in emerging markets. It isn't the only catalyst, however, as the promise of superior returns in an emerging industry drives both new and old firms into the fray, depending on their risk/return tolerance and estimations. There is also a **bandwagon effect**, created by the large number of organizations adopting an innovation simply out of a need on the part of their executives and technology managers to keep up with their peers. The pressure to jump on the bandwagon then prompts yet other organizations to adopt the innovation. Even laggards fear appearing too different from adopters and strive to avoid the risk of being stuck with below-average performance if other competitors profit from adopting a technology. Virtually any innovation—regardless of the ambiguity of return on investment—has the potential to diffuse in a bandwagon manner. And, as with VC investment, bandwagons can prompt most organizations in an industry to collectively adopt an innovation, even when many of them expect the adoption to yield negative returns.[44]

EXHIBIT 5-4 ■ The Automobile Industry, 1890–1910

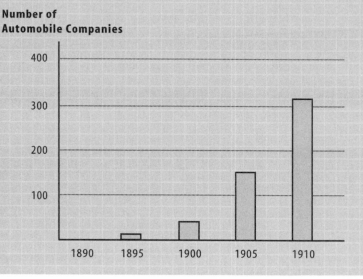

While some firms deliberately strive for leadership, many others simply imitate the success of the leaders. Innovation entails costs that imitation does not,[45] and **fast followers** can hope to learn from the pioneer's investment without making it themselves. If imitators collectively had a motto, it would be the Old West saying "You can tell the pioneer—he's the one with an arrow in his back." As discussed earlier, the primary benefit of being first derives from creating some sort of barrier that is difficult to overcome, thus guaranteeing for the innovating firm a level of performance that is difficult for others to capture. The traditional Schumpeter view of innovation and competitive behavior is that firms are rewarded for innovation and that these rewards are in themselves a form of protection:

> *The absence of competitors and the ability to block competitors are factors that in their own right influence appropriability. . . . This relationship is presumably what Schumpeter had in mind when he declared that perfect competition was incompatible with innovation. "The introduction of new methods of production and new commodities is hardly conceivable with perfect—and perfectly prompt—competition from the start. And this means that the bulk of what we call economic progress is incompatible with it. As a matter of fact, perfect competition is and always has been temporarily suspended whenever anything new is introduced—automatically or by measures devised for the purpose—even in otherwise perfectly competitive conditions." A related but distinguishable argument is this: Absence of competition or restrained oligopolistic competition, by leading to high rates of returns in the industry, generally can serve to shelter firms that do innovative R&D in circumstances*

where, if competition were more aggressive, firms that aim for a "fast second" would drive the real innovators out of business.[46]

Regrettably, this argument was made to identify cases where oligopolistic market structure (i.e., few large firms) acts to protect R&D investment by virtue of non-instantaneous competition. The Gillette example used earlier in the book provides an illustration. With few razor competitors because of global economics and barriers of shelf space, Gillette and Schick can engage in regular R&D one-upmanship. The category orientation of venture capital and the relatively unprotectable soft assets of many startups, however, as well as the uncertainty surrounding the payoff, lead to a much higher level of "me-too" competition in emergent technology.

Even the barriers designed to keep competition at bay can serve to attract new entrants to an industry by drawing attention to it. As shown in Chapter 4, VC funds, for a variety of reasons, tend to concentrate their investments in relatively narrowly defined areas. Steve Jurvetson, managing director of Draper Fisher Jurvetson Partners, admits that investors tend to invest in me-too companies because they have a degree of comfort that they're investing in an established market.[47] Neil Weintraut, of 21st Century Internet Venture Partners, has commented, "We're more impressed to know there are competitors."[48] And startup expert Guy Kawasaki advises entrepreneurs to "acknowledge the enemy. And make up an enemy if there isn't one, because a warning bell goes off in the head of sophisticated investors when they hear, 'We have no competition.'"[49]

High-growth industries, in particular, tend to be characterized by rapid imitation,[50] and the two measures—industry growth and growth in the number of firms—are interrelated. Because of the many diffusion-related factors introduced in both this chapter and Chapter 4, competition can actually be an important component of the evolution and market takeoff of innovations. Mathematical modeling of the S curves of innovation across a variety of industries indicates that a sharp increase in the number of competing firms in a new market precedes a sales takeoff, and that high entry rates are associated with quicker sales takeoff.[51]

Individual versus Industry Experience Curves

An experience curve describes a declining cost of production over time, as a firm becomes more experienced and undertakes continual process change. This declining-cost curve should, in theory, give firms with a head start a lower cost of production and, thus, a competitive edge. The use of this curve as a strategic planning tool has faded as the understanding of industry dynamics has changed and real-world results have put its use in question. As described by UCLA's Marvin Lieberman in 1987,

The learning curve (or "experience curve") has become a central concept in corporate strategic planning. It provides the theoretical rationale for many corporate portfolio-planning techniques and is frequently used to justify aggressive pricing of new products. The popularity of the learning curve as a tool for business strategy reached a peak in the mid 1970s, based on efforts by the Boston Consulting Group to apply to business strategy what had previously been a tool for production planning. Firms were advised to expand output and acquire market share in order to gain a long-term cost advantage over rivals. However, the purported benefits of such learning curve–based strategies often failed to materialize and the concept lost favor during the late 1970s.[52]

It makes intuitive sense that producing something would become cheaper over time as firms become more efficient, and observation in the marketplace confirms lower costs and pricing as industries mature. The fallacy lies in attempting to apply this experience curve to an individual firm rather than to the cumulative market. Both the Boston Consulting Group and Lieberman found that when a diffusion of learning is possible, an experience curve is an industry-wide phenomenon rather than a firm-specific one. Resources and technology knowledge tend to be quite mobile.[53] Therefore, imitating firms can learn from innovating ones, and the imitator often ends up with an advantage, particularly in fast-evolving technology categories. As Andrew Van de Ven, of the Minnesota Innovation Research Program, observed:

> *You usually find that the technological design of the first mover turns out not to become the dominant design that ultimately provides significant profits. There's a reason for that. The first mover, while striking out to develop that new technology, will inevitably make mistakes. And the followers, who are observing the practice of the first mover, can make adjustments in their own technology. As a result, after the first mover has introduced the product to the market, then the second, third, and fourth movers (who have been carefully following the lead) can all of a sudden come through and introduce a more significant, more advanced, and better product or service.*[54]

Since the early period of innovation is marked by experimentation, variation, and competing solutions,[55] the first mover who locks in a commercialization strategy early is likely committing to a less-than-ideal technology platform, which others will learn from and improve on. This is a particular danger for startups, which can often feel pressure from external venture-oriented funding sources to commercialize early. Early commitment may be worthwhile based on the advantages of being first, but it is entirely possible that the platform includes a cost disadvantage, since experience typically leads to improved product performance and decreased costs.[56] One study of 48 "pre-digital" product innovations found that imitators incurred on average only 65 percent of the original innovator's cost of product development.[57] Compounding cost of development problems is the fact that use of "total cost of ownership" models means that imitators will focus on reduced operating-cost models, either internally or for customers, as part of their technology improvements and overall solution approach.

The brief history of web search engines illustrates both the positives and the negatives of moving early. The concept of a search engine is as old as the web, although the first search engines were nothing more than a few hearty souls doing manual indexing and directory creation as a method for helping users find interesting web pages. While attending Stanford University, David Filo and Jerry Yang started and ran Yahoo! in their spare time, simply to keep favorite bookmarks. Web search evolved quickly into automated web crawling (e.g., Excite and AOL) and now consists of much more sophisticated contextual cross-ranking methodologies (e.g., Google). Needless to say, the early manual methods were both more expensive and less effective than Google's automated crawling tools, indexing methods, and algorithms, and each successive generation of firms learned from the earlier ones. Yahoo!—one of the pioneers of the category and still one of the first names that comes to mind in conjunction with the term *web search*—stopped doing searches internally and started "buying" services from Google. It eventually acquired its way back into the search business by purchasing Inktomi and Overture. (*Note:* As will be discussed in Chapter 6, the shakeout phase often presents acquisition opportunities.) Yahoo!'s poor competitive position in search technology could easily have led it to underperform (as was the case for many other pioneers) and did, in fact, open the door for Google—a much leaner firm that is now the clear market share leader in search. Yahoo! did gain some significant advantages by moving first—it established an attractive capital structure, developed a brand, and secured a loyal audience. It then effectively switched its focus to areas in which technology played a less important part. Yahoo! used its first-mover advantage to establish complementary assets (brand, traffic, cash, etc.) that removed its dependence on being the technology innovator. This is a common tactic of successful early movers, without which Yahoo! would have been left with only inferior technology and no future.

Although aggregate industry cost curves are shown graphically as being smooth, they really operate in a stepwise fashion, with successive firms establishing new cost benchmarks. This also holds true for the technology S curve, where successive technologies improve on the innovator's design. An important consideration from the buyer firm's perspective is where the early mover lies relative to the fast followers on the cost and technology performance spectra. While early leaders may have a good reputation and some prominence, they would be wise to parlay these into complementary assets (as Yahoo! did) if their underlying technology platform becomes unattractive. In the case of web content-management and publishing tools, for example, content-management software systems have gone through several steps—from self-built systems to the first generation of external software (with a high price and high operating cost) to much less expensive workflow tools. Firms that committed early—such as Time Warner, with its pathfinder infrastructure in the mid-1990s, and a variety of other firms that installed Vignette content-management and publishing software in the late 90s—found themselves in high-cost infrastructure positions. As *PC Magazine* reported,

> *Most of the low-end products are very close to being turnkey or off-the-shelf products that can be implemented in a few weeks or days with little assistance. Buying a high-end product like Vignette's is more like entering into an agreement with a large consulting firm. Expect installation to take months, with associated high costs, regular service fees, and numerous consultant visits.*[58]

At the time, Vignette was a much better option than building a proprietary solution, but the later competitive variations and greater accessibility to standardized toolsets (a key development in industry maturation that will be discussed in Chapter 6) rendered it a suboptimal solution on both the cost and performance curves for many customers.

Price Elasticity and Imitation

As discussed earlier in the chapter, an innovator has some latitude in deciding whether to price high or low, with higher pricing being an option for capturing revenue in an early adopting inelastic market. This choice disappears as imitation increases in the market. Even the entrance of just one additional firm can create significant price pressure and competition, and a variety of different economic models (as well as common sense) predict that increased price pressure typically follows competition. More importantly, the rise of imitation puts much more emphasis on cost structure and the firm's total cost of ownership, since these measures become benchmarks as other firms enter the market.[59]

From a buyer's point of view, the entrance of additional firms increases price competition and makes it easier to negotiate and get a good deal. By anticipating and keeping a watchful eye out for competition, a buyer can find the best deal (if price is the central decision criterion). In addition to saving buyers money, cost structure has the additional importance of helping buyers to predict which supplying firms are likely to survive and thrive. If early firms have not secured an unassailable first-mover advantage (e.g., capital, a patent, or other structural barriers) and have higher costs, they are likely to be forced out of the industry[60] by firms that leapfrog over them with better economics.

Graphically, the innovation and imitation phases can be shown as having both cost and price curves that decline over time (see Exhibit 5-5). As mentioned, the cost curve is an industry aggregate one, and early-moving firms probably have higher costs than do followers. Since pricing decisions are driven by a combination of cost factors and expected long-term benefits of early market share, price can be (and often is) below the early innovator's cost and therefore may represent a significant negative cash flow for the innovating firm. At the same time, an innovator may never find customers as readily as

EXHIBIT 5-5 ■ Innovation/Imitation Cost and Price Curves Early in Technology's Competitive Life Cycle

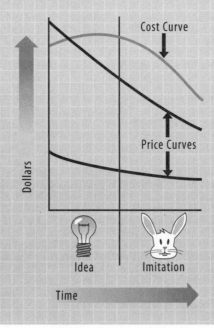

when the competition is underdeveloped, reinforcing the benefits of early discounting when the long-term value of customers is high.

Winning the Wrong Game

Rogers's and Moore's models of technology life cycles and customer segmentation revealed that two somewhat distinct markets exist for technology innovations—an emerging market and a mainstream market. Close examination of these models established that the two markets have significantly different attributes, with the early market being more technically focused, experimental, and willing to tolerate the headaches that come with new products, while the mainstream market wants products that work without hassle. Moore points to a chasm between them, since success with the former is no guarantee of success with the latter. Crossing this chasm is considered to be a key goal in the high-tech industry, where firms tend to sell to one another and use launch strategies focused on early-adopting technology audiences to build buzz. Winning in the early market requires making modifications to suit the few visionary customers. Indeed, one of the classic tradeoffs in engineering design is flexibility versus simplicity. The very early markets demand the former and care little for the latter.

In contrast, success in the pragmatic mainstream market requires focusing on end users over technologists,[61] emphasizing simplicity over flexibility, and standardizing rather than modifying (in order to capture any sort of scale economies). The implication is that one of two strategies is rational in an emerging market:

1. Build a profitable emerging business without concern for the later mainstream market. This could be as complex as building engines for the space shuttle or as simple as focusing on a specific niche.

2. Concentrate on entering the growth phase of the market with some tangible advantage to show for all of the money and effort expended in the emerging phase.

The oft-used expression *first-mover advantage* is often misapplied to the second strategy. Firms can move first and capture the emerging market, only to find that the more pragmatic growth market rejects the product as lacking either the necessary features or simplicity of use. Surprisingly, many technology firms use neither of the above-mentioned strategies. They lose money by moving early *and* end up in a disadvantageous position in the growth phase of the market. Early momentum in this case is probably driven by the goal of a short-term liquidity event more than a long-term competitive position. Quite simply, those that parlay this type of nonstrategic lead into a large capital position will survive; those that don't will not.

The most confident technology-leveraging firms can let others fight it out in the "visionary" segment, knowing that they can deliver products that will fit the mainstream audience's needs much better than can the early innovators. Apple's iPod and Kodak's EasyShare digital camera are examples of products, delivered by "late-to-the-party" firms, that were much more suitable to pragmatists. Five years after the first MP3 player (RioPort) was launched, Apple combined digital rights management, software, hardware, and even the retail experience (the iTunes store) in order to make it easy for the mainstream to play digital music. Kodak was late getting into digital photography, but delivered a camera that could download images via a push-button cradle, software for sharing and printing pictures, and remote processing that demystified digital photography for the mainstream. In Kodak's case, the technology is standards-driven; in Apple's case, it's more proprietary in nature. Both firms were late for the visionary phase, but just in time to address the high-growth period of the mainstream market. They used their organizational skills and a low-cost technology platform to deliver the right product for the pragmatists.

The gamble for incumbents is clear. By waiting, an incumbent firm risks having the market pass it by if a new technology paradigm takes hold while the incumbent continues to invest in the old (e.g., IBM's failure to capitalize on relational databases). At the same time, if a dominant firm can observe and learn from the early market, it can avoid losing money with early commercialization or high-cost and potentially inferior technology and then make prudent decisions as the market moves toward the mainstream. As Chapters 6 and 7 will reveal, the evolution of new categories beyond the innovation/imitation phase presents ample opportunities for incumbents.

Chapter Summary

While the early bird sometimes gets the worm, technology pioneers face daunting challenges in opening new markets and nurturing emerging industries. Moving first does not guarantee success. When conditions are right and barriers can be erected, early movers can hold and benefit from an early lead—but these barriers can be difficult to come by. Even traditional patent-based protection has not proven to be a consistent protective barrier for innovative firms. Without competitive insulation, early firms can still benefit from accelerating the diffusion and adoption of a new technology. A shorter innovation-to-commercialization period can discourage competition and allow the first mover time to establish market leadership. To accomplish this, the firm must overcome a number of resistance points in the market.

The value and price proposition shifts radically during the early market, as a rapid increase in the value of technology is offset by an increase in price pressure and elasticity driven by competitive entry (imitators). Increased competition is an inevitable by-product of the visibility of opportunities created by new technology paradigms, the aggregation of capital, and general bandwagon effects. Following rather than leading has many advantages, as industry experience curves favor later movers, who can have superior cost profiles, avoid locking into early versions of technology, and time entry to better match market demand.

Demand characteristics also change as the life cycle moves through innovation and imitation toward the mainstream. The most significant challenge for many firms is to shift strategic emphasis toward addressing and winning the mainstream market. While the early innovator/imitator battle occurs primarily in the early adopter phase, success with this segment does not foreshadow results in the larger and faster-growth early mainstream market, since the latter exhibits different characteristics. For incumbents in particular, staying focused on the needs and dynamics of this later market is key to success, whether the concern is about being left behind or moving too soon.

Technology Enablers and Horizontal Supply

Unfortunately, there is one inexorable law of technology, and it is this: when revolutionary inventions become widely accessible, they cease to be accessible. Technology is inherently democratic, because it promises the same service to all; but it works (best) if the rich alone are using it.
—**Umberto Eco**, "How Not to Use the Fax Machine"

Thinking Horizontally

Chapter 5 demonstrated that a high-potential innovation, whether recognized for its value to a firm or as an investment opportunity, unleashes a storm of competition. At some point, however, even the most overenthusiastic of entrepreneurs and investors will recognize that they have trailed too far behind the competitive wave, that the competitive set has become ungainly, and that the opportunity for imitation has lost some of its appeal. In terms of the adoption curve, the technology may still be fairly early in its growth cycle, but trumping or capturing the market seems less likely.

The introductory chapter used the California gold rush of the 1850s as an example of how a flood of competition is drawn to new riches. As each additional prospector headed up into the hills to stake a claim, the opportunity became a little less exciting for those yet to get started. By the time 100,000 miners were panning for gold, most of the ideal claims had been staked, and the average expected return was more likely to leave most prospectors firmly in debt than in a mansion on San Francisco's Nob Hill.

At the beginning of the gold rush, simply getting to California with the appropriate equipment was almost a guarantee of a good return. Taking either a 15,000-mile boat ride around the horn of Africa or a dangerous overland journey of the type that waylaid the infamous Donner party, the successful prospector needed to bring along most of what he required in food, clothing, and tools, since suppliers and supplies were scarce. An 1849 report from Sacramento said that eggs were $1 to $3 apiece; a butcher knife, $30; and a pair of boots, $100.[1] Needless to say, firms that supplied the prospectors did quite nicely. Along with the Big Four mentioned in the Introduction, the entrepreneurial Levi Strauss provides an excellent case in point. He came to San Francisco with some rolls of canvas (eventually switching to denim) and built a successful and quite long-lived dry goods and manufacturing firm. Even madams—serving the less material needs of the miners—became wealthy.

The market had grown large enough to attract businesses focused on the 49ers rather than just those intent on finding the mother lode. As these businesses emerged, the emphasis on the prospector's skill as a movable supply train (i.e., a vertically integrated mining company) diminished. It became much more efficient to buy supplies than to attempt to travel overland with them, and this, in turn, made prospecting much more accessible.

The lesson from this historical anecdote is that rather than a period of reduced opportunity, an oversupply of innovators and imitators actually signals the start of a new era of opportunity, while simultaneously fueling the innovation's climb into the steepest portion of the S curve. As the potential of a technology innovation becomes clear, the demand becomes more predictable and large enough to support horizontally oriented firms. For these firms, the targeted opportunity is to supply more of the industry with a necessary component or bundle of relatively homogenous components rather than to compete directly for end users. During the dot-com era, for example, one of the largest IPOs was that of United Parcel Service (UPS), a century-old traditional delivery firm with a focus on technology. UPS delivers roughly half the goods sold over the web; its attractiveness lies in the fact that it helps *everyone* deliver goods.[2] It was able to raise $5 billion by selling only 10 percent of the company to the public. More recently, several digital music providers have been providing the digital distribution platform to firms from Wal-Mart to Dell, which will fuel growth in this category as well.[3]

The emergence of firms that can be thought of as **technology enablers** (or *toolmakers*) spurs more growth and accessibility, but also reconfigures where unique value is delivered in the overall value chain. For the 49ers, readily available supplies de-emphasized what was originally a critical activity of miners and moved the focus toward staked claims (favoring larger established operators). In the digital music industry, access to a strong customer base will eventually become more important than technology development, as the latter becomes more universally accessible. The emergence of enablers allows incumbents with strong and applicable complementary assets to purchase or otherwise acquire key technologies or functionality from specialized firms. After a period of disorder, the appearance of a "new order" in the early market signals the beginning of what will eventually become a shakeout. Competitors are empowered, specialists are able to deliver superior solutions by focusing on a targeted opportunity, and the barriers to adopting and commercializing the technology drop dramatically. This chapter will analyze this period of the competitive technology life cycle and the accompanying upheaval.

What Is Enabling Technology?

Enabling technologies are used to build the critical infrastructure around disruptive innovation. With a technology package that can be plugged into well-understood commercialization/productization efforts (either as a value chain or as a stack component), a new market becomes more modular and therefore more accessible and more affordable. An enabling technology is typically readily available and easily integratable and interoperable with other technologies. Thus, it is a good candidate for becoming an efficient standard.[4]

If these characteristics seem vaguely familiar, it's because they were introduced, back in the discussion of modularity in Chapter 2, as important attributes of the platforms supported by standard-bearers. Many enabling technologies can be classified as platforms. Enablers need these traits for the same reason standard-bearers do—they are required to create the comfort level about availability and predictability of a technology component necessary for pragmatic commercializers to embrace a modular design. Additionally, the cost implications of an enabling technology are an important factor in a growing mainstream market; the above-mentioned attributes of enabling technologies tend to promote lower-cost solutions from both a component and an end-product viewpoint. This description of enabling technology represents a stark contrast to some of the proprietary, hard-coded solutions of early movers, examined in previous chapters. As was also shown, early versions tend to carry higher associated costs.

Adobe Postscript and the Rise of Desktop Publishing

The Adobe Postscript language has been one of the more significant and less touted keys to the growth of personal computing. At the dawn of the PC industry in the early 1980s, if you owned a personal computer and wanted to print something out, your best bet was to hook your computer up to a dot-matrix printer that would output low-quality bitmapped characters. Recognizing this limitation, two engineers at the Xerox research center (PARC)—John Warnock and John Geschke—developed a software language called Interpress, designed to translate the onscreen fonts from Xerox workstations to Xerox printers. Warnock realized that mathematical algorithms could be developed to "describe" each letter; allow users to change font sizes, font types, and resolution; and send information to a printing device.[5] While both engineers sensed the potential for industry-wide adoption of this innovation, adopting a horizontal-enabling posture was inconsistent with Xerox's history of attempting to capture maximum value through fully integrated product offerings. Geschke has said, "They [Xerox] wanted to have an industry standard, but they wanted to control everything at the same time."[6]

Two moves positioned the technology as an enabler:

1. The spinoff of a separate company (called Adobe Systems)

2. The decision to focus on the core technology as a device-independent software platform (called Postscript) rather than build printers

These moves satisfied potential partners that Adobe was sincere in its intention to be a toolmaker and meet the enabling technology provider requirements as discussed on page 150. Adobe initially partnered with Apple and Canon to launch the desktop publishing revolution. For Apple, the concern was less with standards than with building an Apple laser printer that worked seamlessly with Macintosh and Aldus PageMaker software. Rather than pursue proprietary Apple-based development, however, Adobe offered Postscript to others in the personal computer industry, and eventually Postscript became a standard software platform for enabling computers, software, and printers to work together to produce high-quality documents. If Xerox (or Adobe itself) had moved ahead with a vertically integrated document publishing system, it is unlikely that it would have been able to compete effectively with either Apple's desktop system or the eventual PC standard, as alternative enabling technology would almost certainly have emerged. Even if its technology had not become the single industry standard, Adobe's introduction of a key technology in a modular fashion would have moved the industry away from a proprietary, vertically integrated, digital-typesetting model and put the focus on the devices and applications.

A good way to illustrate the ability of an enabling technology to both accelerate and change the structure of a new technology-driven market opportunity is to examine a market where such an enabler has *not* yet appeared and visualize what will change if and when it does appear. Space exploration is a 40-year-old technology category that has yet to make it past the early adopter phase. Space exploration faces a daunting set of technology challenges, especially when it involves sending humans out of our planet's atmosphere and bringing them back again in one piece. The Apollo program, in particular, is widely considered to be one of the top engineering feats of all time. During the early space race between the United States and the USSR in the 1960s, however, the predominant goal was centered around the short-term focus of being first to market—referred to by NASA's contractors at the time as "go fever"—rather than long-term cost effectiveness. Engineers and scientists such as Werner von Braun envisioned a gradual and comprehensive product family–based approach, designed to launch the United States permanently into space travel, but their vision was pushed aside in favor of the goal of reaching the moon first, simply to demonstrate the power of political ideology. This approach was mirrored by NASA's rival space agency in the Soviet Union. As a result, in their quest to be first—first into space, first into orbit, and, eventually, first to the moon—both programs relied on inefficient and proprietary technology with severe limitations. The Apollo space capsule was relatively successful (except for *Apollo 1*), but was described as "probably the most complex thing ever put together by humans . . . the electrical system alone had 30 miles of wire."[7] It's difficult to imagine how this early version could be eventually put into wide-scale production or use.

Clearly, NASA used a "brute force" approach to the Apollo mission in terms of both money spent and the use of early versions of technology, including the reliable but costly and inefficient *Saturn V* rocket (pictured in Exhibit 6-1). Like the lunar capsule, the *Saturn V* was quite complex, with over 1,000,000 parts.[8] This proprietary, early-version approach was again used for the space shuttle, creating an only moderately reliable but staggeringly expensive reusable spacecraft. (Estimates are as high as $500 million per flight.[9]) As a result, "first versions" of both moon landings and manned orbital flight are in the "marketplace," but it's safe to say that space travel is still at the very beginning of both diffusion and technology S curves. As a chronicle of the Apollo program points out, "The race left us with little hardware to show for all of our effort."[10] The marketplace proof is also compelling: Currently, a ticket into space costs roughly $20 million, and seats are quite difficult to come by.

Characteristics of the imitation phase of the life cycle, discussed in Chapter 5, lead to the prediction that a number of entrepreneurial firms will enter the space travel market with improved and less costly products, a phenomenon that is slowly occurring. The X PRIZE Foundation offered $10 million to the first private imitator to successfully build and launch a manned spaceship able to reach an altitude of 100 kilometers, return safely, and repeat the exercise within two weeks. Over two dozen private firms competed for the prize, creating the group of imitators predicted by our earlier model and driving down both the cost and the price of space travel while increasing product performance. Pre-booked tickets for some of these early ventures are as low as $100,000, less than 1 percent of the $20 million paid by millionaire Dennis Tito to fly aboard a Russian Soyuz spacecraft in 2002. These tickets are still relatively pricey, particularly when you consider the immense risk associated with the early products that will be released.

EXHIBIT 6-1 ■ Diagram of the *Saturn V*

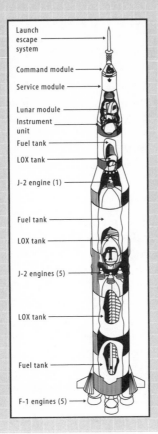

Launch escape system

Command module

Service module

Lunar module

Instrument unit

Fuel tank

LOX tank

J-2 engine (1)

Fuel tank

LOX tank

J-2 engines (5)

LOX tank

Fuel tank

F-1 engines (5)

SOURCE: NASA; http://www.nasm.si.edu/galleries/gal114/SpaceRace/sec300/sec384.htm, December 30, 2004.

In order to open up the space travel market for competition, enabling technologies must provide the critical components necessary to create the large-scale, cost-effective supply of "seats" required to meet the needs of a pragmatic market. This toolset, whether in the form of a critical layer such as engines or a bundle of several layers, will eventually become available. The firm supplying it will have a chance to play an important and profitable role in the industry.

A similar cycle of development occurred in normal air travel. In the airline industry, the enabling product was the Douglas DC-3, a plane that made obsolete the early concept of vertically integrated (make it and fly it) airlines, exemplified by the combined Boeing/United Airlines of the 1920s. After the Air Mail Act of 1934 divided airplane production from commercial airline operation, Douglas "enabled" many firms to offer economically feasible passenger service, by selling DC-3 to all airlines. By the end of the 1930s, Douglas had captured 90 percent of the airplane market as a supplier.[11] In doing so, it also ushered in a new era in which air travel was more accessible, more competitive, and lower priced and delivered more value to travelers.

Eventually, there should arise a rocketeering equivalent of the DC-3, enabling the entire space travel industry. The firm that introduces it will have a greater chance of success if it captures a horizontal layer rather than attempting to capture the market demand on all layers. The propulsion layers (engines and fuel systems) seem to be the leading candidates thus far. The victorious X PRIZE competitor Scaled Composites already outsources engine production of its *Space Ship One* to both Environmental Aeroscience Corporation (eAc) and a firm called SpaceDev. Environmental Aeroscience's literature claims that its philosophy is "focused on flight hardware and high volume designs,"[12] a posture indicative of a firm planning on supplying an entire industry. SpaceDev, which powered Space Ship One's winning flights, is also focused on developing a rocket propulsion system that can be supplied to multiple customers. By working on proof of concept but aiming to sell engines to any number of competing companies, both firms will be creating the know-how and tools necessary to jump start the market. Indeed, Scaled Composites is itself an enabler, licensing technology to Richard Branson's newly formed space tourism venture Virgin Galactic.

In the more grounded and mundane world of digital imaging and document management, the progression from multiple relatively proprietary innovators to modular software had a similar effect in the 1990s. The growth of the desktop computer industry, and the inevitable networked structures soon after, created the potential for storing and retrieving documents centrally, remotely, and electronically—essentially the first generation of digital data warehousing. Not surprisingly, however, early systems were complex, expensive, and hard to manage, creating the opportunity for horizontal enablers to step in. As reported in *Network World* magazine in 1994,

> *Imaging products seem to be coming within reach for many buyers, as vendors continue to pull apart proprietary systems into more modular components that run across a variety of common platforms and LAN environments. . . . The onslaught of modular software is welcome news to new users looking to layer imaging on top of existing environments that utilize commodity products.*[13]

Will Scaled Composites' technology enable Virgin to open up space tourism?

©Mike Massee

Similarly, *Computerworld* reported that users viewed some capabilities of document management systems as key, but that most were unwilling to move all their information to a discrete document management system in order to take advantage of those features.[14] This view is exactly what would be expected from the pragmatic early mainstream market. Xerox spinout firm Documentum (now owned by EMC) took advantage of this attitude, creating a cross-platform document management firm that went public with much fanfare in 1996. By working with Informix, Oracle, and Sybase databases and several enterprise resource planning (ERP) systems and by providing functionality via the web for Adobe, Microsoft NT, and Lotus Notes products, Documentum offered a cross-platform tool for managing documents. Designed to enable Fortune 1000 organizations to practically implement document management, Documentum's solution far surpassed those of the early market innovators and imitators.

As earlier examples have shown, the ability to commercialize a key technology component enables a new wave of competition—some of it from customers' newfound ability to solve the problem internally, and some from other technology providers' or vendors' ability to serve markets more effectively. The lower-cost basis and standardization of solutions create additional pressures on early innovators. This period also signals the end of fierce competition for "best" solutions, as the emphasis moves to application of the "accepted" solution. This life cycle transition will be discussed in the next section.

Design Competition, the Era of Ferment, and the Rise of Dominant Design

When a food or drink undergoes fermentation, the goal is to encourage the growth of "good" microorganisms, while simultaneously preventing the growth of those that cause spoilage. Successful fermentation requires special ingredients and carefully controlled conditions.[15] Analogously, the **era of ferment** for a new technology is a period during which good technology grows and multiplies while less promising technology falls by the wayside. In the case of technology, a "good" solution is one that removes the costs associated with the presence of competing technology solutions—confusion, uncertainty, lack of scale, regulatory indecision, etc.[16] As these costs are removed, the commercialization and incremental innovation process can be carried out in a rational way, attracting more of the mainstream market. As mentioned in Chapter 5, a dominant design eventually emerges. This generally agreed-on, standard architecture allows both suppliers and competitors in a market to move ahead with their plans for adopting a technology. Such dominant designs are found in all areas—the Windows operating system is dominant in personal computers; U.S. homes use alternating current; automobiles use gasoline-powered internal-combustion engines and 12-volt batteries; and so on. In some circumstances, there appear to be multiple dominant designs, but this is most often because of clear and unambiguous market separation. Examples include different languages, left-side and right-side steering wheels, and different wireless standards, all used in different countries.

Dominant design is often driven by buyer-influenced factors and selection rather than merit-based determinants (e.g., the "best" technology).[17] As an example, the well-documented battle between VHS and Betamax to become a videotape standard had little to do with which design was better or who was first and much more to do with the interests of the parties involved in selecting the dominant design. Cusumano, Mylonadis, and Rosenblum described the struggle:

> *A three-year period from mid 1974 to 1977 proved decisive in determining the outcome of the standardization battle that would rage on for another decade. . . . Sony had a clear lead primarily in timing: it would take JVC roughly two more years to match the stage that Sony had achieved by late 1974. But moving first was not sufficient, in itself, to win the prize in this market. How Sony moved and what its principal rivals did also mattered. In retrospect, as Akio Morita, then Sony's president, later acknowledged, he and Masaru Ibuka, then Chairman, made a "mistake" and should have worked harder to get more companies together in a family to support the Betamax format. JVC, in the number two position, did try harder, and was more effective in forming alliances in support of VHS. JVC's more effective campaign to form an alliance behind VHS produced a coalition that matched the Beta coalition's global market power.*[18]

Sony appeared to be a potentially less cooperative partner; therefore, the rest of the industry had an incentive to line up behind JVC's VHS format.

Clearly, marketing and connections with important buyers can trump technological know-how and merit.[19] As the review of technology stacks showed, control of a standard can give the standard-bearer significant power in the industry it participates in. Because of the typical group-wide nature of and incumbent influence over dominant design, a firm that is suspected of abusing its power as a layer provider may find it difficult to transform its proprietary innovation into a dominant design. This seems to have been the case with Sony and its Beta format. Sun Microsystems, in pressing for adoption of the Java programming language to create the computer equivalent of a "dial tone" in the late 1990s, also saw its coalition of support fall apart, as partners became suspicious of its intentions as a standard-bearer and uncomfortable with its tight licensing restrictions. Similarly, while Xerox's vertical mindset made it a suspect provider for industry-wide enabling technology, many PARC spinoffs such as Adobe and 3Com were well received as independent companies. This political interpretation means that having the inter-organizational skills necessary to craft alliances and shape the market is as important as technical competency.

It is concern over loss of control of technology, along with the need for organizational skill sets emphasizing partnering, that creates the opportunity for a horizontal toolmaker approach to displace early proprietary efforts. A design that is offered with industry-wide accessibility in mind is inherently more attractive to others in the market, as are designs that have the potential to be produced and supplied by several firms. The interests of the early market entrants and dominant incumbent firms are, of course, in opposition on this point. A widely accessible tool is not likely to refocus the source of competitive advantage or re-rank the competitive pecking order, whereas a new firm's proprietary embedded technology is.

Consumer adoption of an innovative vertical solution can influence and sometimes set dominant design (as was the case with the rise of the MP3 format in digital music), but significant competitive and political forces attempt to shape the dominant design to meet the desires of incumbents.[20] In the case of complex medical imaging products, for example, standards-based imaging signal–processing systems provided by Mercury Computer Systems are a key modular layer for some of the leading firms in the segment, including heavyweights such as General Electric, Marconi, Philips, and Siemens AG. Embracing Mercury's technology allowed these firms to speed their development cycles and advance

Medical imaging enabled by Mercury Computer Systems

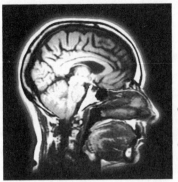

Mercury Computer Systems

product performance toward real-time diagnostics and also to keep out innovative but more vertically oriented firms.[21] Mercury is clearly a horizontal technology supplier and, thus, can be comfortably embraced by the industry. It's one thing for a firm to build a better mousetrap and sell the idea to the industry; it is another to use that mousetrap to try to put other pest control firms out of business.

As mentioned in Chapter 2, standards are often pushed by industry consortia in order to avoid concentrating power in the hands of undesirable proprietary owners. Similarly, industry participants can band together to influence dominant design principles and enable access to modularized technology, whether or not the technology supplier is a given. In the mobile phone industry, for example, Symbian is an operating system company founded and sponsored by Nokia, Ericsson, and Motorola in order to create an open standard for "smart" (data-enabled) mobile phones. In contrast, the CDMA Development Group (CDG) is an industry consortium (which also includes Nokia, Ericsson, and Motorola) that is influencing dominant design in the underlying wireless protocol that makes smart phones "smart." In the case of CDG, the end product is simply agreed-on specifications that enabling technology providers such as Qualcomm can use; Symbian, on the other hand, is itself an enabler. In both cases, the widely accessible nature of the toolsets is influenced by the industry's cooperation in selecting a dominant design.

The S Curve and the Tornado

Geoffrey Moore refers to the period of hyper-growth following the era of ferment and the move toward dominant design selection as the **tornado period**, a metaphor for the powerful forces at work that can destroy and at the same time lift up entire categories and industries. The move from technology embedded in a firm's discrete solution to technology as a potential infrastructure enabler creates a period of escalating demand represented by the steepest part of the diffusion/adoption S curve. It also requires a different focus and skill set on the part of the would-be supplier. Over-customization and over-engineering to satisfy vertical markets—the very traits that firms use to attract early customers—create the risk of being left behind as a variety of segments in the larger market race to embrace new tools. For example, if Douglas had spent too much time focused on custom configurations for the DC-3, it might not have been able to supply the whole market. Documentum did follow a vertical industry and Fortune 1000 strategy and inadvertently allowed more "general market" firms such as Vignette and Interwoven to grab market share in providing the tools for content management systems. Finally, UPS, with the infrastructure to deliver and ship almost anything, was a major beneficiary of the advent of e-commerce related to physical goods, while Webvan—a would-be e-commerce infrastructure provider—stayed heavily focused on groceries and made few inroads in delivering other categories of goods, since it was relying on its own vertically integrated grocery skill set.

Moving Toward Modularity

Webvan's dilemma represents a common problem for startups in their quest to grow and gain market acceptance. One of the important lessons about the tornado period, with its shift to horizontal enablers, is that the factors that allow firms to succeed in an early vertical stack can be diametrically opposed to the factors that allow firms to succeed in the tool phase of the market. As Moore says,

> *Companies that have won great victories in the [early vertical market] and persist in their to-date successful mode of operation doom themselves to become second tier players in the tornado. And [they] play an increasingly marginalized role as the market goes forward.*[22]

In essence, toolmakers allow early firms to seed the market and provide proof of concept. These early firms need to invest in a variety of nontechnical trajectory skills, resources, and personnel in order to understand and service the market and demonstrate commitment to their customer base. Both Calgene and DNA Plant Technology—the first two producers of commercially approved, genetically modified products referred to in Chapter 2—discovered that in order to pioneer the market they needed to invest heavily in a variety of complementary assets, including growing, distribution infrastructure, and consumer education and branding. This investment had an opportunity cost in terms of the availability of funds for basic and applied R&D, licensing efforts, and even patent litigation. Letting these firms pioneer the effort, Monsanto stayed focused on R&D and technology that favored its competitive assets, such as crops resistant to a top-selling Monsanto herbicide called Roundup.

As mentioned in Chapter 2, the skills necessary to service an industry in a modular fashion are different from those necessary to service a market with a complete solution. As the discussion of TiVo illustrates, early vertical market solutions require delivering a complete product that includes whatever the customer needs—whether it is hardware to run a network application, content for a new gaming system, or special boxes for tomatoes.

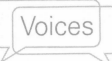

JIM BARTON ON

TIVOLUTION AND COMPETITION

Jim Barton is a cofounder and CTO of TiVo. Prior to cofounding TiVo, Jim was president and CEO of Network Age Software, VP and general manager of the Systems Software Division at Silicon Graphics (SGI), and CTO of Interactive Digital Solutions Company, a joint venture of SGI and AT&T Network Systems created to develop interactive television systems.

Jim observes that, as a startup, TiVo was much less constrained than existing companies in how it approached the question of leveraging the emergence of digital television signal delivery:

Naturally, cable companies approached it from the point of view of compression—"How do you cram more television into the same bandwidth?" But since we were computer guys, we asked, "What can you do with all of this digital information if you have a computer receiving it?" We initially imagined a home media center type service, and got funded based upon this notion. Within 6 months, we researched the available networking technologies and realized that there wasn't enough connectivity and bandwidth in the home. So instead, we took the notion of client-server media delivery and collapsed it into a single box, focused on real time compression and storage, a concept that consumer electronics firms were highly skeptical of. Traditional consumer electronic companies think in terms of embedded systems and small amounts of memory. Again, we're computer guys. . . . We took advantage of the hard disk and our knowledge of integration to essentially build a set-top computer. Fortunately, our investors felt comfortable letting us change direction.

TiVo's managers have followed the common "pioneer" roadmap to success. They selected their own component technology and offered an integrated and easy-to-use complete product. Jim points out that pioneers face the dual challenge of bringing about consumer adoption of a new category and carrying out technology development in an unproven area:

If you are starting a whole new thing, you have to put it all together—especially with something really new, like our category. Since consumers never really saw TV as broken, it had to work flawlessly to avoid discouraging them. Integration and design is a lot of the value in new consumer hardware—all of the components need to work together. We got where we are through integration.

Jim and the TiVo management team saw an opportunity to grab a leadership position, but he isn't surprised that their success has attracted competition from both the incumbent cable companies and their suppliers.

The cable companies were convinced that video on demand was going to work. They only took action in our category when they realized that we were having success. They want to keep control of both their customers and the technology that is used in the home. Left to their own devices, nothing would have happened, but our proving the market has led inevitably to the cable companies and their suppliers following in.

Jim understands that TiVo faces a common dilemma of pioneering firms—their integrated stack is being challenged by existing industry suppliers offering component technology:

> *Our licensing is for the whole system. A lot of people would like us to license component layers, but we got where we are through integration. The problem is that in pulling it apart you can break it. It isn't designed to be pulled apart. The industry technology suppliers who supply most of the cable equipment can use their leverage and channel presence to encourage cable companies to use their equipment, whether their products are as good as ours or not.*

In the end, Jim believes that TiVo is adept at innovating and building end services and products for consumers, while existing cable technology suppliers have more leverage and less revenue conflict with the cable channel. Rather than attempting to compete horizontally, TiVo will compete by continuing to innovate and redefine the market.

> *It comes down to how big the market is and more importantly what is the "real" market. Right now, we see ourselves in the business of helping consumers take advantage of massive amounts of storage in the home. But we recognize that things change. The market that we are after doesn't exist yet, so DVR definitions and analyst-defined market share aren't necessarily relevant. We are continuing to spend on R&D to be ready, and doing it in a direction that has long-term viability. Our platform is built to be extendable, and we see that there are many more markets developing that can take advantage of our basic technology.*

In contrast to building a complete product to open a new market, providing tools to an emerging market involves helping a wide variety of customers become self-sufficient. For software companies, for example, developing **APIs** (application programming interfaces) and documentation is important, while for machinery suppliers, providing technical specs and engineering assistance to customers is critical. In all cases, the organizational skills required for channel development, selling, and servicing of enabling technology are markedly different from those required to provide products and services to end-users. Resources used for the latter are not available for the former.

Following the Short-Term Vertical Path

Chapter 5 discussed the incumbents' dilemma regarding how long to wait for a new technology to develop. Clearly, waiting allows toolsets to emerge that make it easier to eventually make the shift, but waiting always carries with it the specter of an industry reconfiguration that weakens the incumbent's competitive position. An equally complex quandary awaits early innovators and imitators. The pioneering firms that spend time and effort trying to win the early battle must consume resources to do so, leaving less time and money available to develop the technology platform and skills necessary to create a toolset. Essentially, an organization built to win in the early market may lack the resources and mindset to become a winner in this phase of market evolution.

Clear pressures and motivations exist for early movers to pursue the end-user market detour, even if they recognize a long-term horizontal opportunity in the marketplace (which many apparently don't). Those pressures and motivations include the following:

> The VC funding mechanism, with its milestone-based approach, exerts pressure to acquire early customers rather than wait for the market to evolve. As was discussed in Chapter 4, venture money brings with it a focus on liquidity events, a portfolio mindset, and idiosyncrasies related to how a fund's portfolio companies demonstrate their progress.

> Firms that wait risk missing the major liquidity events driven by early growth trajectories and hype cycles. This can create severe competitive imbalances in both capital and market profile, which may result in the firm with a better long-term position (from a technology and toolset point of view) being acquired by a much larger and cash-rich early mover. This is not necessarily a negative, as long as company stakeholders see acquisition as an acceptable next phase or exit strategy.

> The industry gatekeepers of dominant design will almost certainly be reluctant to commit to a design being pushed by a firm with no operating history or results. Unless—or, in some cases, even if—the firm has an extremely high profile, the technology will be an unlikely candidate for dominant design.

The implication is that when firms pursue early vertical markets, they must do so with an eye toward horizontally enabling their product and company in order to thrive as technology companies in the long term. The alternative, particularly if the firm is fortunate enough to have a large infusion of capital through additional rounds of investment or public offering, is to shift perspectives and invest in complementary assets, as Yahoo! did. This is an effective move toward mature incumbent status, where the firm becomes a technology consumer as well as provider.

Can an Innovator Become a Toolmaker?

The cycle that has unfolded over the last couple of chapters is not a particularly attractive one for innovators and early entrepreneurs. Unless they are able to either establish a lasting barrier via some of the methods alluded to earlier or use an early lead to attract a "war chest" of capital, the most likely of their future options are to use acquisition or merger as an exit strategy or to attempt to carve out and survive in a niche. Many of the early firms will simply be "shaken out" of the industry, as enabling tools and a dominant design emerge (events discussed in greater detail in Chapter 7).

Still, some firms do make it through this period. Amazon, for example, started as bookseller and, after investing several hundreds of millions of dollars in distribution centers and logistical infrastructure, realized that it is first and foremost a technology company. As founder Jeff Bezos said, "What gets us up in the morning and keeps us here late at night is technology.... From where we sit, advanced technology is everything."[23]

Currently, retailers such as Target, Toys "R" Us, Nordstrom, and even the number two bookselling chain, Borders Group, use Amazon's software platform for online sales. Rather than attempting to compete across all of these segments in all of these categories,

Amazon is covering as much of the retail market as possible by offering itself up as a tool provider. Amazon's ability to navigate the complex balance between empowering and competing against some of its partners reflects the confidence of the partners that part of their respective industries' core competencies lie outside of the Amazon toolset. The biggest technology threat to incumbents is discontinuous innovation that neutralizes core competencies.[24] In Amazon's case, the partners' sourcing, merchandising, product planning, and brands are enhanced rather than neutralized; Amazon simply provides the selling technology and marketplace. From Amazon's viewpoint, supplying technology has allowed it to capture a larger overall "share of wallet" without the marketing, specialized know-how, and industry-by-industry investment that would otherwise be necessary. Its gross margin as a software provider is as high as 70 percent, while its retail profit margins have been 20 percent or less.[25] There's no doubt that developing the skills and tools to be a software developer and a service provider—including necessary platform items such as a software developer's kit—is a challenge for Amazon, particularly while still performing as a retailer. This dual role has resulted in some platform support–related issues and complaints.[26]

Credibility Issues

"De-integrating" and turning to toolmaking are challenges, regardless of a firm's age. The task is actually much more difficult for existing companies with longer operating histories, standardized methods, established organizational memory, and more complex value networks. For example, Sony could not have hoped to be as effective as JVC in "selling" Beta as a standard to the industry, since its most prominent issue was its overall unwillingness to become a "supplier." Sony's strategy has historically been to "build up the Sony name and reputation and avoid sharing the benefits of Sony innovation with too many levels of distributors," and chairman Akio Morita was clear in stating at the time that "Sony is not an OEM manufacturer,"[27] an unambiguous vote against de-integrating.

An existing firm with enough nerve and imperative to make the shift, however, does have the advantage of an established presence. Amazon's example illustrates the need, discussed previously, for early-entry startup firms to pursue an early market productized entry prior to eventually making the transition to toolmaker. Amazon's clout and demonstrated skills as a retail and technology operator are what made the decision to use its platform palatable to its partners.

Similarly, Nokia's success in licensing its Series 60 handset middleware platform and Toyota's success in licensing its hybrid electric automotive technology to other automobile manufacturers are other examples of cases in which firms have leveraged credible market experience. Their internal results and industry prominence assisted them in establishing their credentials as firms able to create a larger industry pie by shifting from proprietary supplier to dominant design tool provider.

A Willingness to Change

A modular product design requires new kinds of processes carried out by new kinds of organizational structures.[28] Enabling technology providers may have to make significant changes in mindset, staffing, and organization. Embedding an enabling technology platform in an external partner's product is different from managing a simple supplier relationship. The enabler must take a broader architectural view of the enabling technology user's products and be involved in the early planning rather than just the execution of the effort—in many cases building an entire organization around this process. Such tools of the enabler trade as support engineers, account teams, development kit developers, evangelists, and technical writers may not exist in a company built to service end-users. As a Microsoft manager commented about Nokia's effort to sell middleware, "No one would argue that Nokia makes good mobile phones, but it will be very difficult for Nokia to be as good a software maker as it is a handset maker."[29]

Additionally, the enabling firm must have the ability to manage the issues involved in servicing multiple competitors as well as, in some cases, potentially competing against customers.[30] A simple non-disclosure agreement (NDA) is seldom enough to reassure larger customers, who may want to see an organizational design that keeps information partitioned in the enabling company. Finally, in many industries (including the software industry), customer-driven innovation is common.[31] Fostering the user-innovation process requires an approach different from the "build it and sell it" culture that tends to develop in a company delivering complete products to early markets.

The reason all of these factors are mentioned here is that they represent major stumbling blocks for organizations with a legacy. The review of Polaroid in Chapter 2 revealed how a company can fail by not responding to the need to move from an end-user mentality to a component one. Apple is often cited as a company that was unable to make the transition with its operating system. Even if a firm is committed to making the switch, such a dramatic change may require an equally dramatic change in organization and business model. After a few forays into platform licensing, Palm concluded that it needed to split off the entire software division to have a chance at success. Brand issues and internal power struggles were slowing it down, and Palm's larger, revenue-driving hardware group viewed the software division as "giving them an internal edge"[32] rather than as the potential future of the company. This philosophy created resistance among other hardware firms which might otherwise have viewed Palm's OS as a potential enabling platform. For example, the CEO of Handspring, a firm that licensed the software, commented, "In the past, we felt very uncomfortable with Palm, because while we licensed their software, we also felt like we were competing with their hardware."[33] The eventual split allowed the software division to negotiate a strategic investment from Sony, which probably would not have occurred otherwise.

Second-Generation Threats

As early innovators either stay true to a proprietary end-product strategy or struggle with the market shift to more modular enabling, the opportunity arises for a new breed of firms—both startups and incumbents—to step in. The startups may be specifically designed, in terms of both technology and organizational structure, to enable widespread competition with the early innovators/imitators. They are also likely to be heavily funded, since the opportunity is more concrete and quantifiable than it was in the early market. If the second-generation firm is an established company, it is likely to be servicing relevant cross-market needs already and to have the skills and tools to do the job as an enabler.

For Research In Motion (RIM), the makers of BlackBerry wireless e-mail devices, second-generation competition has come from a startup firm called Good Technology. Good Technology, backed by $60 million from two premier venture capital firms (Kleiner Perkins Caufield & Byers and Benchmark Capital), raised most of its money in 2001, well after the launch of BlackBerry. While its product design is based on early market acceptance of and enthusiasm for the BlackBerry device, its focus is on "offering customers flexibility by supporting only industry-standard hardware and platforms. This allows an enterprise to choose their wireless carrier, platform, network and a variety of devices."[34] As Good's CEO remarked, "This category is just getting started, and people don't want RIM to own it."[35]

This focus on cross-platform-enabling software gives Good Technology broader appeal than RIM and a better chance to win dominant design status. As one analyst put it in early 2004,

> The problem with RIM to date has been that you've been tied to the RIM hardware. Though RIM has announced that it is working to make its software work on non-BlackBerry platforms such as Palm and Windows Mobile, they just haven't gone any place. They haven't yet been able to deliver a system that works on the alternative hardware.[36]

For Palm, the second-generation challenge has come from the "mother of all incumbents"—Microsoft. The opportunity in handhelds naturally attracted Microsoft, and the Windows CE operating system, designed as an enabling tool, has given access to the market to many handheld makers, including Dell and Sony. Microsoft, of course, has both the skills and the organizational design (as well as many other complementary assets) to offer a software platform with dominant design potential.

In the case of TiVo, the enthusiasm of early users has clearly brought attention to the category. Michael Powell, head of the FCC, actually referred to TiVo as "God's Machine."[37] The popularity of and excitement surrounding digital video recording (DVR) and the potential value it adds to cable and satellite broadcaster services have naturally made those services want to include DVR functionality in their product lines, and several enablers have emerged. Leading set-top box provider Scientific-Atlanta makes a box that is used by several cable companies; software is available via a firm called NDS; and chipmakers offer the intermediate technology that is working its way into the receiver boxes of some major satellite television providers.

TiVo and Second-Generation Threats

Without a doubt, people who own TiVo digital video recorders love the product. TiVo has done an excellent job of introducing a relatively complicated value proposition—the time shifting of television through video storage—to the early-adopting consumer technophile audience. To introduce this new product, TiVo built an end-to-end plug-and-play solution, including programming guide features.

TiVo followed many of the tactics expected of a successful innovator, including developing an excellent brand, a loyal installed base of 2 million users (as of 2004), and a strong patent portfolio including (as described by the company) "an invention allowing the user to store selected television broadcast programs while the user is simultaneously watching or reviewing another program."[38] It also used its momentum to raise capital in an IPO and garnered investments from some important strategic partners, including Sony and DirecTV.

Despite all of this, the DVR market appears to be an exemplary case of an industry life cycle where a pioneer has demonstrated the market potential, but left the door open for a second-generation toolmaker. Futurist Paul Saffo describes TiVo's key function as a component technology: "In the years to come, TiVo will become a button on some future product, like spell checker did for [Microsoft] Word."[39]

While TiVo has been busy focusing resources on marketing and building out an organization to grab a 3 percent penetration rate as a consumer-facing company, others have been working quietly behind the scenes to develop the next-generation enabling technology needed to allow entrenched incumbents to capture the DVR dollars as the industry grows. One of the primary candidates to deliver the incumbents' toolkit is NDS Group, which already licenses content protection technology and electronic program guide middleware to most of the major set-top box manufacturers, giving them an estimated reach of 40 million households through its partnerships with chipset manufacturers, cable systems, and satellite operators. NDS has observed the benefits of working with cable operators and suppliers as a technology middleware partner, rather than battling them as an end-to-end service. Their XTV platform will have more industry modular technology, and, since it is controlled by Rupert Murdoch, who also controls B Sky B and DirecTV, the satellite operators can push the agenda of an open DVR platform and NDS adoption.

Scientific-Atlanta is another potential enabler with a strong position in the industry. It currently supplies set-top boxes to many of the major cable companies. It also represents tough horizontal competition for TiVo, since it can offer cable operators an alternative DVR solution to embed in their service offering.

These examples illustrate the challenges an early innovator often faces. Once the innovation moves from promising technology needing proof of concept to "the next big thing," heavyweight competitors emerge. This occurs in the era of ferment, during which widescale deployment practicalities and political and economic considerations determine likely winners in the marketplace. Even TiVo (aka "God's Machine") or the BlackBerry (a device so addictive that it's often called "the crackberry") could watch the market move past it. The impatience of firms in adjacent markets to adopt, along with reluctance to trust a proprietary over-verticalized supplier manufacturer, leads to the second-generation threat.

Decomposition and Modularity

Clearly, an innovating firm will be better served if its initial innovation, commercialization, and product strategy are based on a plan to eventually make the firm the tool supplier to the industry. That is, firms that start out with a vertical external orientation may eventually need to participate horizontally in the market. An eventual transition to toolmaker should be a major element of the firm's initial strategy, not an afterthought. For the industry as a whole, decomposition and layer integration happen as the technology ferments and the opportunity arises to climb the S curve. The discussions in this chapter and in preceding chapters have demonstrated that decomposition is less kind to individual innovators and imitators. The clear solution is to build modularity into early efforts, to avoid the challenges and competition that arise from difficulties in re-orientating to become a toolmaker. To design an organizational strategy that will initially approach the market with a complete solution but later provide horizontal tools, three key elements need to be addressed from the outset: modularity in architecture, branding, and organizational design.

Modularity in Architecture

The advantages of making an early aggressive vertical move are speed to market, functionality, removal of some elements of uncertainty, and completeness of the product—in essence, covering the shortest possible distance between two points by developing a tight vertical stack. If doing so means that components of the stack can't be shared or used for other purposes, then the short-term win will be a long-term loss, as the shortcomings of the NASA space programs demonstrated. From an engineering perspective, large multi-product firms—even if they have high degrees of verticalization—find it useful to develop modularity in their offerings, if for no other reason than to create a product family with interfaces that allow parts to be interchanged. For example, Boeing and McDonnell Douglas design their airplanes around common wing, nose, and tail components; automakers design power trains to be used across different car models; and household appliances, power tools, and computer hardware and software are engineered to be used and repurposed for entire product families.[40] More tightly coupled and complex "hard-wired" integration requires a level of coordination that isn't realistic as a method of technology diffusion. Modular architecture (with easily separable components) can reduce the costs of an innovation and encourage its emergence and adoption by other companies.[41]

The implication of the technology platform diagram originally shown in Exhibit 1-7 and redisplayed in Exhibit 6-2 is that even if the early firm pursues only market 1, it needs to design its offering using a modular stack approach and have some sense of which stack layer (or layers) represents the best candidate to be a tool, so that the layer(s) can be the focus of additional research and development.

Branding

One of the benefits of moving first and moving aggressively is the brand association with market/industry leadership that accrues to the firm that does so. This association can represent either a positive or a negative to potential tool customers, depending on how the company and its technology are positioned. Although Intel's ubiquitous co-branding campaign ultimately reduced the power of individual PC makers, its brand positioning conveys to consumers positive attributes about the PC makers that include Intel in their products, and Intel is not seen as a competing force. In contrast, Apple's approach to branding the iPod was to make it part of the Apple-specific product family. By not separating out the underlying AAC files and iTunes access from the hardware, Apple has made partnering more difficult. Palm also created a problem for itself in diffusion of its operating system by associating the Palm brand with both the hardware device and the

EXHIBIT 6-2 ■ When Technology Is the Platform

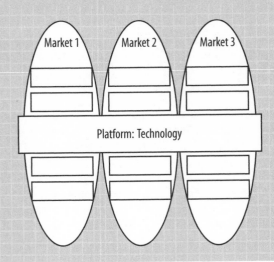

software platform. Internally, Palm executives argued about whether the Palm brand belonged to the hardware or software group, and each side put together a detailed presentation to lobby the board on why it should be allowed to keep the Palm name.[42] The whole exercise sent an ambiguous message to partners. A brand that carries positive benefits associated with a technology element—but does not create competitive concerns—is the most diffusible. The Windows brands (Windows Mobile, Pocket PC, and CE) are much better than the Palm brand in this regard.

Organizational Design

A number of both internally focused and external-facing organizational decisions come into play in serving an industry. If elements of an end-consumer product strategy still exist in a firm that is striving to provide enabling technology, then some internal separation—via physical, organizational, and perhaps even legal structures—is necessary. **Chinese walls** (artificial partitions within the organization) have not proven to be particularly effective in many industries, but sometimes provide reassurance to potential customers. In addition to resolving this conflict of interest issue, the early development of effective infrastructure can facilitate better planning and preparedness for extending a closely held innovation to an entire industry.

On the external-facing side, a company needs to have roles and functions in place that allow product teams to understand what technical specifications and standards are necessary for its enabling product to work for other firms. In the airplane industry, for example, Boeing, Airbus, and others, in order to be successful vendors, need to understand how airlines plan on using their fleets and what gaps exist in the airlines' service offerings. Airbus's focus on fuel efficiency and TCO (total cost of ownership) measures is meant to address the needs of new low-cost carriers and has resulted in major wins for the firm in this segment. In turn, the engine supplier IAE has focused on reliability and cost of ownership metrics in developing engines for Airbus configurations. For companies used to servicing other businesses, this external relationship management comes naturally, as research, customer councils, industry events, and outside relationships are all built into the companies' activities and organizational designs. In a firm that is tightly resourced and heavily focused on the commercialization milestone, however, these functions are largely absent or under-resourced. Without them, it is unrealistic to expect success in the enabling market. In some cases, venture capital firms provide this skill set as part of their participation in the firm, since it is lacking internally. At some point, however, the intention to extend a technology platform outside of the company requires building the external connecting infrastructure to plan and execute the strategy.

Beyond understanding and building connections to the market, the early innovator needs an element of evangelism to convince other companies to embrace its solution. Forrester Research points out that executives must be part technology evangelist and part line-of-business expert.[43] For a large and formidable firm like Microsoft, evangelizing technology presents few risks and is a necessary and customary part of its product development activities. For a smaller innovating firm, evangelism is much riskier, as it can invite competition. A more targeted approach than simply touting the technology via the press should be followed.

In summary, by planning in advance for the increased demand and potential across-the-board desire of incumbents to deploy an innovative technology once its potential is understood, an early entrant firm can avoid the toolmaker flanking maneuver that plagues many innovators. Even if the executive team anticipates accessing favorable capital markets to build complementary assets, setting the groundwork to be a tool provider allows for a viable change in direction if the capital markets are uncooperative or the horizontal opportunity is revealed to be a more attractive way to expand.

Price Pressure and Cost Competition

The preceding chapters have given ample evidence of the existence and drivers of the S curves associated with the demand and supply behaviors of new markets. Throughout the three phases of the innovation life cycle reviewed thus far—invention (the idea), imitation, and enabling (the tools)—a steady downward pressure on cost, a rising value associated with the new category of innovation, and an increase in supplier interest and participation (due to market normalization and clarity of potential) create these behaviors. (This assumes that Moore's chasm is crossed and the technology becomes mainstream.)

Exhibit 6-3 shows the impact of these three phases of the life cycle on both cost and price over time. On the cost side, fast-following firms learn from earlier movers, improving efficiency and helping the technology migrate down the experience curve and up the technology S curve. On the price side, whether an innovator starts high or low, increased competition naturally puts pressure on price, so the cost advantages during the early periods also lead to lower pricing. Not all competitors are equally endowed when it comes to internal cost structure, the product's external TCO, or product performance, and early firms are often at a disadvantage. The toolmaking firms put stress on all industry participants, since they enable incumbent firms with other sources of competitive advantage to enter the market using low-cost and efficient second-generation technology.

EXHIBIT 6-3 ■ The Effect of Enabling Competition on Cost and Pricing in Technology's Competitive Life Cycle

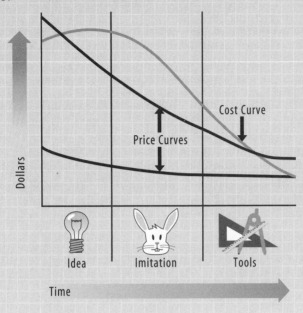

All this creates a watershed moment in the life cycle of a technology innovation, leading to two significant changes:

1. The technology enters the period of dominant design, bringing an end to the frenetic, exciting, and uncertain atmosphere surrounding the innovation's growth and diffusion. In the process, many firms become "odd men out." Relatively few firms emerge as viable long-term winners from this consolidation and shakeout in the industry.

2. The rise of a dominant design and the availability of horizontal tools prime the pump for the aggressive entry of incumbents and signal intensifying competition with less drastic innovation, as the category grows toward maturity.

These events are the primary focus of discussion in Chapter 7.

CHAPTER SUMMARY

This chapter reviewed the third phase of the technology competitive life cycle. As attractive new technology markets become saturated with competition, both existing and prospective firms eventually acknowledge diminishing returns in the category. This dynamic often precedes the high-growth phase of the market. Rather than abandon the new technology opportunity, the more technology-intensive firms can shift focus and concentrate on developing enabling technology that creates access for incumbent firms.

These enabling technology firms, particularly if they have the benefit of the experience curve and potential scale economies, are both higher on the performance curve and lower on the cost curve. They also lack some of the baggage associated with the earlier startups' attempts to bring a complete product to market. This creates an attractive profile for incumbents and also brings the technology a step closer to meeting the pragmatic needs of the mainstream market. Both of these factors can drive diffusion and demand, while attracting support from industry participants that have influence over dominant design and desire technology solutions that support the status quo.

Successful technology enablers need to avoid draining their resources on customization, develop externally facing organizations capable of servicing partners, build the necessary modular architecture into their technology offerings, and position themselves as being more benevolent than threatening. Technology-leveraged firms face a bleak future when they are unable to make significant barrier-creating progress as early end-suppliers, transition to complementary asset–intensive participants, or gain traction as enablers.

Incumbent Adoption and Influence

Success is a lousy teacher. It seduces smart people into thinking they can't lose, and it's an unreliable guide to the future.
— **Bill Gates**, *The Road Ahead*

Watching for Change

This final chapter in Part 2 looks specifically at issues of technology adoption and choice as they relate to established businesses. A number of key incumbent "pluses" have been identified thus far, including complementary assets, relationships, know-how, resources, and influence over dominant design. At the same time, incumbents are widely considered to be "innovation challenged." They are better followers than leaders and, relative to their size, account for a disproportionately small amount of non-process-driven (e.g., disruptive) innovation.[1] This is due to a variety of factors, including organizational inertia, customer expectations, Wall Street earnings commitments, and capital structure.

In the early periods of an industry's life cycle, before product innovation reaches its peak, innovators are likely to play a more significant role than incumbents. In the mature phase, once the new product paradigm has been established, process-oriented incremental innovation becomes more prevalent. As the industry moves toward the mature phase, incumbents become the more capable innovators. As Exhibit 7-1 shows, disruptive product-oriented innovation is paramount in the pre-paradigmatic period; the paradigmatic period is dominated by process-oriented change. The transition occurs as a dominant design takes hold.

Since disruptive innovation is generally not the strong point of incumbents, they need to find and support competence-enhancing technology opportunities that leverage their complementary assets and competitive positions and to avoid competence-destroying situations that render these assets impotent.[2] Incumbents also need to make sure that their assets and core competencies do not become liabilities, as is sometimes the case with **legacy systems**. While a stream of incremental and process-based advancements is key to continued growth and consumer acceptance in established markets, a "big picture" view of paradigmatic innovative change is also necessary. Incumbents need to be watchful for opportunities to acquire, shape, and, when possible, introduce paradigm-shifting disruptive technology. The pre-paradigmatic and paradigmatic periods tend to confront incumbent firms with different opportunities and risks. Therefore, focusing on life cycle timing as it relates to choices and decisions is as relevant for incumbents as it is for newer firms.

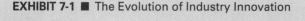

EXHIBIT 7-1 ■ The Evolution of Industry Innovation

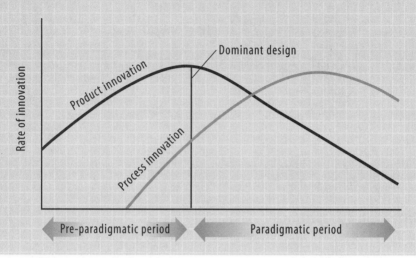

SOURCE: D. Teece, "Capturing Value from Technological Innovation: Integration, Strategic Partnering, and Licensing Decision," *Technology and Global Industry: Companies and Nations in the World Economy*, ed. National Academy of Engineering (Washington, DC: The National Academies Press, 1987).

A Matter of Choice

Dominant design theory, as well as common sense, indicates that some technology archetypes will win out over others and firms that adopt the winning technology will outperform those that don't.[3] Failure to adopt often leads to eventual industry exit. A look at historical innovation in the automobile tire industry illustrates this. A significant winning technological innovation was the Banbury mixer, introduced in the 1920s. The Banbury mixer is used for breaking down or incorporating pigments and fillers into rubber and plastic materials, allowing for the creation of a "tire dough," which can be rolled, shaped, and molded. The process is still in use today as an enabling technology in tire making. A subset of incumbents adopted the technology when it was introduced. Additionally, some new firms with the technology know-how entered the category and built the complementary assets necessary for them to compete as tire suppliers. Some other incumbent firms, however, remained "low tech." The latter firms became uncompetitive and were driven from the industry.[4] Adopting the winning technology involves either engaging in an early and relatively risky trial-and-error period, developing the dominant design, or simply attempting to influence and then quickly adopting the eventual dominant design. Of the three, the optimal outcome for an incumbent firm is to see its internal innovation become the winning design, as was the case with Sony's Walkman and HP's laser printers, but simply adopting is also preferable to ignoring a new paradigm.

Confronting Disruptive Innovation

Much of the contemporary discussion of innovation centers on whether incumbents are "blessed" or "cursed." Interestingly, Tushman and Anderson concluded that industry veterans are most likely to pioneer a breakthrough innovation.[5] They believe that even the innovations that threaten the competencies of an incumbent firm are more likely to be pressed forward by that firm, which prefers to deal with the consequences rather than be hunted down. The one key exception they identify, however, is when an innovation is highly disruptive, both significantly changing the value proposition of the industry and undermining the firm's competencies. This is, of course, the type of innovation that incumbents should be *most* concerned with. More recently, Christensen has asserted that incumbents are adept at managing sustaining (process-related) technologies, but not so adept at dealing with disruptive technologies, since these disruptions often call into question the underlying value proposition of the firm and its complementary assets.[6] MIT's James Utterback explains this critical exception:

> *Identifying the path to the future is an important requirement for survival and success when discontinuities surface. For established firms, getting off the path they are currently on is another, more difficult challenge. The impulse for firms to continue on the path of cash generating technologies is powerful. . . . Established firms are apt to approach discontinuities and conflicting corporate interests with compromise. . . . Bridging a technical discontinuity by having one foot in the past and the other in the future may be a viable solution in the short run, but the potential success of hybrid strategies is diluted from the outset compared to rivals with a single focus.[7]*

The conclusion is that even if an incumbent pioneers a new technology, it may be unwilling to press the technology as a dominant design, and a general inability to deal with disruptive change can lead to the firm's failure.

While incumbents are often aware of candidates for disruptive technology, the organizational bias toward internally developed incremental change may hinder appropriate investigation. Even if it is not developed internally, the enabling technology for disruptive change is typically available, and so the incumbent firm has the potential to impact and influence the dominant design. But larger firms are often torn between a desire to acquire and implement the best available technology solution—which often has been developed outside of the firm—and a desire for control. Additionally, firms with a broad business focus and wide range of interests find it difficult to pursue a technology that requires deep specialization.[8] This factor was evident in the discussion of Xerox/PARC and Adobe Systems in Chapter 6. If the technology innovation is considered speculative, the probability of its being pursued in a large company is further reduced. Finally, Tushman and Anderson's research suggests that the original discontinuous innovation will almost never become a standard, as it is generally an imitator's variation that leads to the dominant design, and that dominant design doesn't even need to be the technologically superior one.[9]

With no internal champion, continued uncertainty, and the potential for the innovation to disrupt the status quo, firms may let the disruptive opportunity pass them by in favor of more incremental change. In this regard, incumbents are neither blessed nor cursed—their destiny is a matter of choice rather than subjugation. If a curse exists, it is manifest in a variety of institutional factors that make decision making extremely difficult. Encyclopedia Britannica was not the early leader in interactive CD production, but the company certainly had made early efforts to use it, had the complementary assets to leverage it, and had the means to acquire the most current technology. With most of its revenue model wrapped up in paper production, however, and a culture driven by the ability to sell large, bound paper volumes, it was understandably reluctant to switch to a new enabling technology that would undermine its assets. It actually *sold off* its CD-ROM division (Compton's) in 1993, in the middle of a decade-long decline in printed sales that eventually reached an 80 percent loss of business![10] The decline of paper volumes in favor of interactive resources was probably out of Britannica's control, but Britannica's timing and role in the CD market and later the online world were a matter of choice. It chose to fight rather than embrace the disruptive change at a key juncture, allowing Microsoft's Encarta to become the clear leader, with over half of the market.[11] The disk drive industry went through several similar cycles, with each successive generation being completely replaced in the market in a few short years. Some established firms continued to hold on to the old paradigm for too long, while newcomers gained traction in the new market.[12]

Managing the Life Cycle versus Resisting Change

While some technology markets exhibit a rapid substitution effect, others experience a more gradual transition, as has occurred in the photography industry in the decade-long move from chemical film to digital imaging. The incumbents in these cases continue to have a short-term tangible opportunity, which is at risk if they move too dramatically and too aggressively. In such situations, the "old" markets may still be experiencing growth and opportunity driven by incremental innovation and appear far too healthy to be abandoned, affording ample reason not to embrace a new design. By embracing the next "new thing," larger incumbents may inadvertently hasten its climb up the S curve and speed the decline of familiar profitable markets. This understanding creates additional motivation for resistance on the part of the most successful firms in an industry.

Whether rapid or slow, technology-induced changes are not necessarily positive for incumbent firms. When faced with a choice between the self-inflicted pain of adapting to a changing industry and the externally inflicted pain of a shifting market, incumbents may find it easier to commit an error of omission than one of commission. The management at Kodak (in eventually embracing digital photography), Hewlett-Packard (in acquiring Compaq in response to changes in the industry), and PeopleSoft (in rewriting most of its code base for the web as the client/server design began to be challenged) made painful and expensive decisions. These decisions all led to severe criticism and scrutiny, since critics viewed the damage associated with the shift to embrace the "next big thing" as primarily self-inflicted. In the case of Kodak, key investor groups immediately challenged the company's strategy of shifting from film to digital technology and asked Kodak to scrap the plan. They also investigated whether to remove Kodak's management, as the firm's stock price plunged. HP's share prices likewise plunged, and a fierce boardroom battle followed the announcement that the company was buying Compaq, a deal that both HP's and Compaq's CEOs felt was imperative to compete in the changing enterprise and desktop computing markets.

In the end, however, avoiding change can be even costlier for both the company and the management team. Leading network provider Novell, for example, waited until well after the Internet had become a clear replacement networking platform before biting the bullet and retooling its product line. As the *Wall Street Journal* reported,

Novell faces an equally important perception problem, that it is late in using standard communications technologies. The company's flagship NetWare product line largely uses a proprietary technology. Mr. Schmidt said his highest priority is in rebuilding the company's products around the standard protocol of the Internet, called TCP/IP, and plans to become a "pure" Internet software leader by summer 1998.[13]

This delay resulted in a wholesale house cleaning of management, precipitous profit and revenue declines, and a permanent loss of category leadership for Novell—all in the midst of an explosive growth in networking driven by the Internet.

When disruptive change occurs, incumbents are eventually forced to adapt, whether or not the industry change is favorable to them. While incumbents are often in an enviable position because of their ability to acquire technology, the timing of adoption and the approach to change depend on the attractiveness and likelihood of the different potential outcomes.

The Rise (and Fall?) of the Video Store

The ubiquitous video store represents an interesting learning lab for studying industry life cycles, as well as the challenges that innovation and technology present to incumbents. The retail video rental industry is fairly new, a by-product of consumer acceptance of the VHS format in the early 1980s. After the typical slow build and era of ferment, VHS became the accepted dominant design, hardware costs dropped, and the rapid climb up the S curve began. The rise of this new format and subsequent studio support led to the rapid entry of hundreds, if not thousands, of small video rental operators—there were 19,000 outlets by 1986.[14]

The more forward-looking and late-entering entrepreneurs applied themselves to toolmaking, preferring to franchise or license in order to reach larger portions of the market than could be developed via self-funded store growth. One of the most prominent entrepreneurial ventures was Blockbuster Video, which was started by a software developer named David Cook. By developing and selling the core retail technology rather than investing in the bricks and mortar, Blockbuster was able to grow rapidly. The chain was then able to leverage this growth into a capital position that allowed it to pursue store and other complementary assets, as other technology became widely available. The industry went through considerable consolidation, which eventually left fewer than five incumbent firms of significant size (with Blockbuster as the clear number one) in a profitable but incrementally changing industry.

One of the industry's biggest challenges—the switch from VHS format to DVD—was managed as an incremental change, since it allowed the video store chains to continue to leverage their existing complementary assets (such as stores, leases, employees, and brand name). Distributors were forced to work cooperatively with the chains because of the importance of the retail channel. Recently, however, a number of technologies representing possible new S curves have emerged. Since the video store chains are deeply entrenched in their complementary assets, some of these changes have not been embraced, as they threaten the chains' core competencies. The rise of Internet-based subscription rental services is one near-term disruption that has the potential to remove the value of stores, as the services use centralized distribution centers and an online storefront and provide for titles to be delivered and returned via mail. These services can carry less inventory than stores and can allow customers to keep movies for an indeterminate amount of time. The startup firm Netflix demonstrated the potential of the category, using an early growth trajectory to raise capital and eventually going public. The capital, in turn, has allowed the firm to build a brand and distribution facilities—complementary assets that secure Netflix a place in the industry.

The major participants in the industry certainly have had the means to appropriate the technology, learn from Netflix, and participate in this new segment. For video store chains, however, this non-location-based model threatens perceived core competencies. As a result, the chains initially moved slowly, despite the availability of the technology—victims of the incumbent **failure framework**."[15] Understandably, Blockbuster, a firm with almost $6 billion in sales, was reluctant to undercut its model for a category segment of less than $500 million, even if failure to do so allowed a new competitor to enter. Its store-based model depends on competencies that are largely irrelevant to the non-location-based model. An aggressive move by Blockbuster would have potentially accelerated migration away from retail locations. As Netflix's CEO Reed Hasting pointed out, "Increased competition will drive consumer interest in the category overall,"[16] something that Blockbuster does not want to see happen. For Blockbuster, the priority clearly is to use the Internet-enabled innovation in conjunction with its current assets, rather than undercut them. As Blockbuster's CEO John Antioco said,

> *Netflix is certainly an alternative for people who want to go online and who like to plan their movie time ahead. They're also willing to wait to get the movies they want. . . . Our own version, The Movie Freedom Pass, is in a thousand stores right now, up from a couple hundred at the beginning of the year, and we plan a full-scale rollout next year. We will also offer an online component, so you'll be able to do the entire transaction online, very similar to what Netflix and Wal-Mart's walmart.com are doing now. But the difference is that you'll also be able to go into the store.*[17]

Wal-Mart was quicker to enter the online rental category, since it already operated in an adjacent category (DVD sales). Without a rental business, it was not threatened by the loss of complementary assets and had little concern about cannibalization. It was able to enter the market relatively painlessly through the acquisition of a Netflix competitor. Wal-Mart, however, did not emulate Netflix's $100–$200 million in losses in a speculative venture to accelerate growth. It, instead, followed a "go slow approach," in order to determine the true profitability of the business and its impact on DVD sales. This process ultimately led Wal-Mart to partner with Netflix, in order to boost its proven DVD sales business rather than compete in rentals. For both Blockbuster and Wal-Mart, the slower approach is dictated by choice, not myopia or inaccessibility, and the threat is considered containable by leveraging preexisting assets.

Video on demand (VOD) and digital video recording (DVR)—the delivery of movies via the airwaves or cable direct to consumers' homes—represent a much more significant threat than Internet-based DVD rental. VOD and DVR remove the need to distribute and return disks, making obsolete many of the assets of Netflix, Wal-Mart, and Blockbuster. This is true disruption; not only are traditional assets made less important, but the retailers may not be able to gain access to the key tools or influence the dominant design in a way that reinforces their assets. A much more significant shift is required, and yet holding back is a much riskier proposition. As Antioco pointed out, "It is naïve at best to think the studios can go it alone when it comes to VOD. And I can promise you, Blockbuster isn't about to sit back and watch that happen.... Battle lines are being drawn. Territory is being staked. And alliances are being forged in the broadband world"[18] Since the key enabling technologies may leverage assets neither held nor acquirable by Blockbuster and other DVD rental retailers (e.g., cable lines, satellite transmission equipment, and set-top boxes), however, it may not be possible for these retailers to participate meaningfully, in which case their role in the industry may eventually be marginalized. In Blockbuster's case, attempts to divert cash and focus on this more disruptive long-term area have created short-term profit pressures, leading to a shareholder revolt. While Blockbuster's management may recognize the upcoming shift, the need to leverage existing assets and deliver short-term profits, combined with a lack of access, may ultimately leave them unable to independently compete after the next technology-driven change in how movies are delivered.

Handling Uncertainty

Chapter 3 mentioned three basic postures that an incumbent firm can take relative to uncertainty. It can attempt to *shape* the market (as Warner Brothers did with DVDs), it can *adapt* to it (as Blockbuster did with DVDs), or it can *reserve the right to play* (as Blockbuster has attempted to do with its video-on-demand initiatives). In the case of the more predictable incremental changes that characterize the paradigmatic period, uncertainty is manageable, and incumbents can choose when and how to adapt. Choices are typically made with great clarity as to the potential consequences, even if the firm chooses not to adapt. When the direction of the market is predictable, with some limited potential choices, incumbents can also choose to attempt to shape the direction of the category, in order to arrive at a favorable outcome.

Alternatively, if the choices involve a potential disruptive change, a firm that tries to shape what is essentially a pre-paradigmatic innovation is basically attempting to influence dominant design. When the technology uncertainty is really just a choice between a few clear options, such as competing standards, shaping has a high potential payout and is a less risky (but by no means certain) path. Warner Brothers' shaping strategy in the DVD market, outlined in Chapter 3, is an example. Disruptive innovations are often the source of significant uncertainty, however, both in concept and in execution. Taking a more aggressive stance in this case, whether through pilot efforts ("reserving the right to play" investments) or full-blown market-shaping initiatives, can yield significant results and allow an incumbent to lock up the market before the explosive life cycle progression is allowed to play out. There is a correspondingly large risk of failure in these cases, however, as there would be for any firm pioneering a disruptive technology change. Previous chapters pointed out that the ways that effective large firms deal with this risk is through skunkworks, separate corporate entities, and corporate venturing, all of which protect the core enterprise if the risk-taking innovator fails.

ChevronTexaco, for example, is using this strategy by making a multitude of investments through its corporate venturing arm (discussed in Chapter 4), thereby gaining experience, know-how, and market "real estate" in a variety of next-generation energy technologies. Identifying the particular technologies that will become dominant designs and commercial successes is not yet possible, but at some point (which, some believe, will be well before fossil fuel becomes scarce) the economics of energy alternatives will disrupt the current oil- and coal-based model. Aside from potential return on capital from venture investments, the payout for ChevronTexaco will be in developing and redeploying complementary assets in such a way as to benefit from the new energy models that become available. ChevronTexaco states that the technologies and products of the funds' portfolio companies "should be applicable across multiple markets and adaptable for use within the energy industry."[19] This indicates the firm's interest in developing enabling technologies that it can leverage.

Again, the alternative to shaping is simply to follow an adaptive strategy. Since the underlying innovation is likely to be available to the adapter eventually in some iteration, the adaptive strategy consists primarily of acquiring capabilities that will allow the firm to leverage the disruptive technology's dominant design, rather than be destroyed by it. In contrast to ChevronTexaco, which took an aggressive stance in alternative energy, GE followed an adaptive strategy with respect to the Internet, focusing on building capabilities for the future. GE waited until 2000 to create two new infrastructure companies—GE Global eXchange Services and GE Systems Services—in order to provide Internet data exchange and operations infrastructure to support e-commerce. GE did this without having a clear picture of how its individual product markets would evolve as a result of e-commerce.[20] GE was accused of inertia by many,[21] because of its late entry and lack of focused application. But the need to protect existing businesses, such as running proprietary trading networks, as well as uncertainty over which of the many Internet ferment era technologies would become permanent, led the firm to use an adaptive strategy. GE was eventually able to apply standard protocols to the development of infrastructure that is now both used inside the company and offered as a technology platform for others through an independent operating company.

Proprietary Risk

The largest risk to incumbents using an adaptive strategy is that the core technology of a new dominant design will be tightly protected and unavailable, leaving the incumbent in a highly disadvantageous competitive position. Chapter 5 pointed out that while patents rarely, if ever, confer perfect protection, protected or proprietary technology can create a winning formula for the innovator when it does exist. The most obvious example is drug discovery, where a significant innovation can immediately shift competitive share, as the incumbent is unable to acquire the compound. For example, the pharmaceutical firm Roche introduced a hepatitis C drug that captured over 50 percent of the market in less than a year, taking the dominant market share from Schering-Plough. Roche's drug Pegasys does not require mixing or dosage adjustment[22] and is generally believed to have fewer side effects.[23] The disruptive market share shift could represent a billion dollars for each of the companies involved. As would be expected, pharmaceutical firms aggressively try to avoid these disruptive shifts by developing innovation internally and by acquiring innovation externally before it hits the market. Other types of firms also need to consider both the opportunity and the risk if a proprietary disruptive technology becomes a dominant design. The impact of Microsoft's operating system on the other participants in the personal computer market illustrates the potential hazards associated with a proprietary dominant design.

A proprietary mouse trap—DuPont's Harvard-based OncoMouse

© by the President and Fellows of Harvard College

On those rare occasions when a patented or copyrighted or otherwise proprietary technology becomes the preferred solution, the payoff can be quite large. Both Alexander Graham Bell, whose telephone patent is considered one of the most valuable ever issued, and the management team of Searle, which controlled aspartame (Nutrasweet) patents, would attest to this. Less well-known inventor Jerome Lemelson also secured and profited from a variety of patents. In his case, the patents covered the code and pattern recognition that formed the preferred basis for bar code scanners, ubiquitous in grocery stores and virtually every logistics application. Many executives who had never even heard of Lemelson found that their firms were required to pay royalties to the billion-dollar Lemelson Foundation while the patents were in force. If Harvard's patented breed of mouse with a genetic disposition to cancer[24] (licensed to DuPont and branded as the OncoMouse) becomes the standard, lab researchers will find that they also face potential royalty or rights issues. Similarly, standardization around proprietary radio frequency identification (RFID) tag technology could create a Lemelson of the airwaves, and SAP may be moving toward becoming this proprietary supply chain standard in such markets as consumer packaged goods, producing a financial windfall. As mentioned earlier, an industry's participants often seek to avoid a proprietary standard for just this reason.

In particularly competitive industries or those where end-users exert influence on what component technologies become a part of the dominant design, there is significant risk that a proprietary standard will become dominant. If the proprietary standard is embedded in a product designed around a vertical stack and customers find the new paradigm attractive, virtually the entire market could be ceded to the new technology provider. This was the situation for Xerox with xerography in the 1960s, and for Hewlett-Packard with inexpensive laser jet printer technology in the 1990s.

Finally, if a firm has capabilities and complementary assets that are unusually aligned with one potential technology design or if a firm will be cut out of the market if another design takes hold, it may be willing to take larger risks. Local telephone companies (telcos), for example, are quite naturally placing large investment bets on DSL, since consumer acceptance of DSL will extend the life of their expensive copper wire networks. Eventually, they hope to provide a variety of high-end data services (Internet protocol–based telephony, video conferencing, and video on demand via DSL) in order to continue to derive value from a significant complementary asset that will otherwise come under pressure from wireless, satellite, and cable alternatives. These billion-dollar bets on DSL, if successful, will allow the telcos to leverage their unique infrastructure and will ensure their future presence in the telecommunications industry.

The Shift to Open Innovation

In general, the pure, old-school model for innovation, with its internal focus and closed-system approach to R&D, is becoming obsolete. As Randy Komisar points out, "Historical vertical integration allowed companies like AT&T and IBM to harvest their R&D directly into their own organization. That has changed—the amount of outside competition and innovation has fragmented markets."[25] Emerging in its place is a new paradigm, referred to as **open innovation**, which seeks to leverage internal and external sources of ideas and bring them both to market.[26] As U.C. Berkeley's Henry Chesbrough argues,

> In many industries, the logic supporting an internally oriented centralized approach to R&D has become obsolete. Useful knowledge is widespread in many industries, and ideas must be used with alacrity if they are not to be lost. These factors create the new logic of open innovation, which embraces external knowledge in conjunction with internal R&D. This logic offers new ways to create value, along with the continuing need to claim a portion of that value.[27]

Even in the pharmaceutical field, technology is now advancing across a wider range of opportunities at a quickening pace. No firm can hope to keep up with all the potential areas of opportunity, and incumbents, by working with dedicated research firms, can avoid the more expensive and unpredictable outcomes of go-it-alone strategies.[28] The implication is that elements of an adaptive strategy must always be in an incumbent's playbook, even if the firm is traditionally an innovation driver.

Incumbent Adoption and Bandwagon Pressure

Whether or not an incumbent is truly excited about an emerging disruption, the sheer number of other organizations adopting the innovation can cause bandwagon pressure.[29] Like the herding effect, the bandwagon effect provokes organizations in the industry and adjacent to it to adopt an innovation simply to "keep up." This helps drive dominant design and propel movement up the S curve. As discussed in Chapter 5, bandwagon pressures can exist either because non-adopters fear appearing different from adopters or because they fear under-performing. Another large factor in the diffusion and adoption of innovation is the social networks of technology decision makers. Both the bandwagon effect and social network pressure represent points of leverage for firms interested in accelerating an agenda of disruptive change. Indeed, creating a climate of fear and the impression that firms are falling behind is a valuable tool in enterprise software sales, where herding behavior is prevalent.

The positives of the bandwagon effect are that it relieves some of the uncertainty pressure on incumbents, is a sign of the emergence of a dominant design paradigm, and reinforces the new dominant technology platform. In keeping with the old saying "Nobody ever got fired for choosing IBM," a firm's managers can reduce their technology risk simply by doing what everyone else is doing. If its resource base and strategy are well aligned with the change, a firm may emerge with an improved competitive position. At the same time, the bandwagon effect can dampen the opportunity for incumbents to embrace a new technology for competitive advantage in the paradig-matic period. Since not all firms are equally endowed, bandwagon pressure can even cause some firms to act against their own self-interests, especially if they are ill suited for the switch. **Efficient choice** (e.g., the payoff for the firm) is only one factor in a firm's decision. It also faces pressures from within and outside the industry to adopt new technology, regardless of impact.[30]

Playing Favorites: Industry Shakeout

The entire competitive life cycle, including the final phase in which a clear picture of the disruptive change emerges and incumbent adoption occurs, is represented in Exhibit 7-2. Overlaying the S curve on this graph would show the new innovation reaching and then passing the inflection point as incumbent adoption takes hold.

Since the commercial application of the innovation is at this point reaching maturity, it is almost certainly a profitable technology to supply and adopt. Cost has been driven to levels where mass market pricing is feasible, while a competitively contested market has driven prices down, accelerating customer demand. A rare and proprietary solu-tion has obvious advantages over this competitively driven scenario, since the price curve would be more under the control of the technology owner and the industry cost curve would be less relevant. But Exhibit 7-2 illustrates that, to be competitive, most firms—with the exception of proprietary technology providers—will need to operate using a cost-effective technology solution and have access to complementary assets. For technology-oriented firms, participation comes from supplying firms that possess these assets or from acquiring them.

EXHIBIT 7-2 ■ The Typical Competitive Life Cycle of Technological Innovation

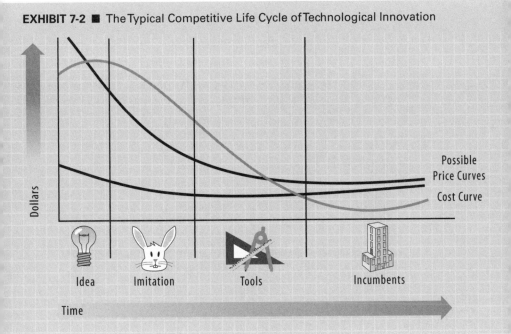

Cost structure varies by individual firm, and higher-cost firms, as well as those without sufficient complementary assets, will become uncompetitive. Early market imitators and innovators whose technology doesn't align with the dominant design will also find that they can no longer compete in the market. Additionally, for incumbent firms, not successfully adapting to the new technology will lead to failure, as it did for the non-adapting firms in the tire market when the Banbury mixer made its entry. The result is a shakeout—a sharp rise in the exit rate of firms from the industry—as both incumbents and startups fail to make the technology shift.[31] An oft-cited study by Michael Gort and Steven Klepper documented this trend across 46 industries, including the tire industry shakeout shown in Exhibit 7-3.[32] The number of firms in the tire industry peaked soon after the emergence of the Banbury mixer, despite continued growth in automobile sales.

While the amount of time between innovation, imitator, and shakeout has been compressed in the current information age, the findings are still considered to be directionally valid.[33] A study of the local area network (LAN) equipment market, for example, validated both the behavior of the price curve—which trended downward at a rate of 17 percent per year—and the rise, peak, and shakeout of participating firms after design characteristics became standardized.[34] The study points out,

> As the market matured, the technical features of individual products (such as processor speed and memory) were increasingly less important to buyers. More important were demand-side notions

EXHIBIT 7-3 ■ The Tire Industry Shakeout

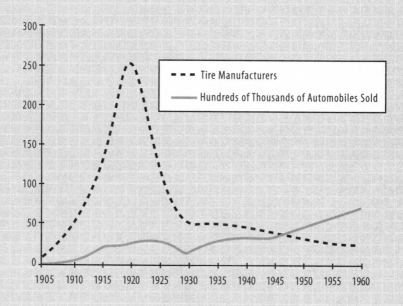

SOURCE: Based on M. Gort and S. Klepper, "Time's Path in the Diffusion of Product Innovation," *Journal of Economics*, September 1982.

such as ease of installation and integration with existing systems, and broader measures of customer service and technical support. Increasing importance of these "softer" product characteristics favored a more concentrated market structure.[35]

This does not signal that a market has reached a mature, "sunset" phase. The LAN equipment market continued to grow at a double-digit rate, and the auto industry was by no means mature in 1925. It does mean that a few well-rounded and more competitive firms will dominate and that success will derive from mature core competencies rather than from innovation alone.[36] While inventive activity continues and patent filings do not cease,[37] the nature of the innovation becomes more process oriented and less disruptive.

The evolution of the industry and of technology enabling online business-to-business marketplaces and e-procurement demonstrates the entire life cycle—from pioneering idea through shakeout.

The Evolution and Shakeout of Online Exchanges

The technology promise of online business-to-business marketplaces comes primarily from a combination of more competitive bidding, catalog synchronization, and supply chain efficiency. The corresponding expected benefit for a business of using an online marketplace model is reduced cost of goods, with a potential payoff of tens or even hundreds of millions of dollars per year for the typical Fortune 1000 firm.

Global consumer goods giant Unilever, for example, was having difficulty realizing scale efficiencies as it grew through acquisition of such firms as Ben & Jerry's and Bestfoods. To address this problem, it put in an Ariba-powered procurement system in order to consolidate, coordinate, and globalize the purchase of materials, replacing inefficient and redundant purchasing processes that impacted input costs. Through these efforts, combined with other procurement efficiency initiatives, it was able to save almost $500 million per year.[38]

The marketplace exchange industry has followed the typical technology industry life cycle. Readily identifiable points of pain (such as that identified by Unilever) helped attract funding for the first set of technology pioneers. These were vertically specialized and closed platform suppliers, such as Chemdex, Aluminum.com, and PaperExchange. Hefty early liquidity events driven by the hype cycle, such as Chemdex's $11 billion post-IPO valuation,[39] attracted the capital to fuel a horde of imitators. With low barriers to imitation, the competition soon multiplied, reaching well over a thousand firms.[40]

These firms were soon put under pressure by horizontal tool firms, such as Ariba, Commerce One, i2, and Manugistics, which provided software that enabled incumbents to enter the fray directly. Transora, for example, was founded by a consortium of 50 of the largest consumer products firms and used the Ariba and i2 platforms to offer marketplace tools to member firms. In response, the largest supply chain software firms, such as Trilogy and SAP, introduced second-generation sourcing and procurement tools that were better integrated with their software stacks, allowing them to better serve their customers. This has put pressure on the early tool providers, just as they put pressure on the early vertical closed platform firms.

The combination of oversupply, horizontal shift, capital scarcity, second-generation threats, and incumbent participation has led to a severe, if not surprising, shakeout in the industry. The sector, which rocketed from roughly 200 firms in 1997 to over 1,500 in 2001, had dropped back down to well under 200 by the end of 2003, through acquisition, consolidation, and shutdown.[41] As one analyst reported, "By coming out visibly and with so much hype, the independents really put fear in the heart of the old economy, but at the same time, they invited the old economy to come take a look."[42] *CFO* magazine was more direct in its 2001 review of the marketplaces: "The old economy did more than look. It came, it saw, it conquered."[43]

Exchanges will continue to grow and improve procurement processes, much to the delight of both industry and supply chain software incumbents. Many of the early participants were attractive, early-momentum plays for their investors, but will not be a part of this change.

Consolidation Opportunities and Errors

The shakeout period can also be a period of consolidation, representing significant strategic opportunities for incumbents and disaster-saving exit strategies for newer firms. A significant part of the industry concentration observed in the networking equipment market, for example, was driven by Cisco's acquisition of other firms. Cisco made over 20 significant acquisitions in a period of five years, focused primarily on filling in technology portfolio gaps. While many of the acquired firms had innovative core technologies, only Cisco had the market presence to rapidly leverage these technologies for their maximum value. In maturing and consolidating industries, innovators can have difficulty getting access to follow-on capital to build these capabilities internally. Once a dominant design emerges, late entrants are at a distinct disadvantage.[44] With neither Gartner's hype behind them nor the necessary capital, they have less chance of long-term success.

Complementary Asset Acquisition Opportunity

For a successful firm focused on continuing to develop complementary assets, a laggard firm that has "missed the boat" with respect to a disruptive technology presents an excellent target, since it has the assets but not the appropriate technology platform. Large pharmaceutical mergers, for example, are often meant not just to address inadequate pipelines, but also to acquire necessary sales and marketing capabilities. Enterprise software firm PeopleSoft's acquisition of smaller firm J.D. Edwards is another example. While PeopleSoft was successful in building and moving to a cross-platform web product, J.D. Edwards had great difficulty in migrating away from the

AS/400 environment, a 20-year-old proprietary IBM platform that many mid-sized users were tied to but that was not well suited to the disruptive force of the Internet. However, J.D. Edwards did have access to customers and customer applications coveted by PeopleSoft. A company spokesman expressed PeopleSoft's view:

> We [and J.D. Edwards] do not play in the midmarket now in the same places. We play in the services industry; they play in manufacturing, distribution and asset intensive industries. . . . With the acquisition of J.D. Edwards, we believe we can accelerate around the midmarket. This acquisition gives us a lot more scale in these international regions, with more feet on the street and more presence in those markets.[45]

The merger helped PeopleSoft to increase in both scale and coverage in the ERP market while leveraging J.D. Edwards's assets. For J.D. Edwards, the merger was a superior alternative to continuing to pursue a challenging technology "catch-up" strategy.

The Danger of Buying Backwards into the Life Cycle

The most prominent innovator technology firms are often those that enter a market early. While slow post–dominant design entrants are at a disadvantage, the life cycle model has shown that a fast-following imitator strategy can often allow firms to develop technology platforms that are superior to those of earlier innovators, since technology improves and costs decline over time. This feature of the industry experience curve represents a major hazard for incumbents, which can be tempted to acquire a prominent early non-winner to make up for their own late-moving position, despite the inferior technology platform of the early firm. Conventional wisdom holds that acquisition can accelerate a firm's entry and technology capability, doing in weeks or months and at reduced expense what might otherwise take years.[46] In emerging technology markets, however, the earliest firms may not have state-of-the-art technology, and acquisition of such firms will erase the benefits that normally accrue to a firm that waits for a standard enabler to emerge: The incumbent instead puts itself onto a high-cost platform. The incumbent is essentially buying backwards into the life cycle. Consider the case of Primedia, one of the world's largest magazine groups. After failing to get many of its magazines repurposed for the Internet, Primedia decided to buy About.com, a large player in the online media marketspace, identified at that time as a probable winner. Thomas Rogers, then CEO of Primedia, was quoted as saying, "We are convinced that this transaction saves years of development time and cost."[47] In reality, Primedia acquired a firm with poor last-generation technology that did not integrate into Primedia's existing operations.[48] About.com also commanded a high premium over its true value because of its prominence, despite a weak balance sheet and severe negative cash flow. The acquisition was disastrous for Primedia, which sold off About.com four years later at a substantial loss. Many of the individual magazines found the About.com platform to be unworkable and were forced to investigate other platform options. Primedia would have been much better off using one of the rapidly emerging publishing/content management–enabling technologies (either open source or Microsoft based) or acquiring a smaller firm with a sound platform but less in the way of complementary assets, such as the online magazine Salon.com. Similarly, Yahoo!'s acquisition of Internet broadcaster Broadcast.com and several of Microsoft's acquisitions were, in retrospect, unnecessary, expensive, and ill advised.

General Merger and Acquisition Risk

As the Introduction to this book emphasized, a merger and acquisition strategy is not without risks and often leads to eroding enterprise value. Mergers and acquisitions of large firms are most successful if consolidation (resource and activity sharing) occurs.[49] And consolidation involves large risks and challenges in integrating suppliers, customers, personnel, and information systems. More importantly, business processes and cultures may not mesh, leading to a decline in performance in the acquired unit. Often, the cost savings and improved performance expected to result from consolidation do not occur.

Differences between large and small firms in cultures and business processes can be extreme. The contrast between startups and incumbents in both company and employee profiles was highlighted in Chapter 1. This creates significant risk that, post-acquisition, the leadership of the startup will scatter. Loss of independence, differences in corporate culture, and naïve expectations about post-acquisition reality are problems for startup leaders.[50] Additionally, factors such as employee burnout, a loss of motivation after receiving the windfall from harvesting a venture, resentment among the acquirer company's employees over the payout received by the acquired firm's employees, loss of guidance from outside venture capital investors, and distractions resulting from the transaction can all quickly kill the momentum of the acquired startup. Thus, the leverageability of the technology and ecosystem assets of the startup should be a key variable in selecting startups as acquisition targets.

ADAM FEIN ON

INDUSTRY SHAKEOUTS AND LIFE CYCLE LESSONS FROM ONLINE EXCHANGES

Adam J. Fein, Ph.D., is the founder and president of Pembroke Consulting, Inc., a firm that helps senior executives of wholesale distribution, manufacturing, and B2B technology companies build and sustain market leadership. He is a Senior Fellow at the Wharton School of Business's Mack Center for Technological Innovation and was named to *Supply & Demand Chain Executive* magazine's list of "Top Industry Analysts to Know," based on his in-depth work in the wholesale industry. He has published several books for the National Association of Wholesaler-Distributors and numerous articles about the expansion and consolidation of competition.

Adam believes that, in emerging industries, visibility of the innovating concept is a key factor that attracts early imitating firms. This has become a more prominent variable in the digital age:

> The visibility of innovation is now a primary driver of the speed of new entry. New concepts that are in the public domain or based on a well-known breakthrough will immediately attract a lot of opportunistic entry and rush of new startups. The history of the early tire industry [see Exhibit 7-3] illustrates this community effect because there was a critical mass of people who were aware of what was going on and how to take advantage of it. The Internet magnifies visibility, so the speed of entry following innovation has increased. Innovation has historically

clustered geographically or in communities, but the B2B marketplace explosion demonstrated how the whole process has accelerated.

Adam notes that since business models based on emerging technologies are often unclear, the period of dramatic expansion in the number of firms preceding a shake-out is marked by experimentation, optimism, and opportunism.

Many startups in the B2B space were experiments, since no one knew what the ultimate model for the online marketplace would be. This period of experimentation is a natural by-product of innovation.

In an article in the *California Management Review,* Adam says:

During the boom period, an unsustainable glut of competitors is attracted by forecasts of high growth and promises of exceptional returns. In the case of B2B Internet exchanges, there were clearly more firms than the market could support. The fuel was free-flowing capital that was less interested in creating long-run profitability than in creating a compelling story so that venture capitalists and owners could cash out.[51]

As Adam points out,

Beyond venture capital firms, there are many others with a vested interest in certain types of technology being adopted, who hype certain types of change. This seems to be occurring in the RFID market, for example. Wal-Mart's interest in RFID is the event that is being used to stoke interest in the category. Potential suppliers to the industry are hyping innovation and trying to convince everyone else to either invest or buy.

Adam's view is that early competitive crowding is driven by new entrants. Since enabling firms lower barriers, in most cases it is less risky for incumbents to wait until they can better understand which models are likely to win out. The maturing market can often create opportunity for incumbents, as the competitive field thins during a shakeout:

In today's environment, there are many more enablers with a vested interest in sharing innovation. They lower the barrier to imitation considerably. Some dot-com consulting firms, for example, took solutions developed for one company and resold them to as many others as possible. The widespread use of these so-called e-consultants ensured that knowledge diffused rapidly to any company that was willing to pay.

For instance, incumbents did not really have to react quickly to the alleged threat of B2B exchanges because the Internet did not change the basic structure, functioning, and purpose of many markets. In these industries, incumbents have built-in advantages with their trusted brand names, customer relationships, systems that are readily convertible to the Internet, and financial depth.

In my opinion, there are very few first-mover winner-take-all markets, so it is prudent to use discretion. This is different for VC-funded firms, of course. Many startups are "built to flip," changing the definition of a successful startup and making early momentum much more meaningful.

To some extent, shakeouts are not necessarily bad because they are the result of innovation. In the early stages of market evolution, product or service variations are essentially experiments for what will actually be used sometime in the future. Assuming that the technology has not become obsolete, many startups end up selling their entire companies for a fraction of the total capital originally required to build and create their technology. The incumbents have the opportunity to generate actual economic profits and drive adoption.

Finally, Adam cautions that despite the recognizable pattern of boom and bust innovation, the biggest issue for most firms is discerning where the industry is in its life cycle:

There is usually sharp disagreement about where you are in the life cycle. As John Maynard Keynes once said, "The markets can remain irrational longer than you can remain solvent."

Implications of Change for Small Incumbents

Although the concept of category disruption tends to focus on large, scale-driven businesses, some disruptive technologies also can have a permanent negative effect on the attractiveness of an industry, from a smaller, "operating" firm perspective. In some cases, disruptive technology favors scale. Capital-intensive manufacturing technology changes or retail and supply chain systems that lower cost for large chains, for example, can create an imbalance of competitive capabilities that favors large-scale operations. Additionally, some technologies disintermediate (remove middlemen) or reconfigure the value chain in a way that eliminates the need and opportunity for certain small incumbents. The travel booking industry, for example, has come under severe pressure from the Internet, which allows direct bookings and easier price comparisons. Even while online bookings accounted for less than 20 percent of total travel sales (this number continues to grow rapidly), the channel created a substitute and enabled airlines to cut commissions—the key traditional source of revenue for travel agents. In addressing the 35 percent decline in the number of travel agencies, the Congressional National Commission to Ensure Consumer Information and Choice in the Airline Industry found that consumers "benefited greatly" from changes in the travel distribution system, particularly the Internet, even though travel agents were "adversely affected."[52] When a disruptive change has scale or value chain implications, smaller incumbents need a revised business model, a shift in focus to new differentiators, or an exit strategy.

Other disruptive changes may actually enable new, smaller firms to compete if they remove the advantages of scale or if the toolmaker provides the scale for the industry. An example of an innovation that removed the advantages of scale is new steel production technology that allows mini-mills to be much closer to end-users. According to a Paine Weber analyst, "The costs of building conventional blast furnace/oxygen furnace steel works shielded the steel giants from new rivals for decades. Now, with low-cost mini-mill technologies, it has become easier for new firms to jump into the (market), and to do so profitably."[53]

Another example is the RenderWare software suite for the video game development industry. The platform provides a set of open and extensible tools, allowing game developers to focus on content and game play. They don't need to "re-invent the wheel" by creating technology and engines for each and every platform and game, nor are they required to invest heavily in proprietary technology. This has meant that smaller creative studios have access to the necessary technology and can effectively compete in the gaming market (as producers, not as distributors). The gaming studio with the most to lose from a level playing field is Electronic Arts (EA), the industry leader. EA's recent acquisition of RenderWare's parent company may be an attempt to hedge against the impact of enabling technology. Even the travel agency industry—a potential victim of the most recent disruptive shift brought about by Internet-based travel booking technology—benefited from an earlier innovation. American Airlines' Sabre and United's competing Apollo reservation system were introduced as booking tools for the industry in the mid-70s, empowering independent travel agents as information intermediaries.

Some enablers provide the scale for the entire industry, removing scale as a firm-specific source of advantage. Internet providers PSI and UUNET (now part of MCI), for example, emerged as wholesalers rather than vertically integrated retail ISPs, allowing thousands of smaller ISPs to launch. In addition to providing the Internet backbone, point of presence locations, and hardware, they eventually added e-mail, domain name registration, and technical support, so that ISPs could launch without the expense of building any of their own infrastructure. UUNET's costs were lower because of its massive scale, and smaller firms were able to compete on an even playing field for this portion of ISP service by dealing directly with UUNET or through an aggregator. Commenting on UUNET's program, an executive from one small provider said,

> We didn't have the time or resources to build our own Internet operations. We talked with other ISPs about obtaining a service that would allow us to resell their access, but it was very expensive. The ISP Program offered us a cost-effective plan that made our decision a lot easier. We are very excited about the new program and about working directly with these technology vendors.[54]

On-demand computing may eventually play this role across a variety of applications, turning IT services into a "utility" and removing many of the scale barriers to deploying enterprise software that currently favor larger customers. According to the CTO of technology consulting firm CAP Gemini, "In ten years, of the 10,000 largest companies in the U.S., only about 200 will be big enough to be their own utility, and only about 100 of those will choose to do it themselves. The driving economics . . . will force the rest into a utility provisioning strategy."[55]

The removal of scale has as many implications for large incumbents as it does for small ones, as the mini-mill steel production example showed. While smaller producers benefited, "big steel" was clearly the market share loser in the transition. The rise of mini-mill technology kicked off what was described as "a 20-year battle between the giant integrated mills such as U.S. Steel and their mini-mill tormentors."[56] Removing scale as a valuable source of competitive advantage leaves many companies in a difficult competitive situation, since an emphasis on scale causes large operations to carry massive overhead. They also lack the flexibility of small firms.

Finding a Niche

For pure technology-providing firms, the dominant design, toolmaking, and shakeout scenarios paint a bleak picture. Any number of small opportunities exist, however, for firms to exploit niches and vertical markets. As will be shown in Part 3 of the book, a firm with a particular advantage or expertise in a vertical market may be able to use a **focus strategy** to design technology solutions specialized enough to avoid the competitive run-up and shakeout, particularly if the market offers only limited attractiveness. A printer technology firm, for example, could specialize in printing systems specifically for kiosks and rely on vertical knowledge and flexibility to compete effectively in this well-defined portion of the market.[57]

This is a self-limiting strategy, however, as too much success and market demand will attract competition. Toolmakers with good product architecture can realign their horizontal offerings vertically, as IBM has done with its WebSphere products,[58] and both investors and incumbents will line up to attack a visibly attractive segment. A company called Changing World Technologies has developed the 21st-century version of the philosopher's stone (the name alchemists used to describe the elusive substance that would transmute base metals into gold). Its philosopher's stone is thermal depolymerization (TDP), which promises to "produce high-quality oil from almost any carbon-based waste product. This includes discarded computers, infectious medical waste, mixed plastics, sewage, slaughterhouse refuse, tires and even chemical waste containing benzene, PCBs and other carcinogens."[59] Basically, Changing World Technologies claims that it can efficiently turn garbage into energy. If this technology proves to have a limited but economically feasible application (such as only for slaughterhouse waste or tire piles), it will undoubtedly survive nicely. If the technology has a broad-based application, however, they can expect large-scale competition and patent-skirting variants that challenge for dominant design.

Another problem with this narrow, niche-specific approach is that it runs counter to the goal of venture capitalists—to hit "home runs." Often, the right approach for the smaller firm is to remain low profile and secretive, so as not to attract the attention of larger firms or new entrants.[60] But this is exactly the opposite of what the investors and board members of hype-seeking, VC-funded firms want. As a result, a niche strategy often becomes a fallback position for firms that have lost the mainstream life cycle battle but still have the resources left to survive independently. At this point, upside and additional capital are limited by cash flow constraints, forcing the firm into an operational mode restricted to incremental changes and leaving it vulnerable to either market shifts or the next wave of disruptive change.

Pure Research

Another option that a technology-driven firm can consider is to remain a pure innovator—in essence, a research and design house. Universities tend to excel in pure research, but don't necessarily excel in technology transfer, technology application, or a continuous stream of innovation. Since focusing on research for profit means that research eventually needs to be applied, a pure research firm is most viable and valuable in partnership with large incumbent firms. Many firms simply sign on with partners on a research and development for hire basis. This is a low-risk but highly limiting strategy, however, since revenue streams disappear when the contract ends, allowing the partner to reap the long-term benefits of the IP. Rather than operating on a research for hire basis, a firm can gain greater leverage over technology development by retaining some intellectual property (IP) rights, which can be used to capture upside.

Bell Labs adopted this approach successfully for some time, contributing technology to more than two dozen ventures, several of which experienced liquidity events.[61] A British firm called Central Research Laboratories (CRL) has partnered with industry consortia and individual firms to turn pure "basic research" into applied research, since many firms can no longer afford basic research on their own. In the case of its agreement with Federal-Mogul (a $6 billion global manufacturer and distributor of vehicular components for automobiles), for example, the plan was to jointly try to develop CRL's electrodeless lighting (EDL) technology. Federal-Mogul funded further development of this filamentless technology to generate products to replace conventional lighting systems on the rear of automobiles, in exchange for an exclusive option to license the technology. A variety of drug discovery firms use this model, as do some gaming software firms. Many chip designers also focus on design—using a **fabless** (no fabrication done in-house) model and working with one set of manufacturers on products and another set to actually produce chips.

Valuable and leverageable IP is, of couse, a necessity in pursuing this path. Substantial funding is also necessary, as the time to market can be quite long, the innovation process is unpredictable, and significant resources are required to defend IP. Millennium Pharmaceuticals, for example,[62] raised $2 billion from partners in order to execute this strategy. Both Bell Labs and CRL have been hampered by the financial difficulties of their parent companies.

Entering the Era of Incremental Change

Between cycles of discontinuity are periods of incremental change. Since dominant design triggers hyper-growth in many cases, the **era of incremental change** is not necessarily one of low growth, but merely one with a more predictable basis for competition. The factors required to succeed in the era of incremental change favor incumbents and innovative firms that are—or are willing to become—mature firms. A mature firm emphasizes manufacturing, sales, and other core competencies that form the base of a firm's complementary assets, and they put a premium on efficiency.[63] Organizational factors also become more important as process, organizational learning, and more formalized roles drive efficiencies and the exploitation of incremental innovation.

Whereas disruptive change requires throwing out the rulebook and creating new value chains, incremental change involves listening to customers, making profitable improvements, and maximizing value.[64] Incumbents' tendency to adhere to their "winning" formula of incremental change is why many as far back as Schumpeter have said that incumbents are not capable of true innovation—at least not without extraordinary effort. A survey in *CIO Insight* magazine found that addressing innovation is much less of a driver of changing business processes than is cost reduction, productivity improvement, or other efficiency goals.[65] Continuous process improvement for the incumbent is typically incremental. The ability to continue to improve incrementally makes incumbents formidable competitors on well-defined battlefields, capable of creating, profiting from, and dominating product categories. Earlier in this book, the resource-based view of competitive strategy was introduced, with its underlying assumption that firms are heterogeneously endowed in their capabilities. Know-how, reputation, assets, and core competencies clearly position some firms over others.[66] As Teece pointed out, "Winners in the global marketplace have been firms that can develop timely responsiveness and rapid and flexible product innovation, coupled with the management capability to effectively coordinate and redeploy internal and external competencies."[67] These **dynamic capabilities** allow firms to incrementally innovate in a way that leverages advantages they have acquired in an industry.

In the area of memory chips and microprocessors, for example, innovating challenger firms really don't have the option of in-house production, given the high level of manufacturing expertise needed to layer silicon correctly. They simply can't compete with the industry's dominant manufacturing firms in this area. Xilinx points out that fabless companies have the benefit of being able to focus solely on their core value-add; they can access the most advanced semiconductor process technologies without being burdened by the huge capital costs associated with building and running a chip factory (building costs alone can now be upwards of $2 billion).[68] Additionally, innovation has been primarily incremental—in its logic devices, Xilinx went from 150 microns of spacing between circuits in 2001, to 130 in 2002, to 90 in 2003—but not truly disruptive. Xilinx and newer firms typically now follow a fabless route, outsourcing manufacturing rather than fabricating in-house. They cannot compete with Intel, Motorola, IBM, and other mature firms, which continue to innovate in inexpensive, high-quality manufacturing, and can only hope to partner with them. Until a disruptive change occurs, these larger firms will benefit from internal incremental process improvements and product development, as well as growth-driving improvements introduced by other innovators, such as Xilinx.

The combination of access to innovation and incremental improvement capabilities is a powerful one. Sony's personal stereo, the Walkman, is an example of a "radical" innovation followed by a long period of incremental model variation (20 new models a year) based on features, packaging, and appearance.[69] These incremental changes emphasized Sony's consumer insight, manufacturing prowess, and ability to put products into the consumer electronics channel.

Predicting a Jump in S Curves

The long-term view of industry evolution is represented by overlapping technology S curves (Exhibit 7-4). While one technology delivers on its promise, incremental improvement continues, and successful firms profit, multiple candidates for the next big thing are plotting the overthrow of the status quo. The trajectories of these other new technologies are shown as the emerging candidate curves in Exhibit 7-5. Many of these new technologies never take hold, either because the supporting infrastructure, market demand, and complementary industries don't develop or because the technology itself fails to deliver on its promise.

Nuclear energy presents an excellent example. Nuclear fission was once expected to be one of the greatest disruptive technologies of our time. Light water uranium-based fission reactors originally promised to offer a clean and unlimited source of electricity,

EXHIBIT 7-4 ■ Industry Evolution from One Technology to the Next

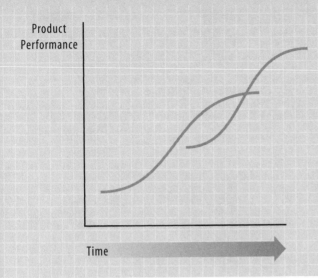

EXHIBIT 7-5 ■ Emerging Candidates for a Disruptive S Curve

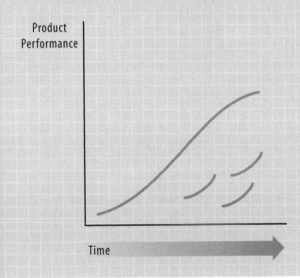

expected to be "too cheap to meter." From the late 1960s to the early 1970s, the cost data and growth rates for nuclear power suggested a disruptive change that would end U.S. dependency on coal. Between 1970 and 1980, coal-generated power dropped from roughly 55 percent of electricity production to 45 percent, while nuclear power rose from 2 percent to 12 percent. From all early indications, the coal industry and power plant construction and management industry were facing major discontinuity,

Too cheap to meter?

Photodisc/Getty Images

and both would need to retool for uranium or face extinction. Except in a few countries, that isn't at all what occurred. In the United States, nuclear power generation topped out at roughly 20 percent of total energy capacity,[70] and almost half of that capacity was brought on line in order to fulfill existing contracts established in the early 1970s. No nuclear plants have been ordered in the United States since 1978, and more than 100 reactors have been canceled, including all of those ordered after 1973.[71] Construction costs, operating costs, regulatory compliance, waste disposal, security concerns, and public opinion have all created a far different scenario than that envisioned at the start of the nuclear age, while continued incremental change in conventional plants raised the bar further. A number of other potential new technologies—including co-generation, fuel cells, and photovoltaic nanotechnology—may turn out to represent disruptive S curves for power generation, but light water fission-based technology has not proven to be one of them.

In the much different world of computer operating systems, OS/2 is an example of a potentially disruptive technology that didn't climb the S curve, exhibiting its own meltdown of sorts. In the 80s, IBM's OS/2 was expected to be the disruptive successor to DOS and the "future" of computing. IBM ran into a series of problems, however, as users found early versions of the software slow and clunky. Venture capitalist Stuart Alsop went so far as to say in 1991 that "every single decision [IBM has] made about operating systems so far has been wrong."[72] As a result, Microsoft was able to press its installed base leverage and position the Windows rather than the IBM operating system as the dominant technology. This cycle may repeat itself. Linux, although much touted as an open, secure, and stable replacement for Windows, suffers from disputes over ownership and evidence that it may not offer a lower total cost of ownership.

Several analysts (such as the Meta Group), pointing to Linux's rapid growth in market share, predict that open source Linux will capture more than 50 percent of the market and change the economics of software. Others (such as IDC) believe that rather than disrupting the software industry, Linux may merely be replacing UNIX, Microsoft's other major challenger. They cite Microsoft's continued dominance in market share and a drop-off in UNIX's sales that has matched Linux's rise.

Most of the popular literature focuses on firms' executive-level myopia regarding disruptive change and emphasizes the potential risks of ignoring new technologies that upset the markets' natural order. But the cases cited here indicate that there are actually two types of potential errors that incumbents may make: overreaction and overconfidence.

Overreaction (Error of Commission)

Continuously plotting the potential trajectories from the high-growth portions of candidates' S curves, as shown in Exhibit 7-6, would create an alarmist attitude toward virtually every new technology that emerged. The hype cycle reinforces this alarmist posture. In the OS/2 case, Lotus, Borland, Ashton-Tate, and other software makers that committed heavily to OS/2 were not against change, but merely "rode the wrong horse." Anticipating a high-growth trajectory and disruption, they all placed large bets on OS/2, with disastrous consequences. As mentioned in Chapter 3, former Intel CEO Andy Grove, using an engineer's vocabulary, described the ambiguity underlying the potential disruptors as a signal versus noise issue. He cited the use of x-rays to produce semiconductors as an example of a case where Intel was unable to determine whether a new technology was going to create wholesale changes in the industry.[73] Overcommitment to x-ray–based production innovation would have damaged Intel severely.

EXHIBIT 7-6 ■ Overreaction and Overconfidence Errors

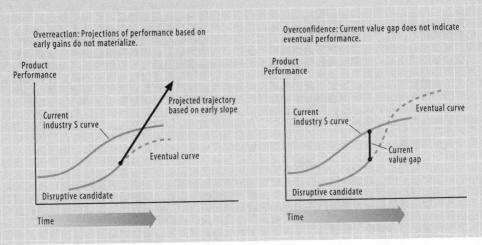

Overreaction: Projections of performance based on early gains do not materialize.

Overconfidence: Current value gap does not indicate eventual performance.

Product Performance

Projected trajectory based on early slope

Current industry S curve

Eventual curve

Disruptive candidate

Time

Product Performance

Current industry S curve

Eventual curve

Current value gap

Disruptive candidate

Time

Overconfidence (Error of Omission)

Looking solely at the performance gap that occurs upon the early entry of a new technology (also shown in Exhibit 7-6) would lead executives to dismiss every new non-incremental innovation as a poorly performing alternative. IBM was unquestionably unimpressed with the early version of Microsoft Windows. Grove refers to this dismissal of early disruptive innovation as the **trap of the first version** and admits having himself called Apple's Macintosh "a ridiculous toy."[74] Research has indicated that disruptive technology does not necessarily meet a short-term recognized need of the current market,[75] nor does it necessarily represent the best technology.[76] VHS certainly did not do either, and the battle over rewriteable DVDs doesn't seem to hinge on performance.

Grove's recommendation is to keep a "paranoid eye" on potential disruptors and to watch for changes in competition, complementors, and market behavior.[77] As discussed earlier, firms can also apply "uncertainty-based" strategies in order to identify and, in some cases, help shape the next significant technology change. Beyond that, accepting rather than fighting progress is a feasible choice, but it often entails making very difficult decisions counter to the wishes of current customers, employees, and shareholders.

The S Curve Jump

Eventually, a disruptive technology from among the candidates does take hold, creating magnitudinal rather than steady changes in the nature of the category. This gives rise to secondary inflection points, as apparently mature and stable sectors jump from one flattening S curve to the next high-growth one. As the current S curve flattens, the successor technology takes hold. The new paradigm represented by the successor technology can potentially change the entire go-to-market strategy, economics, competencies, complementary assets, and/or internal organization necessary for success. Over time, a market may jump S curves several times, as shown in Exhibit 7-7. In each instance, current incumbents—if they are neither diligent nor willing to greet the future—will become low-tech competitors and risk obsolescence. As the industry moves to a new order, each inflection point signals the beginning of new markets and a new market structure for a product category, as well as a decline in competitiveness (preceding a shakeout) for companies that continue to cling to the old technology. In the "new world" of Windows and web-based computing, any software vendor that tried to stick with client/server or DOS-based applications would have experienced this decline and become obsolete. Similarly, in the future, everything from coal-burning power plants to unnetworked game consoles and basic circuit-based telephony (POTS) will eventually be challenged. The best incumbents in all of these industries will be neither taken by surprise nor **sunsetted** by shifts in dominant design when they occur.

Ambidextrous Organizations

The ideal incumbents are **ambidextrous organizations**; that is, they are capable of generating and mainstreaming radical innovation—and, thus, of capturing markets for themselves—while still maintaining the organizational architecture necessary to build,

EXHIBIT 7-7 ■ Jumping S Curves

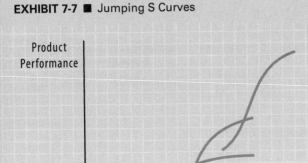

protect, and capitalize on the complementary assets that drive incremental success. Unlike early vertical startup entrants, incumbents can use well-established infrastructure to dominate markets. While they are not immune to mistakes, these firms have the high level of organizational resilience necessary to adapt to changing environments.[78] Apple developed the Macintosh, for example, by ignoring the limitations and assumptions built into the LISA platform. Many pharmaceutical companies partner in order to acquire drugs to keep their pipeline full when necessary,[79] but also work on internal development that will make their own products obsolete before others do so for them. IBM provides manufacturing and engineering assistance to fabless semiconductor companies, while also supporting internal R&D. Intel, while keeping manufacturing proprietary, also thinks in a "sequential platform" context—it is always planning the next generation of processors, while improving and marketing current ones.[80] Sony has been able on occasion to make internally generated innovation the winning technology. It maintains a group called CSL (Computer Science Lab), whose researchers fiercely guard their right to pursue pure science without pressure to work on projects with obvious practical implications. So far, more than half the research from CSL has eventually ended up in Sony's research and development arm, where engineers turn it into something that can be packaged and sold.[81]

Many organizations that could be considered ambidextrous are still constrained by a vertical proprietary mindset, such as the one behind Sony's historical innovation pattern. The ultimate endpoint in ambidextrous capability is the ability to manage existing businesses, foster breakthrough innovation, and also embrace open horizontal innovation when appropriate to avoid losing out in the face of competition from an industry enabler. Firms such as Nokia and Toyota have developed platforms that appear to be taking them in this direction.

Contradiction and tension are inherent in deriving both discontinuous and incremental innovation simultaneously, and those companies that can manage this duality outperform those that cannot.[82] Ambidextrous success is a senior management challenge,[83] and the companies succeeding at it share the common characteristics of strong leadership and a culture that supports and drives change when necessary. In the cases of Apple and IBM, periods when leadership was lacking generally coincided with periods of low growth and only incremental innovation. A multitude of studies have indicated that many less successful companies stay in their comfort zones, investing in the past rather than the future[84] and riding the old S curve into obscurity.

CHAPTER SUMMARY

This chapter focused on the impact on incumbents of the industry evolution that occurs as discontinuous innovation gives way to the era of dominant design. Innovative technology is usually available to incumbents through internal research, external acquisition, or the use of horizontally enabling technology. Incumbents also typically have the opportunity to reinvent themselves around an industry's new S curve, but some don't avail themselves of this opportunity because they find it too difficult to abandon hard-won core competencies and revenue streams. The uncertainty surrounding disruptive technology gives incumbents an excuse not to act, but they would be better advised to influence a coming disruptive change in a manner that favors their asset base—or at least invest in gaining knowledge that will assist them in recognizing when the time is right to adapt and, if necessary, retool. Perhaps most important for incumbents is to look out for the emergence of potentially dominant proprietary designs, either developed by competitors or available internally. The former represent a significant business threat, and the latter a chance for a firm to significantly enhance its competitive position.

The progression of a disruptive technology from ferment era candidate to dominant design leads to a period of industry shakeout and consolidation. As process innovation takes the spotlight from more radical technology innovation, incumbents that avoid self-inflicted obsolescence will find the market re-emphasizing execution, cost structure, and the core competencies that typically accrue to larger firms. Just as significantly, opportunities will emerge to acquire additional technology capabilities from capital-challenged innovators and to acquire complementary assets from established firms that have failed to make the transition from one technology platform to the next.

The principal difficulty for incumbents is determining which innovations have the potential to "jump" past the current technology and thus deserve serious attention and a committed response. Even a firm willing and able to change can easily overreact to a dead-end technology or a manageable technology threat or underreact to a technology that appears to lack potential but, in fact, becomes a disruptive force in the incumbent's industry. Several examples demonstrated that making a wrong bet can have long-term repercussions. Firms need to be ever vigilant on both fronts.

The ideal situation is for a firm to become both ambidextrous and a proponent of open innovation. The ambidextrous firm has the skills and infrastructure that the most successful firms use to compete and dominate in maturing categories, can adapt quickly to market changes, and still fosters enough innovation to drive proprietary dominant design. Ambidextrous firms are well positioned in the long term, as they can co-opt the technology of innovators when needed, recognize when change or acquisition is required, and also drive innovation and designs that cannot be readily co-opted by others. In addition, by embracing an open innovation mindset, they can fully leverage internal innovation when appropriate.

Overall, through an analysis of the life cycle and market evolution, this part of the book has identified opportunities and threats for both challengers and incumbents attempting to introduce and diffuse paradigm-changing technology that will have a substantial impact on customers and competitors. The introduction of disruptive technology can break down the existing competitive criteria and create an opportunity to change the industry's status quo. As a technology moves through the cycle of innovation, imitation, enablers, and incumbent entry, windows of opportunity open and close for various firms.

One of the underlying lessons of the chapters in Part 2 is the importance of developing barriers as a method of protecting what may otherwise be short-lived leads, both for firms that supply technology and for firms that anticipate using technology for a competitive edge. Part 3 will cover the important topic of competitive advantage and effective methods of locking in early promising results to create a more permanent advantage.

part 3

COMPETITIVE
ADVANTAGE

Part 1 highlighted a variety of means for placing technology and innovation in both a contextual and a systemic framework, in order to understand their value as part of a business ecosystem. Methods were developed for positioning new technologies in relation to an overall system of value creation, a firm's resource base, alternatives in the marketplace, necessary partnerships, complementary assets, and overall product delivery, since all of these determine strategic options for firms with a potential stake in an innovation.

Part 2 examined concepts relating to technology evolution and industry life cycles, as well as the impact of timing on innovation and strategic technology choice. An innovation's value changes as the industry and markets it serves evolve. Factoring in likely industry and market behavior and outcomes over time gives a firm much greater insight into how to approach innovation and the introduction of new technology in an industry than does a simple industry snapshot.

While the perspectives differed, both Part 1 and Part 2 emphasized competitive behavior and choice as key variables in the fate of both firms and industries. As Bruce Henderson, founder of consulting firm BCG, said, "All strategy depends on competition." It follows that finding ways to keep competition at bay (or, in the case of new entrants, overcoming such obstacles) should be at the core of every firm's strategy. Part 3 looks at how technology helps shape the array of strategies that insulate a firm from competition, thereby elevating performance and promising long-term success. It also examines how new entrants can recognize and attempt to overcome these barriers when they are present.

Chapter 8 presents an overview of key concepts relating to competitive advantage, including broad discussions of what is meant by the term, how to measure it, and ways to acquire it. Although less closely tied to technology than the other chapters, Chapter 8 establishes a foundation for developing more detailed methods of assessing the role of information technology and general innovation in achieving competitive advantage. Chapter 9 looks at traditional sources of competitive advantage and how technology supports and drives them. Finally, Chapter 10 focuses on competitive barriers that are specific to technology markets.

Paths to Competitive Success

8

It is not from the benevolence of the butcher, the brewer, or the baker that we expect our dinner, but from their regard to their own interest.

—**Adam Smith**, *An Inquiry into the Nature and Causes of the Wealth of Nations*

"Talk to the Hand": Is Competition Inevitable?

To business executives, profits are a good thing. Profits translate into a multitude of benefits for a firm's stakeholders, including profit-sharing bonuses, higher stock prices, more capital for expansion, and spectacular holiday parties. *The Economist* magazine defines profits as the main reason firms exist.[1] Excess profit—profit beyond the minimum return justified by the capital invested, risks taken, and resources committed—is even better. It is particularly coveted, since the excess translates into more of the above-mentioned benefits for the firm. Executives are often compensated handsomely for their over-achieving ways, through stock options, bonuses, or other executive perks. And firms with better results have more flexibility in charting a future path.

Economists, on the other hand, believe that excess profits generally signal a failure of competition in markets. Adam Smith, in his book *Wealth of Nations*, spoke of an **invisible hand**, representing a set of market forces that ensures that the optimal economic outcome results when entities act rationally. In simple economic terms, market demand can be thought of as a series of individual consumer decisions of the form "at price X, a consumer A will be willing to buy item Y." All of these individual decisions together form a **demand curve** which shows the relationship between the quantity demanded of a product and its price, holding everything else constant. This demand curve predicts total market demand at each price point. Suppliers react to consumer demand, and as long as they see an opportunity to make an adequate risk-adjusted return on capital, they will continue to add supply to the market (see Exhibit 8-1). The expanding supply will result in lower prices and draw more buyers in, until a point is reached at which it is no longer attractive to expand supply. The end result is the most product at the lowest possible price for consumers. As Todd Buchholz puts it, in describing Smith's views of the invisible hand, "Prices and profits signal to entrepreneurs what to produce and what prices to charge. High prices and high profits sound alarms in the ears of entrepreneurs, screaming at them to start producing a certain good."[2]

EXHIBIT 8-1 ■ Profits Entice Competitive Entry

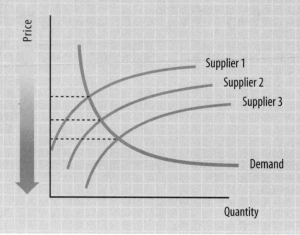

One of the more intensely competitive industrial battles—albeit in the cartoon world rather than the real world—was the bitter rivalry between Spaceley Sprockets and Cogswell Cogs on the classic television show *The Jetsons*. These two fictional industrial titans were broad-line manufacturers, intent on winning the market of the future at all costs. Every Spaceley innovation was quickly met with a response from Cogswell, and vice versa, eliminating the opportunity for an uncontested market. As Cogswell said, "There's only one thing worse than war and that is business, and Spaceley has declared business on us."[3] It was clear that if Spaceley didn't supply the market with all it needed and wanted, then Cogswell would recognize the opportunity and take up the slack. Similarly, if Spaceley Sprockets didn't continue to drive down costs and make sprockets cheaper, then Cogswell Cogs or another competitor would. In this view of the world, it is not possible to make excess profits for any significant period of time—their mere existence will attract competition, and the competition will drive out the excess profits. This principle extends to innovation as well as overall supply. In the world of Adam Smith, market forces continually work toward better and/or cheaper products, and the better/cheaper products always win. As the prisoners' dilemma illustrated (see Chapter 4), however, the invisible hand doesn't always work. Breakdowns in frictionless economics provide the opportunity for some firms to do better than others in terms of profit performance or do worse in terms of product performance. Such breakdowns occur when a firm is able to create and protect a capability that can't be easily duplicated by others or to establish barriers that others have difficulty overcoming.

The Quest for Competitive Advantage

Achieving a protectable and heterogeneous position involves creating a **competitive advantage**—a sustainable, unique capability or barrier that allows the firm to outperform other firms or insulate itself from competition. In a well-managed company, protection from competition, in most cases, will lead to improved financial perform-ance. By definition, therefore, the pursuit of competitive advantage should be the goal of every firm and a driving force behind competitive strategy.

Does this mean that every planner's obsession should be how to deliver excess profits? Not necessarily. Does it mean that developing unique capabilities guarantees competi-tive advantage? Again, not necessarily. Since competitive advantage is defined in terms of outperforming the competition, the first step in the pursuit of competitive advan-tage should be to define **outperformance**. Excess profits are only one of many possi-ble measures. After outperformance has been defined and metrics have been selected, the second step is to determine which unique capabilities and barriers are most likely to lead to its achievement. Aligning goals with capabilities is a logical exercise and key to crafting a firm-specific strategy.[4] Just as a marathon runner focuses on endurance over speed, a firm should focus on capabilities in line with its objectives. A unique capability that isn't relevant to the desired goals of the firm is of little value.

Outperforming

One of the biggest television success stories of 2000 was the show *Survivor*, which put 16 people together in a jungle and let the manufactured "tribe" vote one member off each week. When the field had been reduced to two people, those who had been voted off selected the final winner, who walked away with $1 million. Despite the implica-tions of the show's name and its location, *Survivor* was really about politics and alliances. Fellow contestants—not the elements—determined who stayed, who was voted off, and who ultimately won. Many contestants mistakenly believed that their physical survival skills or contributions to the tribe would make them the most valu-able player and, therefore, the show's winner. In fact, winning involved outperforming in the alliance-building and psychological arenas. This was made clear by the show's logo, which prominently displayed the tag line " Outwit, Outplay, Outlast." The even-tual winner of the first season of *Survivor* (there have been many sequels since) was a man named Richard Hatch, who focused specifically on these performance metrics. He has been widely quoted as pointing out that none of the other competitors really understood what the key success criteria were. As *Time* magazine reported, "Richard Hatch used group-management skills to build protective alliances, describing his plan to viewers with the glee of a dinner-theater Iago."[5]

As in the *Survivor* example, determining the metrics on which to "outperform" is a crit-ical decision for firms. There are numerous possibilities, including ROA, EVA, P/E ratio, PEG ratio, stock price, profit margin, market share, revenue, volume, and cus-tomer satisfaction. For the owner of a small private firm, outperforming may simply mean being able to take eight weeks of vacation while competitors take two, or giving back more to the community than other firms do, while still remaining competitive. For publicly traded companies, Wall Street analysts and fund managers will usually select those metrics that seem most important to the particular industry. CEOs, well aware of the measures used by the financial community and the impact of these met-rics on stock price, will shift their focus to them, thus creating a standardized set of tar-gets for the industry.

Even if the set of metrics becomes standardized, however, the competitive benchmarks do not, because of differences in the ways various firms define the industry/market. The use of multiple metrics can create ambiguity in evaluating firms' relative performance. Take, for example, the battle between television networks CBS and NBC. In television, ratings are a standardized measure of success, but many different types of ratings are used. While CBS claimed to be number one because it had the largest viewing audience, NBC claimed victory in the more profitable 18–49 prime-time demographic. In the *Wall Street Journal*, CBS's chairman, Les Moonves, was quoted as saying, "At the end of the day, I don't care what you're selling. It's about being profitable. Too many people just rely on 18 to 49."[6] In the same article, NBC chief Jeff Zucker argued, "We've invested our money in prime-time programming, and that's paid off to make us, by far, the most profitable network in prime time."[7] Both are claiming victory based on views of the market driven by different metrics.

Harvard Business School's Michael Porter pointed out that strategy is about being different: "It means deliberately choosing a different set of activities to deliver a unique mix of value."[8] This implies that there can be several winners in an industry, and that non-homogenized measures should be not just accepted but encouraged. One of Porter's primary examples is discount airline Southwest Airlines. Southwest takes a unique approach to the airline business: It encourages direct rather than agency-initiated bookings; flies a fleet of identical aircraft; emphasizes point-to-point, multiple-stop routes, rather than the common hub-and-spoke system; and offers few customer "frills," instead favoring faster turnaround time and cheaper airfares. Porter underscores Southwest's focus on delivering superior value for certain types of travelers on specific routes that take advantage of its point-to-point business design, rather than the traditional hub-based system used by many of the larger airlines.[9] Taking this argument a step further shows that metrics designed to create a one-size-fits-all view of the airline industry will not provide an accurate picture of Southwest's performance, nor will they show whether Southwest or American Airlines, for example, is the "better" performer. Traditional measures of performance in the airline industry, such as customer load factor and average revenue per seat mile, might be more important for American Airlines, while cost containment might be more critical for Southwest.

Exhibit 8-2 demonstrates that focusing on passenger load or revenue per available seat mile would raise a red flag about Southwest's performance relative to that of American and other carriers with similar results. As mentioned, however, Southwest is not emulating other carriers, instead focusing most of its efforts on low cost per seat mile, which makes the other metrics less critical. During the third quarter of 2004, Southwest's low-cost approach allowed it to earn a profit, while American ran significant deficits, despite its better performance on seat revenue.

Divergent target metrics should naturally lead to the development and support of different technological capabilities. For major carriers such as American, for which revenue per available seat mile is a crucial metric, investing in technology supporting this focus—such as complex pricing systems and loyalty schemes—has been a priority. For Southwest, the relatively low average seat price makes costs and commissions much more of an issue, so its early focus has been on investing in direct booking technology and ticketless travel.

EXHIBIT 8-2 ■ Metrics Comparison for American Airlines and Southwest
Airlines, Third Quarter, 2004

	American	Southwest
Passenger Load	77.9 percent	72.7 percent
Revenue per ASM	$.0862	$.085
Cost per ASM	$.0943	$.076

ASM = Available Seat Mile

SOURCE: Company 10Q's, third quarter 2004, via SEC/Edgar database.

Even with respect to a standard overall metric such as profitability, the implications of different strategies need to be taken into account. One model may contribute steady but unspectacular profits, while another might create superior profits in some years and deficits in others. The 2001–2003 travel recession and 2004–2005 oil price increases have proven that although Southwest's model may yield less profit in good times, it may ultimately be less variable, resulting in a more viable and predictable long-term trajectory for Southwest.

Spatially, Abell's three-dimensional model developed in Chapter 3 shows that each firm's individual market definition may be different, representing only a subset of the overall market space. Abell points out that differences in business definition can make comparisons irrelevant. He also points out, however, that the choice of "spaces" can create between firms important relative differences that should not be ignored, even if market definitions and approaches appear to differ.[10] Significantly, he asserts that the larger industry space should be used in considering whether a competitor's outperformance on a key characteristic (such as cost) is capable of creating the sort of competitive shift discussed in Part 1 of this book. Southwest's business initially looked so different from that of the major carriers that it would have been easy to dismiss Southwest as a competitor, as the larger carriers did for quite some time. Given the larger industry definition, however, Southwest's clear cost advantage should have been a major source of concern, shifting the metrics that really matter for all carriers. At this point, Southwest appears to be one of the most stable and successful major U.S. airlines, and its model may represent the future for all airlines.

Selecting Outperformance Metrics

As was just demonstrated, selecting appropriate metrics to drive outperformance is critical. In public firms, holistic goals usually take a backseat to more measurable financial performance that reflects shareholder interests. The financial goals can be either long term or short term, depending on which stakeholders are calling the shots. In a startup with a VC-controlled board, the measures are likely to be focused on a liquidity event or growth and market share, since a willingness to "swing for the fences" is an important element of an attractive VC investment.[11] For a small business, cash flow or customer loyalty may be the focus, since such businesses value stability and debt avoidance.

The interesting implication of the multifarious outperformance metrics is that more than one firm can "outperform," as long as their metrics are different. Among privately held companies particularly, one firm can outperform by claiming the largest market share while another does so by being the most profitable—and they can both declare victory. In publicly held companies, this is less often the case, since certain metrics (growth, cash flow, dividends, earnings, etc.) in each sector drive stock prices and competitors are benchmarked against one another, guaranteeing that they compete vigorously. These metrics are usually well understood and tied to executive compensation.

Even different public firms in the same industry, however, can be subject to different expectations with respect to metrics. This presents a challenge, particularly when two of the most often cited performance metrics—growth and profits—are in opposition. Even if it is assumed that valuation is driven by future discounted cash flow estimates (although some believe that it is not), firms may face a choice between current cash generation and future cash potential. An "old world firm" may see a firm one-tenth its size (in sales) sport a similar market valuation, based on expectations about its future earnings. The larger firm would likely see a dramatic drop in its valuation if it suddenly abandoned an emphasis on current cash flow to invest in a growth strategy, while the smaller firm would be similarly punished for forgoing growth for short-term profits.

Using a Balanced Scorecard

Once outperformance metrics have been set, a firm should "tool up" to succeed on the appropriate measures. For a company to succeed in outperforming others, its technology choices need to be aligned with its key initiatives and capabilities and these, in turn, need to be aligned with its strategy and overall vision. Just as a marathon runner needs the right shoes, diet, and time commitment to go along with her focus on endurance, a firm must match resources and action with vision. One tool increasingly used to create this alignment is known as a balanced scorecard. A **balanced scorecard** is essentially an explicit list of measures of the key variables for a particular business in achieving its strategy and vision. The broad areas typically covered include the following perspectives: finance, customer, internal business processes, and learning and growth.

For each of these areas, a set of objectives, measurement criteria, targets, and initiatives is established. The purpose is to create organization-wide visibility of the metrics that matter, provide a method of measuring the organization's efforts to improve these metrics, and identify gaps between strategic initiatives and the firm's measures, processes, and capabilities. A framework for a balanced scorecard is shown in Exhibit 8-3.

As Dr. David Norton, one of the creators of the balanced scorecard methodology, has said,

> The balanced scorecard retains traditional financial measures. But financial measures tell the story of past events, an adequate story for industrial age companies for which investments in long-term capabilities and customer relationships were not critical for success. These financial measures are inadequate, however, for guiding and evaluating the journey that information age companies must make to create future value through investment in customers, suppliers, employees, processes, technology, and innovation.[12]

EXHIBIT 8-3 ■ Balanced Scorecard Framework

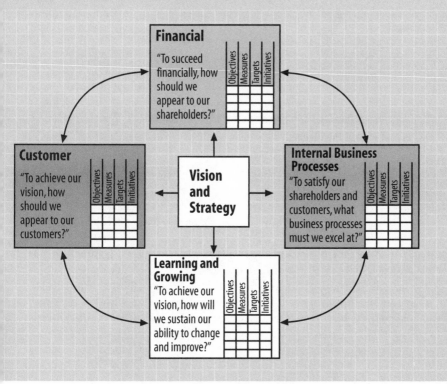

SOURCE: The Balanced Scorecard Institute, Rockville, MD 20852; http://www.balancedscorecard.org.

This approach brings clarity to the concept of outperforming and how it ties into unique capabilities. The scorecard method is designed specifically to reinforce a company's definition of what "winning" means for the firm. Once the definition has been set, the firm can proceed to assess whether it has the capabilities necessary to achieve these goals and address the gaps that need to be bridged. If a company's goal is to grow from $100 million to $1 billion in sales or to become a market share leader, it needs to invest in growth-related capabilities that will allow the firm to reach the desired growth trajectory. As Porter and others have pointed out, however, the key to positioning is sacrifice. Other measures may have to suffer in order for a firm to reach its goals in the chosen performance criteria.

Uniqueness

Once a firm has settled on the appropriate driving metrics for its business, the next step is to identify opportunities to create barriers that will prevent competitors from putting pressure on those metrics. For example, a firm wishing to achieve a competitive advantage that will allow it to gain both high market share and high margins needs to prevent competitors from undercutting it on price or perceived product value. One way for the firm to do so is to become a low-cost producer. This would allow it to undercut on price or spend a greater amount on marketing, while retaining higher profits. A firm in this position might focus, for example, on patentable or proprietary processes, unique formulations, or unique systems capabilities, which would lower its costs vis-à-vis competitors.

Another traditional method the firm might employ is **differentiation**. Rather than focus on cost, it might pursue unique capabilities that would allow it to charge a higher price or produce a product that was not easily imitated. The optimal situation, of course, would be to offer a better product at a lower cost. Consumer packaged goods companies have mastered this, in everything from breakfast cereal to detergent. These strategies are discussed in greater detail in Chapter 9.

Whatever strategy is chosen, the firm's unique capabilities need to be focused on achieving the desired outperformance metrics. A firm that has excelled at developing low-cost products, for example, might have trouble using differentiation to stake out a less price-driven position. Similarly, a company operating with patents that historically ensured a significant level of insulated differentiation may find it difficult to operate in an environment where patents are less relevant. Polaroid operated for many years with what was described as "a veritable fortress of patents" protecting its instant photography business.[13] As digital photography and one-hour developing emerged as substitutes for Polaroid's instant photography product set, however, those unique patented capabilities became progressively less relevant. As a result, Polaroid lost its advantage and was unable to participate in the move to digital photography in a way that ensured a competitive and profitable position.

Uniqueness can be derived from one of three sources: resources, capabilities, and external/environmental factors.

Resources

Brands, sources of supply, patents, proprietary processes, and location-based assets are all considered to be resources. Resources can be either tangible or intangible. A hotel operator who owns the best piece of beachfront real estate in Laguna Beach has a tangible resource that gives it an inherent resource advantage over the operator of a hotel built across the road from the beach. If the first hotel carries the Ritz Carlton brand name, the first hotel operator also has an intangible resource that would likely cause his hotel to be preferred, even if the second hotel had equivalent property. "Classical" views of competitive advantage tend to focus most heavily on resources in evaluating a firm's position. More recent perspectives emphasize the systemic way in which the resources are used as a critical part of establishing a unique advantage.

Capabilities

Organizational skills, distribution channels, and experience are examples of capabilities that can create uniqueness. In the automobile-manufacturing arena, for example, GM is attempting to reduce time-to-market for new cars by creating an organization and technology infrastructure that gets new designs into production faster. Thanks to sophisticated virtual-design methodologies and digital manufacturing design, an engineering team can now complete five products in the same amount of time formerly needed for one. The reduced cost means that GM can sell fewer cars and still make a profit on a product line.[14] According to Georgetown professor Robert Grant,

> *A capability is the capacity of a team or resource to perform some task or activity. While resources are the source of a firm's capabilities, capabilities are the main source of its competitive advantage. . . . Creating capabilities is not simply a matter of assembling a team of resources: capabilities involve the complex coordination of patterns between people, and between people and other resources.*[15]

This view—that a firm with resources and the ability to leverage those resources can create a unique and difficult-to-imitate set of capabilities—is known as a **resource-based view** of the firm. Organizations build on previous efforts, over time developing routines and processes to make things happen. These routines and processes are unique and can have a positive impact on the firm's competitiveness.[16]

Part 2 of the book pointed out that while capabilities can provide incumbents with powerful advantages, firms can become uncompetitive by hanging on too long to old routines and processes. The ability to change and adapt is in itself a capability that can separate winners from losers. As Tushman asserts,

> *The most successful firms maintain a workable equilibrium for several years (or decades), but are also able to initiate and carry out sharp widespread changes . . . when their environment shifts. Less successful firms, on the other hand, get stuck in a particular pattern. The leaders of these firms either do not see a need for re-orientation, or they are unable to carry through the necessary frame breaking changes.*[17]

The implication is that the ability to innovate is tied to a firm's organizational capabilities and culture as much as it is to the available resources.

External/Environmental Factors

Government support, favorable regulation, monopoly power, and customer profiles are all external/environmental sources of uniqueness. Airbus's ability to enter the airline market, for example, was greatly enhanced by its unique support—in the form of $13 billion in subsidies—from European governments. The U.S. government has asserted that subsidies to Airbus enabled the European aircraft consortium to offer airplanes at artificially low prices and to provide below-market financial incentives to purchasers.[18] Similarly, government-protected domestic franchises create unique capabilities for some wireless carriers, both in dominating home markets and in creating cash flow that can be used to compete internationally.

What all three of these sources—resources, capabilities, and environmental factors—have in common is that they create an imbalance among the competition, which gives the firm possessing the uniqueness the advantage necessary to outperform the others. Interestingly, all three tend to be more likely to accrue to larger companies, which have a history, resource base, and government lobbyists in place.

Deriving Uniqueness from Technology and Innovation

Methods for deriving uniqueness from innovation include developing a new product, finding a new way of solving a production problem, and creating a new offering that enhances the position of the company or its products with a previously unrecognized customer segment. As seen in Part 2, developing technology—especially information technology—as a source of uniqueness is often difficult, since it is typically modular and subject to imitation and dispersal through horizontal enablers. This does not eliminate technology as a source of uniqueness, but places it in a supporting, rather than leading, role. Consider Gillette's development of the Sensor razor, discussed in Chapter 1. Gillette wanted to take its superior understanding of the shaving customer, its distribution infrastructure, and its brand and translate them into a unique product that would drive both margins and market share. To do so, it needed to combine these assets with new manufacturing processes and technology. Technology is quite often enabling, putting other unique attributes to work. Chapters 9 and 10 will look in greater detail at the role of technology in developing unique capabilities.

The most common misconceptions about competitive advantage come from confusing what a firm is good at with what is unique and difficult to duplicate in the market. Phrases such as "Our competitive advantage is based upon the energy and commitment of our staff" and "Our competitive advantage is the importance we place on education and information" are thrown around by firms as if they were the only ones to have ever thought of training and motivating employees. Perhaps the most common phrase is "Our competitive advantage is our people." It is embraced by hundreds if not thousands of firms, both large and small. Understanding what in a firm is unique and difficult to duplicate requires looking beyond *what* the firm is good at to *why* the firm is good at it. While a software firm such as PeopleSoft may have developers who write fantastic code, the toolsets for collaboration, project management techniques, and methods for integrating new applications with the existing platform may be more valuable than the individual developers. Although a firm needs good people, its culture—which determines how it attracts, assimilates, and leverages the people—is often the more critical component.

MICHAEL SCHRAGE ON

COMPETING ON TECHNOLOGY CAPABILITY

Michael Schrage is co-director of the MIT Media Lab's E-Markets Initiative and a senior advisor to MIT's Security Studies Program. He advises several Fortune 1000 organizations on the economics of innovation through rapid experimentation, simulation, and digital design, and also performs nonclassified work for the National Security Council, DARPA, and the Pentagon's Office of Net Assessment. He teaches and runs workshops on "innovation economics" and new product development at MIT executive education programs and frequently moderates panels and programs on these themes. He is also a columnist for *CIO* magazine, serves on the editorial advisory board of the *Sloan Management Review*, and has written several books on innovation-related topics.

Michael believes that information technology can be used for competitive advantage, and points out that mastering technology is not a given for all firms:

> *Just like hiring talent, deploying capital, employing advertising, and managing inventory, some firms are simply more capable in managing IT. I reject the notion that IT is a commodity that is interchangeable between organizations. The idea that one SAP implementation is the same as another, or that Amazon's interface and shopping experience is the same as eBay's or InterActiveCorp's is simply ridiculous. It is possible that the investment in IT as a differentiator is over-weighted, but the real question is "What aspect of our lack of return in infrastructure investment is a function of the IT itself, rather than the quality of our processes and people to get the return?"*

The concept of alignment is critical in Michael's view. IT investment is most powerful as a competitive tool when applied in conjunction with a firm's other capabilities:

> *Too many organizations don't understand the congruence between innovation in the business model and innovation in the technical infrastructure that supports the business model. Investment in capacity and investment in capabilities are different. Oftentimes, unfortunately, neither aligns with how the company competes and makes money.*

> *Management needs to decide what implementations they are willing to organize themselves around. Once you decide what kind of business you want to be—leader, low-cost provider, innovator, fast follower, and so on—then you can build your infrastructure accordingly.*

> *For example: Wal-Mart obviously wants to be the EDLP/low-cost firm, so an initiative like RFID that lowers supply chain costs makes sense for them to aggressively pursue. Clearly if you are Wal-Mart, your economies and insights come from the use of data to support low pricing. If you are another retailer, though, you'd better be using the information differently, because you cannot "out Wal-Mart" Wal-Mart.*

Michael emphasizes that this notion seems to sidetrack many firms, which simply look at what others are doing without sufficient sensitivity to what their organizations are capable of or a clear notion of how they compete and make money:

> *Business value is created by translating technical capacity into business capabilities. Too many leaders simply want to do what everyone else is doing, and leave it to middle management to ex-post figure out how to derive value from technology. In attempting to compete on technology, you need to decide how rigorous and serious you are about efficiency, effectiveness, and alignment in your organization. We all can't dunk like Michael Jordan, sumo wrestlers can't be pole-vaulters, and American Airlines can't be JetBlue.*

> *The essence of operation research is optimization, but you need to know what to optimize. Airlines using hub-and-spoke business architecture optimize different factors than JetBlue and Southwest, which optimize point to point. The difference is in the business models, rather than who has the better yield-management software.*

An often-overlooked bright spot that Michael identifies in the digital transformation of many businesses is the potential for flexible organizations to experiment, gain experience, and more rapidly react to innovation:

The line in the VC community is that the earliest Christian got the best lion. With IT, it can be more dangerous to be too early than too late. That's why so many organizations have adopted a policy of fast followership.

But the cost of experimenting with innovation is extraordinarily low, if you manage it properly. The interesting question is "How do you do more experimentation better, faster, cheaper?" The Internet is a fantastic tool to get usable knowledge cheap—it is easier and less expensive to be both experimental and a fast follower. Organizations that can realign the economics of innovation with the disruptive influence of digital media can both learn more and move from experimentation to production more quickly.

Creating Barriers

In addition to outperforming the competition (by out-innovating, out-producing, and out-costing), there is another option for achieving a unique capability—putting up roadblocks. In practice, this entails finding ways to inhibit competition so that a firm's uniqueness can be based simply on the absence of barriers faced by competitors, thereby creating the equivalent of a firm-specific "Diamond Lane." As was shown in the six forces model, barriers to entry are one factor that helps create an attractive competitive situation. Traditional barriers include scale, capital, regulation, and protectable technology, but other methods for creating competitive barriers are often much more relevant to technology companies. Developing switching costs, for example, involves creating friction that makes it easier for consumers to stay with a particular product and therefore acts to reduce consumers' propensity to seek out and select competitive products. Network externalities can create unduplicable value by virtue of a customer's connectedness with other users. Finally, installed base and standards also give certain firms leverage that can't be easily overcome.

These types of barriers are perhaps least appealing to economists and policy makers, since they discourage competition, have a propensity to create winner-take-all markets, and set the stage for an **oligopoly** or **monopoly**. While patents have time limits and monopolies can be regulated, firms such as Oracle, Intel, and Microsoft (and perhaps Cisco, AOL, and SAP) can effectively use these less traditional barriers to keep a hold on their customers that cannot be easily broken. Chapter 10 will focus specifically on these methods of competitive advantage, and when and how they apply to technology markets.

> ### Developing Unique Capabilities at Fair Isaac

How does a company turn an $800 stake into a position as the dominant provider of analytical models and decision software for credit scoring? Fair Isaac first introduced the concept of credit scoring in 1958, and its FICO scoring method has become the industry standard for consumer lenders worldwide. Fair Isaac scoring is used by roughly 75 percent of all mortgage originators, credit card issuers, banks, and small business lenders to evaluate the credit worthiness of potential borrowers. Along the way, Fair Isaac has developed a number of unique capabilities that have allowed it to create a sustainable competitive advantage in the credit-scoring field.

❏ *Brand.* Fair Isaac's FICO brand is synonymous with credit origination evaluation and risk management and is not readily interchangeable with substitutes.

❏ *Proprietary Process.* Fair Isaac employs what has been referred to as an "army" of mathematicians and scientists,[19] who have developed proprietary "black box" predictive models. These models have been refined into a difficult-to-duplicate set of business rules for determining when and how to offer and extend credit in a risk-responsible way.

❏ *Unique Technology.* Fair Isaac possesses a number of proprietary technologies for predictive intelligence. Business rules have been coded into software "engines," which can be integrated with customer data warehouses.

❏ *Switching Costs.* Fair Isaac has created another form of insulation by integrating the software into customer systems and encouraging customers to establish processes that embed Fair Isaac's scoring methods. It is very difficult for a customer to then change providers or extract itself from the relationship.

❏ *Experience Curve.* Fair Isaac's obvious expertise, which would be difficult to duplicate, is complemented by its "neural network" concept, which lets the software "learn" over time, as it is used by customers. This creates an experience curve in the customer environment, making Fair Isaac software more effective.

These unique capabilities have turned Fair Isaac into a steady growth firm and highly profitable cash flow generator, with an estimated 65 percent market share in the credit evaluation industry.

Sustainability

The term *competitive advantage* is almost always prefaced by the word *sustainable*. Doing something first provides only a temporary advantage, which will yield results only in the short run. Unsustainable competitive advantage is not necessarily bad, since a firm still gains a period of excess performance. In this case, a simple discounted cash flow or ROI calculation will determine whether the effort is worthwhile. If the unsustainable advantage leads to the creation of a sustainable advantage through insulation or the locking in of a leadership position (as is sometimes the case when a firm is first to market), it may also be worthwhile even with a sub-par ROI.

Sustainability is challenged by both imitation and depreciation.[20] A decline in the ability of a unique resource, capability, or environmental factor to bring about outperformance leads to a loss of competitive advantage. Because of the rapid pace of innovation, technology-based uniqueness tends to be less durable (shorter lived) than resource- and capability-based uniqueness. How much of a problem imitation is depends on a number of factors. Chief among these are whether government protection (patents/copyrights) is possible and enforceable and how obvious and transferable the technology's advantages are to other firms.

The primary danger for executives lies in assuming that an advantage is sustainable when it is not. Apple, for example, made tremendous gains by giving some of its computer lines a radical exterior design, which led to increased market share. Since installed base is critical in the operating system industry (there will be more on this in Chapter 10), the advantage gained more than justified the investment. It would have been dangerous, however, for Apple to assume that the new exterior design represented a sustainable competitive advantage. In fact, the design was easily replicated by Compaq and quickly became less relevant to the consumer decision-making process. Potential sources of a more sustainable competitive advantage for Apple include its integrated technology stack approach and innovative culture, both of which are catalysts in Apple's ability to create a continuous stream of first-to-market innovations.

Of all the sources of uniqueness identified here, tangible assets are the most easily imitated. A physical location, new piece of equipment, new formula, or (as in the case of Apple) new exterior design can be acquired by other firms. Intangibles and capability-based uniqueness are more variable in their inimitability. A new manufacturing process, if not well guarded, can be co-opted through competitive hiring, industrial spying, taking a factory tour, or simply reading the latest trade journals. If well guarded, however (like the formula for Coca-Cola), it can be quite sustainable. Similarly, some sources of supply, such as British Petroleum's oil field rights or De Beer's diamond franchise, are highly protectable; in other cases (like that of coffee and other agricultural products), imitation will be rapid if the uniqueness is associated with superior financial performance.

Barriers and environmental factors are perhaps the most sustainable but also the most capricious. As Chapter 10 will discuss, well-managed networks or platforms can create a significant source of sustainable heterogeneous advantage, but can also become meaningless if a platform shift occurs. The strong monopolistic positions of AT&T and Standard Oil were unassailable right up until the government changed the environment and both were broken into pieces. Consumer behavior is another environmental factor that can change, thus affecting the attractiveness if not the longevity of a firm's unique capabilities. Uncontainable customer interest in owning certain varieties of tulip bulbs sustained high profits for the technology owner in the 1600s, until the public suddenly realized that the new tulips, while aesthetically pleasing, weren't worthy of the dramatic price escalation and discrimination that had characterized the tulip craze. Knowing how short-lived consumer fads can be, Gemmy Industries competes instead on capabilities.

Competitive Advantage: A Fish Tale

One form of competitive advantage is capability based—having a set of internal skills that other organizations can't duplicate. Since many innovations have at their core unprotectable technology that is easily imitated, organizational capability is often a primary source of competitive advantage.

"Don't Worry, Be Happy"

Courtesy of Gemmy Industries Corporation

An excellent case in point is Gemmy Industries, a novelty goods manufacturer with battery-powered dancing hamsters and singing Christmas trees to its credit. One of its biggest items to date has been Big Mouth Billy Bass—a mounted plastic fish with a motion sensor that sings the songs "Don't Worry, Be Happy" and "Take Me to the River." During the height of Billy's popularity, luminaries including Presidents George Bush and Bill Clinton and Queen Elizabeth were proud and well-publicized Big Mouth Billy Bass owners. Four of the keys to Gemmy's success were[21]

❏ Using a highly flexible manufacturing system that could grow quickly to meet demand,

❏ Making intelligent decisions about distribution to maximize margins,

❏ Using speed to fend off copycats, and

❏ Managing the life cycle—shutting down production before sales cratered, to avoid being left with warehouses full of "last year's hit."

As a Gemmy spokesman said, "There's really no way to manage a hot product—you just run as fast as you can while you have it."[22] Gemmy followed this roadmap to create an early market for the product and, based on early market results, rapidly expanded to the mass merchants, which retailed Billy for roughly $30. Like many of Gemmy's other products, the product itself was easily duplicated, requiring roughly 60 days of lead time for circuitry. Also, Gemmy used contract-manufacturing factories in China, which could easily be procured by competitors. By managing a rapid deployment, however, it was able to lock up the key channels for the short term—and with a fad product, the short term is all that really counts. The entire Big Mouth Billy Bass phenomenon lasted less than 12 months.

The risk of this strategy is that the speed of innovation causes rapid depreciation of the assets of companies that rely on intangible rather than hard assets.[23] Using the ability to "run fast" as a primary competitive advantage means that the firm can never afford to slow down. A firm such as Gemmy must continually safeguard this fast-to-market capability or lose its ability to outperform the competition.

Is Competitive Advantage Necessary for Success?

Implicit in the viewpoint that competitive advantage is necessary for success is the assumption that any attractive business will draw competitors up to the point where it is no longer attractive. To the extent that this assumption is true, it requires that a firm either identify methods for gaining a competitive advantage or accept that the business will be relatively unattractive. In some cases, economic market imperfections make competitive advantage unnecessary.

Attractiveness Is in the Eye of the Beholder

A college student might consider writing a software program for distribution as shareware over the Internet to be worthwhile if it returns roughly $20 per hour in voluntary payments from satisfied users. The student in question would not be concerned about long-term profits or other entrants, just about making a living wage and a return on the effort invested. Contract software development firms and many local service businesses fall into this general category, although one could argue that reputation, experience, proximity, and customer experience/referrals are in themselves unique attributes possessed by these firms. The risk of having no source of uniqueness is that someone else may come along and put the noncompetitive firm out of business. This is most likely to happen within larger segments. In retail, so-called category killers (large superstores) from Home Depot to Starbucks have used a lower cost structure and scale to do just that.

An Attractive Business May Not Draw Competitors If Its Attractiveness Is Not Transparent

Most economic theories assume that perfect information is available, so individuals and firms can make rational choices. Economists frequently cite "imperfect information" as a condition that interferes with the invisible hand. Even if no competitive barriers exist and a business is attractive, competitors need be aware of it in order to make a rational entry decision. A small firm may profitably "fly under the radar screen" and not attract competition. Larger firms such as Cargill, McKesson, and Bechtel are said to be widely profitable, but are secretive enough about their profits to avoid attracting attention to vulnerable segments. A disadvantage of using public financing mechanisms (both venture capital and traditional equity markets) is that these avenues often require aggressive and active promotion of the business. This draws attention to the possibility of profits and draws in competitors.

Outperform or Outlive

Rather than simply enhancing performance metrics and bonus programs, the pursuit of competitive advantage can in some cases determine whether a firm survives. Rapid innovation can quickly make a firm and its products obsolete, particularly in technology-driven markets, which are prone to winner-take-all cycles.

Winner Takes All

Customers accrue many benefits from making the same choices as other customers. The result can be an increasing distance between the share of the leader and those of competitors as the scale begins to tip, creating momentum for the leader and a death spiral for competitors. The unique barriers in many technology industries tend to magnify market leadership and secure market share distribution, so long as customers remain on a given platform. As Shapiro and Varian put it,

> The old industrial economy was driven by economies of scale, the new information economy is driven by the economics of networks. . . . Consider Microsoft. Microsoft's customers value its operating systems because they are widely used, the de facto industry standard. Rival operating systems just don't have the critical mass to pose much of a threat. . . . If everyone else uses Microsoft Word, that's even more reason for you to use it too.[24]

In such situations, what emerges is not vibrant competition between number one and number two, but a single dominant firm (or platform) and a variety of niche players, which must create a significant market upheaval in order to gain major market share.

Rapid Innovation

While the misguided phrase "Internet time"—an oft-used justification for making poor management decisions and putting tactics before strategy—seems to have passed into the history books, technology markets clearly move at a very fast pace. Moore's Law, named for Intel founder Gordon Moore, predicted in 1965 that computing power would double every 18 months, a prediction that has held true for almost 40 years (see Exhibit 8-4). In the software industry, Rapid Application Development (RAD) has made it possible to create faster, more flexible software projects through componential architecture and parallel development. In complex manufacturing businesses, digital design and collaboration tools are greatly reducing time-to-market. Finally, in pharmaceuticals, genomics is creating more compounds and more targets for fighting disease. This technological speed creates a higher risk profile, since industries can shift much more quickly. Firms cannot rely on inertia as product life cycles become more compressed.

Buyer Behavior

As discussed in Part 2, technology buyers are keenly aware of both network externalities and rapid innovation cycles. Their buying behavior reflects a number of rational factors, including a concern about obsolescence and a resistance to behavioral change. The risk of obsolescence drives buyers toward a more forward-looking perspective on the market. Buyer questions such as "Who is likely to emerge as the leader?," "What innovations are on the horizon?," and "Will this product become obsolete?"—designed to elicit the predicted winner—highlight the importance of a discernible and long-lived competitive advantage. High levels of technological change

EXHIBIT 8-4 ■ An Illustration of Moore's Law: Integrated Circuit Transistors per Square Inch, 1970–2000

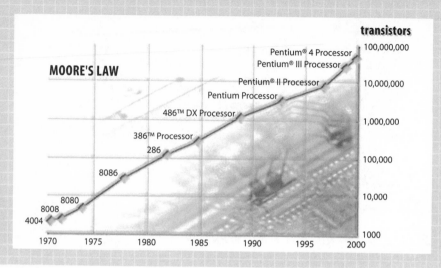

SOURCE: http://wikipedia.org/wiki/Image:Wgsimonmooreslaw001.jpg.

and heterogeneity lead to buyer uncertainty, and this uncertainty tends to result in barriers to the addition of new vendors to buyer decision sets.[25] The implication here is that a product needs to exhibit significant superiority in order to gain a foothold.

CHAPTER SUMMARY

The purpose of this chapter was to create a framework for the discussion in Chapters 9 and 10 of competitive advantage as it relates to technology. As was shown, classical economics demonstrates that market forces tend to work against excessive profits and other elevated results; therefore, a heterogeneous and protectable capability is necessary for a firm to outperform others in the field.

One of the key requirements is that an organization's capabilities be aligned with its goals. Using tools such as balanced scorecards becomes important in ensuring that a firm pursues capabilities and resources that match its end game. The goals and nature of outperformance can be varied. While many industries have institutional pressures that create standard benchmarks for performance, different competitors in an industry can pursue disparate outperformance metrics, leading to multiple winners. Both Abell and Porter support this viewpoint and endorse the pursuit of uniqueness. Both also warn against the emergence of certain capabilities that overshadow all others, leaving a firm in an uncompetitive situation despite the presence of unique capabilities. A firm that successfully develops a significant cost-reducing innovation might eliminate the market opportunity for another firm competing on quality, for example, despite the differing focal points of the two firms.

Tangible and intangible resources, capabilities, and external/environmental factors were all considered as sources of uniqueness. The effectiveness of each source in a particular case depends on how insulated it is from appropriability by other firms. Combining resources and capabilities seems to offer the most powerful insulation, as it can turn duplicable resources into an unduplicable capability. Barriers play a particularly important role when technology is a source of competitive advantage. While technology can be imitated, switching costs, network effects, standards, and platform issues can give a firm an unlevel playing field from which to drive results.

Finally, while gaining a competitive advantage is implicitly or explicitly a goal of all firms, it is imperative for technology-oriented firms. Technology-oriented markets exhibit unique characteristics related primarily to the importance of selecting the perceived winner and avoiding the extra costs associated with choosing a non-winning firm.

Technology and Traditional Sources of Competitive Advantage

You think you're the only writer who can give me that Barton Fink feeling? I got twenty writers under contract that I can ask for a Fink-like thing from.

—Studio director **Jack Lipnick,** conversation with Barton Fink in the movie *Barton Fink*

Lemonade with a Twist

On a slow, hot summer day, some kids with nothing better to do decide to set up a lemonade stand on the northwest corner of a busy suburban intersection. The kids charge $.25 for a glass of lemonade—a nickel above their $.20 per glass cost ($.05 each for the lemon, sugar, ice, and cup). The $.05 markup seems like a fair profit, and $.25 appears to be a price that customers are willing to pay for lemonade, since the stand is doing a brisk business. Another group of kids—unwittingly pushed on by the invisible hand discussed in Chapter 8—see the lines of customers at the stand and decide to set up a competing stand on the southeast corner of the same intersection. Unlike the first group, however, one of the proprietors of the second stand happens to have access to a lemon tree—in fact, his family owns the only lemon tree in town. As a result, the second group doesn't need to purchase any lemons. Since it doesn't have the expense associated with lemons, the second group's cost is only $.15/glass. The group is immediately faced with a strategic choice: It could set its price at $.20 and take a majority share of the business or set its price at $.25 and earn twice the per-glass profit of the original entrepreneurs. Opting for market share, the second group elects to charge $.20, a price that the first group cannot match without sacrificing all of its profits. As a result, the first group decides to pack up and head home to watch television, rather than spend the afternoon selling lemonade at cost. While watching the afternoon movie, however, the kids notice that their parents have failed to lock the liquor cabinet, giving them access to a rather unique ingredient for their lemonade. They return to their original corner and sell their vodka-spiked lemonade for $1 a glass, successfully capturing a profitable share of the market. Both groups are happy—having little to fear from competitors (although a lot to fear from their parents).

This brief story illustrates the simplest view of the classical source of competitive advantage—that a firm's competitive strength comes from its being either cheaper or different. Thus, depending on its aim and capabilities, a business may opt for a *low-cost* or *differentiation* strategy. Most strategy texts depict the choices in terms of a matrix with four quadrants (see Exhibit 9-1), to reflect the fact that a low-cost or differentiation strategy can be either broadly applied or more narrowly targeted—an approach referred to as a focus strategy. A fifth option, called a best-cost provider position, is often overlayed on the matrix, showing that firms sometimes create a unique value/quality position for themselves in the market. These strategic alternatives, and the role of technology in gaining and supporting them, will be discussed over the course of this chapter.

Cost-Based Strategies and the Role of Technology

Cost-based strategies, if sustainable, provide a powerful competitive advantage for individual firms. Quite simply, cost advantages give a firm the flexibility to pursue options unavailable to other firms. With a lower cost base, a firm has the ability to win on price and gain market share and volume. Alternatively, the firm may choose to win on profit margin and reinvest for further competitive advantage, adding features or service levels in order to offer a superior bundle at a comparable cost or adopting other tactics that fit with the firm's goals. As we saw in the lemonade example, cost advantages allow a firm to follow a market share or profit-maximizing strategy that cannot be duplicated by others with similar results. If the group without the advantage of a lemon supply had attempted to match the second group's price of $.20, it would have been operating at zero profit. The second group, however, would have had the choice of pursuing profitability at $.20 or dropping the price further to expand market share. The unambiguous benefits of lower cost make it a significant advantage for firms that have it.

EXHIBIT 9-1 ■ Generic Competitive Strategy Matrix

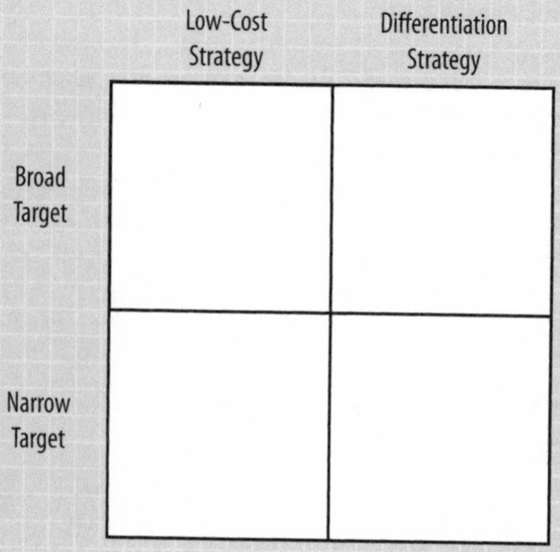

	Low-Cost Strategy	Differentiation Strategy
Broad Target		
Narrow Target		

SOURCE: Based on M. Porter, *Competitive Advantage: Creating and Sustaining Superior Performance* (New York: Free Press/Macmillan, 1985).

Perhaps the most recognizable real-world success in the pursuit of low-cost advantage is the retailer Wal-Mart. In an industry known for relatively thin net margins, Wal-Mart's cost of goods is estimated to be 5 to 10 percentage points lower than that of its competitors,[1] which translates into customer value, good service, and superior operating performance. Much of this advantage has been gained through exploiting technology. Wal-Mart leveraged both its unique resource base and its scale to remove costs from the supply chain, eliminate inefficient processes, make better decisions, and transfer costs back to suppliers that aren't willing to invest as heavily in technology infrastructure as Wal-Mart.

Technology and Wal-Mart's Cost Leadership

From its world headquarters in Bentonville, Arkansas, Wal-Mart has pursued a path of technology-based cost leadership, which has made it one of the most efficient retail operators in the world. Wal-Mart has grown at a double-digit annual pace, becoming one of the world's largest and most profitable companies. This continued excellence is even more impressive when you consider that the company employs almost two million people.

Wal-Mart has used information technology as a method of driving out cost throughout most of its history. Sam Walton's organization is credited with "setting the wheels in motion" for electronic data interchange[2] by putting scanners and satellites in stores, creating store-level and chain-wide real-time visibility into inventory and product mix. This allowed Wal-Mart to implement a collaborative planning, forecasting, and replenishment program, essentially moving to just-in-time replenishment of products at both the store and the warehouse level. This greatly reduced inventory-carrying costs for both the retailer and its suppliers and allowed them to optimize each store's mix.

According to a McKinsey report, in 1987 Wal-Mart had just a 9 percent market share but was 40 percent more productive than its competitors.[3] Leveraging this advantage, by the mid-1990s Wal-Mart had increased its share to 27 percent, while its productivity advantage had widened to 48 percent. The rise in the productivity gap is due to Wal-Mart's focus on a "productivity loop," which continuously drives up sales efficiency and drives down cost.[4] Cost savings are reinvested in new cost/price leadership initiatives. Wal-Mart Executive Vice President and former CIO Kevin Turner asserts that Wal-Mart's information systems give it "a competitive advantage and help the company maintain one of the lowest expense structures in retail."[5] The technical operation is on a centralized platform, using a homegrown, common source code that can be deployed worldwide. More importantly, Wal-Mart's scale allows it to require its vendors to conform with Wal-Mart's desired way of doing business. As Michael Schrage has pointed out,

> Consider Wal-Mart's $4 billion-plus investment in its "Retail Link" supply chain system. What's intriguing is not the multibillion-dollar nature of the company's IT infrastructure initiative, but the fact that it has had at least an order-of-magnitude impact on its suppliers' own supply chain innovations. That is, Wal-Mart's own $4 billion expenditure has likely influenced at least $40 billion worth of supplier investments in systems and software.[6]

The real question is whether the technology itself is the source of competitive advantage or whether Wal-Mart's scale and supply chain capabilities are the underlying source. In this case, as in many others, the technology enables the capability, but one cannot exist without the other; the combination of the two is the true source of the uniqueness that leads to Wal-Mart's cost efficiency and cost-based competitive advantage. The aforementioned McKinsey report echoes this sentiment: "The technology that went into what Wal-Mart did was not brand new and not especially at the technological frontiers, but when it was combined with the firm's managerial and organizational innovations, the impact was huge."[7]

While "Drive cost out" is almost a mantra for most managers, low costs aren't always a source of competitive advantage. As Chapter 8 pointed out, the criterion for competitive advantage is uniqueness—in resources, capabilities, or environmental factors. If a cost-reducing initiative is freely available to others in the industry and doesn't leverage a unique capability of a particular firm, it won't permanently change the competitive playing field. As Part 2 discussed, whereas proprietary large-scale IT investment was once expected to allow many firms to heterogeneously change the cost basis of competition,[8] these early-generation information systems have been replaced by more widely available tools, creating less IT-based leverage for individual firms.

Even without uniqueness, however, cost-removing technology can improve the value offered by all competitors and broaden or improve the attractiveness of a market as a result. For example, technology that allows advertising agencies to post their work securely on the web for clients to review has reduced delivery charges, production expenses, and costs associated with in-person meetings. This has resulted in greater productivity and lower costs for agencies. The first agencies to put this technology in place may even have had a short-term competitive advantage (although the model in Part 2 predicts that the demand was probably limited and the cost of implementing was probably high). Since this technology is more or less available to all agencies without many scale-, technical-, or patent-related barriers, it is unlikely to create a long-term heterogeneous advantage that allows any individual firm to lower its cost structure below that of other firms; it simply will lower the cost of advertising agency overhead. These lower costs should increase the efficiency of advertising dollars, allowing client firms to spend more on media rather than overhead. Industry expansion based on lower costs has, in practice, occurred in a number of industries, including textiles, electronics, telecommunications, and certain software industries, where the trend has been toward lower cost of goods and higher industry-penetration rates. It has not necessarily led to a competitive edge for individual firms (except where economic friction, such as capital investment or union labor, created temporary issues for certain competitors).

To see how a unique technology-driven cost reduction differs from an industry-wide cost-reducing opportunity as a source of competitive advantage, consider the following illustration. What if a single major advertising agency developed a proprietary collaboration tool for the editing of television commercials that reduced film, talent, and directing costs by 50 percent? With a lower cost of production, the agency would suddenly be able to make it more economical for advertisers to produce TV ads, reducing the significant fixed-cost barrier that keeps many potential advertisers off television. As word spread of the agency's low-cost production capability, it would begin winning more clients and would benefit from the usual competitive advantage virtuous spiral— lower costs, more market share, and greater profits. The technology, in the form of a proprietary tool, would propel the firm forward.

As mentioned earlier, however, proprietary tools are hard to come by and protect. The generally level playing field created by widely available tools is a large factor in why a herding mentality exists in many classes of technology investments. While firms are required to make certain investments to maintain the status quo, an information technology "arms race" (like most arms races) is generally much more attractive to the arms suppliers than to the buyers. If the return on investment is attractive, the industry as a whole should be motivated to adopt new technology. Without a low-risk implementation plan and a high ROI, however, foot dragging is inevitable. Knowing that the entire industry must move together makes IT directors and CIOs reluctant to invest in unproven technology. Geoffrey Moore elaborates on this dilemma:

> *IT professionals are expert at networking with each other, even across company and industry boundaries if need be, to discuss the ramifications of the latest technology. These groups are united by the need to answer a single question: Is it time to move yet? . . . Pragmatists want to all move at once, to minimize the risk of moving either too early or too late. When the herd migrates, the industry must follow, and thus no one gets caught out lacking support. Also, whatever protocols get adopted at that time will be the go-forward de facto standards.*[9]

This situation creates both a challenge and an opportunity for firms that expect to apply technology as a lever for gaining a competitive advantage. As Nicholas Carr, an editor at the *Harvard Business Review*, has pointed out, what drives sustained competitive advantage is scarcity, *not* ubiquity. Standardization and commoditization of technology infrastructure have reduced the potential for competitive advantage and created risks of omission, rather than opportunities to gain an edge. Carr is a bit extreme in his view, suggesting that the new rules of IT management are to spend less, follow rather than lead, and focus on vulnerabilities, not opportunities.[10]

While this attitude of "throwing in the towel" and simply trying to maintain the status quo may be appealing to most firms, Chapter 3 pointed out that the resource bases of competitive firms can be decidedly heterogeneous, creating the opportunity to leverage homogenous infrastructure in unique ways. As *Computerworld* noted in rebutting Carr's overgeneralization, "You can get real business advantage with technology. You just don't get it from products, services and information. You get it from processes, skills and execution—the same things that let any business differentiate itself in ways that don't involve IT."[11] An executive at Microsoft put it more succinctly: "I have access to golf clubs, but I am not Tiger Woods."[12]

Firms such as Wal-Mart and Frito-Lay have demonstrated that the early use of third-party, open, or nonproprietary technology, when applied to firm-specific opportunities and assets, can lead to success. The use of proprietary technology, when appropriate, also can create unique cost-based advantages, as not all technology can be classified into commoditized toolsets. Duke's Robert Price points out that there are two classes of technology involved in the functioning of an enterprise—necessary and sufficient:

> *Devising successful strategies (i.e., those that yield competitive advantage) involves being able to discern those technologies that are required to be competitive, but are not of themselves sufficient to yield competitive advantage. These are the "necessary" technologies. Successful strategy also involves being able to discern those technologies, either existing or potential, that secure competitive advantage by differentiating a firm from its competitors. These are the "sufficient" technologies. Say, for example, a firm that makes bicycles wishes to distinguish itself by making the lightest weight bike. It should focus its attention on the technology of lightweight materials and architectures. All the other technologies that go into a bicycle are necessary, but should not be the focus of the firm's attention. Although this seems straightforward enough, in business practice the ability to distinguish between necessary and sufficient technologies is surprisingly rare.*[13]

Using Technology to Drive Out Cost

As the lemonade allegory demonstrated, superior cost structure can be a source of competitive advantage. Two methods exist for examining a firm's cost structure and cost activities as a value chain, in order to find ways to drive out cost: (1) looking at the individual components with an eye to eliminating activities or increasing efficiency or (2) examining the linkages between activities.

Consider the generic value-added manufacturing diagram in Exhibit 9-2. A firm that wants to decrease design costs can realize cost reductions either by changing the design process itself or by creating efficiencies in its methods of connecting the design process with the purchasing, production, distribution, marketing, and support processes.

EXHIBIT 9-2 ■ Cost-Reducing Opportunities in a Traditional Value Chain

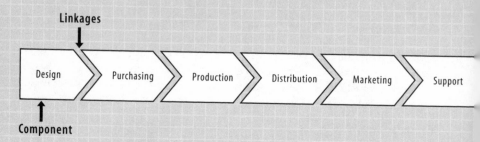

Opportunities to increase efficiency or lower the cost structure for discrete activities can come from any and all of the primary functional areas of a firm. How the company purchases product, for example, might be enhanced through global procurement, how it tracks and predicts potential customer buying patterns addressed through the use of sophisticated predictive models or business information/CRM tools, and how it builds products improved through ERP, factory automation, and other tools. As discussed previously, many of these applied solutions might be fairly widely available and not in themselves create an unbalanced playing field. When applied to an individual firm's resource base, however, the solutions can vary tremendously in leverageability.

Links between the component functions offer many additional opportunities for cost efficiency. An example is the frequent use by large packaged goods manufacturers of enterprise resource planning (ERP) systems to coordinate purchasing and production activities. Tightening the link between material needs and procurement naturally leads to less production surplus, waste, and inventory outages, reducing cost while increasing sales. This linkage can also allow a large manufacturer to leverage purchasing scale, leading to a non-duplicable lower cost of materials.

One of the shortcomings of viewing activities in a traditional value chain configuration is that the number of linkages that can be addressed is limited. Modern companies are made up of a complex set of interrelationships, often referred to as a **value network** rather than a value chain. As the diagram in Exhibit 9-3 makes clear, many interdependencies exist even within the modern firm. As author Verna Allee has said,

Value chain thinking is rooted in an industrial age production line model. . . . The key to reconfiguring business models for the knowledge economy lies in understanding the new currencies of value. A value network generates economic value through complex dynamic exchanges between one or more enterprises, its customers, suppliers, strategic partners, and the community.[14]

EXHIBIT 9-3 ■ Interconnectivity in the Modern Firm

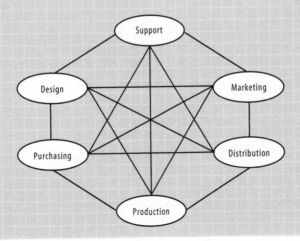

Modern companies also connect with external elements, creating even more linkages, such as those exploited by Wal-Mart. The illustration of a value network in Exhibit 9-4 incorporates some of these external linkages. The additional linkages lead to many more opportunities for achieving cost efficiency, as well as a greater need for tools to manage the interrelationships. When a firm is viewed from this perspective, technology has much more potential as a cost-reducing tool. Consider retailer JCPenney's decision to allow Hong Kong shirtmaker TAL Apparel to collect data directly from the store's point-of-sale systems, run the data through proprietary demand models, and then use the results to make production and stocking decisions on JCPenney's behalf. Product is drop-shipped directly to the stores when necessary. The tighter coordination is designed to decrease excess inventory while also decreasing out-of-stocks. For shirts supplied by TAL, JCPenney has reduced the amount of central warehouse inventory from six months to virtually zero. The linkages exploited in this case are the ones among the stores, the retailer's procurement and merchandising departments, and the external manufacturer. The result is an opportunity to drastically reduce physical product in the system, while having a positive impact on the consumer.[15]

EXHIBIT 9-4 ■ A Firm's Internal and External Value Network

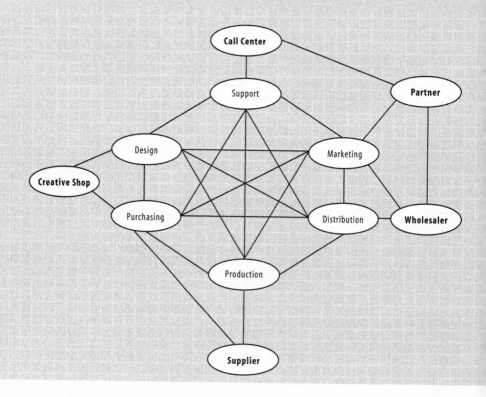

JCPenney's high inventory levels before it implemented this arrangement reveal the challenge faced by many larger enterprises. Their sheer size and complexity (and great number of linkages and dependencies) can create diseconomies rather than economies of scale, turning a major potential source of competitive advantage into a risk for the business. Most of the largest software firms (Oracle, Microsoft, SAP, IBM) have put a great deal of effort into developing integrated toolsets to assist large enterprises like GM in approaching their businesses as networks, working toward greater global efficiency and leveraging their unique configurations.

General Motors Steers Away from Costs

Designing an automobile is a complex task, and cost is a key factor in the success or failure of a new line. A poorly designed automobile will have a "bill of materials" (the list of parts necessary to manufacture the car) that unnecessarily drives up the price of the car, as well as creates inefficient production processes. Changes to one process may affect many others in a cascading fashion, adding expense to the manufacturing process.

Overall expenses associated with design and production can be quite high—in the billions of dollars—since manufacturers have traditionally taken 3 to 4 years to bring a car into production.[16] GM hopes to find ways to reduce these costs by shifting to a systems-intensive virtual-design process for modeling cars and linking processes and suppliers digitally. According to GM vice president Frank Colvin, "These powerful computer platforms have made it possible to reduce the development process to 18 months, and we're now aiming for 15 months in our new vehicle development programs."[17]

By developing in cyberspace, GM can rapidly alter preliminary designs, alert multiple vendors to changes in a bill of materials, test designs without full-scale model building, model manufacturing equipment, assemble repair manuals, and speed up a variety of other activities necessary to get a product to market. GM is also developing a virtual design library, which will allow for iterative modeling[18] and greater organizational learning, as well as the ability to bring new vendors up to speed more rapidly. Cross-referencing will eventually permit GM to share design "best practices" from one car make to another and to identify platform components that can be used across models. Early attempts at platform-based automobile manufacturing have proven that cost savings are possible, but have not yet achieved stellar results in producing high-quality and unique car models.

With better toolsets, perhaps one day cars will be staged the way Dell stages computers—as components ready to be assembled into customized vehicles on a built-to-order basis for consumers. The benefits for consumers would be a wider variation of designs at a lower cost. For GM, the payoff would be reduced inventory and planning risk, greater economies of scale, and the ability to more closely match customer demand.

When "Cost" Doesn't Matter

Using technology to reduce key cost components is not a new concept. Models governing the economics of capital as a substitute for labor were first developed by John Hicks and Alfred Marshall early in the last century. If a dollar invested in a new machine is more productive than a dollar spent on an employee, then a firm will usually choose to spend its money on new machines. If it chooses not to, it risks losing ground to competitors that use their capital more efficiently. Technology has clearly transformed many manufacturing sectors into highly automated industries. The *Wall Street Journal* describes this as a "new blue-collar world" and points out that a steel plant which at one time would have employed 4,000 workers can now produce the same output with less than 400.[19] Many food-processing plants have control centers that a few decades ago would have seemed more probable on the *Starship Enterprise* than in agricultural facilities. While the remaining jobs often require more skill and thus command higher pay, the overall trend is toward a smaller payroll. The economic model driving the switch is simple—the costs of capital, installation, and depreciation/useful life of the technology weighed against the gains in efficiency and productivity. Replacing ongoing operating costs with a one-time capital investment is not a new phenomenon and is often the impetus for technology investment. *Baseline* magazine's ROI Awards provide several illustrative IT-related examples:[20]

> An energy firm spends $50,000 to automate a manual bid-tracking process by putting in place a groupware application. By saving 50 brokers one-half hour per day, it expects to gain $600,000 in additional productivity.

> A firm that makes pacemakers spends $800,000 to install a record-management system that reduces compliance documentation preparation time by 80 percent. Staff reductions, lower communication costs, and higher productivity deliver an estimated $2 million in cost savings.

> Toyota spends $9 million to develop a bar code–based system to track the movement of cars to dealerships, reducing double billing and reporting and tracking costs.

To capture the various costs and thus make an informed decision about the true cost-reduction opportunities presented by infrastructure software, firms must use a **total cost of ownership (TCO) approach**. The principle of TCO is to combine capital outlay, maintenance, and activity-based costing models to determine the true cost of a new technology. TCO models reveal that the actual capital cost outlay can sometimes be virtually irrelevant in decisions about technology. For example, Linux, a free operating system, has been slow to catch on because of the costs of maintenance and documentation, and Sun's Solaris operating system growth was hampered by its dependence on Sun's expensive hardware.

A feature shared by all of the ROI Award winners cited previously is the difficulty of measuring the potential benefit of actual cost savings, as well as the actual costs of the new solution. This is a potential problem in assessing the true impact of large-scale technology projects aimed at achieving cost advantage. Where the goal is to drive out cost, technology can be a less than ideal enabler, particularly because of integration costs, maintenance and support costs, and ambiguities in process change.

> **Integration Costs.** The actual cost of technology is typically a very small portion of the total installation/integration cost. Although particularly true of software, this is also true of other manufacturing-based technology solutions. When training, integration, support and administration, expected downtime, and other costs are factored in, a large-scale information systems project can have a cost of anywhere from $10 million to $100 million or more, of which as little as 10 percent (or less) may be the actual software cost. The personnel to manage the applications, the cost of implementing and the eventual savings from the new processes, and revenue lost or gained through changes in downtime all have a potentially larger impact on a firm's cost structure than does the software cost itself.

> **Maintenance and Support Costs.** The ongoing costs of training, maintenance, and support of enterprise software, as well as many other types of new technologies, can be substantially higher than the original capital outlay. For example, the maintenance costs associated with the custom satellite software discussed in Chapter 3 were significantly higher than the initial investment.

> **Ambiguities in Process Change.** New technology solutions often require company production and organizational processes to change, with unpredictable consequences. Barings PLC, one of the world's largest merchant banks, was brought to ruin by the trading activities of an individual trader in Singapore in the early 1990s. Computer trading was undoubtedly seen as an attractive efficiency-raising and cost-reducing advance in financial markets. But, by eliminating the visibility and managerial oversight that characterized trading activities in earlier decades, it also allowed a single trader to lose billions of dollars in the derivatives markets.[21] In less dramatic cases, factors such as employee turnover due to job description changes, training costs, employee in-fighting, and downtime when systems fail can create significant variation from expected post-technology-implementation costs.

A study by Forrester found that fewer than 25 percent of IT administrators track TCO,[22] primarily because of these difficulties. It should be no surprise that vendors frequently offer this information to buyers to demonstrate the advantages of their solutions. Comparative cost of ownership is a significant piece of the enterprise software sales toolkit, and the inherent ambiguity makes it a particularly attractive tool, as multiple vendors can (and often do) declare victory on the TCO battlefield.

As *CIO Magazine* pointed out in discussing the simple exercise of determining the total cost of ownership for desktop PCs, the soft costs of technology are both significant and elusive:

> *Just look at all that gets rolled into TCO: the direct costs of user support, hardware maintenance, software updates, training, lost productivity while users (and coworkers) try to figure out what's gone wrong, security, downtime, administrative costs and a host of other headings—including depreciation and finance charges. With a laundry list that long, coupled with the increasing cost of hiring, it's no surprise that a business's TCO [for a PC] quickly climbs to about $10,000 a year. Technical advances drive it down, but the people-related costs in the calculation push it obstinately back up.*

> *The ability to determine some of those costs isn't as straightforward as you might imagine. Not only can it be hard to pinpoint precisely how to apportion some easy-to-measure items (the time your purchasing department spends on acquiring desktop PCs and the time your help desk spends sorting out end user fumbles) but some costs are almost impossible to measure. These gray areas include the cost of lost downtime, peer-to-peer support and time spent on user-solvable problems. Time and again, TCO models show that a huge slew of the overall TCO lies in such imponderables—typically around 50 percent, if not higher.[23]*

A study of purchasing managers by *Purchasing* magazine found that over 60 percent don't even try to calculate these imponderables or do so by simple estimation.

Unfortunately, but not surprisingly, "build vs. buy" decisions are often made incorrectly because of a lack of true cost analysis. A homegrown software system may be cheaper in the short run, but require extra personnel to maintain and upgrade it, raising expenses by hundreds of thousands or millions of dollars a year. Proper assessment requires a systemic perspective, with a focus on people and processes as well as technology.

Finally, since ongoing costs result from a firm's processes, ongoing cost savings come from the ability to enable process change, not just improve information flow. While improved information flow identifies opportunities to remove cost and reconfigure operations for greater efficiency, those efficiencies can be captured only with corresponding organizational change. Software that enables global purchasing to enhance buyer power, for example, is effective only if the organization reconfigures itself and the procurement process to allow for global purchasing. This may mean different job descriptions, approval processes, and requisition authority, as well as greater centralization. Cost savings are enabled by information, but are achievable only via organizational change. The alternative is a lack of alignment between a project's tactical and strategic imperatives, the loss of potential cost-based advantages, and a potential *increase* in cost structure due to an infrastructure that doesn't match the process.

The Pitfalls of Cost-Based Strategies

While low cost is an unambiguous universal benefit (in economic, if not environmental, terms), it is easy to become over-reliant on cost-based advantage. If a superior cost structure drives a firm's low-price position—which, in turn, drives market share—a firm may become complacent about adding features that are critical to market demand or reluctant to invest in them for fear of increasing its cost structure. A firm over-positioned on price as its primary customer benefit can find itself vulnerable as soon as a better-priced alternative emerges, since it is fostering price loyalty rather than consumer loyalty. The combination of unwillingness to invest and price-based positioning can eventually have dire consequences.

As discussed in Chapter 7, incumbents are generally very good at incremental improvement. As industries evolve toward maturity, the emphasis on production efficiency increases, causing firms to focus on cost reduction. Firms unable to keep up with the pack are culled from the industry over time. Professors Boyan Jovanovich and Glenn MacDonald observed, however, that eventually it is innovation rather than continued "squeezing" of costs that determines the winners and losers in an industry.[24] In looking at the automobile tire manufacturing industry, for example, they found that several key innovations allowed firms with a more high-tech innovative approach (at least relative to the state of the art in the early 1900s) to develop significant cost/scale advantages, which eventually drove many "laggards" out of the market. These laggards were initially quite capable of competing on cost, but the cost advantage disappeared because of a lack of innovation.

CATHY BENKO ON

TECHNOLOGY AND COMPETITIVENESS

Cathy Benko is Deloitte Consulting's National Technology Sector Leader, and she was previously Deloitte's Global eBusiness Leader. She has been named one of the industry's "25 Most Influential Consultants" by *Consulting Magazine* and is a recognized expert on the topic of business transformation. She is also co-author, along with Professor F. Warren McFarlan of the Harvard Business School, of the book *Connecting the Dots: Aligning Projects and Objectives in Unpredictable Times.*

Cathy believes that while it is possible to achieve a favorable competitive position through technology, some key conditions need to be met. First, Cathy points out that companies must have a clear focus on how they intend to compete:

If properly aligned, your IT strategy is an integral part of your overall business strategy. This means taking into account your position within your industry and knowing how you choose to differentiate yourself in the marketplace. For example, companies such as Wal-Mart and Dell have focused on being world-class operationally, and JetBlue on being a low-cost provider. Understanding how you do (or plan to) differentiate gives you a guidepost to how your technology initiatives can play an important part in achieving your overall objectives.

In analyzing the information tools available, you need to determine whether the software itself provides an opportunity for competitive advantage, or whether your tools are essentially more commodity-oriented building blocks. At the end of the day, there are few technology advantages that are truly sustainable, so your strategic resources and business capabilities need to take this into account.

Cathy has also observed that there is more to leveraging technology than simply articulating a corporate vision and expecting the organization to follow. A much more detailed roadmap is needed, which evaluates a company's portfolio of technology and projects against the overall strategic goals of the firm:

Strategy often is formulated at a very high level, but doesn't always easily correlate to what is happening elsewhere in the organization. Companies often need to get more granular in articulation of their strategies so that they can better connect their infrastructure projects with their strategy. For example, while strategic documents might contain objectives such as increasing market share by 10 percent or breaking into new markets, there frequently is not a clear connection between these objectives and whether a new HR or ERP system contributes to helping the company leverage the capabilities necessary to make this happen. The roadmap that bridges the strategic intent with more "block and tackle" elements like platform and software selection is as important as stating the strategy itself. Many companies assume that this will just happen—and it simply doesn't work that way.

In times of uncertainty, Cathy observes that firms are often better off with an adaptive rather than predictive model. But competitive success has less to do with whether the firm is consciously leading or following, and more to do with organizational characteristics:

We are all morphing to a new set of ways to do business whether we are aware of it or not. How effectively companies can adapt depends on a set of four traits: The first is how eco-driven you are. This entails an understanding that you rely more heavily on value networks and relationships rather than a vertically integrated orientation. The second is whether you can look outside in rather than inside out. While many organizations acknowledge that customer and business partner viewpoints are important, the primary level of focus is often internal. The third is to be what I call fighting trim. This is a question of how quickly you can spot marketplace trends and then respond appropriately. Finally, the organization needs a house in order mindset. The "art of the possible" keeps changing, so you have to have an infrastructure that is capable of identifying and embracing change as adaptively as possible.

From the vendor viewpoint, a clear value proposition for a new technology solution will attract the firms further along with developing the traits described above. More enlightened organizations will readily see the value proposition, and value both the early learning and marketplace exploitation. The followers unable or unwilling to explore the value risk becoming laggards. While it may not be prudent to be bleeding edge, the window for firms that continually morph their value propositions can be substantial.

While many external factors can affect a firm's competitiveness, Cathy's comments highlight the fact that firms can make their own luck by having a clear strategic focus, evaluating the activities that are designed to achieve it, and developing an organization capable of identifying and reacting to new technology opportunities.

Differentiation-Based Strategies and the Role of Technology

Uniqueness, if important to customers, can be a powerful source of competitive advantage for a firm. Unlike cost, differentiation is a highly ambiguous measure—multiple valuable and unique attributes can exist, and multiple firms can win. In the fast food market, McDonald's presses for speed and product consistency, and Burger King for flexibility, while Taco Bell rolls out streams of new products using a product platform approach. In the automotive industry, various manufacturers rely on safety, innovative design, youthful appeal, engine power, service departments, and a variety of other attributes to differentiate their products in a highly competitive marketplace. Once these objectives are set, technology can become an important facilitator. A firm positioning itself as an on-time performer in the trucking industry, for example, may need sophisticated IT, such as GPS- and computer-aided routing, not used by other firms.[25] Likewise, McDonald's focuses on increasingly sophisticated technology to automate kitchen processes and achieve consistency, while Taco Bell concentrates on technologies that make its restaurants resemble assembly plants rather than kitchens, in order to facilitate menu flexibility.[26]

Understanding the Customer

One of the primary drivers of success in differentiation is an in-depth understanding of the target customer base, used both to identify opportunities for differentiation and to determine how to convincingly convey uniqueness to the market. A firm must determine which product characteristics are relevant to the targeted consumers and then emphasize those characteristics over others.

❑ *Relevance.* Cost is clearly relevant to almost all consumers—making something cheaper has nearly universal appeal. Product attributes, on the other hand, may or may not be appealing to critical audiences (both sales channels and end users). Does coffee from the Brazilian rainforest have enough appeal to overcome another brand's claim of best taste? Do consumers care about 100,000-mile warranties? Does John Madden's name on a football video game matter as much as the game play? Without an in-depth understanding of customer attitudes and behavior, these types of questions are impossible to answer, and failure to answer these questions may lead to investment in irrelevant attribute differentiation.

❑ *Tradeoffs.* Successful differentiation often relies on making choices—safe rather than sporty, flexible rather than easy to use, healthy rather than indulgent. While this is not always the case (as discussed later in the chapter), many successful differentiation strategies require placing strong emphasis on certain features/attributes at the expense of others. Designing a car for maximum speed and handling will involve sacrificing some of the smoothness and comfort of the ride in order to have a tight suspension. Similarly, a car designed for a smooth ride will not corner as effectively as a sports car. By trying to succeed on both dimensions, the manufacturer risks succeeding at neither—and failure to identify the right set of tradeoffs can result in suboptimal differentiation.

Generating Uniqueness

Another driver of success in differentiation is the ability to generate uniqueness, once opportunities have been identified. Since the purpose of competitive advantage is to outperform, it follows that focusing on difficult-to-duplicate differentiation is more meaningful than establishing easily replicable differences. As discussed earlier, proprietary processes, patentable ideas, know-how, and technology married to a firm's unique resource base all facilitate technology-driven innovation that is hard to duplicate. Consultant Michael McGrath describes using **vectors of differentiation** to deliver difficult-to-imitate differentiation to customers.[27] The premise is to identify a specific differentiation strategy and then concentrate innovation efforts on that particular vector. SAP, for example, identified information integration as the focus of its enterprise software strategy early on. As McGrath wrote,

> *SAP's original product release, R, integrated manufacturing and accounting information into a single common application. In its next generation, R2, SAP continued the integration with releases that added more integrated functions, such as order processing, purchasing, and shipping, as well as additional materials management and integrated accounting. Competitors followed SAP, but could never catch up as SAP continued to add more integrated capabilities. In the 1990s, SAP released R3 and added integrated capabilities for human resources, sales force automation, taxes, and the like. It continued to add capabilities along this vector for large multinational corporations. . . . Competitors that tried to compete on the same basis were unable to keep up with SAP's movement along this vector.*[28]

In order for a differentiation strategy to be effective, the market or industry it is applied to must value attribute diversity over homogeneity and low price. Markets for pure commodity products such as oil, produce, and pork bellies tend to be driven by large-scale volume production and standard unit costing, rather than product differentiation (although an occasional differentiated product can find a niche, even in these markets). In any case, a firm evaluating the relative opportunity created by a differentiation strategy should take both the market's diversity of preference *and* preference for diversity into account.

Analyzing Value Delivery

Porter has asserted that, like cost-based advantages, differentiation strategies can arise out of an analysis of the firm's value chain or value network.[29] By examining both the way value is delivered and the linkages, firms can find opportunities for meaningful differentiation. Rather than attacking procurement from a cost-based perspective, for example, a firm may aggressively seek out unique procurement strategies in order to differentiate itself. There is no doubt that rainforest-produced coffee beans are not as cheap as plantation-grown ones, but they may create a product that captures the imagination of retailers and consumers. Similarly, the ability to replace a lost credit card anywhere in the world within 24 hours could distinguish one credit card issuer from another, making this support linkage a differentiating factor.

Abell views differentiation from a more functional viewpoint. Since the purpose of products and services is to perform functions for the customer, the choice of *what* functions are provided and *how* the functions are provided can, in effect, constitute a differentiation strategy.[30] For example, in the web-hosting industry, one firm may choose to provide just site hosting services; another may combine site hosting, development, and back office functions; and a third might focus on simply helping customers move existing database content to the web. Further, the approach of the first firm might be to offer server-side web-based tools, while the latter two might sell client-side software. Again, the keys are the extent to which these differing approaches are relevant and appealing to distinct sets of buyers and the ability of the firms to offer something unique in the space.

Technology's role as an enabler in the pursuit of differentiation for competitive advantage is fairly straightforward. The limitless array of technology can be used in many ways, which generally can be classified as taking one of three approaches to creating a potentially unique application:

1. As an integral part of a product or service,

2. Indirectly in the production of the product or service, or

3. Through the delivery of the product or service.

An example of a direct application is toy manufacturer LeapFrog's use of microchips and software to create unique interactive books for children. The technology is part of the product design. Gillette's use of proprietary production processes to manufacture superior blades is an example of an indirect application. While the blades may be somewhat unique, the manufacturing process is primarily where Gillette generates an innovative edge. Finally, Amazon applies its technology platform to merchandise, recommend, and deliver both of these manufacturers' products in unique ways. Each of these areas represents a potential source of differentiation via technology.

Reality versus Perception

Simply differentiating the product itself through any of the three methods just mentioned is often insufficient, since success in differentiation is generally thought of as a victory more of marketing than of technological prowess. Perception of a product or service's attributes is as critical as the actual veracity of the positioning. Are certain headache remedies safer than others? Milder? More appropriate for women? The ingredients in these products are often identical, but buyers' preferences and perceptions of the products are not. Matching a product to a segment creates opportunity, whether or not the product is meaningfully differentiated on the dimension. At the same time, lack of true differentiation calls sustainability into question. Claims and minor modifications in products or product delivery systems can be readily replicated. More complex differentiation, through product attributes and unique capabilities, creates a more stable barrier. Technology can play a key role in both the reality and the perception of a differentiation strategy, as it has for Toyota and Porsche.

> *Toyota Quality versus Porsche Performance*

It's not really surprising that Toyota/Lexus was ranked number one in 9 out of 12 vehicle segments in a 2003 J.D. Power quality survey. Lexus has consistently been ranked number one overall, and Toyota number one among high-volume brands in quality. In a historical context, however, it is a bit of a surprise to see how far Toyota has come. As the head of Saatchi & Saatchi (Toyota's advertising agency) put it in 1998,

> *Even a decade ago, the notion of a luxury Japanese car was a contradiction. There was no heritage for such a product. The perception among Americans was that Japanese cars were functional, but*

not high performance or high quality. Toyota's motivation with Lexus was to create a car that was superior in every performance element to Mercedes—and would cost less. This car brand would also communicate important messages about Toyota quality that would improve the desirability of their other vehicles such as Camry and Landcruiser. This was really important—promote the top of the range, the very best quality.[31]

Lexus was launched with the tag line "the relentless pursuit of excellence," a slogan that embodies quality as the vector of differentiation selected by Toyota. According to Toyota vice president Robert Waltz, "At Toyota and Lexus our goal is to build quality into our cars, not just fix problems as they occur."[32] Toyota has revolutionized the way cars are built and institutionalized its approach in the form of the Toyota Production System (TPS). TPS is an integrated and interdependent manufacturing and design system that can be thought of as a triangle where one side is philosophy, one side is technology, and the other side is management.[33] The primary focus of the system is on problem solving, continuous improvement, and waste reduction at the factory-floor level, with the goal of total quality improvement. While much has been written about the behavioral aspects of the system, in order to make TPS a reality Toyota also needed to leverage information systems to aid in information flow, improve planning, shorten the supply chain, and adjust/share production sequencing.[34] Pioneering just-in-time management processes, for example, should be thought of as a victory in the areas of both process change *and* information flow. By creating a superior manufacturing environment, Toyota has been able to capture a very valuable perception—that it produces reliable, high-quality, affordable automobiles.

While Porsche also appears near the top of the quality lists in most automobile surveys, even the most loyal of Porsche owners probably wouldn't identify "dependability" or "value" as their reason for driving one. Porsche has also been able to leverage technology to achieve significant differentiation, but has chosen a much different vector on which to do so. At Porsche, the philosophy is to develop racing machines for competitive use and then apply the knowledge and experience gained to produce genuine sports cars for the road. Porsche's positioning is "the car of the future—an idea that underlies everything we do." New materials such as carbon fiber, aluminum, and ceramics have been used to improve performance over the years, as have innovations in suspension and transmissions. Porsche also pumps out a steady stream of patent applications from its Weissach Development Centre. This has allowed the company to differentiate itself as *the* manufacturer of high-performance and innovative cars. While there is scant evidence that it is more innovative than other car manufacturers, Porsche uses highly visible performance technology as the key differentiator and thus is perceived as a clear leader in this high-performance automobile category.

The Pitfalls of Differentiation

As discussed, cost is an absolute, whereas differentiation can be clouded with ambiguity. Therefore, recognizing what differences buyers will perceive as valuable requires an external focus. A misstep can result in added cost, or "negative" value, if a product's or service's perceived features do not match customers' needs and desires. This is a particular danger for newer firms with little customer or operating history and no infrastructure for determining what customers actually want (a description of most startups). "Technology in search of a market" results from differentiation that's not attached to specific value. It's no wonder that many startups, lacking appropriate customer insight and interaction, fall victim to this strategic error.

Additionally, changing customer preferences and substitute offerings can cause a differentiated product or service to lose its luster rapidly. Where development cycles are long or capital investment is high, this can be a significant risk. OPEC's oil embargo in the 1970s, for example, changed consumer preference from large, powerful automobiles to smaller, fuel economy–focused ones virtually overnight. American companies were not prepared for this shift, and fuel-efficient Japanese exports to the United States doubled in four years.[35] The shift in preference toward minivans and SUVs in the 1990s created a similar shake-up in the industry. In both cases, another pitfall of a differentiation strategy can be observed: Differentiation can often be imitated, removing the opportunity for uniqueness that drives performance. Once customer preference for a new characteristic becomes apparent, others will move into the market space. Both small, high-mileage cars and SUVs became *de rigueur* for automobile manufacturers after the shifts became apparent.

While differentiated products and services can be imitated, a temporary differentiation advantage can still be parlayed into a less imitable perception of category leadership. Porter identifies a number of **signaling criteria**, which influence a buyer's perception of value. These include image/reputation, time in business, installed base, visibility, and market share,[36] all of which can accrue to early leaders. An early leader can use these and other factors identified in Part 2 of the book to, in essence, "differentiate its differentiation," based on a position of category leadership. Michelin was able to capture a leadership position as a manufacturer of safe, reliable tires, for example, by pioneering and perfecting the radial tire. Whether other competitors are able to develop tire features that add safety is less relevant than the perception that, overall, Michelin makes the safest and most reliable tires. Michelin has continuously reinforced this message and directed its differentiation toward this perception.

Choosing a Narrow or Broad Customer Target

As illustrated by the matrix in Exhibit 9-1, both cost and differentiation strategies can be either narrowly or broadly focused, depending on how much of a total category a firm chooses to concentrate on. Abell views the choice of target customer groups as an exercise in narrowing the scope of a firm's activities to take advantage of its ability to tailor its offering to the particular needs of a definable segment.[37] Two of the most important issues in determining how tightly to focus are (1) the extent to which individual segments are homogenous and unique in their needs and (2) the ability of the firm to develop unique advantages aimed at a segment.

While focused segmentation can be based on self-identifying characteristics—as in the case of analgesics or drinks aimed specifically at the athletic segments (think Advil and Gatorade)—from a technology perspective the point is to tailor a value chain to match the characteristics of the target market. Web hosting, for example, is generally becoming a commodity, but a number of firms have carved out successful niches by understanding the unique workflow and business rules in specific fields, such as college athletics, nonprofit fund raising, racing events, real estate, and investment advising. Each of these fields possesses some set of unique characteristics that makes a customized web-hosting product vastly superior to generic, broad-targeted web hosting. A provider hosting nonprofits may need unique reporting and tracking tools for the IRS, while a real estate site would need three-dimensional property-display tools and multiple listing service integration. Such a tailored approach to establishing a value chain is a more sustainable strategy than relying on simple positioning.[38]

In other cases, a broader approach makes more sense, since the amount of value-tailoring needed is minimal. While instant messaging (IM) technology certainly appeals to a number of well-defined segments, including teens, colleges, and specific enterprises, the way IM is used by these different segments is quite similar. A broadly focused horizontal platform strategy is, in most cases, practical and gives participating technology firms a much larger potential customer base to work with. A firm with a narrower focus risks losing potential economies of scale, making its product less attractive despite the segment focus. (Chapter 10 will discuss the network effect issues associated with this decision.)

In the IM market, one of the few exceptions to the broadly focused strategy is in messaging products for the securities industry. The need for compliance documentation and heightened privacy and security concerns cause IM for this industry to have a different value configuration and workflow. Reuters, which services this industry, was able to develop an IM focus strategy by designing a product with this exceptional segment's specific workflow issues in mind. The Reuters example illustrates the importance of understanding firm-specific skills related to the segment when choosing a focus strategy. Reuters actually partnered with Microsoft for the technology, but it was Reuters' reputation, knowledge of the audience, and sales channels into financial services that made the service viable. A focus strategy requires both opportunity and capability. Domain expertise and cost-based advantages applicable to the segment(s) of choice will put a firm in a much better position to succeed. These capabilities can be excellent arguments for a firm to pursue a focused path.

Other reasons for taking a focused approach to a marketplace include the absence of a (or, at least, a reduced) competitive set in the segment, a limited market size, or a complex set of requirements for meeting the needs of the segment. As discussed earlier, pursuing an available market can also provide a potentially attractive beachhead for eventual broader market penetration.

Pursuing Low Cost *and* Differentiation

The fifth space in the classical view of competitive advantage is occupied by firms that choose to pursue both low cost *and* differentiation. As shown in Exhibit 9-5, this is referred to as the **best-cost provider** option. Toyota is an example of a company that is pursuing both a differentiation strategy and a low-cost production strategy. For its Lexus line, Toyota sees low cost and quality as simultaneous, rather than mutually exclusive, goals. In the book *Built to Last*, James Collins and Jerry Porras introduce a

EXHIBIT 9-5 ■ Expanded Strategy Matrix

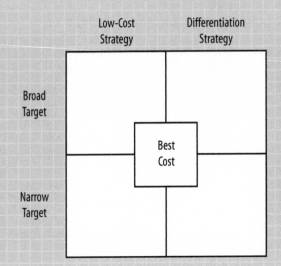

SOURCE: Based on M. Porter, *Competitive Advantage: Creating and Sustaining Superior Performance* (New York: Free Press/Macmillan, 1985); and A. Thompson and A. Strickland, *Strategic Management and Concepts* (New York: McGraw-Hill Higher Education, 2001).

concept known as **the tyranny of OR**, which postulates that most firms force themselves into making tradeoffs—such as "You can have it on time OR on budget" or "You can have low price OR quality."[39] The best solutions and the most outstanding companies don't accept artificial tradeoffs; instead, they focus on doing both. In the case of the strategy matrix, success in both a low-cost strategy and a differentiation strategy would certainly provide better insulation and superior results, if managed correctly.

Pursuing a combination of low cost and differentiation creates the danger of being flanked. A firm that focuses on both cost and uniqueness risks becoming a suboptimal choice for each customer. With limited resources and multiple goals, the firm may be stretched too thin and fail, rather than succeed on either measure. Within set quality parameters, a buyer focused on price would select a lower-cost option, while one focused on a particular differentiated characteristic might find another product that was more attractive on the differentiation axis. In the low-cost wristwatch market, for example, a new entrant trying to use a best-cost strategy to take on Swatch would inevitably be faced with a comparison between its models and Swatch's designs, while also being required to fend off even lower-cost options. Since flanking presents an opportunistic point of entry for innovators, firms attempting to be the best-cost provider are more susceptible to a disruptive threat, as innovation can occur on either the cost or the performance axis. For this reason, pursuing a best-cost provider position should not be seen as a move toward mediocrity on two axes, but rather a pursuit of excellence on both. If the executives in a contact management software firm (such as ACT!) want to avoid startup competition, they certainly need to be aware of the price of their product relative to that of competitors. More importantly, they also need to balance the low price driving economies of scale they can achieve through a horizontal offering with the need to avoid losing business in key vertical markets to segment-focused generic competition. Packaged goods companies provide the most visible examples of this strategy successfully executed. Firms such as Morton Salt and

Anheuser-Busch are highly efficient producer/distributors, and they are equally adept at differentiating their products.[40] Where low cost is driven by scale, focus strategies will not be particularly effective unless the focus segment has sufficient scale. With a large enough segment or broad strategy, however, a best-cost provider position can be a powerful facilitator of competitive advantage.

CHAPTER SUMMARY

This chapter introduced the primary traditional generic strategies for achieving competitive advantage—focused or broad low cost, focused or broad differentiation, and best-cost provider. A low-cost position can be achieved through removing high cost or inefficiency either in discrete functions of the firm or in the reconfiguration of the value network both inside and outside of the company. Cost-based competitive advantage is especially powerful, given the universal desire of buyers to pay less, but it can also be harnessed as a method for achieving higher margins. If profits are reinvested in further low-cost innovation, a firm can create a virtuous spiral and develop an insulated position, while also providing some protection from others that are also harnessing disruptive technology changes. Although proprietary technology for lowering cost structure is hard to come by, a firm can apply available technology to firm-specific processes and characteristics (such as scale or product-specific production know-how) to create difficult-to-imitate cost advantages. Matching strategy to resources is critical.

Competitive advantage–yielding differentiation can be achieved through the product itself, the production process, or the overall solution delivery—changing the way a customer problem is solved. Even when real differentiation exists, it is important to position the product or service appropriately, since perception is a critical component of differentiation. Both the actual product differentiation and the perception-creating process depend on a thorough understanding of the customers and the industry. Differentiation strategies are easiest to employ where market preferences vary and product differences will be valued.

Even if a firm does not have a broad advantage in either differentiation or cost, it is possible to create such an advantage for a segment of the market. Such a narrow, or focused, strategy allows a firm to leverage unique resources applicable to a particular category subset. For a focus strategy to be viable, it must be possible to identify meaningful segments with highly varied needs. When an underlying product platform is easily adaptable across segments, a broad strategy may be more appropriate.

These strategies form the foundation of traditional thinking about competitive advantage, since they are designed to create heterogeneity in an industry's most critical performance drivers, leading to superior performance by firms that can take advantage of them. Chapter 10 will consider alternative strategies for creating this same type of advantage.

Technology-Specific Sources of Competitive Advantage

10

"Is Orr crazy?"
"He sure is," Doc Daneeka said.
"Can you ground him?"
"I sure can. But first he has to ask me to. That's part of the rule." . . .
"And then you can ground him?" Yossarian asked.
"No. Then I can't ground him."
"You mean there's a catch?"
"Sure there's a catch," Doc Daneeka replied. "Catch-22. . . .
Anyone who wants to get out of combat duty isn't really crazy." . . .
[Yossarian] let out a respectful whistle. "That's some catch that catch-22,"
he observed.
"It's the best there is," Doc Daneeka agreed.

—**Joseph Heller,** *Catch-22*

A Triumph of Habit

Chapter 9 looked at traditional cost- and differentiation-based sources of competitive advantage. This chapter will examine other sources of competitive advantage somewhat unique to—or at least highly relevant to—technology-dependent markets.

Rather than compete solely on cost or feature differentiation, firms can also take advantage of structural barriers to provide nonduplicable value. A fascinating example of structural barriers in action is described in the late Stephen Jay Gould's essay on the history of the typewriter keyboard. The layout of a standard keyboard (known as a QWERTY keyboard, in reference to the sequence of letters in the upper left-hand portion of the keyboard) is considered by many to be suboptimal, as it places four out of five vowels off the "home row," emphasizes the left hand, and requires extension of the weaker fingers for some oft-used letters. Anyone viewing a QWERTY keyboard for the first time would have a hard time seeing anything but an arbitrary grouping of letters. As Gould wrote:

> *Clearly QWERTY makes no sense. . . . This claim is not just conjecture based upon idiosyncratic personal experience. Evidence clearly shows that QWERTY is drastically suboptimal. Competitors have abounded since the early days of typewriting, but none have supplanted or even dented the universal dominance of QWERTY for English typewriters. The best known alternative, DSK, for Dvorak Simplified Keyboard, was introduced in 1932. Since then, virtually all records for speed typing have been held by DSK, not QWERTY,*

typists. . . . As touch typing by QWERTY became the norm in America's typing schools, rival manufacturers (especially in a rapidly expanding market) could adapt their machine more easily than people could change their habits—and the industry settled upon the wrong standard.[1]

Although Gould was a cultural anthropologist, his essay on QWERTY has its roots in economic theory, particularly the work of economist Paul David. David interpreted the events leading up to QWERTY adoption as both a victory for randomness and a sign of "market failure."[2] This brings us back full circle to the theme introduced at the start of Chapter 8: Economists tend to see market failure in an unfavorable light, even if it makes good business sense.

The structural barriers in the case of the QWERTY keyboard consist of a variety of factors, including an installed base that is (and has been) resistant to a new layout, institutionalized incompatibility driven by the teaching of typing in the QWERTY format in schools, hardware incompatibility, and software written around the present keyboard layout. Clearly, a large constituent base, with the ability to help determine the standard, became invested in the status quo early on, creating somewhat of a catch-22 for challengers. In addition, the fact that the DSK keyboard was a proprietary patented device constituted another reason not to embrace it. For a typewriter or keyboard manufacturer, the use of a patented keyboard layout rather than an open standard could have resulted in an unfavorable change in the distribution of profits, given the need to pay royalties to a new intermediary value partner—the owner of the patent.

EXHIBIT 10-1 ■ The QWERTY and DSK Keyboards

The relative advantage of DSK over QWERTY has been the subject of ongoing heated debate, which will not be continued here. Rather, the example will be used as a segue to a discussion of the nature of barriers shaping competition in technology markets. This chapter will examine several types of barriers, including classic network effects, complementary network effects, compatibility and standards, lock-in and switching costs, platform efficiencies, and installed base leverage, all of which assist in institutionalizing certain solutions and create barriers for rivals.

Network Effects

Bob Metcalf, an inventor of Ethernet technology and a 3Com founder, developed a simple mathematical equation called Metcalf's Law:

$$V = N^2$$

where V is the value of a technology and N is the number of individual nodes, or participants using it. The logarithmic relationship between the size of a network and its value for each network participant reflects the role that interconnectedness plays in creating utility in many classes of technology and particularly in information technology. Think of the telephone, e-mail, and music file-sharing—they all become much more valuable to each user as other users are added to the system, creating a **network effect**.

Suppose a computer science student, studying at a college in a parallel universe where e-mail hadn't been invented yet, suddenly saw the code for the Microsoft Exchange Server and Outlook flash across her computer screen from outer space. If only this one student had access to this miraculous tool, its value would be negligible. The student's e-mails would represent nothing more than the sound of a virtual tree falling in the woods. If other students in the department had e-mail, however, she could at least exchange notes with fellow classmates, and her e-mail system would begin to have value. This increase in value for the student would come about through interconnectedness with other students, rather than any change in the actual technology. Add professors to the system, and the department could start to conduct class business online. Add the entire university, and the student could conduct an array of education-related activities, including library inquiries, schedule planning, tuition payment, and perhaps even finding a date. This exercise demonstrates that value for the individual e-mail user increases dramatically as N becomes larger.

The underlying implication of Metcalf's Law of network externalities is that the more users there are on a common system, the more value the system has. UC Berkeley's Carl Shapiro and Hal Varian refer to this phenomenon as "demand side economy of scale."[3] Normal supply side economies of scale create a favorable situation when suppliers, through their market dominance, are able to stake out a low-cost position that makes them largely unassailable, without a major market disruption or investment. This is Wal-Mart's virtuous cost circle in action. Similarly, a network effect creates the same dynamic, but on the demand side for users of a product. The scale of the network of users makes the value of the dominant product much higher than that of alternative technological solutions, whether or not the alternatives are superior.

This logarithmic interconnectedness has the effect of exacerbating leadership and making it difficult to break into a market with a new technology. The winner-takes-all profile of a market with a network effect is illustrated in Exhibit 10-2. The **network value gap** between the leader's and the follower's products increases over time as the size of the leader's network grows.

The leader in Exhibit 10-2 is maintaining twice the market share of the follower. As the leader's network grows, however, the value of its product increases substantially relative to the value of the competitor's product, even though their market shares remain stable. At some point, the value gap may become so great that it becomes difficult for the secondary competitor to remain viable. Markets are thought of as **tipping** when they reach a point where one competitor's interconnectedness value is so much higher than that of the competition that the market is no longer contestable, leading the competitor to exit, as shown in Exhibit 10-3.

EXHIBIT 10-2 ■ A Progressively Increasing Value Gap Caused by Network-Based Value

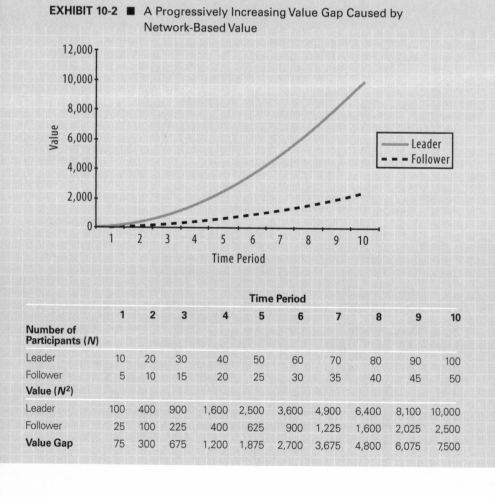

		Time Period								
	1	**2**	**3**	**4**	**5**	**6**	**7**	**8**	**9**	**10**
Number of Participants (N)										
Leader	10	20	30	40	50	60	70	80	90	100
Follower	5	10	15	20	25	30	35	40	45	50
Value (N²)										
Leader	100	400	900	1,600	2,500	3,600	4,900	6,400	8,100	10,000
Follower	25	100	225	400	625	900	1,225	1,600	2,025	2,500
Value Gap	75	300	675	1,200	1,875	2,700	3,675	4,800	6,075	7,500

EXHIBIT 10-3 ■ Market Tipping

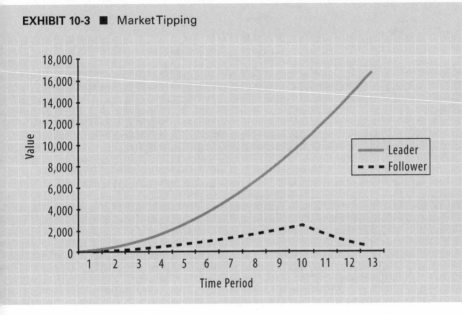

The rapid rise of the MP3 music format is a perfect example of a network effect in action. From its inception, MP3 was considered by industry executives to be the QWERTY of the music industry. The sound quality is average at best, and the format lacks the key tracking and digital rights management features offered by alternative formats (Real Player, Windows Media, Liquid Audio, AAC) designed to avoid rampant piracy. For these reasons, the format was dismissed as a nonviable alternative[4] and was not favored by most within the industry. The industry as a whole instead pursued a common format through the Secure Digital Music Initiative (SDMI). What MP3 did have to offer was high compression (the ability to make files smaller), a lack of "sensitivity" to the legal issues surrounding copyright protection, and, most importantly, mechanisms for creating interconnected value in the format (in the form of Napster and other file-sharing services). All three of these factors are network multipliers, since they foster the sharing and exchange of files. As a result, the value of putting music files in MP3 format quickly outpaced that of other formats and made MP3 the de facto standard. Napster, the original file-sharing service, was itself a beneficiary of the network effect, as its large number of interconnected users created a network where music was most likely to be available, thereby encouraging others to join. The shutdown of Napster simply created an opportunity for other networks to rise in its place. Other examples of network size leading to a value gap and competitive advantage include eBay in the market for used goods and AOL in instant messaging.

> ## AOL and Instant Messaging—Metcalf's Law in Action

The mechanism for AOL's most popular feature—instant messaging—is relatively simple. A user of AOL's Instant Messenger (IM) service has a list of other AOL users who have agreed to become his or her "buddy." The user is notified whenever one of the designated buddies is online. Likewise, all the buddies are notified when the user goes online. A central AOL server acts as a matchmaker between IP addresses (the distinct numerical addresses that identify computers on the network) so that a user and his or her buddies can send instant messages to each other in real time. The value of IM service for any user is proportional to the number of buddies also using the service.

While AOL offers two versions of the service (AIM and ICQ), it has purposely avoided interoperability with competing messaging services from Yahoo! and Microsoft (MSN). MSN messenger clients cannot "find" AOL IM users online. As a result, new users have an incentive to use AOL's system. For the average AOL user, switching instant messaging services would mean no longer knowing when and how to reach the buddy list. This acts as a significant barrier, preventing the defection of users to a rival network. Many AOL IM customers have signed up for multiple services, regardless of what single application they might prefer.[5]

The mathematics of Metcalf's Law indicates that this is the appropriate strategy for AOL to follow. Creating a non-platform-dependent network would give all IM service companies networks of equal size and, thus, equal technology value, eroding AOL's value gap. Not surprisingly, the smaller players (who lack users) are lobbying hardest for interoperability. The FCC has also taken an interest in opening up this market.

Switching costs are a powerful competitive advantage for AOL in its quest to remain the platform of choice for Internet users. The power of AOL's network also gives it leverage to pressure others to adopt the AOL IM protocols on AOL's terms.

Harnessing Network Power

Since the network effect benefits market leaders by creating a value gap, it follows that market leaders should be highly cognizant of opportunities to create network effects. By doing so, they may be able to lock in leadership, even as markets expand rapidly. Would Netscape, with an estimated 80-plus percent share of the browser market in 1995, have had more success against Microsoft if it had created a stronger network among its users? Can GE's bomb screening and bomb detection equipment firm, InVision Technologies (also with a dominant market share), secure its lead by creating greater interconnectedness among individual machines? The answer in both cases, based on developing network value, is almost certainly yes, although the tactics may vary. Netscape, for example, could have built in more network-leveraging services, such as instant messaging, to encourage users to connect to each other, thus creating a value gap with Internet Explorer. In the absence of this value gap, Microsoft was able to leverage its considerable portfolio of complementary assets to compete with Netscape and, eventually, leave Netscape far behind. To secure its lead, perhaps GE InVision could build an infrastructure that would allow data about unusual readings to be shared among devices in different airports, creating a neural network that would make its products more valuable than those of smaller competitors. Such tactics transcend the cost or differentiated feature sets offered and create asymmetrical value delivery through interconnectedness.

Like supply side scale, market leaders should pursue demand side "multiplier" advantages whenever possible. While some markets are naturally network-oriented, facilitating a network effect can create an additional source of competitive advantage even in markets where this is less obviously the case. Airlines that allow reward miles to be portable to noncompeting carriers, for example, increase the value of the reward miles they give out. A software company that holds user conferences or developer forums creates contact networks that remain relevant only if users stay on the platform. Even a health club, simply by organizing tennis "ladders" and social events for members, creates additional value through the interconnectedness of its membership.

The Limits of Networks: Avoiding Diminishing Returns

In some cases, networks without coordination can undergo demand side **diseconomies of scale**. U.C. Berkeley economist Brad Delong believes that, in building networks, the most valuable connections are made first;[6] therefore, there are generally diminishing returns. Some network members can even act as "contaminants"[7] and actually reduce network value through their behavior or inattention to the network. This, of course, conflicts with Metcalf's Law—or, at least, puts a cap on the value gap that network externalities can create. If the value of additional users is less than the cost to current users—in performance, ease of use, reliability, etc.—then the network effect will reach its limit as an insulating barrier. In the case of music sharing, for example, as Napster and other similar services moved from being small, word-of-mouth file-sharing services to global phenomena, problems began appearing as a result of scale, reducing the value of the services. These problems include fake songs, poor recordings, and slow downloading. Similarly, "spam" has reduced the value of e-mail, even as e-mail has become a necessity for the majority of users. Even without negatives such as spam or file "spoofing," additional users on large networks can remove more value than they add, as the sheer number of members lowers the value of the network and diminishes the overall network multiplier. An oversized online job board may showcase too many poorly screened candidates, when an employer simply wants a few good ones. As the eBay community has grown, eBay members have complained about shoddy bidding practices, outdated auction-management rules, and poor search engine capability, in addition to an ongoing fraud problem.[8]

The solution is to either limit the size of the network or establish rules and tools that create order rather than chaos as the network gets larger. Social networking websites, for example, require users to have common, established relationships in order to enter a network. eBay has community rules and policies designed to avoid transactional anarchy and has created feedback mechanisms to enhance the value of interconnectedness. Even simple message boards can benefit from moderators who establish order as the network's size increases. This highlights an interesting contrast between truly open systems and well-managed platforms: Open systems may be self-limiting, as the size of the user base undercuts the orderliness of the product evolution, while platform management (discussed later in the chapter) can facilitate network value as networks increase in size.

Overcoming Network Barriers

Clearly, the network effect underlying Metcalf's Law can be and is used to create an unbalanced playing field and competitive advantages for market leaders. Just as size alone cannot guarantee an everlasting low-cost position or leverageable advantage for market leaders, however, it cannot guarantee success through network value. A variety of opportunities exist for challengers to break through network barriers. As has been the case throughout this text, such an opportunity for a challenger equates to a threat for an incumbent.

■ **Segmentation.** As mentioned earlier, all interoperable users are not created equal, and sizable networks can suffer from diminishing returns as they grow larger. Suppose 50 percent of all Internet users use an AOL Instant Messenger product, but 90 percent of a specific firm's project team members use the Microsoft version; the Microsoft product will have a higher interoperability value for the team, despite its smaller network size. The relevant audience is the much more important metric, which hints at a strategy for overcoming the barriers created by network effects: By finding relevant segments and pockets of high-value interconnectedness, challenging companies can overcome network externalities. This is done by creating a more relevant "pool" of interoperability, where each node has a higher value. In the desktop software arena, for example, both Adobe and Quark have managed to thrive in the shadow of Microsoft by picking specific audiences (those in digital design and desktop publishing, respectively) that require specialized tools and place high value on interoperability. Another example is online dating services that pre-screen and closely match users, making each member in the network much more valuable and interesting than those in an unscreened dating site open to the great "unwashed" Internet masses.

Just the *promise* of more tightly coupled and relevant interoperability can help win over a segment if no clear interoperable winner has yet emerged. This is a result of the perceived future value of the technology with the network in place, even if the network has yet to materialize. Aggressive evangelizing efforts for new technologies are often conducted partially to foster the perception that future value will be created by a large number of relevant users. This tactic is more achievable with a tighter and more manageable pool of customers.

The strategy ties back to Michael Porter's generic focus strategy, outlined in Chapters 8 and 9. If a company has a unique capability that allows it to better meet the needs of a particular target market, then focusing on that narrower market will potentially allow the firm a degree of competitive advantage. In the case of network value, if a firm is able to address a definable market and capture a network effect more efficiently than can a broad-based competitor, it will create a value gap that serves as a competitive barrier.

■ **Value Increase.** Another way to overcome the structural barriers created by network effects is to change the value side of the equation. A truly innovative product can add enough value to overcome the value gap created by interconnectedness. Consider, once again, instant messaging: A high-quality videoconferencing and file sharing–enabled instant messaging service might create incentives for switching, despite the presence of buddy lists on a competing IM product. Gauging whether enough value exists to overcome a network externality (or other barriers) is a difficult task, however, as promoters of the Dvorak keyboard discovered.

Metcalf's Law is conceptual and directional, not mathematically precise. The value of interconnectedness varies from situation to situation, relative to the value of performance, and not all interconnectedness is created equal. In other words, N^2 is a directional statement about the relationship between value and interoperability, not an exact formula. Where the network multiplier is weaker (e.g., $V = N^{1.5}$), it represents less of a barrier. In console gaming, for example, the ability to share games with others is a relatively weak network effect that influences platform choice but can be overcome by a consumer's desire to gain access to a particular feature or software title. Microsoft gambled that the Xbox's better graphics and more mature software titles would cause users to switch from Nintendo and Sony PlayStation2. The value-increase tactic has been used throughout the history of the console gaming industry, as companies have introduced major performance enhancements as a method of breaking the relatively weak interconnectedness of neighborhood game sharing. Interestingly, the rise of Internet-based gaming will lead to a much larger network multiplier, based on building both larger and more tightly coupled networks through online interconnectedness. As a result, it should become much more difficult to overcome the network effect in the future. The days of significant swings in installed base and console platform market share may soon come to an end, unless far more revolutionary changes are introduced in future systems.

> ### Palm Pilot and Network Value

In order to establish itself, Palm initially used a high-performance strategy to overcome the pull of the Windows OS network effect and switching costs. The discussion of Palm in Chapter 2 highlighted how Palm's management used an early integrated stack to create a highly attractive product, relative to alternatives in the handheld market. This stack was attractive enough that the use of a proprietary OS, hardware, and software was not an issue for consumers.

Palm's dominant lead has steadily eroded, however, as Windows CE-based handhelds have gained market share at the expense of Palm and Palm-compatible devices. With an early lead, Palm did create some switching barriers—including encouraging users to adopt the Palm desktop and unique handwriting language called "Graffiti" for entering data into devices. They also fostered a developer's network, to create additional software and, therefore, additional reasons for Palm users to stay on the platform. With such a tremendous lead in handhelds, however, creating a winner-take-all market would have been the best way for Palm to secure its lead. Increasing the emphasis on interconnectedness among users of Palm PDAs—a network effect—would have been a powerful way for Palm to protect its market leadership position by creating a value gap.

Palm's handhelds have an infrared beaming device that allows them to communicate with one another, creating this opportunity for interconnectedness. A lack of compelling applications, however, has limited the usefulness of "beaming." Better groupware applications and more support for the use of digital business cards, kiosks, and other applications that raise the value of Palms (particularly when others in the room have them) could have swept Palm into a much more secure position. The network-driven value gap between Windows CE and Palm would have allowed Palm to rely less on price in trying to drive out CE-based competition, since Palm could have delivered network value that Microsoft could not. The lack of price pressure as a higher-scale, low-cost producer could also have allowed Palm to reinvest and stay ahead.

■ **Regulation.** "Natural" supply side monopolies develop for goods and services with high fixed costs, where it is assumed to be most efficient for a single provider to offer the service. Utilities typically fit into this category and are almost always regulated to protect consumers from the absence of the competitive market forces that would normally keep service levels high, prices low, and profits in check. Both California's disastrous experiment with free market energy and the massive losses generated by telecommunications infrastructure firms provide further evidence of the benefits of a regulatory approach over a true laissez-faire attitude in some cases.

Traditional economic thought (Alfred Marshall et al.) assumes that monopolies should be regulated or otherwise dealt with in the public interest. While many "public choice" economists may dispute this,[9] the current environment has created an opportunity for both consumers and firms "injured" by monopolistic competition to pursue regulatory relief. Given the court cases involving Microsoft, AOL, and cell phone providers, the focus seems to be on ambiguous, network-based monopolistic power. Regulatory relief, therefore, remains an option for overcoming significant network externalities, if a winner-take-all market has developed.

NYU professor Nicholas Economides has argued, however, that strong network externalities can create what equates to a **natural monopoly** for certain services—consistent with the winner-take-all behavior of these markets.[10] This viewpoint, in addition to having social repercussions, indicates that regulatory relief risks upsetting a natural market equilibrium, as well as the maximized consumer value proposition. For a successful network good, as the number of users (N) increases, the cost of the product/service (whether or not it decreases as a result of economies of scale) will eventually fall below the utility (value) of the product, creating an attractive consumer proposition. Take, as an example, the hypothetical parallel universe without e-mail mentioned earlier: $20 a month for the use of e-mail software would seem to be a high price if only two users had access to the system, but would represent a much more reasonable value if the entire campus participated. As Economides articulated:

> *In summary, we have the paradoxical situation where the winning firm (that has high market share) is at the same time the company that sells at a low price. Sacrifices in price pay off in higher market share, and market share is more valuable when the industry has network externalities, since higher sales signify higher value. In this process, consumers benefit from the low market price.*[11]

Upsetting this balance could create a situation where no viable business proposition existed, since the value of each network would be smaller and therefore less than that of the natural monopoly. The price would presumably be higher as well, with fewer users to absorb the fixed costs (R&D, legal, marketing, etc.) associated with production and sales. As an illustration, consider the situation in which the cost to produce and distribute a product in scale is 20, the firm seeks a 50 percent margin, and 10 interconnected users make up the market ($N = 10$). Then a literal application of Metcalf's Law would yield

$$\text{Price} = 40 \qquad\qquad \text{Value} = 10 \times 10 = 100$$

In this scenario, the single producer would be profitable, and users would each be paying a price below the value they place on the product. However, if regulators decided to break up the firm into two entities, giving each half of the market ($N = 5$ for each), each new entity would likely experience higher costs (because of less scale) and lower value (because of smaller network size). If their costs went up to 30, then even if they were willing to accept only a 25 percent margin, price and value would be as follows:

Firm 1 price = 40   Value = $5 \times 5 = 25$
Firm 2 price = 40   Value = $5 \times 5 = 25$

Breaking up the demand side monopoly in this simple case would make the market unattractive. In attempting to gain access to an attractive but dominated market via regulation, a firm would be wise to anticipate a potentially less attractive end result if the network effect is strong.

Value Networks and Complements

As demonstrated earlier in the book, providing "complete" products often requires coordination with complementary goods providers and partners. Both the concept of value networks and the concept of stack layers are pertinent in discussing structural barriers that create competitive advantage. The internal combustion engine and the companies that produce the automobiles employing it, for example, have a significant structural advantage in the form of gas stations on virtually every corner. Hydrogen- and electrical fuel cell–based technology providers, without this ubiquitous source of fuel distribution, face a significant uphill battle in displacing the gasoline-powered engine. Similarly, a robust network of developers can make one software platform much more attractive than another.

Referred to as an **indirect network effect**, this relationship can be viewed as sort of a modified Metcalf's Law, where N (in $V = N^2$) represents the number of partners and complementary suppliers rather than the number of end users. Naturally, complementary goods suppliers emerge as the size of the installed base increases (in this way, the two Ns are interrelated). Facilitating this secondary network effect through partner and complement development accelerates the growth of the overall value gap between a solution provider and its potential competitors. As the size of the complement's market grows, scale economies and competition can reduce costs to the purchaser, amplifying the indirect network effect.

Clearly, a support network is a critical factor in the successful adoption of anything new. Most consumers are pragmatists,[12] hesitant to acquire new technology without a demonstrated support network. In making decisions about the purchase of a new brand of automobile, the strength of the dealer service network, parts suppliers, and skilled mechanics is an important issue for consumers. GM's Saturn division focused heavily on building a dealer network in order to create a new car brand consumers would be comfortable buying. Likewise, the availability of DVD software (primarily movies) and retailer shelf space dedicated to software have driven the rapid adoption of DVD hardware.

Overcoming Value Network/Complement Barriers

As with the user-based network effect, a significant change in the value proposition brought about by an innovation can overcome the value gap created by interconnectedness. A beachhead can be established by segmenting users and finding those for whom the value proposition is highest and the value of complementor interconnectedness is lowest. For stereo equipment, there are audiophiles; for new gadgets and software, there are technophiles. Early-adopting enthusiasts exist for new cars, skis, games—virtually all product and service categories. Part 2 of the book pointed out that this early adopter beachhead is important, since these users can often be highly influential in determining whether the mainstream audience will accept a new technology. In the book *The Tipping Point*, Malcolm Gladwell develops the **law of the few**, pointing out that targeting a small but influential group can lead to the wide-scale popularity of a new paradigm.[13] He refers to this group as "connectors, mavens, and salesmen." Geoffrey Moore talks about these early market adopters as innovators and visionaries.[14] The value of a nonstandardized solution is highest for them; others follow once the solution's utility has been proven.

Part 2 also pointed out that this audience can be approached in one of two ways—as a stand-alone profit segment with low price elasticity or as an important bridge to a larger market. If the technology in question has a high probability of eventual adoption (like HDTV or a new automobile model), then targeting an enthusiastic segment is an opportunity to price high. However, the more that product value will be driven by network value—or a network's perceived future value—the more critical it becomes to cultivate as many early users as possible. It may be prudent to price lower to accelerate the growth of the network and create more visible incentives for complementors to support it.

The Xbox had very strong pre-order sales, and many Xboxes were immediately re-sold for twice the retail price, as early supply was outstripped by demand. Keeping the price competitive with that of other consoles, however, caused the Xbox to be seen as having a very high potential mass market installed base (and lots of enthusiasm)—important value factors for both users and developers. In contrast, a few years earlier 3DO priced an equally revolutionary gaming console at two to three times the price of other consoles in the market. While the 3DO console may have been worth the price on a stand-alone basis, its pricing was indicative of a niche product strategy that did not rely on the potential interconnectedness value of either a consumer base or software developers. For potential complementors, this made it a less attractive platform to support.

Compatibility and Standards

As the discussion on networks revealed, there can be strong incentives to develop technology that is incompatible with that of the competition, if the goal is to leverage proprietary network economies. The payoff of a closed network is the value gap illustrated in Exhibit 10-2. If a firm participates in multiple stack layers (essentially developing its own complements), making these other layers incompatible with competitive platforms can reinforce the closed network. Microsoft's "Halo" game for the Xbox and Nintendo's "Mario" franchise, for example, are designed to lure users to their respective platforms and are not produced for other platforms. Halo 2 in particular, with its online multi-player component, is designed to attract and capture new network partic-ipants. As a Microsoft executive put it,

> *You know what? Those million-plus subs [Xbox Live subscriptions]*
> *that we're going to have going into next generation, they're not going*
> *to want to leave their friends. They're not going to want to leave*
> *their communities . . . so they're going to buy Xbox. They're not*
> *going to go to some other communities and start establishing*
> *friends. They're in the club, man.*[15]

But planned incompatibility can also slow adoption. If complements are required, compatibility with other stack layers or value chain members may be needed. Both the failure of quadraphonic sound to overtake stereo as a music standard[16] and the slow adoption of 56K dial-up modems can be attributed to uncertainty, resulting in a delay in support by necessary complementors. Even though incompatibility is good for the platform, it can be disadvantageous for the downstream supplier.[17] Whereas it was to Microsoft's benefit to release an Xbox-only Halo 2 game, other game firms would nat-urally prefer to reach as broad an audience as possible. As mentioned in Part 1, this can lead to a reluctance to support proprietary platforms.

Establishing **standards** can accelerate adoption and create a larger pool for the devel-opment of network value, with benefits to most constituents. It can be attractive to incumbents, particularly if they can use their influence to avoid changes in either the competitive status quo or the value configuration. Complementors and consumers appreciate the reduced uncertainty. Even innovators arguably have an interest in embracing standards, since some innovations might never get off the ground without them.[18] While open standards can do all of this, a firm is clearly much more competi-tively insulated if it has at least partial control over the standard, since it can create a unique and heterogeneous competitive position.

Fighting for Standards

Although there is typically strong and often organized opposition to a firm that is pressing for closed standards, firms can pursue a number of strategies to gain leverage for their proprietary technology.

> *Embedding a proprietary component* into a standard is one way to gain at least some control or profit opportunity. Rambus's DRAM patents and Lemelson's bar code patents, mentioned earlier in the book, are each valued in the billions of dollars, as a result of their having become embedded in de facto standards. The current legal environment seems to discourage hidden **submarine patents** or delayed ownership claims, however, particularly if they are seen as inhibiting diffusion or are the result of intentional deception. Both examples just cited have been the focus of intense litigation.

> *Contributing to consortia* allows industry participants to gain access to each other's portfolios, fosters rapid diffusion, and makes it less problematic for firms to embed technology in the industry standard. For example, a group called MPEG LA offers a complete MPEG-4 Visual Patent Portfolio License (covering video compression and decompression technology patents across multiple countries), which allows MPEG technology users to obtain access, in a

single transaction, to essential MPEG-4 Visual patents owned by many patent holders, rather than negotiating a direct license with each of them individually. Since various MPEG patents are held by all the firms listed in Exhibit 10-4, it is clearly easier for firms to license via the consortium. The licensors also benefit, via both royalties and their own freedom to operate using the MPEG standard. The CDMA Development Group (known as CDG) has a similar goal in the cell phone industry. The firms that participate are interested in a more rapid evolution and deployment of systems based on WCDMA (Wideband Code Division Multiple Access), which essentially lets everybody in an area use the same narrow band of spectra and separates calls by encoding each one uniquely. The goal is to develop open worldwide standards to accelerate progress of the technology. One of the key IP holders—Qualcomm—both sells chipsets and collects well over $100 million per quarter in royalties, while others can use the CDMA standard with a known model and IP rights.[19]

> *Alliances* with other dominant firms can also accelerate acceptance of a firm's solution. Sun Microsystems' aggressive efforts to establish multiple partnerships for the diffusion of its Java language and Microsoft's attempts to gain early support for a variety of products were designed to create a market default toward the standards controlled by the firms. While the terms of an alliance typically need to be quite favorable to attract early support for a proprietary standard, the payoff can be significant over the life of the IP if others are also attracted (or coerced) into adopting it.

> *Giving the technology away* is a more extreme manifestation of the strategies just mentioned. Giving away key components of a technology can facilitate widespread adoption. RealNetworks, Inc. has offered its player as a free download, and Adobe Systems freely offers its Acrobat Reader, in an attempt to woo users to their standards. They can then require others to pay for key pieces, such as server technology or encoding software, and also sell proprietary upgrades, based on the standard that they control.

EXHIBIT 10-4 ■ MPEG LA Licensors

Canon, Inc.	Microsoft Corp.
Competitive Technologies, Inc.	Mitsubishi Electric Corp.
Curitel Communications, Inc.	Oki Electric Industry Co.
France Télécom, S.A.	Robert Bosch GmbH
Fujitsu Limited	Samsung Electronics Co., Ltd.
GE Technology Development, Inc.	SANYO Electric Co., Ltd.
General Electric Capital Corp.	Sharp Kabushiki Kaisha
Hitachi, Ltd.	Sony Corp.
KDDI Corp.	Telenor Communication II AS
Koninklijke Philips Electronics N.V.	Toshiba Corp.
LG Electronics Inc.	Victor Company, Ltd.
Matsushita Electric Industrial Co., Ltd.	

SOURCE: MPEG LA website, http://www.mpegla.com/m4v, January 15, 2005.

Downstream Standards Decisions

For other stack participants, understanding standards is a necessary part of the product planning process. Attempting to sell cars with the steering wheel on the left in Japan would be more difficult than following accepted practice in the country, which holds that steering wheels belong on the right side. Similarly, software is much more salable when it conforms to the hardware environment used by the target audience. Embracing a single standard is seldom a source of competitive advantage, however. As Michael McGrath points out, competing by choice of standard is a tenuous tactic: "Differentiation based on standards is difficult to rely on. A company can't control establishing a standard, although many would like to. It's also difficult to stand out with a standard as vector of differentiation, since almost by definition most other competitors will convert to the same standard."[20]

Lock-In and Switching Costs

Historically, to own a cellular phone has been to experience firsthand the power of lock-in. Every time mobile phone consumers gave out their phone number, put it on a business card, or found another way to put it into someone else's address book, they made changing their phone service a little more costly. Since the phone number traditionally stayed with the carrier, all of the user's contact information would become outdated if she or he switched to another provider. The FCC recognized this and—believing that phone number portability would increase competition in the industry—mandated that users in the United States be given the option of keeping their phone numbers. This move implicitly acknowledged the power of phone number **lock-in** in creating competitive advantage. The *Wall Street Journal* referred to this change as "a seismic shift in the wireless industry, expected to spark an increase in churn."[21] In addition to phone numbers, however, mobile instant messaging and paging services, carrier-supplied phone e-mail, and even ring tones all represent other self-inflicted barriers to users' easily changing service. The investment in the phone hardware also creates a barrier to service switching, as does use of the hardware as a storage device. As new carriers offer lower-cost plans and new features become available, users may not be willing to take advantage of them because of the above-mentioned barriers.

These barriers represent **switching costs**—additional expenses and inconveniences incurred if a consumer opts to switch to a competitive product or service. These costs of exercising competitive choice make the incumbent provider the lower-cost producer in the eyes of a current customer, since staying with the existing provider avoids an expense that is incurred by switching.

Fostering Sources of Lock-In

Lock-in and switching costs are especially powerful forces when technology is heavily integrated into systems or processes. As a result, they are virtually ubiquitous in information systems.[22] Take, for example, a hypothetical manufacturing firm that has invested in PeopleSoft software to run its human resource applications. In addition to having spent $2 million on training across the organization and another $2 million on application integration, the firm pays a licensing fee of $500,000 each year. If a license-free, open-standard software package were announced that did exactly what the PeopleSoft application did, would the manufacturing firm switch and save the $500,000 per year? Probably not, since the costs of retraining and reintegrating would be $4 million. These switching costs would keep the manufacturer locked in, making it more cost-effective to remain with PeopleSoft's products. As systems become more complex and interdependent, the costs of switching become ever higher.

It is important to make a distinction between switching costs and sunk costs. **Sunk costs**—as money already spent—are, in theory, irrelevant to future decisions. In the example shown in Exhibit 10-5, the software customer would have a difficult time justifying a switch from package A to package B, since the **business case** assumes that the $3.7 million one-time investment in package B would yield only a $250,000 annual business benefit. However, the $1.6 million investment in package C would yield $1 million in annual savings, in the form of lower licensing and staffing costs, and have a payback period of roughly 18 months. If package A was put in only 12 months ago, does that change the attractiveness of changing to package C? The answer, of course, is no; it is still just as attractive to make the move despite the switching costs. The $4.4 million invested in package A has already been spent—that is, it is a sunk cost—and is not relevant to the business decision. In practice, however, few companies would make the decision to switch, because the $4.4 million has already been invested, and switching would mean acknowledging that a poor decision had been made. This, in itself, represents another form of self-inflicted lock-in. It is artificial in nature and creates potential cost issues for firms that focus on sunk rather than switching costs.

The scenario just discussed is most likely to be the case for a firm with only a short-term focus on the roadmap for an industry's technology. It is also the result of locking in with a vendor without getting the vendor's commitment to assist customers in

EXHIBIT 10-5 ■ Comparative Costs of Hypothetical Enterprise Software Packages

	Package A (current)		Package B		Package C	
	One-Time (Sunk)	Ongoing	One-Time	Ongoing	One-Time	Ongoing
Hardware	$ 400,000		$ 200,000		$ 100,000	
Training	$2,000,000		$2,000,000		$ 500,000	
Integration	$2,000,000		$1,500,000		$1,000,000	
TOTAL	$4,400,000		$3,700,000		$1,600,000	
Annual						
Licensing		$ 500,000		$ 500,000		$ 250,000
Staff		$1,500,000		$1,250,000		$ 750,000
Annual Savings (vs. current)		N/A		**$ 250,000**		**$1,000,000**

capturing additional business case revenue through product improvements. As *Harvard Business Review* editor Nicholas Carr pointed out:

> *Given the rapid pace of technology's advance, delaying IT investment can be another powerful way to cut costs—while also reducing a firm's chance of being saddled with buggy or soon-to-be obsolete technology. Many companies, particularly during the 1990s, rushed their IT investment either because they hoped to capture a first mover advantage, or because they feared being left behind. Except in rare cases, both the hope and the fear were unwarranted. The smartest users of technology—here again, Dell and Wal-Mart stand out—stay well back from the cutting edge, waiting to make purchases until standards and best practices solidify.*[23]

From a technology user's perspective, part of the message in this lesson is to avoid switching costs/lock-in until an obvious best solution has been identified. It also points out the importance of recognizing lock-in and planning business relationships accordingly.

A *Baseline* magazine article on major lighting supplier Osram Sylvania's reliance on SAP highlighted the considerations and dilemma:

> *[Osram's CIO] could lock himself more into SAP's embrace—in effect betting his company's electronic business future on its German partner—or pursue a safer strategy that lessened its dependence on one supplier of its enterprise software needs. Other companies report similar quandaries about how to manage their increasing dependencies on single software companies whose growing portfolios of products underpin their most fundamental processes. Carreker Corp., a supplier of consulting and software to banks, for instance, is in the midst of restructuring its business processes because it is finding it easier to conform to PeopleSoft software than change it; Odwalla has found the best way to get what it needs to manage its energy juice manufacturing business is not to scream at its primary enterprise business software vendor, Oracle, but to promote its partner in public and get free training and consulting in return; and payroll processor ADP has taken a tough-love stance with IBM, putting Big Blue's software team on a rigorous development tracking system it calls the Train; it also makes a point of airing any difficulties at least twice a month. And where Life Time Fitness found its exercise club and health food business constricted by its reliance on Microsoft software, JetBlue Airways embraced Microsoft software as a key means of achieving a cost advantage as a discounter.*[24]

While the large companies mentioned in the *Baseline* article were able to be proactive in attempting to manage the roadmap and their relationship with their technology platform provider, most mid-size and smaller companies have less influence and must recognize that overcommitment to a technology platform makes them potentially vulnerable.

Oracle brought out this risk both when it attempted to change the licensing terms for customers using difficult-to-migrate data warehouse products and through its acquisition of PeopleSoft, which many feel will force PeopleSoft users to migrate to additional Oracle services.

Practically speaking, the pitfalls for consumers of overdependence on a supplier are obvious and include vulnerability to price spikes, shortages, and quality-related issues. Consider the results of the OPEC-induced energy crisis of the 70s and the many virus issues surrounding Microsoft's operating systems in the 21st century. For a technology provider, taking an overly predatory approach to a committed user base—either through pricing action or through product-quality negligence—has long-term implications that can overcome short-term gain. Just as the energy crisis forced Americans to make usage and supply changes to lessen their dependence (for a time) on Middle Eastern oil, an overly disruptive business change can undermine the economic advantage gained from the presence of switching costs. The real long-term benefit of lock-in is the ability to inexpensively cultivate additional product investments and thus expand the scope of business with the customer base.

Overcoming Lock-In

As Exhibit 10-5 demonstrated, significantly enhancing performance can eliminate the barriers of lock-in (except the psychological ones) by tipping the cost–benefit scale through business case benefit. Michael Porter confirms this: "If switching costs are high, then new entrants must offer a major improvement in cost or performance in order for the buyer to switch from an incumbent."[25]

Hypothetical package C in Exhibit 10-5 delivered $1 million in additional annual total cost of ownership (TCO) benefits and, theoretically, could have been priced at an upfront cost of several million dollars to the customer. It is unlikely that the vendor would make the sale at this price, however, given the other upfront expenses associated with switching. This highlights the dilemma faced by a technology vendor employing a performance-based or long-term TCO strategy. The switching costs force the vendor to adopt an artificially low price initially to win the business. This undermines the value created by the competitive advantage that the vendor should have due to the performance of its products. For a vendor in this situation, the strategy should be to focus on downstream payments, which can be matched against downstream benefits, and set the initial investment at the price necessary to make switching feasible.

In industries with lock-in potential, therefore, a view toward the entire lifetime value to the customer is necessary. This will create a more favorable business case for setting the initial cost low enough to help overcome the switching costs associated with lock-in. Consider once again the cell phone example: The combination of service fee discounts, handset subsidies, and incentives necessary to motivate a customer to switch creates an immediate deficit for the carrier, which can be overcome only by locking the consumer into future revenue streams. In addition to the switching cost tactics mentioned earlier, two-year contracts and service cancellation penalties are designed to protect carriers from losing customers before they can recapture the costs associated with switching users from other vendors.

Another method of overcoming lock-in is to find the "lynchpins" and "kingpins"—the key influencers who can force change on other users. As discussed earlier, interconnectedness plays an increasingly important role in capturing efficiencies; it also plays a role in capturing value through the network effect. As a result, driving change through the most influential partners in interconnected networks can force other partners or network participants out of a lock-in situation. For example, getting the central e-mail administrator in a corporation to switch from Lotus Notes to a Microsoft Exchange Server can force thousands of field salespeople to switch from other e-mail clients to Outlook. Similarly, by focusing on Wal-Mart and Target, a radio frequency identification (RFID) technology supplier can ensure that the entire packaged goods industry is forced to adapt to new methods of tracking inventory. Wal-Mart's CIO has said, "It [RFID] will become a requirement, like EDI, because if we can't track your product, it's an added cost for us that we have to pass on to our customers."[26] This logic and Wal-Mart's market power give Wal-Mart both the justification and the ability to set technology direction and change the status quo.

Platform Efficiencies

In the discussion of technology stacks in Chapter 2 and the earlier discussion in this chapter, achieving layer ownership and being a standard bearer emerged as an important method of establishing a dominant position in an industry. A key characteristic of a robust platform is a technology that underpins customer solutions and on which further applications are built. Ownership of a technology stack layer, and the resulting ability to influence the total customer solution, is, of course, a heterogeneous capability and represents an excellent source of competitive advantage. The examination of some of the largest technology firms—Microsoft, Oracle, Intel—has made it clear that the leverage they exert creates both an opportunity to capture higher profits and some security against volume loss or obsolescence.

As a solution becomes "hard-wired" into customers' systems, one of the obvious barriers introduced is the switching cost. Getting a technology to the center of an interconnected business solution creates a variety of interdependencies and investments that make it painful for customers to defect. Many of the examples alluded to throughout this book—from the investment in games that follows a dependency on a particular gaming platform to the custom applications work that is built on top of ERP applications—provide clear illustrations of how customer commitment to a platform keeps the provider entrenched. The PeopleSoft example demonstrated that the higher the integration commitment, the less chance a customer will defect to another solution.

Developing and Managing a Platform

A well-managed platform can both grow and accelerate the demand for a technology. There is a symbiotic relationship between aspirant platform providers and their customers and complementors. Perhaps the most important aspect of a well-thought-out platform orientation is to facilitate an ecosystem that promotes the growth of the platform. The need for completeness in products and services—a concept introduced in Chapter 2—creates the opportunity for a platform provider to coordinate activities and interfaces, set architectural direction, and create momentum that makes the platform attractive to support.

Platforms are limited if a secondary set of providers does not form around them. Similarly, broader application and deeper market penetration create a bigger potential market, which attracts new ecosystem participants. The discussion earlier in the chapter and elsewhere in the book on standards highlighted that uncertainty often slows commitment. Platform leaders can create faster-growing markets by removing uncertainty.

Another of the ways for a technology firm to capitalize on the platform characteristics of a product is to leverage the platform to sell additional products and services. A combination of ongoing revenue streams, ancillary product offerings, and new releases captures revenue that is insulated from competition. While the initial battle for product acceptance may be quite competitive and highly contested, these other sources of revenue and growth can be developed within a much more protected market mindset. As in monopolistic settings, pricing can be oriented more toward customers' willingness to pay than competitive pressure.

Still, management of these revenue streams requires a thoughtful sensitivity to the potential loss of platform leverage. The overuse of leverage to capture what are perceived as unfair and undeserved profits can trigger a platform revolt. The Oracle licensing changes mentioned earlier in the discussion of lock-in led many previously loyal users to either cancel upgrades or move to competitors.[27] In another example, chip maker Rambus, which holds key DRAM patents, has seen the rest of the industry ally against it because of perceived heavy-handed and underhanded tactics.[28] The discussion of stack-based strategy in Chapter 2 stressed the importance of allowing in outside partners in order to maintain industry-wide endorsement of a platform choice. In planning future releases, a vendor needs to find ways to offer upgrades with value, while avoiding disruption of the product's platform characteristics. Recall that requiring a "re-connection" of integrated elements is, in effect, a platform shift and sacrifices the competitive advantage gained through customer commitment and integration.

An additional key benefit of having a product become a platform is the influence gained over the direction and architecture of the industry's future product development. The ability to drive the industry toward solutions that the incumbent favors helps the incumbent to avoid yielding competitive advantage to others. The incumbent has the opportunity to design a future that includes a continued favorable position for itself. As Siebel Systems gains clout as the leader in customer relationship management (CRM) systems, for example, other hardware and software vendors planning CRM segment strategies or needing a CRM component for their solution will find it necessary to work closely with Siebel. Along the way, Siebel will be able to exert influence on the next generation of products and gain support for a product roadmap that meets its goals. As Siebel moves from salesforce automation to customer relationship management to business process automation, it continues to redefine the market in ways that favor its solutions over potential competition.

Managing a platform as a source of competitive advantage is a balancing act, for which the payoff is a robust market, the ability to continue to press for new revenue streams, and a secure, more predictable future for the firm. As discussed earlier, over-leveraging the platform advantage can weaken and eventually destroy the platform by creating user resolve to switch. The appropriate leverage will vary based on the interdependencies, investment, and choices available. An outsourced e-mail provider, for example, cannot exert much leverage if the customer's e-mail and IP address are easily movable. However, once the customer starts to build applications on top of the e-mail provider's platform (such as a web-based application that generates e-mail and address book–based actions), then the leverage is higher, as is the opportunity for the provider to seek out new pockets of revenue. The conclusion to be drawn from this is that developing a platform as a source of competitive advantage requires a well-crafted plan to create customer investment, integration, and dependencies.

Professors Annabelle Gawer and Michael Cusumano identify four key areas in planning for and developing a successful platform-based competitive advantage:

> *Determining firm scope.* Generally, once a platform advantage has been gained, a wider scope of business creates more uncontested sources of potential revenue for the firm. Lack of choice for customers, however, can lead to less desire for integration and hard-wired dependency, in turn weakening the platform. Staying within a reasonably well-defined scope gives third parties greater incentive to develop applications that further secure the platform. While this may narrow the short-term opportunity, it increases the long-term leverage created by platform-based competitive advantage.

> *Determining architecture and modularity.* Creating an infrastructure for integration increases the odds of both third-party vendor and customer commitment to investing in integration, which serves to secure the platform. As discussed in Chapter 2, determining what technology to make modular and what to keep proprietary is a key strategic decision for a firm. Well-defined layers and interfaces stimulate innovation, but an overly open and modular approach can lead to an easy migration away from the platform, undermining the platform owner's control.

> *Shaping relationships with complementors.* Finding complements that contribute to platform-based advantage through integration, innovation, and investment (like gaming software for a game console maker or "big six" consultants/integrators for enterprise software application development) is critical to expanding and securing the platform.

> *Organizing internally.* Earlier sections demonstrated that making and executing decisions in the three key areas just discussed requires a properly oriented organizational structure and skill sets, as well as an executive mindset that balances the tradeoffs.[29]

Understanding the life cycle of a platform is also crucial in developing a successful platform-based competitive advantage. As Michael McGrath points out,

> *For high technology companies, the most important judgment for senior executives pondering their product development portfolio is "what is the remaining lifecycle of our primary product platforms." When a primary product platform enters its decline, the entire business is threatened if the company doesn't react in time.*[30]

The life cycle characteristics of platforms tend to favor upstarts, since incumbent firms are tempted to ride the existing platform too long while innovation emerges elsewhere.

ANNABELLE GAWER ON

PLATFORM LEVERAGE

Annabelle Gawer is a member of the Strategy and Management Department at INSEAD, directs INSEAD's Executive Education programs, and is a lecturer on technology strategy at Imperial College, London. She graduated from MIT with a Ph.D. in management of technological innovation and also holds an MSc in industrial engineering from Stanford University (1992). She is an expert in high-tech strategy and author (along with Michael Cusumano of MIT) of the book *Platform Leadership: How Intel, Microsoft, and Cisco Drive Industry Innovation.*

Annabelle's book highlights the strategic value to firms of successfully developing a platform and assuming the role of network orchestrator. Annabelle identifies the primary importance of controlling a platform as part of a broader goal to grow a market and structure it in one's favor:

> *Collaboration and cooperation between firms is particularly important with complex systems and where specialization and modularization occur. Platform leadership can be looked at in terms of both creating value and capturing value in these cases.*
>
> *As a platform leader, you create value by making it possible for many other companies to innovate around your platform, which is necessary to deliver value for end users. You are orchestrating product innovation through activities such as setting standards, disclosing interface information, and supporting design specifications. As a result, you encourage and accelerate the growth of your market.*
>
> *But in addition, there is an aspect of capturing value. The objective of platform leadership is not just to create the market, but also to derive long-term benefit from it. The primary method of capturing value is by influencing the direction of innovation in a way that favors both your design and long-term plans.*

Annabelle points out that not all markets will evolve to support modularized product platform layers and dominant platform leaders. The dominant platform in some cases will remain embedded in an integrated stack:

> *While new categories often first appear in the form of tightly integrated products, it isn't accurate to generalize that in all cases they will always evolve into modularized platform-based categories.*
>
> *Two key conditions must be met: The first is that the size and profitability of the market has to be large enough to attract specialization and modular providers. A smaller niche market may not support this. Secondly, the platform should provide potential versatility for .other applications. "Can the platform be expanded or used for different uses?" If it is narrowly dedicated to a single purpose, the attractiveness of a modular platform is again limited.*
>
> *Specialization and modularization is a strong possibility where these conditions are met. But if the tight integration of layers adds enough value, the tightly integrated product can still win.*

While controlling a platform with a large installed and complement base creates a source of competitive advantage for the firm, this advantage can erode if ecosystem partners switch to or support other platforms, creating a platform shift. Annabelle recognizes this danger, and she councils a proactive long-term platform development plan that is market rather than partner driven.

> *Part of successful platform management requires not losing sight of the customer who buys the end product. While you need to maintain close relationships with developers and complementors, at the end of the day, the end-user—the customer—makes a choice of purchasing the end product. You have to keep providing the best product.*

> *This sounds simple but can be quite difficult to manage. There is a danger of being so committed and involved with managing your existing platform and complement relationships that you become blind to a threat coming from a different place. You need to be aware of what is happening externally and evolve your platform in a way that encourages the developers of complements to support you. You can't be held hostage by them.*

From the partner's viewpoint, Annabelle notes that it makes sense to be diligent in selecting which platform to support, but that the reality of the marketplace may force your hand or at least limit your decision-making latitude:

> *You need to do your homework as a partner about the various platform options. But in some cases, there aren't a lot of platform choices. Even if choice exists, cross-platform commitment is a matter of resources. Of course, it is preferable and improves bargaining power to support multiple platforms, but this isn't always possible in the short term.*

> *Your dependence on a platform comes with risk. In the end, the better platform choice is the standard that is likely to win by creating momentum in both installed base and network . . . rather than simple technical superiority. As a partner, your real interest should be in who can grow the market and is most likely to succeed.*

This last point highlights the virtuous circle that makes platform and layer ownership such a powerful competitive position. It also clarifies why maintaining a platform leadership position has such a high strategic importance.

Avoiding Platform Leverage

From the customer (and partner) perspective, interoperability and portability in applications allow for an easier move from platform to platform and decreased supplier leverage. When possible, to avoid becoming an unwitting and unwilling cash machine for the platform provider, customers should have long-term contractual agreements protecting their interests with respect to changes in licensing, forced upgrades, and other leverage points. Closer partnering, user group participation, and the firm's agreement to visibly support and promote the platform also enhance customer leverage.

For smaller companies, the ability to counteract supplier leverage is somewhat more limited. The greatest leverage is often found on the tails of the S curve—in working early on with small providers for which the account is significant enough that concessions will be made or, alternatively, in working with a very large dominant design provider in which case market forces and other large customers will protect the interests of all platform users. An example of the former is a small insurance firm working with a local web-hosting company/developer; the small firm has the opportunity (although many don't exercise it) to reach a prenegotiated agreement on support levels, code transfer, and upgrades. An example of the latter is a small company working with a very large provider such as Yahoo! or eBay; any unreasonable changes by the provider will likely give rise to objections from the most vocal customers and will also trigger competitive reaction to lure dissatisfied users from the platform. When the supplier is large relative to the customer yet small enough to avoid competitive reaction, however, the customer is likely to have little or no leverage.

Overcoming Platform Leverage

For a nonincumbent challenger, breaking into a market with entrenched platform-based competition is a difficult task. Pursuing switchers requires overcoming lock-in costs and developing relationships and skills that provide for smooth product migration. It also requires convincing customers in the targeted industry that the well-thought-out future offered and evangelized by the current platform supplier represents an inferior path. Since platform owners can inadvertently create a platform shift for their users, watching for opportunities created by disruptive shifts offers one potential window for challengers. In managing the move from client/server to Internet-based application delivery, for example, many software firms rewrote their applications so extensively that the incentive for customers to stay with the platform was eliminated. Many upstarts were able to step in as a result.

Incumbents obsessed with managing the existing platform may create another potential source of opportunity for challengers. A disruptive platform-shaking innovation may, in fact, shed light on the path an industry will eventually follow, but still not be embraced by the current platform leader. Consider again the airline industry, where the existing carriers continue to use a hub-and-spoke system, since their business model is built on it, while customers are discovering that low-cost point-to-point airlines actually offer a superior choice in many cases.

Christensen sees this as the primary Achilles heel of leading organizations and observes that, in the computer disk drive industry, overemphasis on current customer platforms led to a recurring theme of obsolescence.[31] As discussed in Chapter 7, industries can be characterized as following a series of S curves (see Exhibit 10-6); as the potential for one platform begins to flatten out, a new technology takes its place. Since customers and the supplier are both heavily invested in the older technology platform, they tend to resist platform shifts and redouble their efforts to maximize the existing platform's value. As shown earlier, McGrath sees this point as a critical juncture in the life of a firm. Andy Grove refers to the tendency to underreact at this juncture as the **inertia of success**, which creates an opportunity for new firms to step in and develop platforms that ultimately take the industry to a new level.

This opportunity is created partly by the emergence of new customers who do not have the switching costs of the existing buyers. The established customer base tends to follow later, once it becomes clear that a new solution's short-term cost is worth incurring

EXHIBIT 10-6 ■ Jumping S Curves

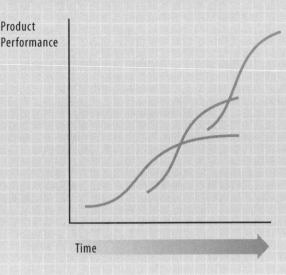

because of its long-term value potential. While new customers don't have the switching cost issues, they still need to see evidence that the new platform will be robustly supported and that the vendor will not abuse the power that comes from the customers' commitment. Before buying an Xbox, for example, customers needed to feel comfortable that plenty of game software would be available at a reasonable price. And before incorporating a patented drug delivery system, other pharmaceutical firms must understand the terms that govern their freedom to use the technology. Since savvy customers understand both the importance and the risks of platform choice, the platform challenger needs to demonstrate that it has the ability to take on the role of platform leader and a willingness to repudiate a profiteering mentality.

Installed Base Leverage

An **installed base** is, of course, a feature of companies with an operating history. It is established by building up a customer base over time and developing an ongoing relationship with these customers. An installed base is most relevant to platforms, since the range of future choices for an installed base should be limited by the past product choices that define them as "installed." For example, the number of Sony PlayStation owners dictates the market potential of new games (as it is limited by the number of Sony console owners), as well as the purchase choices that can be made by these Sony owners. In contrast, owners of the board game Monopoly are much less definable as an installed base, since the board game lacks platform characteristics.

Installed base size can yield economies of scale and is thus a potential source of competitive advantage. Additionally, a large installed base attracts more complements, influencing others to join.[32]

Harnessing Installed Base Advantages

Economies of scale and complement development aside, building an installed base rather than simply capturing discrete transactions creates more opportunities to create structural barrier–based competitive advantage. The heterogeneous advantages for incumbent firms of possessing an installed base of users, which can be used to create an unbalanced and advantageous playing field, include the following:

> **Credibility.** The presence of a vibrant customer base indicates that the company can produce a workable product that meets customer needs at an acceptable price. The more similar existing customers are to a prospect's business, the greater this influence becomes. Vertical industry–focused case studies are heavily used in many technology industries to foster this credibility and to demonstrate to prospects that the supplier is a "player" in their market. In pursuing new prospects, a supplier that can demonstrate experience in developing solutions pertinent to the customer has an advantage that does not accrue to all firms.

> **Referral business opportunities.** Referral-based business is both cheaper and easier to close than other types of business, since customers do the marketing on behalf of the vendor. Encouraging customers to recommend and evangelize the product creates a trusted sales force unavailable to the competition.

> **Low-cost access.** Finding and reaching the right customer decision-maker can be an expensive proposition. With proper relationship marketing, a firm with an installed base has a conduit directly to key contacts in the right firms. It also has the attention of this audience and doesn't need to send as many messages about its offerings as does the prospecting firm. This allows the firm to much more easily sell upgrades, next-generation products, and complementary goods.

> **Interoperability.** The promise of simplicity and interoperability between different applications creates the potential for capturing market share in related product areas. Whether by bundling additional extensions or merely providing a suite of products designed to smoothly integrate, the owner of an installed base has opportunities that are not as readily available to the competition.

> **Influence.** Like layer and platform ownership, an installed base allows the base's owner to press for the vision of the future that is most favorable to the firm. This gives the installed base owner far greater influence than other competitors and keeps the installed base owner entrenched.

> **Lock-in.** As outlined earlier in the chapter, locking in a customer base has tremendous competitive benefit because of the cost imbalance between switching and staying. Needless to say, it is not possible to have lock-in without first having an installed base.

> **Information.** A relationship with customers can be used to develop a conduit for information on purchase plans, technology paths, desired product/service upgrades, and other variables that are important from a planning perspective. This insight is unique and valuable and gives an incumbent firm with an installed base significant competitive benefits over a potential challenger.

Two proverbs apply to these installed base advantages:

1. To the victor go the spoils.

2. History is written by the winners.

Firms can capture the heterogeneous benefits just discussed and improve their economic performance by developing an installed base orientation.[33] A company with a base of customers can both harvest additional profits and help set the future direction of its market. This requires focusing on customers in terms of a set of *relationships* rather than a set of transactions. The distinction can best be seen by comparing online retailer Amazon.com to a primarily offline retailer such as Sears. By capturing customer information and purchase behavior and focusing on relationship marketing, Amazon.com can identify products likely to be of interest to individual consumers and notify those consumers of other products they might like, influence future purchase decisions, and even save information on products that customers have considered buying. When a customer returns to the Amazon.com "store," he or she will have a shopping cart full of these items, as well as suggestions for new items that also fit the customer's profile. This is in stark contrast to the traditional shopping experience at Sears, where employees have no personal memories of what the customer has purchased in the past and when he or she last visited. Information on the customer's size, color and brand preferences, or complementary purchases is not available either. The traditional transaction-based approach means that each shopping experience is a unique event, giving Sears little leverage over other competing retailers, while Amazon's relationship-oriented, installed base approach creates some nonduplicable advantages for the consumer. The movie *The Sixth Day* presents a vision of the future in which a computer at the front of a Gap clothing store automatically recognizes an established customer and makes suggestions for new items he might want as he walks in the door. Nordstrom's currently follows a similar approach by using a highly trained sales staff. No matter what type of "technical" approach is used, the value of a customer base increases substantially when its members are approached and managed as an installed base.

Installed Base and Vulnerability

Firms with installed bases also have more to lose. Along with having cannibalization issues, they need to keep their customer base satisfied and thus are required to dedicate resources to supporting the customer base and their relationships with it. The aforementioned enterprise software firm Siebel Systems, for example, is deeply wedded to the traditional large-scale enterprise software integration model. Many of its clients have large switching costs (and licensing fees) that Siebel helped to cultivate. Although a software "rental" model (such as that offered by upstart competitor Salesforce.com) with much lower per-user price points could shift the industry's value configuration and business model, Siebel cannot easily embrace it. Siebel needs to continue to support and cultivate its existing customers while not ceding the new market. This presents a dilemma if the new business paradigm shows potential. As ZDNet reported:

> *IT research firm Forrester predicts that growth in hosted CRM revenue will outpace traditionally licensed CRM revenue over the next four years. However, hosted revenue will remain a fraction of the*

total CRM software market. . . . Siebel has been slow to identify the trend. Last year, Chief Executive Tom Siebel downplayed the demand for such services, saying, "It makes an intuitively comfortable argument—but for some reason, it's just not how people want to buy software."[34]

In response, Salesforce.com CEO Marc Benioff said:

Why should [Siebel's] attempt to re-enter the ASP [rental] market be any different? Siebel's entire business philosophy is to sell expensive software to big companies with deep pockets and reap the rewards of maintenance fees and license renewals. If history is a guide . . . it won't be pretty.[35]

Many others have echoed this sentiment, including CRMGuru founder Bob Thompson, who said the following:

I give a Siebel/ASP solution low odds for success, for much the same reasons that full-fare airlines like United failed to beat discounters like Southwest, or that full-service computer companies like IBM and HP struggle to win profitable business against the ultra-efficient Dell.[36]

As earlier discussions in the book about both Dell and Southwest have shown, as innovation shifts industries from old models to new, opportunities are created for challengers. Essentially, Siebel, like many incumbents with large installed bases, is the keeper of the status quo. Existing installed bases reinforce this role and encourage incumbents to stick with it. The result is that resources are allocated to maintain projects designed by existing customers and to protect short-term revenue models at the expense of exploring projects that may reflect the future direction of the market.[37] To the extent that the installed base remains loyal and productive, this isn't a problem. It is simply a choice about existing versus new market opportunities. For a challenger, however, the incumbent's choosing to stay with the existing paradigm creates an opportunistic entry point. In cases where the new technology is disruptive, the opportunistic entry point will evolve from a niche/flank position to the dominant one. As part of this industry transition, the incumbent's installed base will begin to migrate, leaving the incumbent out in the cold. This trend has been documented in a number of industries ranging from automobiles to disk drives.[38]

CHAPTER SUMMARY

Following a discussion of traditional sources of competitive advantage in Chapter 9, this chapter looked at other structural barriers that exist in many technology-intensive industries, particularly the IT arena. These barriers create competitive advantage primarily through value gaps and cost asymmetries inherent in product usage.

Network effects are derived through user interconnectedness and result in value creation related to demand side economies of scale and market share. As illustrated by Metcalf's Law, a leader's product can have a higher value than those of other market participants simply because a higher number of its users can interact with one another. This value gap is a powerful source of competitive advantage. Network externalities, developed by offering activities and product features that focus on enhancing network value for users, can be used to secure ongoing dominance. Network value may diminish, however, if the network beneficiary does not establish rules and create tools to keep the market orderly and ensure ongoing interconnectedness value. In other cases, overcoming network effects requires focused market segmentation, radical performance improvement, or disruption through regulatory mechanisms.

Complementors also represent a source of network value, and fostering a robust network of complements can create a value gap for leading firms and thus be a source of competitive advantage. Early customers can base value on the potential for complementor development, even before the complements exist. In order to establish a market beachhead, firms need to embrace tactics that foster the perception that robust networks will be built in the future.

The proper posture toward adherence to and influence over compatibility and standards can also create (or reinforce) a firm's competitive standing. Nurturing positive network feedback can help a firm's technology emerge as a standard, but the firm may be left with an incompatible and poorly supported offering if the process is not managed correctly. Through a variety of tactics, such as alliances or participation in standards consortia, a firm can turn the emergence of a standard from a winner-take-all event into one in which the firm simply has leverage. For the standards aspirant, gaining traction and focusing on other stack participants is important. This is a somewhat unilateral tactic, however, as commitment to a standard is seldom a source of long-term competitive advantage for downstream firms.

Switching costs and lock-in affect the cost side of the equation by creating a user-specific cost difference for challengers attempting to win business from the incumbent. As on the value side, these extra costs associated with new solutions can be an asymmetrical source of advantage for existing providers. Again, radical performance improvement is one way to overcome this problem. Structuring pricing to minimize upfront expense and capture lifetime value can also counteract switching costs in cases where the challenging firm has a superior overall proposition.

Platform ownership and leadership is another source of asymmetry, allowing the owner to grow the market size and set the category direction and product roadmap, steering toward a future where the platform leader continues to play a key role. Control over platforms also creates both switching costs and network externalities, on which the platform incumbent can capitalize through recurring revenue streams, sale of additional products and services, and licensing fees from either users or other layer providers. Addiction to this revenue stream, however, can lead incumbents to make poor long-term platform decisions, allowing challengers to either initiate or take advantage of platform shifts.

Finally, an installed base provides a unique source of competitive advantage by signaling acceptance of the firm by the industry, supplying a low-cost sales channel for additional products and services, influencing future customer decision making, and providing customer insight not readily available to other firms. The presence of an installed base does give rise to cannibalization concerns, however, that can leave openings for challengers and restrict the strategic options available to the incumbent firm.

While the benefits are clear for technology suppliers, technology buyers should be aware of the barriers described in this chapter and avoid self-inflicted damage from the costs associated with them. Thoughtful planning that focuses on interoperability, appropriate vendor choice, modularity, and contractual protection when necessary can lessen the impact of some of the market imperfections that typically allow vendors to capture high profits.

ENDNOTES

Introduction

Epigraph: Charles Darwin, *Origin of Species*, 1859, Chapter 3.

1. Sandra D. Atchinson, "A Perfectly Good Word for WordPerfect: Gutsy," *BusinessWeek*, October 2, 1989.

2. International Data Corp. research director Mary Wardley, in *Macweek*, April 24, 2000.

3. Legal Technology Institute, University of Florida, Fredric G. Levin College of Law, "Application Service Providers: An In-Depth Look into the Future Use of ASPs in the Legal Profession," Fall 2000.

4. Dataquest data, referenced in N. Newman, "From Microsoft Word to Microsoft World: How Microsoft Is Building a Global Monopoly," NetAction White Paper, http://www.netaction.org/msoft/world/msword2world.html.

5. Legal Technology Institute, *op. cit.*

6. Jared Diamond, *Guns, Germs, and Steel* (New York: W. W. Norton & Co., 1999).

7. Guest is better known for writing the famous phrase "It takes a heap o' livin' in a house t' make it home," which, as far as I can tell, has no practical application to the topic at hand.

8. *Time*, December 27, 1999.

9. Piper Jaffray, analyst report, December 1998.

10. Amazon S-1 filing, SEC EDGAR Database.

11. Amazon 1998 10K filing, SEC EDGAR Database.

12. Andersen Consulting Supply Chain Practice Report, referenced in *Computerworld*, January 3, 2000, http://www.computerworld.com/news/2000/story/0,11280,40476,00.html.

13. Piper Jaffray, *op. cit.*

14. The group, called "Shopper Connection," included CDNow, Reel.com, eToys, Outpost, Preview Travel, and Fogdog, among others.

15. Boston Consulting Group Study, "The State of On-line Retail 3.0," commissioned by Shop.org, April 2000.

16. J. W. Gurley, "How Low Can You Go," CNET, December 21, 1998, http://news.com.com/how+low+can+you+go/2010-1071_3-281193.html.

17. Data provided to the author by VentureOne.

18. Venture Economics cited in D. Bloom, "Optical Bubble," *Red Herring*, March 6, 2001.

19. Fred Wang of Trinity Ventures quoted in C. Koo, "Venture Capitalists Turn Lemming over Optical Networks," October 25, 2000, http://www.thestreet.com/_tscs/tech/telecom/1142666.html.

20. Study by Alan Jacobwitz cited in Shannon Faris, "Seeking Entrepreneurial Origins: Are Entrepreneurs Born or Made?" Kauffman Center for Entrepreneurial Leadership, Clearinghouse on Entrepreneurship Education, December 1, 1999 (DIGEST Number 99-1).

21. California State Railroad Museum website, http://www.csrmf.org/doc.asp?1D=279.

22. A. Friedlander, "Infrastructure: The Utility of the Past as a Prologue," Corporation for National Research Initiatives Paper, Reston, VA, 1997.

23. R. Riegel, *The Story of the Western Railroads* (New York: Macmillan, 1926), p. 133.

24. J. Stover, *American Railroads* (Chicago: University of Chicago Press, 1961), p. 146.

25. *Ibid.*, p. 175.

26. A. Grove, *Only the Paranoid Survive* (Garden City, NY: Doubleday, 1999).

27. H. Petroski, *The Pencil—A History of Design and Circumstance* (New York: Alfred A. Knopf, 2003), p. 196.

28. Robert D. Putnam, *Bowling Alone: The Collapse and Revival of American Community* (New York: Simon & Schuster, 2000).

29. T. W. Malone and J. F. Rockhart, "Computers, Networks and the Corporation," *Scientific American*, Vol. 267, 1991, pp. 92–99.

30. *Ibid.*

31. J. Sapsford, "As Cash Fades, America Becomes a Plastic Nation," *Wall Street Journal*, July 23, 2004, p. A1.

32. John Seely Brown, Foreword to *Understanding Silicon Valley: The Anatomy of an Entrepreneurial Region*, by M. Kennet (Stanford: Stanford University Press, 2000).

Chapter 1

Epigraph: George Carlin, *Braindroppings* (New York: Hyperion, 1998), p. 75.

1. C. Pistorious and J. Utterback, "A Lotka-Volterra Model for Multi-Mode Technological Interaction: Modeling Competition, Symbiosis and Predator Prey Modes," *Technology Management in a Changing World*, Proceedings of the Fifth International Conference on Management of Technology, Miami, Florida, February 27–March 1, 1996.

2. P. Ghemawat and P. del Sol, "Commitment versus Flexibility?" *California Management Review*, Summer 1998.

3. G. Dosi, "Sources, Procedure, and Microeconomic Effect of Innovation," *Journal of Economic Literature*, September 1988.

4. L. Branscomb and P. Auerswald, *Taking Technical Risks* (Cambridge, MA: MIT Press, 2001).

5. A. Cooper and C. Smith, "How Established Firms Respond to Threatening Technology," *The Academy of Management Executive*, Vol. 6, No. 2, 1992.

6. R. Langlois, "Schumpeter and the Obsolescence of the Entrepreneur," UConn Department of Economics Working Paper No. 2002-19, August 2002, http://ssrn.com/abstract=353280. (Also published in *Advances in Austrian Economics*, Vol. 6, 2003, pp. 287–302).

7. J. A. Schumpeter, *Capitalism, Socialism, and Democracy* (New York: Harper and Brothers, 1942).

8. J. Pinto, *Controls Intelligence & Plant Systems Report*, September 2000.

9. Branscomb and Auerswald, *op. cit.*, p. 70.

10. D. Dunn, "Philips Fills Gap in Wireless LAN Portfolio—Acquisition of Systemonic," *EBN*, January 6, 2003.

11. Philips Press Release, December 19, 2002, http://www.semiconductors.philips.com/news/content/file_919.html.

12. J. Gans and S. Stern, "The Product Market and the Market for 'Ideas': Commercialization Strategies for Technology Entrepreneurs," *Research Policy*, February 2, 2003.

13. KPMG Planning Process Assessment Service Brief, "Tools for Improving Financial Performance," 2001, http://www.bearingpoint.com/library/publications/pdfs/FS_PPA_SolBrfv2.pdf.

14. Ghemawat and del Sol, *op. cit.*

15. L. Aragon, "Head Count: Heads' Heads Roll," *Red Herring*, November 13, 1999.

16. "Wall Street Plays Numbers Game with Earnings, Despite Reforms," *Wall Street Journal*, July 22, 2003, Section A1.

17. *The McKinsey Quarterly*, No. 2, 2001.

18. L. Bourgeois, I. Duhaime, and J. Stimpert, *Strategic Management: A Managerial Perspective* (Orlando, FL: Dryden Press, 1999).

19. M. Master, "Guy Kawasaki Offers a Start-up Mentality to Big Business," *The Conference Board*, 2004.

20. T. Peters, *A Passion for Excellence: The Leadership Difference* (New York: Random House, 1989).

21. Al Reis and Jack Trout, *The 22 Immutable Laws of Marketing* (New York: HarperBusiness, 1993).

22. J. McGroddy, "Raising Mice in the Elephant's Cage," in Lewis M. Branscomb and Philip E. Auerswald (Eds.), *Taking Technical Risks: How Innovators, Executives, and Investors Manage High-Tech Risks* (Cambridge, MA: MIT Press, 2001), pp. 83–91.

23. C. Christensen, *The Innovator's Dilemma: When New Technologies Cause Great Firms to Fail* (Boston: HBS Press, 1997).

24. "Dell Build to Order Manufacturing," Accenture Case Study, http://www.accenture.com/xd/xd.asp?it=enweb&xd=industries%5Ccommunications%5Chigh-tech%5Ccase%5Chigh_dell.xml, accessed August 1, 2004.

25. IDC report in *Electronic News*, May 2000.

26. D. DeLong, "Analysts Skeptical of Dell's Aim to Dominate Global PCs," *Newsfactor Network*, June 20, 2001.

27. Tom Peters, "The Mythology of Innovation," *Stanford Magazine*, Summer/Fall, 1983.

28. http://www.lil-abner.com/kickapoo.html, accessed July 2, 2004.

29. M. Schrage, "What's That Bad Odor at Innovation Skunkworks?" *Fortune*, December 20, 1999.

30. Interview with Vinod Khosla, *Harvard Business Review*, July 2000.

31. Technology Funding, Inc.

32. F. Scherer and D. Harhoff, "Technology Policy for a World of Skew-Distributed Outcomes," *Research Policy*, Vol. 29, 2000.

33. A. Stinchcombe, "Social Structure and Organizations," in J. G. March (Ed.), *Handbook of Organizations* (Chicago: Rand McNally, 1965), pp. 142–193.

34. R. Komisar, cited in S. Smith, "Learn This Start-up Lesson Now: Get Your Goals in Line with Your Passion, and You'll Be on the True Path to Success," *Entrepreneur*, October 15, 2001.

35. D. Teece, "*Managing Intellectual Capital: Organizational, Strategic, and Policy Dimensions* (New York: Oxford University Press, 2002), Chapter 5.

36. http://www.ChasmGroup.com.

37. Data calculated from USDA Nationwide Food Consumption Survey, Continuing Survey of Food Intakes by Individual, 1994–96, and reported in M. Jacobson, "Liquid Candy," Center for Science in the Public Interest report, 1998.

38. National Soft Drink Association, "Soft Drink Fact Sheet," http://www.nsda.org/SoftDrinks/History/funfacts.html.

39. M. McGrath, *Product Strategy for High Tech Companies* (New York: McGraw-Hill, 2001), p. 72.

Chapter 2

Epigraph: Dave Barry, *Dave Barry in Cyberspace* (New York: Crown Books, 1996).

1. T. Bresnahan and S. Greenstein, *The Economic Contribution of Information Technology: Value Indicators in International Perspective* (Paris: OECD, 1998).

2. M. Iansiti, "Technology Integration: Matching Technology and Context" in *The Technology Management Handbook* (Boca Raton: CRC, 1999).

3. M. Iansiti and J. West, "Turning Great Research into Great Products," *Harvard Business Review*, May-June 1997, p. 69.

4. C. Baldwin and B. Clark, "Managing in an Age of Modularity," *Harvard Business Review*, October 1997.

5. *Ibid.*

6. J. Mahoney and R. Sanchez, "Modularity, Flexibility and Knowledge Management in Product and Organization Design," *Strategic Management Journal*, Vol. 17, 1996.

7. G. Graff, G. Rausser, and A. Small, "Agricultural Biotechnology's Complementary Intellectual Assets," U.C. Berkeley, 2001.

8. S. Simon, "Biotech Soybeans Plant Seed of Risky Revolution," *Los Angeles Times*, July 1, 2001.

9. P. Phillips and D. Deirker, "Public Good and Private Greed: Strategies for Realizing Public Benefits from a Privatized Global Agri-food Research Effort," presented at AARES Pre-Conference Workshop on Biotechnology, January 22, 2001, Adelaide, Australia.

10. Graff, Rausser, and Small, *op. cit.*

11. M. Cusumano and A. Gawer, "The Elements of Platform Leadership," *MIT Sloan Management Review*, Spring 2002, p. 51.

12. D. Rasmus, "Unix—Make Your Choice Based on a Business Decision," *Manufacturing Systems*, June 1994.

13. G. Moore, *Inside the Tornado* (New York: HarperBusiness, 1995), pp. 69 and 160.

14. C. Morris and C. Ferguson, "How Architecture Wins Technology Wars," *Harvard Business Review*, March-April 1993.

15. Microsoft SEC 10K filing, year ending June 30, 2003.

16. Intel SEC 10K filing, year ending December 27, 2003.

17. *Ibid.*

18. Cusumano and Gawer, *op. cit.*, p. 51.

19. Baldwin and Clark, *op. cit.*, p. 84.

20. Moore, *op. cit.*, pp. 69, 160.

21. Morris and Ferguson, *op. cit.*

22. G. Hamel and Y. Doz, "The Use of Alliances in Implementing Technology Strategies," in M. Tushman and P. Anderson (Eds.), *Managing Strategic Innovation and Change: A Collection of Readings* (New York: Oxford University Press, 1997).

23. *Polaroid Corporation: Digital Imaging Technology in 1997* (Boston: HBS Press, 1997).

24. *Ibid.*

25. M. McGrath, *Product Strategy for High-Tech Companies* (New York: McGraw-Hill, 2000), p. 53.

26. W. Clifford, "Disruption in a Networked World: Capitalizing on Patterns of Structural Succession," CGEY CBI Working Paper, December 2001.

27. M. Heinzl, "Growing BlackBerrys Overseas," *Wall Street Journal*, November 13, 2003, p. B3.

28. Morris and Ferguson, *op. cit.*

29. R. Hacki and J. Lighton, "The Future of the Networked Company," *The McKinsey Quarterly*, No. 3, 2001.

30. Morris and Ferguson, *op. cit.*

31. P. Anderson and M. Tushman, "Technological Discontinuities and Dominant Design: A Cyclical Model of Technology Change," *Administrative Science Quarterly*, 1990.

32. S. Baron, Stanford Ph.D. dissertation, cited in Robert Sutton, "Force of Habit," *CIO Insight*, October 2002.

33. R. Sutton, "Force of Habit," *CIO Insight*, October 2002.

34. "Consumer Demand and the Emerging Markets for Recordable DVD," IDC-Pioneer Electronics study, 2002, http://www.pioneerelectronics.com/pioneer/files/IDCwhitepaper.pdf.

35. B. Wilson, "Should Apple Go Intel?" *Newsfactor Network*, April 4, 2002.

36. C. Baldwin and B. Clark, "How Palm Computing Became an Architect, *Harvard Business Review*, October 1997, p. 84.

37. P. Dillon, "The Next Small Thing," *Fast Company*, Vol. 15, June 1998, p. 97.

38. Cusumano, and Gawer, *op. cit.*, p. 51.

39. H. Varian and C. Shapiro, Introduction to "The Art of Standards Wars," *California Management Review*, 1999.

40. Cusumano and Gawer, *op. cit.*, p. 51.

41. D. Goodin, "Microsoft's Holy War on Java," CNET, http://news.com.com/2009-1001-215854.html?legacy=cnet, last modified September 23, 1998.

42. C. Christensen, *The Innovators' Dilemma* (New York: HarperBusiness, 2000), Chapter 1.

43. A. Cooper and C. Smith, "How Established Firms Respond to Threatening Technologies," *Academy of Management Executives*, Vol. 6, No. 2 (1992).

44. G. Hartmann and M. Myers, *Technical Risk, Product Specification, and Market Risk—in Taking Technical Risks* (Cambridge, MA: MIT Press, 2001).

45. B. Markham, B. Tevelson, and T. Houghton, "What's So Strategic About Sourcing?" *Executive Agenda* (AT Kearny), Vol. 4, No. 2, 2001.

Chapter 3

Epigraph: John Steinbeck, *The Grapes of Wrath* (New York: Heritage Press, 1939).

1. United States Patent and Trademark Office.

2. T. May, "In Search of Better Relations for Vendors, CIOs," *Computerworld*, December 3, 2001.

3. S. Gupta, PWC partner interviewed in "Is India Viable for Call Center?" *CommWeb*, March 21, 2001, http://www.commweb.com/showArticle.jhtml?articleID=7616951.

4. Wharton School, "When Back Office Work Moves Overseas," CNET, http://news.com.com/2009-1069_3-964069.html, last modified November 3, 2002.

5. W. Clifford, *Disruption in a Networked World*, Cap Gemini White Paper, December 2001.

6. J. Steinbeck, *The Grapes of Wrath* (New York: Heritage Press, 1939).

7. I. Sender, "Generic Drugs Give Big Pharma Big Pain," *NY Post*, November 10, 2002.

8. D. Wessel, "It's How We Use Computers That Counts," *Wall Street Journal*, November 14, 2002.

9. M. Porter, *How Competitive Forces Shape Strategy* (Boston: HBS Press, 1979).

10. House Subcommittee on Aviation Hearing on Effect of Fuel Price Increases on Airlines and Passengers, October 11, 2000.

11. D. Kasler, "Power Prices a Drain on Jobs," *Sacramento Bee*, September 6, 2001.

12. J. Gose, "Cogeneration," *Utility Business*, July 2002.

13. Porter, *op. cit.*

14. A. Grove, *Only the Paranoid Survive* (Garden City, NY: Doubleday, 1999), p. 29.

15. A. Brandenburger and B. Nalebluff, *Co-opetition* (New York: Doubleday, 1997).

16. D. Lyons, "Cheapware," *Forbes*, September 6, 2004.

17. Bloomberg, "Industry Jumps on De Beers's Retail Bandwagon," February 3, 2004.

18. R. McMillan, "Linux's Proprietary Booster: Larry Ellison Sees Big Changes in the Age of Linux," *Linux Magazine*, November 2002.

19. N. Bunckley, "Pay Phones a Dying Breed in Cellular Age," *Detroit News*, March 14, 2004.

20. D. Abell, *Defining the Business—Starting Point of Strategic Planning* (Englewood Cliffs, NJ: Prentice Hall, 1980), pp. 17, 30.

21. *Ibid.*

22. Porter, *op. cit.*

23. E. Iwata, "Juniper Attacks Cisco with Smart Bomb Accuracy," *USAToday*, January 30, 2001.

24. A. Cunningham, Interview with Stanford University for "Making the Macintosh: Technology and Culture in Silicon Valley," online project, http://library.stanford.edu/mac/.

25. "Trends in Contact Lenses," Bausch & Lomb Annual Report to Vision Care Professionals, December 2001.

26. Vision Council of America, 1999 survey, http://www.visionsite.org.

27. K. Croies, "Will Custom LASIK Boost Growth? Analysts Say Yes, but Also View Emerging Technologies and Favorable Demographics as Growth Generators," *OptiStock Refractive Surgery Edition*, September 2003, http://www.optistock.com/mw/2003_09all.htm.

28. P. Bye, S G Cowen Analyst report, cited by Optistock, http://www.optistock.com/mw/2003_09all.htm, September 2003.

29. J. Barney, "Firm Resources and Sustained Competitive Advantage," *Journal of Management*, Vol. 17, 1991.

30. *Ibid.*

31. M. Meyer and J. Utterback, "The Product Family and the Dynamics of Core Capability," *Sloan Management Review*, Vol. 34, Spring 1993.

32. E. Corcoran, "Routers for Sale," *Forbes*, April 16, 2001, p. 53.

33. C. Christensen, *The Innovator's Dilemma* (New York: HarperBusiness, 1997).

34. P. Evans and T. Wurster, *Blown to Bits* (Boston: HBS Press, 2000), Chapter 1.

35. T. Levitt, "Marketing Myopia," *Harvard Business Review*, September-October 1975.

36. Christensen, *op. cit.*, p. 16.

37. R. Weisman, "Network Router Showdown: Cisco vs. Juniper," *Ecommerce Times*, October 6, 2003.

38. Christensen, *op. cit.*

39. Grove, *op. cit.*, p. 107.

40. From G. Lynn, J. Morone, and A. Paulson, "Marketing and Discontinuous Innovation: The Probe and Learn Process," *California Management Review*, Vol. 38, No. 3 (1996).

41. From H. Courtney, J. Kirkland, and P. Viguerie, "Strategy Under Uncertainty," *Harvard Business Review*, December 1997.

42. *Ibid.*

43. Wharton School, "The Brains Behind the DVD," CNET, http://news.com.com/2009-1040-867543.html, last modified March 25, 2002.

Chapter 4

Epigraph: Thomas Edison, cited in W. Wachhorst, *Thomas Alva Edison* (Cambridge, MA: MIT Press, 1981).

1. Clarence Ditlow, executive director of the Center for Auto Safety, quoted in *The Christian Science Monitor*, September 22, 2000.

2. Data from Morningstar Farms and California Tomato Growers Association.

3. Bureau of Economic Analysis, "Price Indexes for Selected Semiconductors 1974–96," February 1998, cited in "DRAM Pricing—A White Paper," Tachyon Semiconductors, Naperville, IL, September 2002.

4. M. Tushman, P. Anderson, and C. O'Reilly, "Technology Cycles, Innovation Streams, and Ambidextrous Organizations: Organizational Renewal Through Innovation Streams and Strategic Change," in M. Tushman, and P. Anderson (Eds.), *Managing Strategic Innovation and Change: A Collection of Readings* (New York: Oxford University Press, 1997).

5. L. Hillenbrand, *Seabiscuit* (New York: Ballantine, 2003).

6. R. Agarwal and B. Bayus, "The Market Evolution and Take Off of Product Innovations," *Management Science*, 2002.

7. R. Rumelt, "Numbers 101: The Diffusion of Innovation," Anderson School at UCLA POL, 2002–2005.

8. G. Tarde, *The Laws of Imitation* (New York: Henry Holt, 1903).

9. A. Grubler, "Time for a Change: On the Patterns of Diffusion and Innovation," in Jesse H. Ausubel and H. Dale Langford (Eds.), *Technological Trajectories and the Human Environment* (Washington, DC: National Academy of Engineering, 1997).

10. E. Rogers, *Diffusion of Innovations*, 4th ed. (New York: The Free Press, 1995).

11. G. Moore, *Crossing the Chasm* and *Inside the Tornado* (New York: HarperBusiness, 1999).

12. A. Hargadon, "Diffusion of Innovations," in *The Technology Management Handbook* (Orlando, FL: CRC Press, 1999).

13. Moore, *op. cit.*

14. Rogers, *op. cit.*

15. Moore, *op. cit.*

16. D. Evans and P. Jovanovic, "An Estimated Model of Entrepreneurial Choice Under Liquidity Constraints," *Journal of Political Economy*, Vol. 97, No. 4 (August 1989).

17. Various studies by Hellman, Puri, Lerner, and Gompers.

18. P. Gompers and J. Lerner, *The Money of Invention: How Venture Capital Creates New Wealth* (Boston: HBS Press, 2001).

19. A. Bhide, *The Origin and Evolution of New Business* (New York: Oxford University Press, 2000).

20. P. Milgrom, "Putting Auction Theory to Work: The Simultaneous Ascending Auction," Stanford University working paper 98-002, 1998.

21. J. Paulos, *Innumeracy: Mathematical Illiteracy and Its Consequences* (New York: Vintage Books, 1990).

22. J. Zider, "How Venture Capital Works," *Harvard Business Review*, November 1998.

23. W. Sahlman and H. Stevenson, "Capital Market Myopia," *Journal of Business Venturing*, Vol. 1, 1985.

24. C. Mackay, *Extraordinary Popular Delusions and the Madness of Crowds* (New York: Barnes & Noble, 1989), originally published 1841.

25. *Ibid.*

26. C. Reed, "The Damn'd South Sea," *Harvard Magazine*, May-June 1999.

27. Mackay, *op. cit.*

28. C. Christensen, *The Innovator's Dilemma* (New York: HarperBusiness, 2000).

29. Sahlman and Stevenson, *op. cit.*

30. "Beyond the Bubble," *The Economist*, October 9, 2003.

31. N. Tredennick, "An Engineer's View of Venture Capitalists," *IEEE Spectrum*, September 2001.

32. M. Grinblatt, S. Titman, and R. Wermers, "Momentum Investment Strategies, Portfolio Performance, and Herding: A Study of Mutual Fund Behavior," *American Economic Review*, Vol. 85, 1995.

33. A. Oehler and G. Chao, "Institutional Herding in Bond Markets," Bamberg University working paper, 2000.

34. D. Repin, "Riskpsychology.net—Study of Risk Propensity Models," MIT, 2003.

35. A. Ginsberg, "Blue Chip Entrepreneurs," *Stern Business*, Fall/Winter 2001.

36. Cited in C. Hill and G. Jones, *Strategic Management*, 5th ed. (Boston: Houghton Mifflin, 2001), p. 362.

37. "How Mergers Go Wrong," *The Economist*, July 22, 2000.

38. *Ibid.*

39. J. Byrne and B. Elgin, "Cisco: Behind the Hype," *BusinessWeek*, January 21, 2002.

40. Ginsberg, *op. cit.*

41. J. Lerner, "Xerox Technology Ventures," Harvard Business School Case 9-298-109, 1997.

42. A. Campbell, J. Birkinshaw, A. Morrison, and R. van Basten Batenburg, "The Future of Corporate Venturing," *MIT Sloan Management Review*, Fall 2003.

43. H. Chesbrough, "Designing Corporate Ventures in the Shadow of Private Venture Capital," *California Management Review*, Spring 2000.

Chapter 5

Epigraph: Gabrielle Tarde, *The Laws of Imitation* (New York: Henry Holt & Co., 1903).

1. *The Catholic Encyclopedia*, Vol. 7 (New York: Robert Appleton Company, 1910); and J. Man, *Gutenberg: How One Man Remade the World with Words* (New York: Wiley, 2002).

2. G. Basalia, *The Evolution of Technology* (Cambridge: Cambridge University Press, 1987).

3. *Ibid.*

4. R. Srinivasan, G. Lilien, and A. Rangaswamy, "First In First Out? The Surprising Effects of Network Externalities on Pioneer Survival," ISBM Report 14, Penn State University, 2002.

5. G. Anders, "He Who Moves First Finishes Last," *Fast Company*, September 2000.

6. Srinivasan, Lilien, and Rangaswamy, *op. cit.*

7. M. Lieberman and D. Montgomery, "First-Mover (Dis)Advantages: Retrospective and Link to the Resource-Based View," *Strategic Management Journal*, 1998.

8. As cited by R. H. Ziedonis in Committee on Intellectual Property Rights in the Knowledge-Based Economy, National Research Council, *Patents in the Knowledge-Based Economy* (Washington, DC: National Academies Press, 2003).

9. *Ibid.*

10. A. Hargadon, "Retooling R&D: Technology Brokering and the Pursuit of Innovation," *Ivey Business Journal*, November/December 2003.

11. K. Dobyns, *History of the United States Patent Office* (Fredericksburg, VA: Kirkland Historical Society, 1999).

12. J. Gleick, "Patently Absurd," *New York Times Magazine*, March 12, 2000.

13. M. Popper, "Altera: The New Prince of Programmable Chips?" *BusinessWeek*, July 26, 2000.

14. A. Ries and J. Trout, *The 22 Immutable Laws of Marketing* (New York: HarperBusiness, 1993).

15. L. Capozzi, "Creating Preference for Internet Leaders," presented at the Manning, Selvage, and Lee Media Summit '99, on September 23, 1999.

16. M. Lieberman, "The Learning Curve, Diffusion and Competitive Strategy," *Strategic Management Journal*, Vol. 8, 1987.

17. R. Van den Broek, "Bioworld," *Forbes*, May 31, 1999.

18. D. Teece, *Managing Intellectual Capital* (Oxford: Oxford University Press, 2002), Chapter 5.

19. A. Grubler, "Time for a Change: On the Patterns of Diffusion and Innovation," in Jesse H. Ausubel and H. Dale Langford (Eds.), *Technological Trajectories and the Human Environment* (Washington, DC: National Academies Press, 1997).

20. G. Moore, *Inside the Tornado* (New York: HarperBusiness, 1995).

21. Grubler, *op. cit.*

22. Committee on Innovations in Computing and Communications: Lessons from History, National Research Council, *Funding a Revolution: Government Support for Computing Research* (Washington, DC: National Academies Press, 1999), Chapter 6.

23. *Ibid.*

24. R. Greenwald, R. Stackowiak, and J. Stern, *Oracle Essentials : Oracle9i, Oracle8i & Oracle8*, 2nd ed. (Cambridge, MA: O'Reilly, 2001).

25. R. Whiting, "IBM Eclipses Oracle," *Information Week*, May 7, 2002.

26. C. Christensen, *Innovators' Dilemma* (New York: HarperBusiness, 2000).

27. M. Kanellos, "AMD Compatibility No Problem for Intel Chip," *CNET*, February 13, 2004.

28. Moore, *op. cit.*

29. J. Hoppes, "Personal Technology Journalists' Influence on the Diffusion of Innovation—Case Study: Walt Mossberg," Ph.D. thesis, Georgetown University, 2001.

30. "Managing Vendors," *CIO Insight*, November 2002.

31. A. Alter, "ROI 2003—Do You Have Any Faith in Your ROI Numbers?" *CIO Insight*, March 17, 2003.

32. Author's interview with C. Robbins-Roth.

33. R. Foster, *Innovation: The Attackers' Advantage* (New York: Summit Books, 1987).

34. M. Tushman, P. Anderson, and C. O'Reilly, "Technology Cycles, Innovation Streams, and Ambidextrous Organizations: Organizational Renewal Through Innovation Streams and Strategic Change," in M. Tushman and P. Anderson (Eds.), *Managing Strategic Innovation and Change: A Collection of Readings* (New York: Oxford University Press, 1997).

35. *Ibid.*

36. M. Marriott, "Lots of Players, Little Harmony," *New York Times*, January 8, 2004.

37. J. Utterback, *Mastering the Dynamics of Innovation* (Boston: HBS Press, 1996).

38. R. Adner, "A Demand-Based View of Technology Life Cycles," Insead, Paris, March 2004.

39. L. Hillenbrand, *Seabiscuit* (New York: Ballantine, 2003).

40. K. Train, presentation to the California Air Resources Board (CARB), September 2000.

41. *Ibid.*

42. E. Von Hippel, interviewed in *Advertising Age*'s Business Marketing, January 1994.

43. P. Smith and H. Philip, *Wheels within Wheels: A Short History of American Motor Car Manufacturing* (New York: Funk & Wagnalls, 1968), as reported in S. Klepper and K. Simons, "Industry Shakeout and Technological Change," Carnegie Mellon, 2001.

44. E. Abrahamson and L. Rosenkopf, "Social Network Effects on the Extent of Innovation Diffusion: A Computer Simulation," *Organization Science*, May/June 1997.

45. R. Nelson and S. Winter, *An Evolutionary Theory of Economic Change* (Cambridge, MA: Belknap/Harvard, 1982), Chapter 12.

46. *Ibid.*

47. D. Needle, "The Myth of First Mover Advantage," Internetnews.com, April 5, 2000, http://siliconvalley.internet.com/news/article.php/3541_333311.

48. *Ibid.*

49. G. Kawasaki, "Time to Money," *Forbes*, March 22, 1999.

50. E. Mansfield, "Technical Change and the Rate of Imitation," *Econometrica*, Vol. 29, 1961.

51. R. Agarwal and B. Bayus, "The Market Evolution and Take Off of Product Innovations," Marketing Science Institute Report 02-111, Cambridge, 2002.

52. Lieberman, *op. cit.*

53. D. Filson and R. Gretz, "Strategic Innovation and Technology Adoption in an Evolving Industry," Claremont College working paper 2003-08, March 2003.

54. A. Van de Ven, interviewed in *Industry Week*'s "Why Companies Don't Learn," August 19, 1991.

55. M. Tushman and P. Anderson, *Managing Strategic Innovation and Change* (New York: Oxford University Press, 1997).

56. Lieberman, *op. cit.*

57. E. Mansfield, M. Schwartz, and S. Wagner, "Imitation Costs and Patents: An Empirical Study," *Economic Journal*, 1981.

58. J. Rapoza, "The High End," *PC Magazine*, March 20, 2001.

59. Supported by the work by Jovanovic, Klepper, and Tushman/Anderson cited elsewhere.

60. S. Klepper, "Entry, Exit, Growth, and Innovation over the Product Life Cycle," *American Economic Review*, Vol. 86, 1986.

61. Moore, *op. cit.*

Chapter 6

Epigraph: Umberto Eco, "How Not to Use the Fax Machine," in *How to Travel with a Salmon and Other Essays* (New York: Harcourt Brace, 1994).

1. S. Wiegand, "The California Gold Rush: An Era Remembered," *Sacramento Bee*, January 18, 1998.

2. "Week in Stocks," *Computerworld*, November 22, 1999.

3. N. Wingfield, "With the Web Shaking Up Music, a Free-for-All in Online Songs," *Wall Street Journal*, November 19, 2003.

4. CEFRIEL, "Classification of Enabling Technologies," Startel report II-9, Politecnico de Milano, ICT Center for Research, Innovation, Education, and Industrial Labs Partnership.

5. R. Cringely, *Accidental Empires* (New York: Addison-Wesley, 1992), Chapter 11.

6. W. Chesbrough, *Open Innovation: The New Imperative for Creating and Profiting from Technology* (Boston: HBS Press, 2003), p. 84.

7. P. Dickson, *Sputnik: The Shock of the Century* (New York: Walker Publishing 2001).

8. W. Reynolds, *Apollo: The Epic Journey to the Moon* (New York: Tehabi/Harcourt, 2002).

9. A. Cha, "Shuttle Tragedy Renews Focus on NASA Contractors," *Washington Post*, February 2003.

10. Reynolds, *op. cit.*

11. From the PBS series "Chasing the Sun," 2001.

12. eAC website, http://www.hybrids.com/about.html, October 1, 2004.

13. L. Musthaler, "Modularity Eases the Imaging Purchase," *Network World*, December 12, 1994.

14. B. C. Cole, "Document Management, Groupware Close Gap," *Computerworld*, March 3, 1997.

15. San Francisco Exploratorium, "The Accidental Scientist: Science of Cooking," http://www.exploratorium.edu/cooking.

16. M. Tushman and P. Anderson, *Managing Strategic Innovation and Change* (New York: Oxford University Press, 1997).

17. *Ibid.*

18. M. Cusumano, Y. Mylonadis, and R. Rosenbloom, *Strategic Maneuvering and Mass Market Dynamics: The Triumph of VHS over Beta* (Boston: HBS Press, 1992).

19. D. Filson and R. Gretz, "Strategic Innovation and Technology Adoption in an Evolving Industry," Claremont College working paper, March 2003.

20. Tushman and Anderson, *op. cit.*

21. C. Fine, "Clockspeed-Based Strategies for Supply Chain Design," *Production and Operations Management*, Vol. 9, No. 3, Fall 2000.

22. G. Moore, *Inside the Tornado* (New York: HarperBusiness, 1995).

23. R. Hof, "Reprogramming Amazon," *BusinessWeek*, December 22, 2003.

24. M. Tushman and P. Anderson, "Managing Through Cycles of Technological Change," *Research Technology Management*, 1991.

25. N. Wingfield, "New Chapter: In Latest Strategy Shift, Amazon Is Offering a Home to Retailers," *Wall Street Journal*, September 24, 2003.

26. E. Behr, "Will Amazon.com's Growth Strategy Work?" *eWeek* case study, December 4, 2003.

27. Cusumano, Mylonadis, and Rosenbloom, *op. cit.*

28. R. Sanchez and J. Mahoney, "Modularity, Flexibility, and Knowledge Management in Product and Organizational Design," *Strategic Management Journal*, 1996.

29. K. Fitchard, "Nokia's New Math: How Dividing Mobile Software Will Multiply Business and Add Up to Smartphone Supremacy," *Wireless Review*, December 1, 2003.

30. M. Cusumano and A. Gawer, "The Elements of Platform Leadership," *MIT/Sloan Management Review*, Spring 2002.

31. E. Von Hippel, "Horizontal Innovation Networks—By and for Users," MIT/Sloan Working Paper 4366-02.

32. P. Tam, "For Palm, Splitting in Two Isn't Seamless," *Wall Street Journal*, June 27, 2002.

33. *Ibid.*

34. Good Technology corporate literature.

35. H. Green, "The Squeeze on BlackBerry," *BusinessWeek*, December 6, 2004.

36. R. Enderle, "The Enderle Group," reported in J. Fortt, "New Software Challenges for BlackBerry," *San Jose Mercury News*, February 4, 2004.

37. P. Krane, "FCC's Powell Declares TiVo 'God's Machine,'" *AP News*, January 2003.

38. R. Shim, "TiVo Sues Echostar over DVR Patent," TiVo press release, January 5, 2004.

39. R. Shim, "Five Tech Firms at Crossroads," *CNET*, September 8, 2004.

40. Sanchez and Mahoney, *op. cit.*

41. Cusumano and Gaewer, *op. cit.*

42. Tam, *op. cit.*

43. S. Whitmore, "Forrester Weeds Out Problems for 'High Performance IT,'" *PC Week*, April 1995.

Chapter 7

Epigraph: Bill Gates, *The Road Ahead* (New York: Penguin, 1996).

1. S. Klepper, "Entry Exit Growth and Innovation over the Product Lifecycle," *American Economic Review*, June 1996.

2. M. Tushman and P. Anderson, "Technological Discontinuities and Dominant Design: A Cyclical Model of Technological Change," *Administrative Science Quarterly*, Vol. 35, 1990.

3. B. Jovanovic and G. MacDonald, "The Life Cycle of a Competitive Industry," *Journal of Political Economy*, April 1994.

4. *Ibid.*

5. M. Tushman and P. Anderson, "Managing Through Cycles of Technological Change," *Research/Technology/Management*, 1991.

6. C. Christensen, *Innovators' Dilemma* (New York: HarperBusiness, 2000).

7. J. Utterbeck, *Mastering the Dynamics of Innovation* (Boston: HBS Press, 1994), Chapter 9.

8. R. Goodman and M. Lawless, *Technology and Strategy* (New York: Oxford University Press, 1994), Chapter 17.

9. Tushman and Anderson, "Managing," *op. cit.*

10. P. Evans and T. Wurster, *Blown to Bits: How the New Economics of Information Transforms Strategy* (Boston: HBS Press, 2000).

11. Interview with R. Bach, Microsoft Presspass, November 22, 1999.

12. Christensen, *op. cit.*

13. D. Clark, "Novell Joins Internet Marketing Fray with Software for Corporate Networks," *Wall Street Journal*, August 20, 1996.

14. G. DeGeorge, *The Making of a Blockbuster: How Wayne Huizenga Built a Sports and Entertainment Empire from Trash, Grit, and Videotape* (New York: Wiley & Sons, 1997).

15. Christensen, *op. cit.*

16. P. Patsuris, "Blockbuster Takes on New Strategy vs. Netflix," *Forbes*, April 21, 2003.

17. Interview with Blockbuster CEO J. Antioco, Motley Fool, July 29, 2003.

18. D. Lieberman, "Consumers Still Wait for Video on Demand," *USAToday*, February 6, 2002.

19. http://www.chevrontexaco.com/technologyventures/invest_tech/diversified_tech.asp, October 8, 2004.

20. D. Frantz, "To Put G.E. Online Meant Putting a Dozen Industries Online," *New York Times*, March 29, 2000.

21. "While Welch Waited," *The Economist*, May 17, 2001.

22. "Roche Hepatitis C Treatment Gains Half of Market Share from Schering-Plough," Kaiser Daily HIV/AIDS Reports, December 23, 2003.

23. M. Herper, "Schering-Plough Gets Guts," *Forbes*, September 24, 2003.

24. E. Marshal, "DuPont Ups Ante on Use of Harvard's Oncomouse," *Science*, May 17, 2002.

25. Interview with Randy Komisar.

26. H. Chesbrough, *Open Innovation: The New Imperative for Creating and Profiting from Technology* (Boston: HBS Press, 2003).

27. *Ibid.*

28. A. Pyka and P. Saviotti, "Innovation Networks in the Biotechnology-Based Sectors," University of Augsberg, Germany, July 2001.

29. E. Abrahamson and L. Rosenkopf, " Institutional and Competitive Bandwagons: Using Mathematical Modeling as a Tool to Explore Innovation Diffusion," *Academy of Management Review*, July 1993.

30. E. Abrahamson, "Managerial Fads and Fashion: The Diffusions and Rejection of Innovations," *Academy of Management Review*, Vol. 16, 1991.

31. M. Gort and S. Klepper, "Time Paths in the Diffusion of Product Innovation," *Journal of Economics*, September 1982.

32. *Ibid.*

33. B. Jovanovic, "Michael Gort's Contribution to Economics," *Review of Economic Dynamics*, 1998.

34. M. Doms and C. Forman, "Prices for Local Area Network Equipment," Fed Reserve Bank of San Francisco Working Paper, June 2003.

35. *Ibid.*

36. R. Agarwal and M. Gort, "The Evolution of Markets and Entry, Exit and Survival of Firms," *Review of Economics and Statistics*, August 1996.

37. Jovanovic, *op. cit.*

38. M. Hicks, "Inside E-procurement," *eWeek*, January 7, 2002.

39. J. Bousquin, "Stick a Fork in Ventro's Exchange Business, It's Done," TheStreet.com, February 20, 2001.

40. IDC report, "Marketplace Participants Share Their Tales of Woe," *Network World*, June 4, 2001.

41. G. Day, A. Fein, and G. Ruppersberger, "Shakeouts in Digital Market: Lessons from B2B Exchanges," *California Management Review*, Winter 2003.

42. T. Reason, "This Year's Model," *eCFO*, http://www.cfo.com/article.cfm/3002036/ 1/c_3046576?f=inside cfo, Spring 2001.

43. *Ibid.*

44. S. Klepper and K. Simons, "Innovation and Industry Shakeout," *Business and Economic History*, Vol. 25, Fall 1996.

45. J. Panker, Interview with N. Caldwell, SearchCRM, http://searchcrm.techtarget.com/qna/0,289202,sid11_gci904299,00.html, June 3, 2003.

46. E. Roberts and C. Berry, "Entering New Business: Selecting Strategies for Success," *Sloan Management Review*, Spring 1985.

47. B. Quint, "About.com Acquired by Primedia—Sin or Synergy?" *Information Today*, December 2000.

48. J. Bandler, "New York Times Buys About.com from Primedia for $410 Million," *Wall Street Journal*, February 18, 2005.

49. T. Brush, "Predicted Change in Operational Synergy and Post-Acquisition Performance of Acquired Businesses," *Strategic Management Journal*, Vol. 17, No. 1, January 1996.

50. J. Petty, J. Shulman, and W. Bygrave, "Mergers and Acquisitions: A Means of Harvesting the Venture," *Managerial Finance*, Vol. 20, No. 1, 1994.

51. Day, Fein, and Ruppersberger, *op. cit.*

52. "Airline Consumer Panel Draws Blank on Travel Agency Decline," *Aviation Daily*, November 14, 2002.

53. "Electric-Furnace Steelmakers Reinvent the Supply Base," *Purchasing Magazine*, August 14, 1997.

54. P. DeVeaux, "UUNET Announces ISP Program for Vertical Markets," *America's Network*, March 2000.

55. E. Baker, "The Simplicity Paradox," *CIO Insight*, April 2003.

56. H. Unger, "David and Goliath Forge Bond of Steel," *Purchasing and Supply Management*, January 1995.

57. L. Haber, "Filling a Niche with Products and Service," *Computer Reseller News*, March 1997.

58. B. Fonseca, "IBM Makes New Pitch for Partners," *eWeek*, March 1, 2004.

59. J. Birger, "Can This Company Change the World?" *Money*, July 2003.

60. M. Cheng and D. Hambrick, "Speed, Stealth, and Selective Attack: How Small Firms Differ," *Academy of Management Journal*, April 1995.

61. Chesbrough, *op. cit.*

62. Chesbrough, *op. cit.*

63. Tushman and Anderson, "Managing," *op. cit.*

64. Christensen, *op. cit.*

65. "Business Process Management," *CIO Insight*, August 2002.

66. D. Teece, G. Pisano, and A. Shuen, "Dynamic Capabilities and Strategic Management," *Strategic Management Journal*, 1997.

67. *Ibid.*

68. http://www.xilinx.com/company/press/grounder.htm.

69. S. Sanderson and M. Uzumeri, "Managing Product Families: The Case of Sony Walkman," *Research Policy*, Vol. 24, 1995.

70. EIA Annual Energy Review, 1999.

71. Congressional Research Service, from "Nuclear Energy Policy," Report IB88090, March 22, 2001.

72. L. Hooper, "IBM Is Mustering Its Forces to Save OS/2," *Wall Street Journal*, March 8, 1991.

73. A. Grove, *Only the Paranoid Survive* (Garden City, NY: Doubleday, 1999).

74. *Ibid.*

75. Christensen, *op. cit.*

76. Tushman and Anderson, "Managing," *op. cit.*

77. Grove, *op. cit.*

78. J. Porras and J. Collins, *Built to Last* (New York: HarperBusiness, 1994).

79. Pyka and Saviotti, *op. cit.*

80. M. McGrath, *Product Strategy for High-Technology Companies* (New York: McGraw-Hill, 2001).

81. K. Sibley, "Sony Research Division Reaches Far into the Future," *Computing Canada*, October 26, 1998.

82. Porras and Collins, *op. cit.*

83. M. Tushman, P. Anderson, and C. O'Reilly, "Technology Cycles, Innovation Streams, and Ambidextrous Organizations," in M. Tushman and P. Anderson (Eds.), *Managing Strategic Innovation and Change* (New York: Oxford University Press, 1997).

84. See, for example, Utterback, *op. cit.*, and Tushman and Anderson, "Managing," *op. cit.*

Chapter 8

Epigraph: Adam Smith, *An Inquiry into the Nature and Causes of the Wealth of Nations*, 1776.

1. "Economics A–Z," *The Economist*, http://www.economist.com/research/Economics/alphabetic.cfm?LETTER=P#PROFIT.

2. T. Buchholz, *New Ideas from Dead Economists* (New York: Penguin, 1989), p. 25.

3. "Jetsons 1962," IMDB.com, http://www.imdb.com/title/#0055683/quotes.

4. M. Porter, "What Is Strategy?" *Harvard Business Review*, November-December 1996.

5. "People Who Mattered," *Time: The Year in Pictures*, 2000.

6. E. Nelson, "CBS's Higher Ratings, Low Costs Helped Cut Profit Gap with NBC," *Wall Street Journal*, April 15, 2003.

7. *Ibid.*

8. Porter, *op. cit.*

9. *Ibid.*

10. D. Abell, *Defining the Business: The Starting Point of Strategic Planning* (Englewood Cliffs, NJ: Prentice Hall, 1980), pp. 200–201.

11. M. Bolton, "Methodologies for Evaluating Start-Ups," Woodside Fund Presentation to International Angel Investors, May 16, 2002.

12. Interview with Dr. David P. Norton, co-creator of the Balanced Scorecard, by Craig Eason, World Trade Group, Summit Club press release.

13. Polaroid Corporation, Harvard Business Review Case 9-798-013.

14. S. Gallagher, "GM Plots Digital Turnaround," *Baseline*, November 1, 2002.

15. R. Grant, "The Resource Based Theory of Competitive Advantage," *California Management Review*, Spring 1991.

16. R. Nelson and S. Winter, *An Evolutionary Theory of Economic Change* (Cambridge: Belknap Press, 1982), Chapter 5; and I. Dierickx and K. Cool, "Asset Stock Accumulation and Sustainability of Competitive Advantage," *Management Science*, Vol. 35, 1989.

17. M. Tushman, W. Newman, and E. Romanelli, "Convergence and Upheaval: Managing the Unsteady Pace of Organizational Evolution," *California Management Review*, Vol. 29, No. 1, 1986.

18. P. Turk, "Aerospace—The Subsidy Question," *Europe*, May 1993.

19. "Fair Isaac," *RBC Capital Markets Report*, January 16, 2003.

20. Grant, *op. cit.*

21. D. McGinn, "Big Mouth Billy Bass Case Study," *MBA Jungle*, September 2001.

22. *Ibid.*

23. G. Ip, "Mind over Matter," *Wall Street Journal*, April 4, 2002.

24. C. Shapiro and H. Varian, *Information Rules* (Boston: HBS Press, 1998), Chapter 7.

25. J. Heide and A. Weiss, "Vendor Consideration and Switching Behavior for Buyers in High-Technology Markets," *Journal of Marketing*, July 1995.

Chapter 9

Epigraph: Joel and Ethan Coen, *Barton Fink*, 1991.

1. AMR research estimates, cited in A. Johnson, "35 Years of IT Leadership: A New Supply Chain Forged," *Computerworld*, September 30, 2002.

2. J. Hammond, cited in J. Aisner, "Rapid Response: Inside the Retailing Revolution," *HBS Working Knowledge*, October 12, 1999.

3. M. Schrage, "Wal-Mart Trumps Moore's Law," *Technology Review*, Vol. 105, No. 2, March 2002.

4. J. Maximov and H. Gottschlich, "Time-Cost–Quality Leadership: New Ways to Gain a Sustainable Competitive Advantage in Retailing," *International Journal of Retail & Distribution Management*, 1993.

5. A. Lundberg, "The IT Inside the World's Biggest Company," *CIO Insight*, July 1, 2002.

6. Schrage, *op. cit.*

7. *Ibid.*

8. See W. McFarlan, "Information Technology Changes the Way You Compete," *Harvard Business Review*, May-June 1984.

9. G. Moore, *Inside the Tornado* (New York: HarperBusiness, 1995), Chapter 4.

10. N. Carr, "IT Doesn't Matter," *Harvard Business Review*, May 2003.

11. F. Hayes, "IT Delivers," *Computerworld*, May 19, 2003.

12. J. Vaughan, "At Tech.ED: Microsoft Exec Says IT Has Room to Grow; Company Rolls out New Betas," *Application Development Trends*, June 2, 2003.

13. R. Price, "Technology and Strategic Advantage," *California Management Review*, Spring 1996.

14. V. Allee, "Reconfiguring the Value Network," *Journal of Business Strategy*, Vol. 21, No. 4, July 2000, p. 36.

15. G. Kahn, "Made to Measure," *Wall Street Journal*, September 11, 2003, p. A1.

16. "From Math to Machine," *Tech TV* report, aired February 11, 2003; and S. Gallagher, "Grand Test Auto," *Baseline*, November 2002.

17. M. Lillich, "GM Designs Digital Future for Its Cars—and Future Employees," *Purdue News*, September 26, 2002.

18. S. Rohde, "GM's Virtual Vehicle Revolutionizes Product Design," Report of D. H. Brown Associates, April 2002.

19. C. Ansberry, "A New Blue-Collar World," *Wall Street Journal*, June 30, 2003, p. B1.

20. "Baseline Magazine's ROI Awards," *Baseline*, June 2003.

21. G. Rochlin, *Trapped in the Net* (Princeton, NJ: Princeton University Press, 1998).

22. J. Emigh, "Total Cost of Ownership," *Computerworld*, December 20, 1999.

23. M. Wheatly, "Every Last Dime," *CIO Magazine*, November 15, 2000.

24. B. Jovanovich and G. MacDonald, "The Lifecycle of a Competitive Industry," *Journal of Political Economy*, April 1994.

25. A. Chakraborty and M. Kazarosian, "Product Differentiation and the Use of Information Technology: New Evidence from the Trucking Industry," NBER Working Paper No. 7222, July 1999.

26. E. Schlosser, *Fast Food Nation: The Dark Side of the All-American Meal* (New York: Houghton Mifflin, 2001).

27. M. McGrath, *Product Strategy for High Technology Companies* (New York: McGraw-Hill, 2001), p. 164.

28. *Ibid.*

29. M. Porter, *Competitive Advantage* (New York: Free Press/Macmillan, 1985), p. 120.

30. D. Abell, *Defining the Business: The Starting Point of Strategic Planning* (Englewood Cliffs, NJ: Prentice Hall, 1980), p. 170.

31. K. Roberts, "Creating and Sustaining Global Brands," presentation by the American Chamber of Commerce at Brand China, Shanghai, April 22, 1998, http://www.saatchikevin.com/talkingit/shanghai.html.

32. "Nine Toyota and Lexus Vehicles at the Top of Their Segments," J.D. Power and Associates 2003 Vehicle Dependability Study," PR Newswire, July 8, 2003.

33. G. Convis, article for SAE International, July 2001.

34. S. Mukund, "Lean Roll Out Inside the Automotive Value Chain," I2 Technologies White Paper, June 2002.

35. JAMA statistics.

36. Porter, *op. cit.*, p. 144.

37. Abell, *op. cit.*, pp. 174–175.

38. Porter, *op. cit.*, p. 267.

39. J. Collins and J. Porras, *Built to Last: Successful Habits of Visionary Companies* (New York: HarperBusiness, 1994).

40. L. Bourgeois, I. Duhaime, and J. Stimpert, *Strategic Management* (Ft. Worth, TX: Dryden Press, 1999), Chapter 7.

Chapter 10

Epigraph: Joseph Heller, *Catch-22* (New York: Simon & Schuster, 1996).

1. S. Gould, "The Panda's Thumb of Technology," *Natural History*, January 1987.

2. P. David, "Understanding the Economics of QWERTY: The Necessity of History," in W. Parker (Ed.), *Economic History and the Modern Economist* (Oxford: Basil Blackwell, 1986).

3. H. Varian and C. Shapiro, *Information Rules* (Boston: HBS Press, 1999).

4. Interview with G. Kirby, founder of Liquid Audio.

5. Nielsen NetRatings 2002 IM report.

6. P. Krugman, "Networks and Increasing Returns: A Cautionary Tale," http://web.mit.edu/krugman/www/metcalfe.htm.

7. A. McAfee and F. Oliveau, "Confronting the Limits of Networks," *MIT Sloan Management Review*, Summer 2002.

8. E. Millard, "The Dark Side of eBay," *E-Commerce Times*, June 28, 2002.

9. T. Buchholz, *New Ideas from Dead Economists* (New York: Plume, 1990), p. 247.

10. N. Economides, with F. Flyer, "Compatibility and Market Structure for Network Goods," Stern/NYU Department of Economics Working Paper 98-02, 1997.

11. N. Economides, Interview with J. Irons, http://www.stern.nyu.edu/networks/ms/iv1.html, October 2004.

12. G. Moore, *Inside the Tornado* (New York: HarperBusiness, 1995).

13. M. Gladwell, *The Tipping Point: How Little Things Can Make a Big Difference* (New York: Little Brown and Company, 2000).

14. Moore, *op. cit.*

15. J. Allard, cited in N. Davidson, "More Than a Money Maker, Halo 2 Helps Set Stage for Xbox's Next Generation," *Canadian Press*, November 8, 2004.

16. S. Postrel, "Competing Networks and Proprietary Standards: The Case of Quadraphonic Sound," *Journal of Industrial Economics*, December 1990.

17. N. Economides, "Desire of Compatibility in the Absence of Network Externalities," *American Economic Review*, 1989.

18. Varian and Shapiro, *op. cit.*

19. M. Angell, "Goal for Qualcomm: Repeat Performance," *Investor's Business Daily*, September 1, 2004.

20. M. McGrath, *Product Strategy for High Technology Companies* (New York: McGraw Hill, 2001), p. 76.

21. J. Spencer, "Cell Phone Services Brace for a New Era," *Wall Street Journal*, September 11, 2003.

22. Varian and Shapiro, *op. cit.*

23. N. Carr, "IT Doesn't Matter," *Harvard Business Review*, May 2003.

24. D. Gage and L. Barret, "Learning to Love Vendor Lock-In," *Baseline*, March 2002.

25. M. Porter, *Competitive Strategy* (New York: Free Press, 1998).

26. "Wal-Mart Draws Lines in the Sand," *RFID Journal*, June 2003.

27. D. Verton, "Users: Oracle's Price to Blame," *Computerworld*, March 19, 2001.

28. M. Ingram, "Rambus' Business Is All About Tech—and Lawsuits," *Globe and Mail*, February 19, 2004.

29. A. Gawer and M. Cusumano, *Platform Leadership: How Intel, Microsoft, and Cisco Drive Industry Innovation* (Boston: HBS Press, 2002).

30. M. McGrath, *op. cit.*

31. Christensen, *op. cit.*

32. M. Schilling, "Winning the Standards Race: Building Installed Base and the Availability of Complementary Goods," *European Management Journal*, Vol. 17, 1999.

33. D. Zahay, "The Differential Value of Customer Transactional vs. Relational Data," NIU working paper, presented at the Direct Marketing Educators Conference, 2003.

34. A. Gilbert, "Siebel, IBM Preparing Online Service," CNET News, July 18, 2003, http://news.zdnet.com/2100-3513_22-1027324.html.

35. Interview with Marc Benioff, http://www.customerthink.com/111.cfm, November 23, 2004.

36. T. Robinson, "Siebel Takes (Another) Shot at ASP Model," *CRM Product Review*, October 9, 2003.

37. Christensen, *op. cit.*

38. L. Bourgeois, I. Duhaime, and J. Stimpert, *Strategic Management* (Ft. Worth, TX: Dryden Press, 1999), Chapter 5; and Christensen, *op. cit.*

glossary

adaptive strategy The strategy of waiting for likely technology standards and solutions to emerge prior to making significant investments in product/service lines incorporating new technology.

ambidextrous organization An organization capable of driving both incremental and discontinuous innovation.

angel investor A person, with no formal association with a VC firm or investment fund, who provides backing to very early-stage businesses. Typically, angels are entrepreneurs who have become wealthy (often in technology-related industries). Angels usually invest smaller sums and have much more limited involvement than VCs.

API Application programming interface; a set of instructions or rules that enables two operating systems or software applications to communicate or interface with each other.

backwards integration An organization's attempt to gain control of its inputs by taking control of activities formerly performed by suppliers.

balanced scorecard A measurement-based strategic management system, originated by Robert Kaplan and David Norton, that provides a method of aligning business activities with competitive strategy and monitoring the performance of both activities and strategic goals over time.

bandwagon effect The tendency of organizations to adopt an innovation or pursue a new market simply because their peers do, even if the business model is not clear or justifiable. It is driven by a fear of being left behind or appearing to be out of step with the industry.

best-cost provider A firm that successfully pursues both low-cost and differentiation strategies, incorporating key features at a lower cost and thus capturing a unique and insulated position.

boom-bust cycle An economic pattern in which significant innovation in an industry is followed by a boom in investment, which is followed by a shakeout, as is characteristic of many sectors of the technology industry.

business case An analysis of the business value (typically in terms of the change in future cost and revenue) of a particular project, designed to justify a business decision to spend funds.

capital market myopia The tendency of investors to focus on their self-interests rather than the overall detrimental implications of an investment in the firm receiving funds or the industry as a whole.

category killer A firm (usually used in the context of retail) that offers such a compelling combination of scale and low price that it is capable of driving the majority of competing firms out of business.

category leadership The belief that a company is a leader, which establishes in the minds of buyers, vendors, and others that the company has both staying power and insight into the direction of the category.

challenger firm A new entrant attempting to compete with or displace established incumbents, often via the use of innovative technology.

channel conflict The result of pressure exerted by current sales channels in response to a producer's attempts to disintermediate or introduce alternative channels.

Chinese walls An imaginary wall of separation between two companies or departments controlled by a common parent, established when companies or departments are engaged in activities that would normally be deemed a conflict of interest.

competitive advantage A sustainable resource, capability, or barrier that allows a firm to outperform other firms or insulate itself from competition.

complementary assets The assets, other than technology and intellectual property, used by a firm to bring a product to market successfully.

conjoint analysis A multivariate analysis technique that is used to quantify the value that customers associate with different levels of product/service attributes. Respondents rank various bundles against each other to establish product preferences and the relative importance of attributes. These attributes can be grouped and associated with distinct market segments.

co-opetition A combination of cooperation and competition between rivals or complementors. When they cooperate in growing a market, rivals can compete against each other for share of a larger overall market. Likewise, complementors may cooperate in growing markets while competing over distribution of profits.

corporate venturing Providing venture capital–type funding via the in-house investment fund of a large corporation in order to allow an entity to behave like a startup while accruing strategic benefit for the corporation.

customer lock-in An arrangement that makes it difficult, inconvenient, or expensive for customers to switch to another supplier.

demand curve The graphical relationship between the quantity demanded of a good and its price when other variables are held constant.

differentiation The pursuit of unique capabilities that allow a firm to offer a product or service attribute that is not easily imitated.

diffusion period The period in which an innovation begins to spread rapidly into the marketplace, as a result of consumer and industry behaviors; sometimes referred to as a *tornado*, based on G. Moore's books *Crossing the Chasm* and *Inside the Tornado*.

discontinuous innovation Innovation that performs a function for which no product has existed previously, upending how value is defined or delivered; also referred to as *disruptive innovation*. It typically displaces existing markets and/or creates new ones.

diseconomies of scale Diminishing returns or rising costs attributable to increased size.

disintermediation Removing or making obsolete one or more middlemen or intermediaries between a producer and end consumers.

disruptive technology New technology that causes a significant shift in the status quo, such as a revised method of meeting customers' needs, a process with significantly different economics, or a technology that results in a revision of the value chain.

dominant design The standard design that emerges in an industry, becoming entrenched through the development of supporting infrastructure, assets, and organizational codification.

dynamic capabilities The capabilities that firms have to shape, reshape, configure, and reconfigure assets so as to respond to changing technologies, markets, and customer needs.

early adopters The population segment in the buyer adoption curve that follows very early innovators, precedes the early majority, and is thought to be the most influential in encouraging adoption.

early majority The third identifiable segment within a population that adopts an innovation, following innovators and early adopters. Members of the early majority like to await the outcome of product trial by the two earlier groups; they are more pragmatic in adoption decisions, more mainstream in usage, and much more heavily integrated into existing market and industry infrastructures.

e-commerce Conducting business and/or processing economic transactions, such as buying and selling, through digital means.

efficient choice Allocating resources to maximize risk-adjusted gains.

era of ferment The period in a technology life cycle when various competing technology configurations begin to be replaced by an emerging dominant design that will become a standard for the industry.

289

era of incremental change Following the emergence of a dominant design, a period characterized by better defined and standardized products, incremental improvements to technology, consolidation, and the shakeout of small players. Scale, complementary assets, and process become more crucial as cost-based competition increases.

evangelists Individuals and firms with the role of convincing others to support a particular platform.

excess return Profit returns in excess of what the risk-adjusted cost of capital would normally justify.

fabless Refers to semiconductor companies that don't have their own fabrication plant and instead outsource production to third-party manufacturers.

failure framework A dynamic in which apparently optimal short-term decisions by incumbents lead to an uncompetitive position in the long term.

fast follower An imitator who quickly duplicates an innovation in the hope of taking advantage of the innovator's expensive lessons without the same level of risk or investment.

firm-specific resources Both tangible and intangible assets and resources that reinforce firm-specific skills, including distinctive competencies (unique or special capabilities that allow a firm to perform better than its competitors) and dynamic capabilities (the integration and combination of a firm's resources).

first-mover advantage A competitive benefit that is assumed to accrue to early market innovators but actually applies only if the early advantage produces longer-term barriers.

five forces model A strategic tool frequently used for analyzing the structure and attractiveness of an individual company or an industry. The forces determine both the distribution of profits in the value chain and the intensity of rivalry.

flanking Moving into an area that competitors have not entered (and perhaps are unaware of), rather than confronting them head on in well-defined market spaces.

focus strategy Identifying and targeting narrow markets in which a firm has some unique advantage.

game theory Models designed to help us better understand strategic choices and interactions—in particular, how people or organizations behave when their actions influence the behavior of others.

growth by acquisition A growth strategy, often used by larger companies, that involves acquiring or merging with other companies in order to increase size or gain access to key technologies or capabilities.

hype cycle A cycle by which investments in an industry by perceived leaders create excitement and attract additional investors, rather than dissuading them.

incremental innovation Innovation that takes place within existing market and technology infrastructures. It typically focuses on progressive refinement of existing knowledge in existing markets without challenging underlying strategies or assumptions.

incumbent An established organization, typically with significant market share and experience in a particular segment.

indirect network effect An increase in the demand for and value of a product, service, or technology driven by the availability of complementary goods (e.g., toner cartridges for printers or game software for a gaming platform) and lower price for these complements as the network size increases.

industry life cycle An S-shaped curve describing the supply side performance characteristics of a new product class, from introduction to eventual decline.

inertia of success Complacency and unwillingness to abandon the practices, platforms, and methods that brought a firm success, despite the need for change.

innovation A new idea, method, or device; an improvement to an existing technological product or system; or the act of creating a new product or process.

innovation inertia Resistance to change and preference for the status quo.

innovation phase The period in which an invention is successfully exploited toward becoming a commercially viable product.

innovators In reference to the buyer adoption curve, those who are the very first to adopt a new product introduced to the marketplace.

innovator's dilemma The dilemma that the very factors that help a successful company maintain its preeminent position may also prevent or at least discourage it from introducing necessary disruptive innovation; a term coined by Clayton Christensen and applied in particular to existing customers and channels, both of which pressure suppliers to resist disruptive innovation; similar to the "winner's curse."

installed base A customer base with lock-in, switching costs, or some other relationship that allows the firm to monetize and leverage customers.

invention The process of demonstrating the feasibility of a new and useful concept, process, device, article of manufacture, or composition of matter (or a useful improvement on one of these).

invisible hand A term developed by economist Adam Smith to describe the forces of self-interest that guide the free market through competition to the optimal social outcome. The supplier profit motive and consumer decision making result in production of the right amount of what the consumer wants at an acceptable price.

key influencers The set of early adopters after whom others in the same circle tend to model their behavior.

killer application (killer app) An application that dominates competition or becomes an industry standard by meeting a key customer need.

law of the few The concept that a small but influential group can bring about wide-scale popularity of a new paradigm.

legacy systems Computer systems or applications that are outdated and incompatible with other systems, but too costly to replace or redesign. Their size, scope, and mission-critical function turn them from a source of advantage to a liability as technology progresses.

liquidity event An event that allows a VC to harvest an illiquid investment in a firm (also known as an exit strategy). Common exit routes include initial public offerings (IPOs), buyouts by a third party, and mergers. It represents an exit strategy to the investor, but also sets a benchmark for potential valuations for other VCs investing in the sector.

lock-in A situation in which a customer is unable to easily abandon a service or technology.

modular approach (modularity) An approach to product design that involves dividing a technology delivery system into components, connected by pre-specified interfaces. Third parties can provide many of the components, and components can be used, modified, and maintained independently of the remainder of the system. Changes in one part of the system should not lead to unexpected behavior in other parts.

monopoly Typically defined as a market with only a single supplier of a good or service, but often used to refer to any market in which one firm has considerable power over prices and supply.

multi-layered approach Assembling various technologies on multiple layers to offer a more complete solution, with less emphasis on modularity and outside vendor add-ins; also known as bundled architecture.

natural monopoly A situation in which one firm can supply the entire market at a lower per-unit cost than could two or more separate firms, making it economically undesirable for more than one entity to be in the market. Regulation is often required in order to protect consumers from collection of excessive profits.

network effect The increase in value of a product, service, or technology resulting from an increase in the number of users and their interaction. The increased utility brought about by additional users often further accelerates adoption.

network orchestrator Similar to a platform leader, a firm that plays the role of coordinating various companies and technologies to deliver value. Even without owning the key technology layer, the firm typically sets uniform standards for physical interconnections as well as information flow.

network value gap The difference between the utility of one product/service/technology and that of another, created by the former's larger user base as a result of network effects.

oligopoly A market with a small number of suppliers. The firms can benefit by acting together to control both the supply of a particular good and its market price.

open innovation The process of strategically leveraging internal and external sources of innovation and taking them to market through multiple paths; an alternative to the traditional incumbent method of relying on internal R&D for innovation and attempting to capture R&D value through vertical integration.

open standards A set of technological standards that are not the intellectual property of any firm; typically, recognized standards established by industry-wide or multi-firm organizations and available for use at no cost or with a moderate license fee.

opportunity cost of capital The income that would be earned by investing money in income-generating assets or alternative projects, rather than in a specific capital investment under consideration.

organizational capabilities Applied technical know-how and knowledge about both customers and processes that a firm and its employees gain through experience.

outperformance Performance better than that of the competition on one or more predetermined measures.

platform (company) The foundation, core skill set, or resource base on which a company builds its strategy.

platform (technology) The hardware and software used to run applications or on top of which an end product is built.

platform leadership The role played by a company in establishing the rules, specifications, and roadmap around a technology

stack so that third parties can provide modular solutions that fit with the stack. It is a necessary part of gaining adoption of and maintaining the viability of an open technology platform.

platform shift A change in technology solutions that creates a new technology stack. It can lead to a redistribution of power and profits within a technology solution space.

point of leverage The area that has the most significant impact on a firm or industry's operating results; also referred to as a *point of pain* or *critical success factor*. Innovators try to identify these to ascertain where their technology can offer the greatest value.

price elastic A characteristic of a product or service for which buyers, because of choice or lack of compelling need, have extremely variable demand based on its price. In economic terms, a 1 percent change in price translates to a greater than 1 percent change in demand.

price elasticity A measure of buyers' sensitivity to price, derived from the percentage change in quantity demanded that results from a percentage change in price.

price inelastic A characteristic of a product or service that buyers, because of lack of choice and urgency of need, are willing to acquire with relatively limited concern for the price. In economic terms, a 1 percent change in price translates to a less than 1 percent change in demand.

prisoners' dilemma An example of game theory, illustrating how the noncooperative pursuit of self-interest by two parties can actually make them both worse off.

productization The process of taking a basic technology or set of technologies and adding to it the other elements and supporting layers necessary to sell it as a solution.

rational rate of return The rate of return in line with the risk and cost of capital.

razors and blades approach Offering a basic platform (such as a safety razor) that requires the user to go back to the same company for supporting products (blades). In this approach, unlike the modular approach, the platform-providing firm enforces a closed model so that no others can sell products to platform users.

reserving the right to play strategy The strategy of making investments, establishing partnerships, and conducting exploratory research in areas that have the potential to significantly impact the market.

resource-based view The theory that sustainable competitive advantage results from firms' both acquiring and effectively leveraging and deploying resources, in order to build unique value-creating capabilities.

shaping strategy An attempt by industry participants to steer both participants and consumers toward embracing a certain technology solution before the market determines the dominant designs and accepted standards.

signal versus noise A phrase coined by Intel chairman Andrew Grove to describe the problem in distinguishing between early disruptive change and the much more prevalent everyday competitive activity. The term is based on the broadcasting measure "signal to noise ratio," which compares relevant content (signal) to nonrelevant content (noise).

signaling criteria Aspects of value—including such factors as image/reputation, installed base, time in business, market share, and visibility—that influence customers' perceptions of a firm's ability to meet their needs.

skew-distributed outcome The result when a small number of innovators or innovations in a portfolio contribute most of the total value.

skunkworks An internal group of people given the freedom to approach a project from outside the usual rules of the organization in order to achieve unusual results; often a small autonomous team, with executive support, that is given responsibility for developing something in a short time with minimal management constraints.

soft assets Intangible assets such as ideas, know-how, informal rights over resources, and systems of production.

standards Conditions, guidelines, and protocols set up to allow uniformity and interoperability.

strategic inflection point Point at which a new disruptive innovation begins to change

the underlying competitive landscape or value proposition of an industry.

submarine patent A patent that an inventor files on a device or technology that is evolving or that has not yet been successfully implemented. By applying for additional or expanded claims and by using techniques to extend the patent application process, the filer can keep the details of the patent secret. Once a practical implementation of the device/technology appears on the market, the filer then allows the patent to "come to the surface" and demands royalties. When this tactic is successful, the inventor can broaden the scope of the patent to encompass technologies invented and commercialized by others who unknowingly embed the patented technology into products or further invention.

sunk cost An incurred cost that cannot be changed, no matter what action is taken. Such costs are sometimes mistakenly factored into future decisions.

sunsetted Rendered less relevant or competitive by new developments, as when a technology platform is no longer supported, hastening obsolescence of a product or firm.

switching costs The actual or perceived costs to a customer of moving from one solution to another, which effectively create a lower-cost basis for staying with the current solution.

technology enablers Firms that concentrate on offering technology or a necessary component across an industry, rather than focusing on embedding the technology or component into end solutions; also referred to in this text as *toolmakers*.

technology risk The risk assumed by buyers in selecting a technology solution for which the level of long-term support by other customers, vendors, or complements is unknown.

technology stack model A model for looking at a set of technologies—either modular or more tightly coupled—as part of a complete solution. Each layer interacts with the ones above and below it, and technology must be designed with adjacent layers in mind. The relative dominance and profile of the technology solutions on particular layers determine the competitive structure of the overall industry defined by the stack.

tipping Reaching the point at which the gap in value due to network effects becomes so large that a market is no longer contestable, leading to standards, dominant design, and in some cases effective monopoly.

tornado period A period of rapid diffusion of a new technology solution, often in response to the emergence of dominant design; also called *diffusion period*.

total cost of ownership (TCO) approach A method of determining the true cost of a technology or business solution by factoring in items such as ongoing maintenance, support, implementation/customization, professional development, replacement costs, and process-related changes, as well as the initial investment cost.

trap of the first version The premature dismissal by incumbents of a disruptive innovation due to the poor performance of early versions of the technology.

tyranny of OR, the The belief by management that a firm must make tradeoffs—for example, between cost and quality—rather than aim to achieve multiple goals.

usage-specific resources Resources with a relatively inflexible application, tailored toward a specific purpose or use.

value-based pricing Pricing based on maximizing profits by determining what potential customers are willing to pay, rather than focusing on either sales quantity or production cost.

value chain The progression of activities that actively add value to the end product or service offered to customers.

value network A concept derived from the value/supply chain concept, referring to the set of interrelationships among a firm's internal groups, business suppliers, partners, wholesalers, retailers, and other support services.

vector of differentiation A differentiation strategy in which innovation efforts are focused on making continual progress in a specific direction in order to produce an increasingly difficult-to-imitate product or service.

venture capital Funds that are invested by a third party in a business, either as equity or as a form of secondary debt. Such capital is usually offered by specialist partnerships willing to take a high risk of loss to obtain a stake in firms with high growth potential.

winner's curse The observed fact that the very factors that help a successful company maintain its preeminent position may prevent or at least discourage it from introducing necessary innovation; also known as the "competency trap."

Wintel architecture Industry term for the computer stack based on the Intel microprocessor and one of the Windows operating systems from Microsoft.

Index

About TEXERE

Texere, a progressive and authoritative voice in business publishing, brings to the global business community the expertise and insights of leading thinkers. Our books educate, enlighten, and entertain, and provide an intersection where our authors and our readers share cutting edge ideas, practices, and innovative solutions. Texere seeks to cultivate, enhance, and disseminate information that illuminates the global business landscape.

www.thomson.com/learning/texere

About the Typeface

This book was set in 9.5-point Warnock Pro. Warnock Pro was created in 2000 by Robert Slimbach of the United States. This classic, yet contemporary, typeface is known for being both versatile and elegant.

Library of Congress Cataloging-in-Publication Data

Rochlin, Dave.
    Hunter or hunted? : technology, innovation, and competitive strategy / Dave Rochlin.
    p. cm.
    Includes bibliographical references and index.
    ISBN 0-324-26128-4
    1. Competition. 2. Technological innovations--Management. 3. Technological innovations--Economic aspects. 4. Technology--Economic aspects. 5. Strategic planning. 6. Industrial management. I. Title.

HD41.R63 2006
338.6'048--dc22

2005041890